Implicit Leadership Theories

Essays and Explorations

A volume in
Leadership Horizons, The Series
Series Editor: Mary Uhl-Bien

Leadership Horizon, The Series

Mary Uhl-Bien, *Series Editor*
James R. Meindl, *Founding Editor*

Implicit Leadership Theories

Essays and Explorations

Edited by

Birgit Schyns
Tilburg University, The Netherlands

James R. Meindl
State University of New York, Buffalo

INFORMATION AGE
PUBLISHING

Greenwich, Connecticut 06830 • www.infoagepub.com

Library of Congress Cataloging-in-Publication Data

Implicit leadership theories : essays and explorations / edited by Birgit
Schyns, James R. Meindl.
    p. cm. – (Leadership horizons series)
 Includes bibliographical references.
 ISBN 1-59311-360-9 (pbk.) – ISBN 1-59311-361-7 (hardcover)
1. Leadership. I. Schyns, Birgit. II. Meindl, James R. III. Series.
HD57.7.I47 2005
658.4'092–dc22

                        2005020175

Printed in the United States of America

CONTENTS

PART II
Contents and Generalizability of Implicit Leadership Theories

PART III
Explaining Implicit Leadership Theories

Broadening Up Our Views on Implicit Leadership Theories:
Implicit Followership Theories and Implicit Organizational Theories

SERIES INTRODUCTION

This book is the third volume in the *Leadership Horizons* series. This series, started by Jim Meindl, is devoted to new developments in theory and research on leadership within the context of continuing and emerging organizational issues. In this spirit, the present volume delves into implicit leadership theories (ILTs), and opens intriguing new avenues for research on ILTs, but does so while maintaining an eye on the past. For example, the book offers valuable historical perspectives from those who were "there"—Dov Eden and Uriel Leviatan share the inside scoop on the origination of the concept of ILTs, and Bob Lord traces the evolution of social-cognitive perspectives work on ILTs—while all authors raise interesting questions and offer important new directions to advance this work well into the future. It features a wide range of scholars and perspectives, and practical implications are implicit and explicit throughout the volume. The book offers a valuable resource for researchers, students, and practitioners interested in leadership and social cognition in the workplace.

The idea for the book came about through discussions between Birgit Schyns and Jim Meindl while Jim was visiting the Netherlands. Birgit and Jim lined up contributors early in 2004, and in May, Birgit went to Buffalo, where they collaborated on the Introduction. Later that summer, while this volume was underway, the field of leadership suffered a tragic loss with the sudden death of Jim Meindl. In coping with the loss, the authors and Birgit decided to carry on with the book—that is what Jim would want. As a result, while Jim's presence is strong throughout the book, much the work of managing and editing the volume was done by Birgit Schyns.

Implicit Leadership Theories: Essays and Explorations, pages vii–viii

Jim was truly a leader in the fields of leadership and organizational science, and a devoted mentor and teacher, who always pushed others to view things in new ways. He was dedicated to his students and generous with his intellect. As Birgit noted in an email to me, Jim had a gift for challenging peoples' opinion by asking just the right questions. He was a pioneering presence in the leadership arena, never satisfied with the status quo or willing to be restricted to standard approaches. He explored leadership in novel and fascinating ways, raising interesting questions and producing articles that were as enjoyable to read as they were useful. For all those who knew Jim personally, or know of his work, the hole left by Jim's passing is deep, and hard to fill.

To honor Jim Meindl and his tremendous contribution to the academic profession and the people within it, we plan to devote the next volume of this series to his legacy. This volume will be edited by Boas Shamir, Raj Pillai, Michelle Bligh, and Mary Uhl-Bien and will address follower-centered perspectives on leadership. While it by no means compensates for the loss to the field, we hope that it will serve as a tribute to the tremendous impact that Jim's many years of dedication and intellectual leadership has had on advancing scholarship in leadership and organizational studies.

—Mary Uhl-Bien
University of Central Florida
March 2005

PREFACE: IMPLICIT LEADERSHIP THEORY

Although primitive creatures such as paramecia merely react to their environment in a physical way after bumping into obstacles, more evolved creatures such as humans build symbolic representations of their environments based on perceived features, and they use these "mental models" in controlling actions (Johnson-Laird, 1989). For the past 30 years leadership researchers have applied similar reasoning in maintaining that individuals have "implicit leadership theories" that guide their sensemaking processes when perceiving and reacting to leaders. Built from repeated encounters with leaders, such implicit theories allow individuals to appropriately classify leaders as such when they are encountered; that is, they guide leadership perceptions. Implicit leadership theories also suggest appropriate ways to respond to leaders so that potential social or organizational "bumps" can be avoided.

As the research described in this book shows, interest in implicit theories has been widespread, and it reflects the expanding influence of the social-cognitive perspective that has developed since the 1970s. This research bears on many practical issues involving cognitions, social perceptions, and the effects of various social roles and gender in organizations. Such research recognizes the active, constructive role of perceivers in social and cognitive processes; organizational members are sensemakers, and they respond to the highly personal meaning that they construct for

Implicit Leadership Theories: Essays and Explorations, pages ix–xiv
Copyright © 2005 by Information Age Publishing

organizational events and actors. Indeed, people only know reality in terms of the internal representations they construct. What is particularly intriguing about this perspective is that the meaning construction process occurs primarily at a preconscious, implicit level, and consequently, people have little insight into this process. Further, because the internal representations people construct correspond to in fundamental ways to social and physical realities, they provide effective guidance to actions, thereby subjectively affirming the correctness of one's internal representations.

Several factors make the term "implicit theories" appropriate for describing the systems perceivers use to construct meaning with respect to leadership processes. First, these systems may operate automatically or implicitly, producing effects that are outside of perceiver's conscious awareness because they affect the preconscious choice of symbols used to represent a social stimulus. Second, they are an inherent, implicit part of the sense making process. Unlike paramecia, people do not respond to the world in a direct sense, instead they respond to their internal representation of the world. Third, because implicit theories are rich cognitive structures that not only provide conceptual units but also specify the connections of such units to other constructs, they can be the mechanisms for empirical effects that are implicit and hard to recognize. For example, as noted three decades ago by Barry Staw (1975) in his seminal article, implicit theories can distort perceptions of processes based on knowledge of outcomes. Thus, Staw suggested that implicit theories could provide a type of reverse causality in which knowledge of performance affected the measurement of constructs thought by researchers to cause performance.

In the 1970s such reasoning suggested the potential for an artificial, reverse causality that had obvious implications for the leadership field which was, and still is, dependent on questionnaire-based measures of leadership processes to measure behaviors thought to be antecedents to performance. After Staw's article, implicit theory research quickly established that experimentally manipulated knowledge of performance produced robust effects on ratings of leadership behavior that have proved difficult to eliminate through conventional rater training (Baltes & Parker, 2000). Equally important from a measurement perspective were the consequences of implicit theories for the inductive development of leadership constructs. Calder (1977) criticized the use of first-order common sense constructs as the basis for science, arguing that such constructs had their origin in the implicit theories and sensemaking activities of perceivers. This concern was reflected in a number of early studies which showed that the factor structure of leadership questionnaires could be generated solely from rater's implicit theories (Eden & Leviatan, 1975). Specifically, research shows that ratings of fictitious individuals for whom raters had no behavioral information nicely replicated the factor structure of extant leadership instruments used to describe the behavior of real leaders. This meant that the inductive search for important leadership dimensions may tell us as much about the implicit theories of raters as the actual behaviors of leaders they are rating. Recent perspectives on memory suggest that much if not all information is reconstructed at the time of retrieval. Thus, both the performance cue effect and the effects of implicit theories on the factor structures of behavioral questionnaires may ultimately reflect the reconstruction of memories based on known information and implicit theories.

A fundamental point illustrated by work on implicit theories was that raters were *active* contributors to leadership measurement and leadership perception processes. Indeed, Jim Meindl argued that the contribution of raters was so extensive that leadership could best be understood as a social construction that existed mainly in the mind of perceivers (Meindl, 1995) and was used to understand organizations as a causal system (Meindl, Ehrlich, & Dukerich, 1985). Using archival data Meindl et al. showed that heightened attention to leadership in the scientific and popular literatures occurred when the performance of companies, industries, or nations was extreme. In other words, very good or very bad performance promoted a search for leadership-based explanations of these outcomes. These results were interpreted as indicating that the leadership construct itself involved a sensmaking process in which perceivers explained causality in terms of an oversimplified emphasis on heroic, personal qualities which they equated with leadership. Further, Meindl et al. argued that this "romanticized, larger-than-life" (p. 79) view of leadership involved a substitution of an explanatory, perceptual category for the ill-structured, and difficult to understand causal factors that actually influence organizational performance. In other words, people use their implicit theories to construct a simplified understanding of events that emphasize human qualities rather than the more complex effects of organizational and interorganizational systems.

The work of researchers like Staw, Meindll, and Calder represented attempts to understand implicit theories by applying what Calder termed, second-order scientific theories, in this case attribution theory, to understanding leadership perceptions. Lord, Foti, and De Vader (1984) provided another attempt to apply social cognitive theory by arguing that implicit leadership theories were cognitive categories that had a structure similar to other types of categories used by perceivers to understand their world. Rather than being defined by concrete, specific critical features that distinguished all leaders from all non-leaders, such categories were thought to coalesce around more abstract set of features that were widely shared among *types* of leaders (e.g., educational leaders, political leaders, business leaders, etc.). Leadership perception could then be defined in terms of the match between perceiver prototypes and the characteristics of potential leaders. According to this view, leadership perception was a dyadic level process that involved both perceiver and leader effects. The use of cognitive categories as perceptual structures also allowed for classification based on inferences from performance information as long as the potential leader was seen as a causal source.

Research on implicit leadership theories and the social-cognitive literature on which it was based had a number of consequences for the leadership field. One is that it helped to legitimize the study of perceivers and perceiver processes as essential to understanding leadership. More contemporary research has expanded this perspective to include the emotional as well as cognitive responses of perceivers to potential leaders as critical to understand leadership processes. As second consequence is that an understanding of implicit leadership theories provided a conceptual framework for emerging applied interests. For example, gender bias and the "glass ceiling" confronting female executives could be understood in terms of the greater correspondence of leadership prototypes to typical masculine than to typical feminine gender stereotypes (Heilman, Block, Martell & Simon, 1989). Similarly, cross-cultural differences in leadership could be understood in terms differences in the way that perceivers from different cultures defined leadership. Thus, under the direction of Bob House and colleagues, the massive GLOBE project has compared the leadership prototypes of thousands of raters from more than 60 countries (Den Hartog et al., 1999). A third consequence is that knowledge of implicit leadership theories further eroded the acceptance of overly simplistic trait theories of leadership which implied that there were traits which were associated with leadership effectiveness across situations. Instead, research on implicit theories emphasized the situational and cultural contingency of such leadership traits and the need to assess their fit with the implicit theories of perceivers, or in some circumstances, the prototype created by strong group identities (Hogg & van Knippenberg, 2003). This perspective also emphasized that leadership emergence depended on the fit of an entire *set* of leader characteristics with the prototypes of followers (Smith & Foti, 1998).

As this book shows, research on implicit theories over the past 30 years has enriched our understanding of leadership processes, yet there are still important areas that have not been fully examined. Several of these pertain to issues addressed in this book such as the role of implicit theories in relationships, organizational hierarchies, organizations. Three issues which have not yet received much attention seem particularly important to me. First, implicit theories have been viewed as static cognitive structures. Issue like how these theories are learned, how they change over time, or how they are adjusted to fit different contexts or the emotional states of perceivers have not been widely investigated, although there has been limited recent attention to these questions (Epitropaki & Martin, 2004; Lord, Brown, Harvey, & Hall, 2001). Second, there is no accepted theory specifying the relation of implicit leadership theories to memory processes. The potential of such theoretical development is illustrated by the recent work by Martell and Evans (in press) who finds that performance cue effects on leadership ratings are associated with reliance on semantic rather than episodic memory. The conditioning effect of emotions on memory also is likely to be an important part of this issue. Third, with the exception of the pioneering work of Wofford and Goodwin (1994; Wofford, Goodwin, & Whittington, 1998) the use of implicit theories *by* leaders to guide their leadership actions not been examined. However, leaders, like all humans, construct meaningful interpretations of their environments which then guide their actions. Much could be gained if future leadership research systematically investigated how implicit theories guide the enactment of leadership, particularly if implicit theories were broadly construed to include both cognitive and emotional components. Because both leaders and followers are guided by their implicit theories, one may view them as jointly constructing meaningful leadership processes. Such a joint construction should be facilitated when the dimensions underlying a leader and follower's implicit theories converge.

—Robert G. Lord
University of Akron

REFERENCES

Baltes, B.B., & Parker, C.P. (2000). Reducing the effects of performance expectations on behavioral ratings. *Organizational Behavior and Human Decision Processes, 82*, 237–267.

Calder, B.J. (1977). An attribution theory of leadership. In B.M. Staw & G.R. Salancik (Eds.), *New directions in organizational behavior* (pp. 179–204). Chicago: St Clair Press.

Den Hartog, D.N., House, R.J., Hanges, P.J., Ruiz-Quintanilla, A., Dorfman, P.W. & Associates (1999). Culture specific and cross-culturally generalizable implicit leadership theories: Are the attributes of charismatic/transformational leadership universally endorsed? *Leadership Quarterly, 10*, 219–258.

Eden, D., & Leviatan, U. (1975). Implicit leadership theory as a determinant of the factor structure underlying supervisory behavior scales. *Journal of Applied Psychology, 60*, 736–741.

Epitropaki, O., & Martin, R. (2004). Implicit leadership theories in applied settings: Factor structure, generalizability, and stability over time. *Journal of Applied Psychology, 89*, 293–310.

Heilman, M.E., Block, C.J., Martell, R.F., & Simon, M.C. (1989). Has anything changed? Current characterizations of men, women, and managers. *Journal of Applied Psychology, 74,* 935–942.

Hogg, M.A., & van Knippenberg, D. (2003). Social identity and leadership processes in groups. In M. P. Zanna (Ed.), *Advances in experimental social psychology* (Vol. 35, pp. 1–52). San Diego, CA: Academic Press.

Johnson-Laird, P.N. (1989). Mental models. In M. I. Posner (Ed.), *Foundations of cognitive science* (pp. 469–499). Cambridge, MA: MIT Press.

Lord, R.G., Foti, R.J., & DeVader, C.L. (1984). A test of leadership categorization theory: Internal structure, information processing, and leadership perceptions. *Organizational Behavior and Human Performance, 34,* 343–378.

Lord, R.G., Brown, D.J., Harvey, J.L., & Hall, R.J. (2001). Contextual constraints on prototype generation and their multilevel consequences for leadership perceptions. *Leadership Quarterly, 12,* 311–338.

Martell, R.F., & Evans, D. (in press). Source-monitoring training: Toward reducing rater-expectancy effects in behavioral measurement. *Journal of Applied Psychology.*

Meindl, J.R., Ehrlich, S.B., & Dukerich, J.M. (1985). The romance of leadership. *Administrative Science Quarterly, 30,* 78–102.

Meindl, J.R. (1995). The romance of leadership as a follower-centric theory: A social constructionist approach. *Leadership Quarterly, 6,* 329–341.

Smith, J.A., & Foti, R.J. (1998). A pattern approach to the study of leadership emergence. *Leadership Quarterly, 9,* 47–160.

Staw, B.M. (1975). Attribution of the "causes" of performance: A general alternative interpretation of cross-sectional research on organizations. *Organizational Behavior and Human Performance, 13,* 414–432.

Wofford, J.C., & Goodwin, V.L. (1994). A cognitive interpretation of transactional and transformational leadership theories. *Leadership Quarterly, 5,* 161–186.

Wofford, J.C., Goodwin, V.L., & Whittington, J.L. (1998). A field study of a cognitive approach to understanding transformational and transactional leadership. *Leadership Quarterly, 9,* 55–84.

INTRODUCTION

FROM IMPLICIT PERSONALITY THEORY TO IMPLICIT LEADERSHIP THEORY

A Side-trip on the Way to Implicit Organization Theory

Dov Eden and Uriel Leviatan

PROLOGUE

In 1953, Warner Brothers Studio made a film about the goings-on in a mobile army surgical hospital set in the Korean War battlegrounds. Entitled *Battle Circus*, it starred Humphrey Bogart as a cynical surgeon and June Allyson as a nurse. The film was originally entitled "MASH" but neither the studio nor the director liked this title. It sounded too much like mashed potatoes, so they rejected it and chose "Battle Circus" instead. *Battle Circus* never amounted to much either in the ratings or at the box office. However, it was reissued in 1970 as "M*A*S*H" starring Donald Southerland as Hawkeye, Elliot Gould as Trapper, and Sally Kellerman as Nurse Margaret "Hot Lips" Hoolihan. Its phenomenal success led to the TV series starring

Implicit Leadership Theories: Essays and Explorations, pages 3–14
Copyright © 2005 by Information Age Publishing

Alan Alda as the surgeon and Loretta Swit as "Hot Lips," and it is still being aired today worldwide.

What does M*A*S*H have to do with Implicit Leadership Theory (ILT)? Nothing—and everything.

THE ORIGINS OF IMPLICIT LEADERSHIP THEORY

Warren Norman (1963b) is often credited for bringing the Big Five personality approach into mainstream psychology. While on his way to accomplishing this, Norman, (1963a) began studying the importance of item content in personality surveys. Norman became interested in Berg's (1955; Berg & Rapaport, 1954) work on the "deviation hypothesis." Statistical analysis of deviant test responses had led Berg to the notion that item *content* often is not an important characteristic of test items. Whether item content makes any difference or not became a "hot" issue among psychometricians. Inspired by Berg's hypothesis, Norman's work was based on anonymous "peer nominations," that is, respondents' responses to trait items describing unidentified ratees with whom the respondents had little or no prior acquaintance. Norman and Goldberg (1966) argued that the factor structure that results from trait ratings obtained under these conditions may not be indicative of the *ratees'* personality structure, but may rather be the manifestation of an "implicit personality theory" (IPT) shared by the *raters*. They also proposed using indices of interrater agreement and convergent and discriminant validity vis-à-vis other measures of the same traits to determine the pertinence of such ratings to the ratees' traits.

Controversy emerged as Goldberg and Slovic (1967) tested Berg's assertion further, but found little support for it, and Adams (1967) rejoined that Goldberg and Slovic had misconstrued Berg's hypothesis (see also Watson, 1989). Nevertheless, the most basic question concerning the measurement validity of personality assessment had been broached: does it make any difference what the items say and what the traits of the assessee are? Do personality inventories reveal more about the raters than about the ratees? This led Norman to conduct further research on IPT.

Norman and his colleagues, notably Frank Passini (Passini & Norman, 1966, 1969), studied implicit personality theory in several studies, by asking students on the first day of a new semester, to use 20 items on a personality rating instrument to rate each other despite having no prior acquaintance with each other. These students had been in the same room for less than 15 minutes and had no opportunity for verbal communication. Yet, they rendered ratings that, when factor-analyzed, yielded the *same* factor structure obtained from ratings by individuals intimately familiar with each other, as well as trained professionals' ratings of clients in treatment. Furthermore, throughout this period the repeated confirmation of the five-factor personality structure was solidifying the standing of the five-factor approach to personality theory and assessment. Nevertheless, the nagging cloud of doubt aroused by the factor structure's being *too* stable was casting a shadow over its validity.

OUR IDEA: IMPLICIT ORGANIZATION THEORY

It was the late 1960s. We were taking Professor Norman's course on measurement and assessment as part of the recommended curriculum in the organizational psychology doctoral program at the University of Michigan. It was one of the best courses we ever took. It led us through psychometrics from A to Z with strong emphasis on factor analysis for assessing personality and for investigating personality structure. However, it gave us much more than the intellectual satisfaction derived from mastering psychometric methods; it inspired us to view critically the methods in use in our own disciplinary subfield of organizational psychology. In organizational research, observations are mostly based on respondents' perceptions and the data are collected by means of questionnaires. We began wondering whether this was a credible method or, perhaps, only a reflection of *Implicit Organizational Theory,* that is, an expression of the individual *perceivers' opinions* about how organizational variables related to one another rather than the *true relationships* as they exist in the rated organizations—independently of the raters' cognition and assessment.

The only thing in organizational-behavior related research at the time that seemed remotely similar to implicit theory was Mason Haire's (1950) work on the impressions participants formed of shoppers' character from shopping lists. For example, Haire found that participants rated shoppers appreciably more negatively if their list included instant coffee. New at the time, it was a product that aroused denigration and attribution of laziness and lack of care for the welfare of the shopper's family. The demonstrated impact of information about one characteristic on positive or negative assessments of other characteristics was actually an early form of halo research and was a precursor of the notion of implicit theory, though neither the IPT literature nor the ILT literature referenced Haire's study, nor did Haire contemplate implicit theory. Nevertheless, Haire's research was in our minds as our interest in implicit organization theory developed.

In the most commonly used method in organizational behavior research, respondents are asked to rate—using questionnaire items—their organization, or some aspects of it, in various domains. Based on theoretical reasoning, these items are then grouped together into indices to enhance the reliability of the measurement of the underlying constructs that they are supposed to tap (by some statistical technique such as factor analyses or smallest space analysis). Then the researcher typically seeks statistical relationships *among* the indices, strives to explain the pattern of their interrelationships and interprets them using a theoretical model. Usually it is a casual model, so that each construct is categorized as either a causal variable, a mediator, a moderator, or an end-result (outcome) variable.

When we learned about the notion of IPT in personality research in Norman's course, it dawned on us that the same implicit theory phenomenon could be happening when researchers construct multiple-item indices in organizational behavior research. We wondered: What assurances do we have that respondents in organizational behavior surveys are not rating their organizations on the basis of their own, personal implicit organizational theories (like raters of persons)? For instance, items that rate different aspects of team cohesion may cluster in a specific way—the way dictated by the raters' implicit organizational theories—rather than the way objective and independently-verifiable variables cluster in the real world of the particular rated organization. But then we went one step beyond the IPT of Norman and colleagues by wondering not only about the validity of the factor structures of theoretical variables but also about the validity of the *pattern of relationships among factors*. We wondered whether the relationships between constructs (e.g., between causal, intervening, or end-result variables) found in a set of data actually reflect not objective reality but rather an implicit organizational theory that respondents carry around in their minds. Thus, we were concerned with two potential implicit theories. One concerned implicit relationship *among the particular items* comprising each factor, and the other concerned implicit relationships *among* the factors.

We thought that both of these possibilities would have far-reaching implications because most organizational behavior research was—and still is—based on perceptual data collected by means of questionnaires. Would we get the same factor structure if respondents were asked to use the same questionnaire to describe an unknown or nonexistent organization? The answer would have to await our return to Israel after completing our doctoral studies.

SURVEY OF ORGANIZATIONS (SOO)

We had intimate familiarity with the Survey of Organizations (SOO). The Business & Industry Group (BIG) at the Center for Research on the Utilization of Scientific Knowledge (CRUSK) at the University of Michigan's Institute for Social Research (ISR) had developed this questionnaire instrument for its basic research and for its action-research in organizations (see Taylor, 1971; Taylor & Bowers, 1972; Seashore, Lawler, Mirvis, & Cammann, 1983). The SOO operationalizes Likert's (1961, 1967) theory of organizations. It measures the full complement of organizational variables that Likert posited to be interrelated causally in a manner that points the way to practical application. Interventions designed to improve the causal variables (e.g., leadership, innovation, management policy) result in elevating the intervening variables (e.g., communication, teamwork, involvement, interdepartmental coordination), culminating over time in better results such as satisfaction, performance, and profitability. The evidence supporting this central thesis was the repeatedly-obtained strong correlations among the causal, intervening, and end-result variables measured using paper-and-pencil questionnaire surveys. Such results were evidenced in many studies. These consistently strong correlations led Likert to the inference that higher-level "causal" variables cause higher levels of intervening variables, which in turn transfer causality to the end-result variables, the endpoint in a process that culminates with improvements in management's coveted outcomes. An illustrative example of using the SOO instrument to substantiate Likert's theoretical causal model is the work of the CRUSK team headed by Bowers (1973). They undertook the Inter-Company Longitudinal Study (ICLS) in twenty-three organizations that received different types of OD interventions in a pretest–posttest design using the SOO to measure the impact of these interventions. The ICLS confirmed, among other findings, the causal flow in organizations from "causal" to "intervening" to "end-result" variables, as predicted by Likert's theory. (Under current rules of evidence, such results would be highly suspect for same-source-same-method bias, not strong confirmation of the theory.)

Thus, the SOO was theory-based, widely used, and highly regarded as a validated measuring instrument. However, our knowledge of implicit personality theory led us to question whether the all-important factor structure obtained for the SOO items, as well as the pattern of correlations among the factors, truly reflected organizational reality. Could they be merely a reflection of implicit organization theory? If the answer were to be positive, what is the value of amassing knowledge of cognitive artifacts?

Major parts of the SOO had been translated into Hebrew in a previous large scale organizational study in Israel (e.g., Tannebaum et al., 1974). We adapted the Hebrew version, added the few items from the original that were missing, and set out to test out our ideas empirically.

OUR STUDY

We were teaching organizational behavior classes in several departments in colleges and universities in Israel. We had our students describe "Plant X" using the translated SOO. The only information we provided about Plant X was that it was a medium size food producer located in the central part of the country. At the time, food processing and packaging was among the leading branches of the local industrial economy, and that emaciated description was intended to keep it as nondescript as possible to replicate Norman's anonymous peer-nomination procedure with as much fidelity as possible. Our intention was to provide minimal information to force respondents to tap their implicit organization theories in responding, if they harbored such theories. One thing was clear: if data collected in this manner yielded the same factor structure of the items and the same correlational pattern among the factors as are obtained when using the same questionnaire to measure these variables in "real" organizational surveys, the nonexistent Plant X could not be the source of the interitem variances that are the stuff of which factors are made. Plant X could also not be the source of the covariation among the factors that constitute the foundation of our organizational theories. Therefore, *implicit organization theory* would remain a viable explanation.

We collected data about Plant X from about 250 student-respondents in several courses and subjected the data to factor analysis. As this preceded the era of exploratory and confirmatory factor analysis, we separately factored each of the three categories of variables in the Likert scheme: causal, intervening, and end-result variables. Then we analyzed the pattern of relationships among the factors within each of the groups and the pattern of relationships among the groups of variables. As predicted on the basis the implicit-organization-theory hypothesis, the items factored according to the conceptual variables in Likert's theory. Furthermore, the pattern of relationships among the factors was similar to that obtained under "real" research conditions in actual organizations.

We then did everything imaginable to try to prevent the confirmatory theoretical factor structure and pattern of interconstruct correlations from emerging. We analyzed the responses separately for respondents who had experience working in organizations and separately for those who had no work experience. We analyzed the data separately for those who said they had a specific organization in mind when answering the questions and for those who had not. All these analyses yielded the same factor structure and the same correlational pattern. Finally, we even analyzed the data separately only for those who said they had responded at random; it was clear that they had not responded randomly because the same relationship structures emerged from this analysis also. We realized that this factor structure and correlational pattern were going to emerge regardless of what we did.

We wrote a report of our study under the title of "Implicit Organization Theory" and submitted it to *Journal of Applied Psychology.* We got back a revise-and-resubmit that imposed a page limitation requiring us to reduce length substantially. One reviewer recommended dropping all findings of the relationships between factors and the presentation of the entire organizational model, and reporting only the results for the factor analysis of the leadership items. We were not overjoyed by having to jettison most of our data, and not much evidence would survive to substantiate our claim to have demonstrated implicit *organization* theory. However, given that we had to reduce it, it made sense to retain the leadership factors; after all, they comprised a major part of the first step of our analyses: the inter-item analyses to examine factor structure. Presenting the leadership factors in the first report of our findings—if we were to be limited to reporting just one aspect of our findings— also *seemed* justified on the grounds that this was the closest analogue to Norman and his colleagues' research on IPT that had inspired our own ideas.

This seemed to be appropriate also because the leadership items in the SOO had a long and illustrious history. Bowers and Seashore (1966) had assembled them from the Ohio State University and University of Michigan leadership studies and validated them as indicators of leadership that predicted organizational effectiveness. The SOO leadership items had the cleanest factor structure in the SOO. Furthermore, in our study we obtained the original four Bowers-and-Seashore theoretical leadership factors. Moreover, the SOO leadership items yielded simple structure; each item loaded on one of the four factors and no item loaded on more than one factor. Therefore, we met the page limitation with our revision by reporting only the leadership results. Then, in the revision process, we correspondingly changed the title from "Implicit Organization Theory" to "Implicit Leadership Theory" better to reflect its focus, and *Journal of Applied Psychology* published it under that title (Eden & Leviatan, 1975).

In short, "implicit *leadership* theory" was born of a fluke. Thus began a stream of research that blossomed as organizational psychology got swept into the cognitive revolution that came to dominate social psychology (see Lord & Mahler, 1989, 1991). Many of the issues aroused by the cognitive revolution are addressable by conceptualizing implicit theories and studying them empirically.

It also led to some further developments. From its humble beginnings in our original study of the imaginary "Plant X," ILT has generated a considerable effort to understand the peculiar variables that come into play in leadership ratings (e.g., Hall & Lord, 1995). There have been serious attempts to unravel the mysteries of leadership perception and its implications for leadership research and practice (e.g., Hall & Lord, 1995; Lord & Mahler, 1990). Implicit leadership theory research has been taken as far as the cross-cultural comparison of leadership perceptions in 62 cultures encompassed in the GLOBE study (Den Hartog, House, Hanges, Ruiz-Quintanilla, & Dorfman, 1999). Indeed, this edited volume is itself a testament to thirty years of flowering of implicit leadership theory.

WHAT IF? THIRTY-YEAR-OLD-FANTASIES

Like "MASH" that became "Battle Circus" and then "M*A*S*H," "Implicit Organization Theory" became "Implicit Leadership Theory." Perhaps it is time to reconsider the generalizability of implicit theories in organizational behavior and rediscover implicit *organization* theory. After all, ILT dealt with a limited, mostly psychometric, aspect of organizational behavior. We have often wondered how things would have developed differently had we been able to publish the entire set of results under the title: "*Implicit Organization Theory.*" Here are some of our fantasies about what could have resulted.

We would have cumulative evidence from a stream of validation studies of the MTMM type (Campbell & Fiske, 1959) to offer convergent validation of the recurrent patterns of relations among organizational variables. Research would have discovered the origins of the implicit organizational theories that people harbor in their minds. We would know how, if at all, implicit organizational theories develop and change. Research might have focused on how to mold implicit organizational theories and what impact such engineered implicit organization theories have on organizational members. Research would have revealed the causal relationships between leaders' implicit organization theories and their actual behavior and vice versa. Alternatively, a different, perhaps richer, stream of cognitive organizational research may have flourished. There would be organizational-behavior discourse about implicit theories of group relations and teamwork, decision-making, interpersonal and interdepartmental communication, conflict, negotiation, and the like.

Clearly, there is potential for implicit theories of other organizational constructs and processes. For example, the publication of one experiment on "implicit *stress* theory" (Westman & Eden, 1991) kicked off a spate of follow-up research replicating it and developing its implications for stress management and abatement (Fernandez & Perrewé, 1995; Furnham, 1997; Moss & Lawrence, 1997; Perrewé, Fernandez, & Morton, 1993; Westman, 1996).

One more example is the Pygmalion-in-Management research, which is actually a special case of implicit theory. The Pygmalion effect illustrates the way in which changing one aspect of how managers perceive their subordinates changes how they perceive other aspects of the same subordinates (recall the effect of simply adding instant coffee to a shopping list), changes their expectations of the subordinates, and changes how they treat and manage them. Once led to believe that their subordinates are capable of success, managers treat them accordingly and produce a self-fulfilling prophecy that maintains the integrity of the gestalt; workers who are *expected* to do well *do* do well. Thus, the practical power of implicit theories may reside in the their capacity to evoke behavior that accords the "theory" and can produce productive results—provided it is the "right" theory.

EPILOGUE

There is a cardinal lesson to be learned from how we got from IPT in the 1960s to ILT in the 21st Century. Perhaps most important, had we not been required to take Warren Norman's course in personality assessment, we may not have taken it and may not have known about implicit personality theory. Such cross fertilization from one specialty to another has occurred with other topics as well. For example, Bass has repeatedly told how a doctoral student urged him to read a book in political science. The book was entitled *Leadership* and its author was James MacGregor Burns (1978). In it Burns developed the concept of transformational leadership in the political arena. Within a few years, Bass's (1985, 1998) work transformed management leadership research as transformational leadership came to dominate the leadership literature in organizational psychology and organizational behavior. Another example is the Pygmalion effect, which originated in educational psychology with Rosenthal and Jacobson's (1968) landmark classroom experiment in Oak School and was later "imported" into organizational psychology (Eden, 1990, 2003). It emerged as a line of research within organizational behavior, as evidenced by meta-analyses of the Pygmalion effect exclusively in the Pygmalion-as-Manager realm (Kierein & Gold, 2000; McNatt, 2000). Another example is Axelrod's (1984) work with the prisoner's dilemma and its translation into interorganizational relations and the international arena of diplomacy and relations among nations. Yet another instance is making analogues from organizational theory to international relations (Kahn, 1994). Finally, much of the research on international conflict resolution has borrowed concepts from social psychology and interpersonal conflict resolution. Without any doubt, cross-disciplinary fertilization spawns new scientific discoveries.

   Neither of us continued the line of research that was ignited by our ILT study. This was due partly to the frustration we felt having been forced to give up the far-reaching topic of implicit *organization* theory for the sake of the relatively anemic implicit *leadership* theory. Each of us moved in different directions but followed the gush of publications on this theme, amazed over the years by the interest that our humble study had spawned. Yet, if we may offer advice to organization researchers who are actively engaged in research on implicit theories, it is the ideas that we list under the heading "WHAT IF" above. Who knows? Perhaps we ourselves may renew our active pursuit of implicit theories and the more generic realm of cognitive organizational behavior. This time we'll call it I*O*T.

REFERENCES

Adams, H.E. (1967). Comments on L. Goldberg and P. Slovic's Misunderstanding of I. Berg's hypotheses and their misinterpretation of several studies. *Journal of Counseling Psychology, 14,* 472–473.

Axelrod, R. (1984). *The evolution of cooperation.* New York: Basic Books.

Bass, B.M. (1985). *Leadership and performance beyond expectations.* New York: Free Press.

Bass, B.M. (1998). *Transformational leadership: Industry, military, and educational impact.* Mahwah, NJ: Lawrence Erlbaum.

Berg, I.A. (1955). Response bias and personality: The deviation hypothesis. *Journal of Psychology: Interdisciplinary & Applied, 40,* 61–72.

Berg, I.A., & Rapaport, G.M. (1954). Response bias in an unstructured questionnaire. *Journal of Psychology: Interdisciplinary & Applied, 38,* 475–481.

Bowers, D.G. (1973). *Journal of Applied Behavioral Science.*

Bowers, D.G., & Seashore, S. (1966). Predicting organizational effectiveness with a four-factor of leadership. *Administrative Sciences Quarterly, 11,* 238–263.

Burns, J.M. (1978). *Leadership.* New York: Harper & Row.

Campbell, D.T., & Fiske, D.W. (1959). Convergent and discriminant validation by the multitrait-multimethod matrix. *Psychological Bulletin, 56,* 81–105.

Den Hartog, D.N., House, R.J., Hanges, P.J., Ruiz-Quintanilla, S.A., & Dorfman, P.W. (1999). Culture specific and cross-culturally generalizable implicit leadership theories: Are attributes of charismatic/transformational leadership universally endorsed?" *Leadership Quarterly, 10,* 219–256.

Eden, D. (1990). *Pygmalion in management: Productivity as a self-fulfilling prophecy.* Lexington, MA: Lexington Books.

Eden D. (2003). Self-fulfilling prophecies in organizations. In J. Greenberg (Ed.), *Organizational behavior: The state of the science* (2nd ed., pp. 91–122). Mahwah, NJ: Lawrence Erlbaum.

Eden, D., & Leviatan, U. (1975). Implicit leadership theory as a determinant of the factor structure underlying supervisory behavior scales. *Journal of Applied Psychology, 60,* 736–741.

Fernandez, D.R., & Perrewé, P.L. (1995). Implicit stress theory: An experimental examination of subjective performance information on employee evaluations. *Journal of Organizational Behavior, 16,* 353–362.

Furnham, A. (1997). Lay theories of work stress. *Work and Stress, 11,* 68–78.

Goldberg, L.R., & Slovic, P. (1967). Importance of test item content: An analysis of a corollary of the deviation hypothesis. *Journal of Counseling Psychology, 14,* 462–472.

Haire, M. (1950). Projective techniques in marketing research. *Journal of Marketing, 14,* 649–656.

Hall, R.J., & Lord, R.G. (1995). Multi-level information-processing explanations of followers' leadership perception. *Leadership Quarterly, 6,* 265–287.

House, R., Javidan, M., Hanges, P., & Dorfman, P. (2002). Understanding cultures and implicit leadership theories across the globe: An introduction to project GLOBE. *Journal of World Business, 37*(1), 3–10.

Kahn, R.L. (1994). *Organization and nation states: New perspectives on conflict and cooperation.* San Francisco: Jossey-Bass.

Kierein, N., & Gold, M.A. (2000). Pygmalion in work organizations: A meta-analysis. *Journal of Organizational Behavior, 21,* 913–928.

Likert, R. (1961). *New patterns of management.* New York: McGraw-Hill.

Likert, R. (1967). *The human organization: Its management and value.* New York: McGraw-Hill.

Lord, R.G., & Maher, K.L. (1989). Cognitive processes in industrial and organizational psychology. In C.L. Cooper & I.T. Robertson (Eds.), *International Review of industrial and organizational psychology* (Vol. 4, pp. 49–91. Manchester: Wiley.

Lord, R.G., & Maher, K.L. (1990). Perceptions of leadership and their implications in organizations. In J. Carroll (Ed.), *Applied social psychology and organizational settings* (pp. 129–154). Hillsdale, NJ: Erlbaum.

Lord, R.G., & Maher, K.L. (1991). Cognitive theory in industrial and organizational psychology. In M. Dunnette & L. Hough (Eds.), *Handbook of industrial and organizational psychology* (2nd ed., Vol. 2, pp. 1–62). Palo Alto, CA: Consulting Psychological Press.

McNatt, D.B. (2000). Ancient Pygmalion joins contemporary management: A meta-analysis of the result. *Journal of Applied Psychology, 85,* 314–322.

Moss, S.E., & Lawrence, K.G. (1997). The effects of priming on the self-reporting of perceived stressors and strains. *Journal of Organizational Behavior, 18,* 393–403.

Norman, W.T. (1963a). Relative importance of test item content. *Journal of Consulting Psychology, 27,* 166–174.

Norman, W.T. (1963b). Toward an adequate taxonomy of personality attributes: Replicated factor structure in peer nomination personality ratings. *Journal of Abnormal and Social Psychology, 66,* 574–583.

Norman, W.T., & Goldberg, L.R. (1966). Raters, ratees, and randomness in personality structure. *Journal of Personality and Social Psychology, 4,* 681–691.

Passini, F T., & Norman, W.T. (1966). A universal conception of personality structure? *Journal of Personality and Social Psychology, 4,* 44–49.

Passini, F T., & Norman, W.T. (1969). Ratee relevance in peer nominations. *Journal of Applied Psychology, 53,* 185–187.

Perrewé, P.L., Fernandez, D.R., & Morton, K.S. (1993). An experimental examination of **implicit stress theory**. *Journal of Organizational Behavior, 14,* 677–686.

Porras, J.I. (1979). The comparative impact of different organization development techniques. *Journal of Applied Behavioral Science, 15,* 156–178.

Rosenthal, R., & Jacobson, L. (1968). *Pygmalion in the classroom: Teacher expectation and pupils' intellectual development.* New York: Holt, Rinehart & Winston.

Seashore, S.E., Lawler III, E.E., Mirvis, P.H., & Cammann, C. (Eds.). (1983). *Assessing organizational change: A guide to methods, measures, and practices.* New York: Wiley.

Tannenbaum, A.M., Rosner, M., Kavic, B., Vianello, M., & Weiser, G.(1974). *Hierarchy in organizations.* San Francisco: Jossey Bass.

Taylor, J.C. (1971). *Technology and planned organizational change.* Ann Arbor: University of Michigan, Center for Research on Utilization of Scientific Knowledge, Institute for Social Research.

Taylor, J.C., & Bowers, D.G. (1972). *Survey of organizations: A machine-scored standardized questionnaire instrument.* Ann Arbor: University of Michigan, Center for Research on Utilization of Scientific Knowledge, Institute for Social Research.

Watson, D. (1989). Strangers' ratings of the five robust personality factors: Evidence of a surprising convergence with self-report. *Journal of Personality and Social Psychology, 57,* 120–128.

Westman, M., & Eden, D. (1991). Implicit stress theory: The spurious effects of stress on performance ratings. *Journal of Social Behavior and Personality, 6,* 127–140.

Westman, M. (1996). Implicit stress theory: An experimental examination of the impact of rater's stress on performance appraisal. *Journal of Social Behavior and Personality, 11,* 753–766.

AN OVERVIEW OF IMPLICIT LEADERSHIP THEORIES AND THEIR APPLICATION IN ORGANIZATION PRACTICE

Birgit Schyns and James R. Meindl

ABSTRACT

This paper gives an overview of past and present research on implicit leadership theories. The application of implicit leadership theories in organizational practice is outlined and a broad definition of this concept is given. Research is separated into several streams, namely: information processing and the effects of implicit leadership theories; content and generalizability of implicit leadership theories; and explanations of implicit leadership theories. Research from all streams is summarized. At the end of this chapter, an overview of all the chapters in this book is given.

Implicit Leadership Theories: Essays and Explorations, pages 15–36
Copyright © 2005 by Information Age Publishing
All rights of reproduction in any form reserved.

INTRODUCTION

The concept of implicit leadership theories has become a topic of methodological and substantive research interest since its introduction in Eden and Leviatan (1975). This chapter aims at giving an overview of past and present research on implicit leadership theories. Before we outline the existing streams of research, we will explain the relevance of implicit leadership theories in organizational practice. Finally, we will give an overview of the chapters in this book.

THE APPLICATION OF IMPLICIT LEADERSHIP THEORIES IN ORGANIZATIONAL PRACTICE

Knowledge about implicit leadership theories is highly relevant for organizations. Unfortunately, in comparison to the interest in leadership behavior, this topic is more or less neglected in organizational practice. In this section, we will summarize some of the ideas proposed for the use of implicit leadership theories in organizational practice, as well as offer some new ideas on the topic. In doing so, we wish to make clear that the possible bias that implicit leadership theories bring to the perception of leadership (e.g., Awamleh, 2003; Shamir, 1992) is relevant to leadership practice. Leaders are often the subject matter of questionnaires given to followers, as is the case in the context of 360-degree feedback. Since the feedback from these questionnaires is frequently used to train leaders, an awareness of the subjective biases embedded within them is essential to the appropriate interpretation of the information these questionnaires hold.

An assessment of followers' implicit leadership theories could prove helpful in determining the potential need for *"followers training."* Although this kind of training is unusual in present organizational practice, a training concentrating on followers rather than leaders could prove to be interesting and worthwhile. Encouraging followers to reflect on possible "errors" in their implicit leadership theories could improve the relationship between leaders and followers and may help followers to have more realistic expectations of their leaders. In general, training observers to be aware of their implicit leadership theories and helping them come to make more realistic evaluations of a target (here: the leader) can reduce the effects of negative biases in evaluation processes.

More research is needed on the actual effects of implicit leadership theories on followers' and leaders' behaviors and interactions. We can assume that not only followers' behavior and well-being are influenced by implicit leadership theories (through fulfilment or non-fulfilment of their expectations) but also—subsequently—leaders' reactions. It seems easier for leaders to lead a group that has expectations in line with his/her behavior than to lead a group that has expectation he or she cannot fulfil (e.g., in the case of the Romance of Leadership, Meindl, 1990, see below).

A CATEGORIZATION OF IMPLICIT LEADERSHIP THEORY RESEARCH

The idea of implicit leadership theories has inspired different streams of research. After conducting the initial research on the factor structure of implicit leadership theories (Eden & Leviatan, 1975), researchers working with implicit leadership theories next focused on information processing in leadership (for an overview see Lord & Maher, 1993). This stream of research worked with the idea of applying a certain behavior scheme to a particular target—in this case, the target being the leader (e.g., Calder, 1977; see Figure I.1). In this approach, it is more important how prototypical a behavior is than what behaviors the implicit leadership theories actually consist of (see Fraser & Lord, 1988; Lord, Foti, & de Vader, 1984). Prominent examples of this stream of research are Lord and colleagues' studies on the effect of performance cues on the perception of leaders (e.g., Phillips, & Lord, 1986; Rush, Phillips, & Lord, 1981).

In more recent research from this stream, the effect of implicit leadership theories on the perception and evaluation of leadership is examined (e.g., Awamleh & Gardner, 1999; Schyns, Felfe, & Blank, in review; Schyns & Sanders, 2004). Others have examined the effect of implicit leadership theories in an organizational context (e.g., Nye & Forsyth, 1991). Figure I.2 gives an idea as to how this research is designed.

The second stream of research has drawn more from qualitative and explorative research methods. This stream of research has focused on the content of implicit leadership theories. The aim of this research is to uncover the behaviors and attitudes which form individuals' implicit leadership theories (e.g., Offermann, Kennedy, & Wirtz, 1994). Although this stream of research has in some cases asked their participants to rate differ-

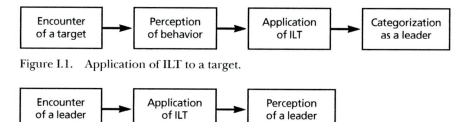

Figure I.1.   Application of ILT to a target.

Figure I.2.   Application of ILT to a leader.

ent targets (such as leaders and supervisors), another area has put the different targets more into focus by looking for differences in different types of leaders (e.g., male and female leaders) or by examining the generalizability of implicit leadership theories across cultures. Although this latter research area also focuses on the content of implicit leadership theories, there are some differences between the two approaches mentioned which can be outlined as follows: Whereas the main aim of the one type of content research is to find out what individuals believe to be the basic characteristics of leaders in general, the aim of the other research area is to profile different subtypes of leaders. Here the actual content of an implicit leadership theory is less important. More important are the overlap or differences that exist between different groups. Research on the content of implicit leadership theories is often more qualitative in nature, whereas research on cross-cultural generalizability and studies attending to the different kinds of leaders tend to use quantitative methods.

Still another kind of research has focused on predicting implicit leadership theories (Keller, 1999), for example, by using personality characteristics and the influence of parents as predictors. Implicit leadership theories are regarded as dependent variables and research in this area aims at explaining how implicit leadership theories evolve. See Table I.1 for an overview of the streams and examples of research questions.

Table I.1.   Research Streams and Sample Research Questions

Stream	Sample research question	Sample article
Factoranalytic research	What is the structure of leadership ratings like, when no leadership is mentioned	Eden & Leviatan (1975)
Information processing	a) How does information given to a participant shape the perception of leadership	Lord (1985) Meindl & Ehrlich (1987)
	b) How do observer's ILT shape the perception of leadership	Shamir (1992)
	c) What effects do ILT have in organizations	Nye & Forsyth (1991)
Contents	What characteristics are stored as characteristics of leaders	Offermann et al. (1994)
Generalizability	What differences exist between different types of leaders	Den Hartog et al. (1999)
Prediction	How can we explain ILT	Keller (1999)

While this categorization of the streams of research is based on the content of the studies, other categorizations could organize research on implicit leadership theories according to whom actually "has" these theories (e.g., do they stem from followers, supervisors, observers?), whom the theories are about, or whether or not implicit leadership theories are used as dependent or independent variables. Studies applying implicit leadership theories may also be based on different research designs, as mentioned above. In our overview, we will make use of the following categorization of research: (a) factor-analytic approach to implicit leadership theories, (b) information processing and effects of implicit leadership theories, (c) content, (d) generalizability of implicit leadership theories, and (e) explanations of implicit leadership theories.

DEFINITIONS OF IMPLICIT LEADERSHIP THEORIES

The definition of implicit leadership theories presented in the pioneering article by Eden and Leviatan (1975) is based on Schneider's (1973) implicit personality theories. Eden and Leviatan refer to implicit leadership theories as "conceptual factors that the respondents brought with them to the measurement situation" (p. 738). Other definitions have also been offered since the beginnings of the research in this area, with definitions being more or less implied by the different research traditions identified above. In the following section, we will summarize the most important ones and add a broader definition of the concept.

Categorization

In the context of information processing, Kenney, Schwartz-Kenney, and Blascovich (1996) define implicit leadership theories as *cognitive structures* containing the traits and behaviors of leaders. They are stored in memory and are activated when individuals are confronted with leaders.

The definition used by Lord and colleagues (e.g., Engle & Lord, 1997) falls into the same tradition. Here, implicit leadership theories begin with a more general classification of a target as leader or non-leader. Subsequently, the judgment and reaction toward the other are based on a *general impression*, rather than the memory of specific behaviors (Engle & Lord, 1997, p. 991).

Offermann et al. (1994) also place their research on the content of implicit leadership theories in the tradition of cognitive categorizations, referring to the work of Lord and colleagues (Lord et al., 1984; Lord, Foti, & Phillips, 1982). For them, leadership is "a cognitive category in memory, organized hierarchically, like all other categories, into three levels" (p. 44). These levels are (1) the distinction between leaders and non-leaders, (2) different types of leaders, and (3) actual leaders (persons). The further content is then comprising positive and negative leader attributes (e.g., tyranny).

In the context of research explaining implicit leadership theories, Keller (1999) uses the same definition as Offerman et al. (1994), namely, Lord's categorization approach, and defines implicit leadership theories in the tradition of *script and schema* approaches (Keller, 2003). Foti and Lord (1987) distinguish between implicit leadership theories as prototypes and implicit leadership theories as scripts. Whereas prototypes refer to a set of characteristics, scripts have a temporal structure involving a process of actions.

Postive and Negative Implicit Leadership Theories

When we consider the literature on implicit leadership theories and its connection to culture and/or gender, we can see that some researchers in this tradition have concentrated on the positive side of implicit leadership theories, that is, they define implicit leadership theories as the opinion individuals have about the characteristics of a successful leader. Although the GLOBE-project generally defines implicit leadership theories as implicit ideas about how leaders *are* and the *expectations* others have of them (Den Hartog et al., 1999), their assessment concentrates on the question as to which leadership attributes facilitate *effective* leadership and use a "should be"-approach (see also Szabo et al., 2002).

Research on the think-manager-think-male approach (Schein, 1973, 1975; Sczesny, 2003) and other research on gender and implicit leadership theories (e.g., promotability; van Engen, Johannesen-Schmidt, & Vinkenburg, 2003) define implicit leadership theories in terms of managers in general (male and female) as well as successful managers (male and female, see Heilman, Block, Martell, & Simon, 1989): The content of ILT in this stream of research comprises of positive, neutral as well as negative attributes (e.g., analytic ability, decisiveness, power need). Some of these definitions also include a differentiation between descriptive and prescriptive norms. The first ones contain beliefs about what women and men actually do; the second ones contain beliefs about what members of both social groups ought to do (Heilman, 2001; Sczesny, 2003). For a summary of elements of implicit leadership theories see Table I.2.

Table I.2.   Elements of a Definition of ILT

Memory	Evaluation	Ascription
Cognitive structure	Positive/negative	Prescriptive
Script/schemas	Effective	Descriptive
Categorization as a leader	Successful	

Overview and Summary of the Definitions of Implicit Leadership Theories

Research in the context of information processing does not focus, for the most part, on the content of implicit leadership theories but on the application of these theories. Those studies that emphasize the content of implicit leadership theories do so in different ways: One in a more explorative way, the other in a more profiling way. While some research groups define implicit leadership theories as theories about good or successful leaders (e.g., Den Hartog et al., 1999), others focus on leaders in general. It may well be that the term's leader and good/effective leader are viewed as equivalent for some participants (though maybe not for all of them).[1] A summarizing definition of implicit leadership theories, which incorporates all approaches, could read: "the image that a person has of a leader in general, or of an effective leader." This definition allows for the possibility that the respective person applies this image to a target person in order to identify this target person as a leader, or applies this image to a person previously labeled as leader.

OVERVIEW OF RESEARCH ON IMPLICIT LEADERSHIP THEORIES

In order to examine implicit leadership theories, Eden and Leviatan (1975) gave students information about a plant (but not about the actual leadership in that plant). The students were then asked to rate leadership on a common leadership questionnaire (the Survey of Organizations by Taylor & Bowers, 1972). The resulting factor structure of the data was similar to the one found in prior research, where participants rated real leaders. This result was replicated by Weiss and Adler (1981), although their hypothesis that cognitive complexity would affect the factor structure of the leadership questionnaire was not confirmed. These early studies on implicit leadership theories were rather explorative in nature and resulted in the idea that the structure of implicit leadership theories would be the same as the structure of evaluations of actual leaders.

Subsequent research followed the lines mentioned above, allowing us to cluster the research into groups concerning information processing, content and generalizability of implicit leadership theories, and the prediction of implicit leadership theories. We will outline the respective research in the following sections.

Information Processing and Effects
of Implicit Leadership Theories

Lord and colleagues conducted a series of experiments on the idea of how information about group performance would impact the ratings of leaders. Already in 1977, Lord argued that the variance found in leadership measures might be due to evaluator stereotypes. Rush, Thomas, and Lord (1977) could replicate Eden and Leviatan's (1975) result on the structure of leadership questionnaires and found in addition that ratings were highly influenced by the information given to participants concerning performance. In 1981, Rush, Phillips, and Lord extended the research on the effect of bogus information on the perception of leadership by introducing a time lag between the information and the actual rating. They manipulated leader's behavior, as well as the performance information, and found that the effect of the behavioral information on participant recall was relatively stable. After the time lag, however, participants' perception of leadership oriented toward the performance information rather than the initial leader behavior.

With these initial studies, a series of experiments began which then led to the following results with respect to implicit leadership theories (for an overview see Lord & Maher, 1993): Information about performance (e.g., of a group or an organization) has an impact on leadership perceptions, which is to say that observers perceive more leadership in cases of success, and that others are seen more as leaders when success is attributed to them. In addition, different types of information processing (automatic and controlled, Lord, 1985) occur depending on whether or not the information given fits the observed outcome or not. The results on performance cues obtained in Lord's studies could be replicated by Larson (1982). Watching videos of groups, the participants received bogus information concerning the performance of these groups. This information had an impact on the evaluation of the group's leader.[2]

In their most recent theoretical outline on information processing in leadership, Lord, Brown, Harvey, and Hall (2001) developed an explanatory model they term a connectionist network. This network explains the different images for different targets and individuals by introducing the concept of contextual constrains. Lord et al. (2001) differentiate four types of contextual constrains and their characteristics: culture (values and norms), leader (goals, affect, and norms), follower (values and goals), and current task (affect and goals). These constrains plus behavioral input (that is the actual leader behavior) form the basis of leadership schemes that can be characterized by six characteristics: dominant, decisive, masculine, extraverted, intelligent, flexible. In this way, Lord et al. (2001) also allow for changes in implicit leadership theories (through the constrains they mention). The topic of change is picked up again later in this chapter.

The notion of automatic and controlled information processing in the context of applying implicit leadership theories is supported by Kenney et al. (1996). They found that individuals rely on prototypes when rating leaders' behavior. Their results indicate that participants recognize category-consistent information more easily than information concerning others for whom the category (leader-worthy-of-influence) was not triggered.

Using a sentence-completion design, Konst, Vonk, and van der Vlist (1999) found that participants engaged in more causal analysis when a person was labeled "leader" than when a person was labeled "follower." Based on the general tendency that people more strongly attribute leader behavior (as opposed to follower behavior) to dispositional rather than situational factors, Vonk and Konst (2003) showed that inconsistent information (followers' behavior explained with their disposition) caused stronger inferences than consistent information (leaders' behavior explained with their disposition).

Implicit leadership theories were also used in experiments on information processing and the perception of leadership. Rather than testing if implicit leadership theories exist, this research focused on the effects of implicit leadership theories. Some examples are summarized below.

Awamleh and Gardner (1999) found no relationship between the implicit leadership theory "Romance of Leadership" (that is, the extent to which individuals attribute responsibility for company performance to leaders, see Meindl, 1998, for further details, see below) and the perception of transformational leadership. The same results were found by Schyns and Sanders (2004). However, Awamleh (2003), Al-Dmour and Awamleh (2002), as well as Schyns et al. (in preparation), found that Romance of Leadership has a positive impact on the perception of a leader as transformational. A similar result was reported by Shamir (1992). Meindl (1990) could confirm this relationship using the rating of political leaders.

Nye and colleagues go one step further by focusing on the actual effect of a match between followers' implicit leadership theories and leaders' actual behavior. Whereas Nye and Forsyth (1991) found that the match indeed had an impact on the ratings of leaders' effectiveness though not on other ratings, Nye (2002) could not confirm this result. She examined the members' attribution of responsibility onto a leader under three conditions: win versus lose, sabotaged versus not-sabotaged material and match between leader and participants' implicit leadership theories. Nye did not find an effect in the match between leader and participants' implicit leadership theories with respect to the attribution of responsibility onto self or the leader.

Still, falling under the category of information processing is the revolutionary approach introduced by Meindl. Meindl and colleagues (Meindl, Ehrlich, & Dukerich, 1985) challenged leadership research in 1985 by introducing the idea that leadership is—first and foremost—a construction of the followers. Meindl called his approach the Romance of Leadership, which refers to the general tendency of individuals (but also a tendency that exists on a societal level) to attribute responsibility—*all* responsibility—for company's success to leaders rather than to other influential factors, such as the economy. Although Meindl (1990) viewed this approach as an implicit *organization* theory dealing with the attribution of company performance, it can also be regarded as an implicit *leadership* theory as the attribution concerns the leader.[3]

In his dissertation, Pastor (1998) picked up the social constructionist approach of leadership and embedded it in a social network approach. In his view, individuals share an image of leadership with those people they are surrounded within their social networks. He found that indeed social network parameters are related to individuals' cognitive structures with respect to leadership.[4]

From the description of research mentioned above, we can see that implicit leadership theories are relevant in information processing. However, we still know little about the content of implicit leadership theories. This topic is addressed in the following section.

The Contents of Implicit Leadership Theories

A second stream of research on implicit leadership theories has focused on the contents of implicit leadership theories. An example is a study by Offermann et al. (1994). The authors used three stimuli to assess the content of implicit leadership theories: leaders, effective leaders, and supervisors. They found eight factors that underlie implicit leadership theories: sensitivity, dedication, tyranny, charisma, attractiveness, masculinity, intelligence, and strength. These were relatively stable across participants' gender and the three stimuli. However, leaders and effective leaders were seen as more positive than supervisors. A similar venture was undertaken by Kenney, Blascovich, and Shaver (1994). In search of attributes of "new leaders worthy of influence," they conducted a qualitative study, asking participants to talk about characteristics and behaviors of leaders. Using data reduction as well as sorting methods, they identified four superordinate categories: learning the groups' goals, taking charge, being a nice person, and being nervous.

The Generalizability of Implicit Leadership Theories

In the following, research on the generalizability of ILT will be reviewed. We understand generalizability in a very broad sense: Generalizability across gender is included in this review as well as generalizability across different cultures. Research considered here also focuses on different ILT with respect to different types of leaders—which is understood as target generalizability. The issue of generalizability can also focus on the individuals holding the ILT—referred to as holder generalizability. In cultural research, the target of the ILT and the holder of the ILT will often share the same culture, thus, target and holder generalizability are intertwined.

Generalizability Across Different Targets

Graves and Powell (1982) conducted interviews examining gender differences in implicit leadership theories. Their results indicate that male and female undergraduates differ when describing traits of an effective leader. Men describe a leader more in terms of instrumental traits, while females use more expressive traits. No difference was found with respect to the description of effective leader behaviors. Both sexes mentioned structuring and consideration-oriented behaviors.

In the context of information processing, Lord et al. (1984) introduced the concept of "family" resemblance between different types of implicit leadership theories. They set up a hierarchical structure of implicit leadership theories: the superordinate level constituted the concept "leader"; the basic level referred to different types of leaders (e.g., business, education, politics); and the subordinate level involved a further differentiation of the basic level (e.g., leaders in different types of business). Family resemblance in this context means that, on a horizontal level (e.g., on the basic level), implicit leadership theories share characteristics. Few of these will be common over all types of leaders, more will be shared only with a few other types of leaders.

The most recent venture in terms of generalizability of implicit leadership theories has been undertaken by Epitropaki and Martin (2004). Referring to the work of Rush and Russell (1988), the authors argue that implicit leadership theories are formed through exposure to social events, prior experiences, and interactions. Therefore, one can expect them to change in ongoing interactions with a leader (although research on stereotypes suggests that cognitive structures and schema are in fact hard to change). In addition to studying the effects of time on implicit leadership theories, Epitropaki and Martin (2004) wanted to test the extent to which implicit leadership theories are different for individuals working in different contexts. Using the Offermann et al., (1994) scale for the assessment of implicit leadership theories, they examined the extent to which implicit leadership theories are stable over time and settings. The results by Epitropaki and Martin (2004) indicate a reasonable generalizability of implicit leadership theories in terms of age, and tenure, that is, these factors do not appear to affect implicit leadership theories. However, they did find differences between male and female employees as well as between employees in different positions and professions (service versus manufacturing).[5] Their assumption concerning stability of implicit leadership theories over time was supported. However, their use of very broad categories can be criticized. A more specific assessment of ILT may well have left open more possibilities to find changes in individual ILT over time (Lord, personal communication, October 13, 2004).

Generalizability Across Culture

The topic of generalizability became more prominent in connection with research on culture and leadership, which examined cultural differences and similarities in implicit leadership theories. As early as 1987, Bryman's study dealt with the generalizability of implicit leadership theories. He examined whether or not the concept of implicit leadership theories, which, at that point, was almost exclusively examined in the United States, is transferable to the UK. In a broader context, Gerstner and Day (1994) examined the generalizability of leadership prototypes across students stemming from different countries. Participants were asked to rate how prototypical particular traits were for a business leader. They found that none of the traits were in the top five prototypical traits for all groups of students.

Posssibly the biggest venture in the area of *cultural generalizability* is the GLOBE project involving 62 cultures (e.g., Den Hartog et al., 1999; House et al., 2004). As cited in Dorfman, Hanges, Brodbeck, and the project GLOBE research team (2004), participants in sixty-two nations were asked to rate items on a scale from 1 = *this behavior or characteristic greatly inhibits a person from being an outstanding leader* to 7 = *this behavior or characteristic greatly contributes to a person being an outstanding leader.* Behaviors / characteristics are divided into six dimensions, namely, charismatic/value-based, team oriented, participative, humane oriented, autonomous, and self-protective (for a detailed definition see Dorfman et al., 2004). Their results indicate that attributes that can be summarized as charismatic leadership are indeed considered important for successful managers in all cultures (Dorfman et al., 2004). Conversely, some characteristics seem to be specific to some clusters of countries. In total, ten clusters were identified (such as Eastern Europe, Germanic, Anglo). Within these clusters, the implicit leadership theories are (for the most part) shared and a picture of what is seen to be important for an outstanding leader can be identified.

Generalizability Across Gender

Research in the field of *gender and implicit leadership theories* has been inspired by the fact that women are underrepresented in leadership positions. As this is true of women in almost all countries, researchers of gender generalizability are also involved in research addressing cross-cultural issues. Research exploring gender and implicit leadership theories often find differences in implicit leadership theories for male and female leaders. Images of leader consist of more stereotypical male than female characteristics as suggested in research on the think-manager-think-male phenomenon (e.g., Schein, 1973).

Schein (1973, 1975) presented a list of characteristics to her participants and asked them to rate the typical (successful) managers and the typical man/the typical woman on these characteristics. She found that persons in general see more overlap between characteristics of managers and men than between characteristics of managers and women. In later replications, this research was extended to different countries (Schein & Mueller, 1992; Schein, Mueller, Lituchi, & Liu, 1996). Heilman et al. (1989) extended this research by including women labeled as managers as well and by doing so increased the correspondence between female characteristics and characteristics of managers. However, the difference between women and successful managers was still higher than the one between men and successful managers. Recently, Schein (2001) found that successful middle managers are now seen as more androgynous at least in some countries (see also Sczesny, 2003).

In an extension of this research, Sczesny (2003, in the tradition of Heilman, 2001) differentiated between prescriptive and descriptive norms, asking her participants to rate characteristics they consider important for leadership and characteristics male and female leaders possess. Whereas she found stereotypic views on descriptive norms, she could not confirm stereotypic views on prescriptive norms. In particular, female participants held a more androgynous view of leadership.

Powell and Butterfield (1979) examined the extent to which the image of a successful leader corresponds with the image of a typical man or women. In line with the results obtained in research on the think-manager-think-male phenomenon, they could confirm that the male stereotype and the manager stereotype are more congruous than the female stereotype and the manager stereotype. Recently, Powell, Butterfield, and Parent (2002) examined the extent to which these stereotypes have changed, reasoning that as more and more women enter top management, a better fit between the female and the leader stereotype should emerge (in the sense of changing stereotypes through bookkeeping or conversion). Contrary to expectations, the image of a successful manager is still male. Interestingly, the same authors (Powell & Butterfield, 1984) have examined characteristics of bad in comparison to good managers. They found that bad managers score lower on both masculinity and femininity in comparison to good managers. This difference was higher for masculinity, indicating that bad managers are seen as more feminine than masculine.

A different approach is reported by Vinkenburg and van Engen (2005; citing van Engen et al., 2003). They concentrated on the promotability of men and women, in particular, on the respective stereotypes that decision makers hold. Their results indicate that managers know that women use more transformational (and thus more effective) leadership styles than men. However, when questioned about behavior that leads to promotion, their participants indicated that these behaviors are less likely to lead to a promotion when shown by women as opposed to men. Interestingly, however, Powell and Butterfield (1994) considered studies on actual promotion (as opposed to promotability) and found a gender advantage for female applicants.[6]

Ryan and Haslam (2005) claim that when women are promoted to top management positions it is often into precarious positions, for example, in companies that are not performing well. In this volume, they follow up these results and seek to explain them in terms of implicit leadership theories.

Explaining Implicit Leadership Theories

Keller (1999) focused on the development of implicit leadership theories. She examined the extent to which personality traits and perceived parents' personality traits have an impact on implicit leadership theories. She found that personality traits indeed influence implicit leadership theories in a way that individuals characterize leaders similar to an ideal image of the self. In addition, idealized leaders have similar traits as those perceived in parents. In her theoretical paper, Keller (2003) extends this view to the expectations individuals have of themselves in relation to a leader, and the individuals willingness to adapt their behavior to leadership models. Other studies may help in explaining implicit leadership theories, such as Pastor's (1998) work on the (shared) social construction of leadership and research on the generalizability of implicit leadership theories, implying that socialization plays a part in the development of implicit leadership theories. Research in this area is relatively new and more is clearly needed.

THE CHAPTERS OF THIS BOOK

In the twelve chapters of this book, we will give the current state of the art in implicit leadership research. Both theoretical and empirical work is presented. Although some of the chapters could be classified into different categories, we have organized chapters according to three basic topics: (a) information processing and effects of implicit leadership theories, (b) the contents and generalizability of implicit leadership theories, (c) the explanation of implicit leadership theories. In the following section, we will briefly summarize the chapters of this volume.

Information Processing and Effects of Implicit Leadership Theories

Judith Nye's contribution focuses on information processing in leadership. She empirically examines the effects of a match between individuals' prototypes and a given leader on the rating of that leader. In addition, she turns to the effects of winning and losing on the rating of the leaders and the effect of sabotaged versus non-sabotaged material. In line with her prior research, she found that implicit leadership theories matter in the evaluation of a leader. Certainly, this highlights the importance of implicit leadership theories in organizational practice.

Tiffany Keller picks up an important topic in the research of implicit leadership theories by concentrating on the effect the match between these implicit theories and leaders' behaviors have in organizational practice. Results of an initial study are presented in which the effect of the above-mentioned match of implicit leadership theories and leaders' behavior on followers' satisfaction is highlighted.

Contents and Generalizability of Implicit Leadership Theories

In their qualitative study, *Andres Müller and Birgit Schyns* concentrate on examining the contents of implicit leadership theories. Using the repertory grid method, they asked their participants to indicate attributes of certain types of leaders (e.g., male and female leader, efficient leaders). Their results show what characteristics individuals regard as important for leadership and indicate that the evaluation of leaders is dependent upon the participants characteristics.

Mary Uhl-Bien introduces the concept of implicit relationship theories. Based on her prior work in the field of Leader-Member Exchange, she examines the extent to which the partners in a leadership interaction not only have implicit leadership theories, but also theories about how the relationship between leader and member should be. This approach offers an interesting extension of the concept of implicit leadership theories.

Deanne den Hartog and Paul Koopman analyze the extent to which implicit leadership theories (in this case of successful leaders) have different contents for leaders in different levels of hierarchy and the extent to which prototypes differ for male and female participants. The researchers indeed found that the image of good leadership differs when different hierarchical levels are involved. In addition, some characteristics were highlighted to a greater extend by female participants.

Sabine Sczesny picks up Schein's approach concerning the think-manager-think-male phenomenon. She provides an overview of results for the phenomenon in different countries. Her approach includes not only the image of a male and a female manager but also the self-image of her participants. She finds that, although the phenomenon still exists, the image of leaders is less traditional than expected. In self-descriptions, both male and female participants rate themselves similarly competent.

Michelle Ryan and S. Alexander Haslam take the think-manager-think-male phenomenon as a background for their study as well, and refer also to the common phenomenon, the "glass ceiling," which is understood as an invisible barrier women face when wanting to progress to high leadership positions. They propose a new concept, the glass cliff, meaning that women not only face barriers when wanting to reach top positions but that—if promoted to a top position—they get promoted in times of unlikely success, that is, when a company is already struggling. Ryan and Haslam propose different explanations for this phenomenon.

Explaining Implicit Leadership Theories

Jörg Felfe examines which followers' characteristics have an impact on the romanticization of leadership. He considers a broad variety of characteristics in his empirical studies, such as demographic variables, Big-Five, self-efficacy, need for structure, and cognitive abilities. He indeed finds that some of these characteristics are related to the Romance of Leadership. In particular, self-efficacy and self-esteem are positively related to Romance of Leadership. Felfe explains his results as follows: the social construction of leadership (the image of a leader) appears in many ways to mirror aspects of the self.

Saba Ayman-Nolley and Roya Ayman focus on the implicit leadership theories of children. In their overview chapter, they show that implicit leadership theories develop early and summarize the existing knowledge concerning children's implicit leadership theories.

Broadening Up Our View on Implicit Leadership Theories: Implicit Followership Theories and Implicit Organizational Theories

Reinout de Vries and Jean-Louis van Gelder's contribution presents a view that can also be placed in the information processing tradition. However, in contrast to the other contributions, they focus on an observer's attribution rather than an actor's attribution. In their study, participants observe a leader-member interaction. De Vries and van Gelder first manipulate the interaction in such a way as to evoke different observer assessments of need for leadership and see if this has an effect on the perception of leadership. In a second study, they manipulate leader's charisma and examines how that affects observers' assessment of need for leadership.

The chapter by *Dorien Konst and Wim van Breukelen* can be put in the tradition of information processing in leadership as well. Similar to de Vries, the authors also focus on implicit theories with respect to followers. These are compared with implicit leadership theories. Konst and van Breukelen view both implicit theories in light of attribution theory, arguing that different reasons are attributed to followers compared to leader behavior. A series of their own studies confirm this idea.

Brigitte Kroon goes one step further and extends our view of implicit leadership theories to the implicit view of organizations. She applies her approach to context of setting up a new business and raises the question as to what kind of expectations the owners may face in the processes of starting up and establishing their company.

AUTHOR NOTE

Please address correspondence to Birgit Schyns, University of Twente, Faculty of Behavioral Sciences, Department of Work and Organizational Psychology, PO Box 217, 7500 AE Enschede, The Netherlands. The authors wish to thank the research departments of the Universities of Tilburg and Buffalo for making this cooperation possible. The authors wish to thank Robert Lord for his helpful comments on an earlier version of this paper. The first author worked on this paper during a stay at the State University of New York at Buffalo.

NOTES

1. The idea that not all individuals equate leaders with good/effective leaders is supported by results reported by Offermann et al.'s (1994) qualitative study. The participants in their study clearly named negative leader attributes (such as power-hungry and manipulative). Participants rated these characteristics a bit lower for effective leaders than for leaders in general.

2. Offermann, Schroyer, and Green (1998) applied this research to leaders' implicit theories about followers' performance. Giving leaders performance feedback as well as an attributional explanation for subordinate performance on a first trial affected the amount of time leaders spent talking to the group in a second trial. In addition, performance feedback as well as an attributional explanation influenced the number of negative leader comments. Finally, the ratings and the reward/punishment recommendations for the subordinates differed depending on the information given.

3. The most recent research on Romance of Leadership focuses on the measurement of that concept in different countries (Schyns, Meindl, & Croon, 2004; for a comparison between Germany, the Netherlands, and the United States). For this purpose, a core instrument that can be used in different contexts is going to be designed. In general, the cultural issue has become more prominent in leadership research in recent years. This development is not exclusive to research on Romance of Leadership, as the following section will show.

4. Rentsch (1990) found a similar result for organizational events (culture and climate).

5. A similar result is reported in a study based on the GLOBE data. Dickson (1997) reports that prototypes of effective leaders are different for employees in different types of organizations, namely, that they vary with the degree to which organisations are "organic" or "mechanistic."

6. However, these results have to be viewed in light of the sample that was examined. Participants were drawn from a U.S. federal government department, that is, a branch that is especially aware of equal rights and obliged to pursue them.

REFERENCES

Al-Dmour, H. & Awamleh, R.A. (2002). Effects of transactional and transformational leadership styles of sales managers on job satisfaction and self-perceived performance of sales people: A study of Jordanian manufacturing public shareholding companies. *Dirasat: Administrative Sciences, 29*, 247–261.

Awamleh, R.A. (2003, April 11–12). *A test of the transformational leadership model: The case of Jordanian banks.* Paper presented at the Academy of International Business (UK Chapter), Leicester.

Awamleh, R., & Gardner, W. L. (1999). Perceptions of leader charisma and effectiveness: The effects of vision content, delivery, and organizational performance. *Leadership Quarterly, 10*, 345–373.

Bryman, A. (1987). The generalizability of implicit leadership theories. *Journal of Social Psychology, 127*, 129–141.

Calder, B.J. (1977). An attribution theory of leadership. In B.M. Staw & G.R. Salancik (Eds.), *New directions in organizational behavior* (pp. 179–204). Chicago: St. Claire Press.

Den Hartog, D.N., House, R.J., Hanges, P.J., Ruiz-Quintanilla, S.A., Dorfman, P.W., et al. (1999). Culture specific and cross-culturally generalizable implicit leadership theories: Are attributes of charismatic/transformational leadership universally endorsed? *Leadership Quarterly, 10*, 219–256.

Dickson, M.W. (1997). *Universality and variation in organizationally shared cognitive prototypes of effective leadership.* Unpublished dissertation, University of Maryland at College Park.

Dorfman, P.W., Hanges, P.J., Brodbeck, F.C., & Project GLOBE research team. (2004). Leadership and cultural variation: The identification of culturally endorsed leadership profiles. In R.J. House, P.J. Hanges, M. Javidan, P.W. Dorfman, V. Gupta, & GLOBE Associates (Eds.), *Cultures, leadership, and organizations: A 62 nation GLOBE study.* Thousand Oaks, CA: Sage.

Eden, D., & Leviatan, U. (1975). Implicit leadership theory as a determinant of the factor structure underlying supervisory behavior scales. *Journal of Applied Psychology, 60*, 736–741.

Engle, E.M., & Lord, R.G. (1997). Implicit theories, self-schemas, and leader-member exchange. *Academy of Management Journal, 40*, 988–1010.

Epitropaki, O., & Martin, R. (2004). Implicit Leadership Theories in applied settings: Factor structure, generalizability and stability over time. *Journal of Applied Psychology, 89*, 293–310.

Foti, R.J., & Lord, R.G. (1987). Prototypes and scripts: The effects of alternative methods of processing information on rating accuracy. *Organizational Behavior and Human Decision Processes, 39*, 318–340.

Fraser, S.L., & Lord, R.G. (1988). Stimulus prototypicality and general leadership impressions: Their role in leadership and behavioral ratings. *Journal of Psychology, 122*, 291–303.

Gerstner, C.R., & Day, D.V. (1994). Cross-cultural comparison of leadership prototypes. *Leadership Quarterly, 5*, 121–134.

Graves, L. M. & Powell, G. N. (1982). Sex differences in implicit theories of leadership: An initial investigation. *Psychological Reports, 50*, 689–690.

Heilman, M.E. (2001). Description and prescription: How gender stereotypes prevent women's ascent up the organizational ladder. *Journal of Social Issues, 57*, 657–674.

Heilman, M.E., Block, C.J., Martell, R.F., & Simon, M.C. (1989). Has anything changed? Current characterizations of men, women, and managers. *Journal of Applied Psychology, 74*, 935–942.

House, R.J., Hanges, P.J., Javidan, M., Dorfman, P.W., & Gupta, V. (2004). *Culture, Leadership, and Organizations The GLOBE Study of 62 Societies.* London: Sage.

Keller, T. (1999). Images of the familiar: Individual differences and implicit leadership theories. *Leadership Quarterly, 10*(3), 589–607.

Keller, T. (2003). Parental images as a guide to leadership sense-making: An attachment perspective on implicit leadership theories. *Leadership Quarterly, 14,* 141–160.

Kenney, R.A., Blascovich, J., & Shaver, P.R. (1994). Implicit leadership theories: Prototypes for new leaders. *Basic and Applied Social Psychology, 15,* 409–437.

Kenney, R.A., Schwartz-Kenney, B.M., & Blascovich, J. (1996). Implicit leadership theories: Defining leaders described as worthy of influence. *Personality and Social Psychology Bulletin, 22,* 1128–1143.

Konst, D., Vonk, R., & van der Vlist, R. (1999). Inferences about causes and consequences of behavior of leaders and subordinates. *Journal of Organizational Behavior, 20,* 261–271.

Larson, J.R. (1982). Cognitive mechanisms mediating the impact of implicit theories of leader behavior on leader behavior ratings. *Organizational Behavior and Human Performance, 29,* 129–140.

Lord, R.G. (1977). Functional leadership behavior: Measurement and relation to social power and leadership perceptions. *Administrative Science Quarterly, 22,* 114–133.

Lord, R.G. (1985). An information processing approach to social perceptions, leadership and behavioral measurement in organizations. In B.M. Staw & L.L. Cummings (Eds.), *Research in organizational behavior* (Vol. 7, pp. 87–128). Greenwich, CT: JAI Press.

Lord, R.G., Brown, D.J., Harvey, J.L., & Hall, R.J. (2001). Contextual constraints on prototype generation and their multilevel consequences for leadership perceptions. *Leadership Quarterly, 12,* 311–338.

Lord, R.G., Foti, R.J., & de Vader, C.L. (1984). A test of leadership categorization theory: Internal structure, information processing, and leadership perceptions. *Organizational Behavior and Human Performance, 34,* 343–378.

Lord, R.G., Foti, R.J., & Phillips, J.S. (1982). A theory of leadership categorization. In J.G. Hunt, U. Sekaran, & C. Schriesheim (Eds.), *Leadership: Beyond establishment views.* Carbondale: Southern Illinois University Press.

Lord, R.G., & Maher, K.J. (1993). *Leadership and information processing.* London: Routledge.

Meindl, J.R. (1990). On leadership: An alternative to the conventional wisdom. In L.L. Cummings & B.M. Staw (Eds.), *Research in organizational behavior* (Vol. 12, pp. 159–203). Greenwich, CT: JAI Press.

Meindl, J.R. (1998). The romance of leadership as a follower-centric theory: A social construction approach. In F. Dansereau & F.J. Yammarino (Eds.), *Leadership: The multiple-level approaches, Part B: Contemporary and alternative* (pp. 285–298). Stamford, CT: JAI Press.

Meindl, J.R., & Ehrlich, S.B. (1987). The Romance of Leadership and the evaluation of organizational performance. *Academy of Management Journal, 30,* 91–109.

Meindl, J.R., Ehrlich, S.B., & Dukerich, J.M. (1985). The romance of leadership. *Administrative Science Quarterly, 30,* 78–102.

Nye, J.L. (2002). The eye of the follower—Information processing effects on attribution regarding leaders of small groups. *Small Group Research, 33,* 337–360.

Nye, J.L., & Forsyth, D.R. (1991). The effects of prototype-based biases on leadership appraisals: A test of leadership categorization theory. *Small Group Research, 22*, 360–375.

Offermann, L.R., Kennedy, J.K., & Wirtz, P.W. (1994). Implicit leadership theories: Content, structure, and generalizability. *Leadership Quarterly, 5*, 43–58.

Pastor, J.-C. (1998). *The social construction of leadership: A semantic and social network analysis of social representations of leadership.* Unpublished dissertation, State University of New York at Buffalo.

Phillips, J.S., & Lord, R.G. (1986). Notes on the practical and theoretical consequences of implicit leadership theories for the future of leadership measurement. *Journal of Management, 12*, 31–41.

Powell, G.N., & Butterfield, D.A. (1979). The "good manager": Masculine or androgynous? *Academy of Management Journal, 22*, 395–403.

Powell, G.N., & Butterfield, D.A. (1984). If "good managers" are masculine, what are "bad managers"? *Sex Roles, 10*, 477–484.

Powell, G.N., & Butterfield, D.A. (1994). Investigating the "glass ceiling" phenomenon: An empirical study of actual promotions to top management. *Academy of Management Journal, 97*, 68–86.

Powell, G.N., Butterfield, D.A., & Parent, J.D. (2002). Gender and managerial stereotypes: Have the times changed? *Journal of Management, 28*, 177–193.

Rentsch, J.R. (1990). Climate and culture: Interaction and qualitative differences in organizational meanings. *Journal of Applied Psychology, 75*, 668–681.

Rush, M.C., Phillips, J.S., & Lord, R.G. (1981). Effects of temporal delay in rating on leader behavior descriptions: A laboratory study. *Journal of Applied Psychology, 66*, 442–450.

Rush, M.C., & Russel, J.E.A. (1988). Leader prototypes and prototype-contingent consensus in leader behavior descriptions. *Journal of Experimental Social Psychology, 24*, 88–104.

Rush, M.C., Thomas, J.C., & Lord, R.G. (1977). Implicit leadership theory: A potential threat to the internal validity of leader behavior questionnaires. *Organizational Behavior & Human Decision Processes, 20*, 93–110.

Ryan, M.K., & Haslam, S.A. (2004). *The glass cliff: Evidence that women are overrepresented in precarious leadership positions.* Unpublished manuscript.

Schein, V.E. (1973). The relationship between sex role stereotypes and requisite management characteristics. *Journal of Applied Psychology, 57*, 95–100.

Schein, V.E. (1975). Relationships between sex role stereotypes and requisite management characteristics among female managers. *Journal of Applied Psychology, 60*(3), 340–344.

Schein, V.E. (2001). A global look at psychological barriers to women's progress in management. *Journal of Social Issues, 57*, 675–688.

Schein, V.E., & Mueller, R. (1992). Sex role stereotyping and requisite management characteristics: A cross cultural look. *Journal of Organizational Behavior, 13*, 439–447.

Schein, V.E., Mueller, R., Lituchy, T., & Liu, J. (1996). Think manager–think male: A global phenomenon? *Journal of Organizational Behavior, 17*, 33–41.

Schneider, D.J. (1973). Implicit personality theory: A review. *Psychological Bulletin, 79*, 204–309.

Schyns, B., Felfe, J., & Blank, H. (in preparation). *The relationship between romance of leadership and the perception of charismatic leadership revisited.*

Schyns, B., Meindl, J.R., & Croon, M.A. (2004, June 10–12). The Romance of Leadership Scale: Structural validations in different countries and contexts. *Proceedings of the 1rst Conference on Cross-Cultural Leadership and Management Studies,* Seoul.

Schyns, B., & Sanders, K. (2004). Impliciete leiderschapstheorieën en de perceptie van transformationeel leiderschap: een replicatie van Duits onderzoek (Implicit leadership theories and the perception of leadership: Replication of a German study). *Gedrag en Organisatie, 17,* 143–154.

Sczesny, S. (2003). A closer look beneath the surface: Various facets of the think manager-think male stereotype. *Sex Roles, 49,* 353–363.

Shamir, B. (1992). Attribution of influence and charisma to the leader: The Romance of Leadership revisited. *Journal of Applied Social Psychology, 22,* 386–407.

Szabo, E., Brodbeck, F.C., Den Hartog, D.N., Reber, G., Weibler, J., & Wunderer, R. (2002). The Germanic Europe cluster: Where employees have a voice. *Journal of World Business, 37,* 55–68.

Taylor, J.C., & Bowers, D.G. (1972). *Survey of organizations: A machine-scored standardized questionnaire instrument.* Oxford: University of Michigan.

Van Engen, M.L., Johannesen-Schmidt, M.J., & Vinkenburg, C.J. (2003, May 14–17). Transformational versus Transactional leadership as a Route to Career Advancement: Doing the Right Thing differs for Male and Female leaders. *Paper presented at the European Congress of Work and Organizational Psychology* (EAWOP), Lisbon.

Vinkenburg, C.J., & van Engen, M.L. (2004). Perceptions of gender, leadership and career development. In R. Burke & M. Mattis (Eds.), *Supporting women's career advancement: Challenges and opportunities.* Edward Elgar.

Vonk, R., & Konst, D. (2003). Effects of behavioral causes and consequences on perceived competence of leaders and subordinates. *Journal of Applied Social Psychology, 33,* 1684–1692.

Weiss, H., & Adler, S. (1981). Cognitive complexity and the structure of implicit leadership theories. *Journal of Applied Psychology, 66,* 69–78.

PART I

INFORMATION PROCESSING AND EFFECTS
OF IMPLICIT LEADERSHIP THEORIES

CHAPTER 1

IMPLICIT THEORIES AND LEADERSHIP PERCEPTIONS IN THE THICK OF IT

The Effects of Prototype Matching, Group Setbacks, and Group Outcomes

Judith L. Nye

ABSTRACT

The present study addressed the impact of three factors, all of which have been theoretically linked to implicit leadership theories, on followers' leadership perceptions. First, the impact of individual differences in leadership prototypes was tested, with the expectation that leaders who more closely matched prototypes would be perceived as better leaders. Second, the role of group performance information on followers' perceptions of their leader was examined; it was hypothesized that followers in winning groups would infer better leadership skills than followers in losing groups would. Third, some groups suffered a setback during group interaction, to investigate whether the setback would affect leadership ratings. Eighty female and 29 male college students competed in small groups in this 2 (group perfor-

Implicit Leadership Theories: Essays and Explorations, pages 39–61
Copyright © 2005 by Information Age Publishing

mance information: win vs. lose) × 2 (material sabotage: sabotage vs. no sabotage) design study. A third continuous factor addressed how well leaders matched followers' prototypes. Analyses revealed that both the leaders who matched follower prototypes and the leaders of winning groups were judged more positively on several measures. Losing leaders were given the benefit of the doubt, however, when groups suffered the setback of flawed materials. These findings suggest that all three factors affect followers' reactions to their leaders in complex ways, and that followers occasionally allow biases to influence their leadership perceptions.

INTRODUCTION

Does anyone know what good leadership is? We all think we do. Despite historian James MacGregor Burns' description of leadership as "one of the most observed and least understood phenomena on earth" (1978, p. 2), most people think they know good leadership when they see it. To do so, we apparently rely upon implicit leadership theories. These theories are detailed, highly abstracted cognitive schemas about what constitutes good leadership, including the traits and behaviors of leaders (Calder, 1977; Eden & Leviatan, 1975; Kenney, Schwartz-Kenney & Blascovich, 1996). Research suggests that individuals construct these theories as a consequence of experience with actual leaders (Brown & Lord, 2001), and exposure to others' thinking on the subject (such as coworkers and the media; Lord & Maher, 1991). Moreover, research has revealed that our own personalities (Keller, 1999) and self-concepts (Hall & Lord, 1995; Lord, Brown, & Freiberg, 1999; Lord, Brown, & Harvey, 2001) may play a role in constructing implicit leadership theories, suggesting that individual differences in such theories exist (Brown & Lord, 2001; Hall & Lord, 1995; Keller, 1999; Lord, Brown, & Harvey, 2001).

Many researchers now believe that for the most part leadership is a social perception formed on the basis of implicit theories (Kouzes & Posner, 1990, 1993; Lord, Brown, & Harvey, 2001; Lord & Emrich, 2001). This premise is not new to the literature; it has been advanced for 30 years or more (Calder, 1977; Eden & Leviatan, 1975; Hollander & Julian, 1969; Mischel, 1973; Pfeffer, 1977). For example, Calder (1977) and Pfeffer (1977) both suggested that leadership is an inference made by the individual based upon his or her interpretation of the leaders' behaviors and group outcomes. When leaders match followers' conceptions of good leadership and meet group goals, followers allow themselves to be influenced by these individuals (Hollander, 1992; Hollander & Julian, 1969; Kenney et al., 1996). Thus, leadership can be conceptualized as a reciprocal process of mutual influence between group members and their leaders (Hollander, 1992; Hollander & Julian, 1969; Lord & Maher, 1991). Much of the recent leadership research has therefore focused on the thinking, and resulting leadership perceptions, going on in the minds of followers (Lord & Emrich, 2001). The study presented in this chapter explored the effects of implicit theories on perceptions of leaders in small ad hoc groups, using a theoretical framework proposed by Lord (Lord 1985; Lord & Maher, 1991).

A MODEL OF LEADERSHIP PERCEPTION

To encompass the complex exchange of influence between leaders and followers, Robert G. Lord and his colleagues have developed a theory that places social cognitive processes at the center of understanding leadership (Brown & Lord, 2001; Lord, 1985; Lord & Maher, 1991). Lord's theory acknowledges that perception of leadership is determined by leader traits and behaviors as well as the social context and the group task. However, Lord also points out that it is the individual's interpretation of these factors, rather than objective reality, that influences leadership (Lord & Maher, 1990). Central to understanding followers' perceptions of leadership in Lord's theory are implicit leadership theories (Brown & Lord, 2001; Lord, Brown & Harvey, 2001; Lord, Brown, Harvey & Hall, 2001; Lord & Maher, 1990, 1991). According to Lord, these theories drive two important processes that shape leadership perceptions, recognition-based and inference-based processes (Lord & Maher, 1990, 1991).

Recognition-based Processes. Perhaps the most obvious of the two processes is based upon recognition: we know good leadership when we see it. That is, we know how leaders should behave, and we expect certain traits and characteristics in our leaders. Lord's theory suggests that we construct cognitive categories of leadership, distinguishing one category from another by its prototype (a cognitive summary of the most typical features of the category). Our prototypes allow us to look for certain traits and behaviors that we associate with good leadership. When we are faced with potential leaders, we size them up based upon our prototypes in a process Lord refers to as *leadership categorization* (Fraser & Lord, 1988; Lord, 1985; Lord, Foti, & Phillips, 1982).

Once the categorization has been made, we once again rely upon our implicit theories to fill in the gaps and reconstruct the leaders' past behaviors (Lord & Emrich 2001; Lord & Maher, 1990). Thus, we are easily able to interpret basic cues for their leadership relevance (e.g., sitting at the head of the table indicates that this individual will be running our meeting; Lord & Emrich, 2001; Lord & Maher, 1990). Fraser and Lord (1988) demonstrated this process by exposing participants to one of three hypothetical managers who varied in terms of how well they matched participants' prototypes (high, moderate, low). They found that the more prototypical leaders were described to be, the more positive participants rated them. This prototype matching effect has been revealed in other studies as well (Bartol & Butterfield, 1976; Fraser & Lord, 1988; Lord, Foti, & De Vader, 1984; Lord, Foti, & Phillips, 1982; Nye & Forsyth, 1991). Interestingly, we are sometimes inclined to recall leader behaviors that did not actually occur, but that are consistent with our theories (Larson, 1982; Lord, Brown & Harvey, 2001; Meindl, 1995).

Research suggests that there is considerable common ground between individuals in their implicit theories. That is, there are some universally-endorsed characteristics of leadership (e.g., intelligence, masculinity, dominance; Den Hartog, House, Hanges, Ruiz-Quintanilla, & Dorfman, 1999; Lord, De Vader, & Alliger, 1986; Offerman, Kennedy, & Wirtz, 1994) that ifluence implicit leadership theories. However, research also suggests that individual differences in prototypes do exist (Hall & Lord, 1995; Keller, 1999; Nye, 2002). It therefore stands to reason that tapping into these individual differences in leadership prototypes could provide considerable insight when predicting an individual's reaction to a stimulus leader (Nye, 2002).

Inference-based Processes. In any given leadership situation, however, we have more information than just leader traits and behaviors to draw upon. We are particularly adept at looking for other information to infer leadership, such as group outcomes (Lord & Maher, 1991). Such inference-based cognitive processes, according to Lord, stem from our belief that the major role of any leader is to help the group achieve its goals. Therefore, leaders who facilitate goal achievement are looked upon as good leaders. Leaders who impede or are ineffective in achieving goals are looked upon as poor leaders. This common inferential process has been named the *performance cue effect,* and has been demonstrated in past research (Binning & Lord, 1980; Binning, Zaba, & Whattam, 1986; Larson, 1982; Larson, Lingle, & Scerbo, 1984; Phillips, 1984; Phillips & Lord, 1981). For example, Nye and Simonetta (1996, Study 1) presented participants with a stimulus group of graduate students as they engaged in a problem solving exercise, and then provided feedback on the group's overall performance. Participants in the good performance condition rated the stimulus leaders as significantly more effective and collegial than did participants in the poor performance condition.

Interestingly, the link between successful groups and effective leaders is so ingrained in our minds that we tend to view them as one and the same. Even followers themselves—individuals who share the same fate with the leader—appear to make the biased connection between group success and good leadership (Lord, 1985; Lord & Emrich, 2001; Lord & Maher, 1991), although perhaps to a lesser extent than observers (Nye, 2002).

Once the leadership inference has been made, we once again call upon our implicit leadership theories to fill in the gaps (Meindl, 1995; Larson, 1982; Larson, Lingle, & Scerbo, 1984; Lord, Brown & Harvey, 2001; Phillips & Lord, 1982).

Of course, we are not blind to the various situational factors that can facilitate or impede group success, regardless of the presence of the group leader. Lord's theory acknowledges that the performance cue effect can be moderated by such factors if they become apparent to the social thinker (Lord & Maher, 1991), calling upon Harold Kelley's (1971, 1973) classic attribution principles of discounting and augmentation to explain this phenomenon. That is, if we become aware of plausible factors other than the leader, we may discount the causal role of the leader. However, becoming aware that the group was successful in spite of inhibitory factors may lead us to augment the causal role of the leader. For example, a leader may be discounted as a plausible cause for group failure if the group had been denied adequate resources to complete its task. However, should the group prevail in spite of this setback, we might attribute their surprising success to the superior skills of their leader. Past research has found support for this notion (Nye, 2002; Phillips & Lord, 1981).

In summary, Lord's model is an ambitious effort to account for the complex processes that occur between leaders and followers in group and organizational situations. It incorporates the preconceptions that we use to identify and judge leaders (recognition-based) as well as our dependence upon past outcome information to assess leaders' effectiveness (inference-based), relying in both cases on our implicit theories of leadership to guide our perceptions. We have learned to recognize that good leadership leads to certain behaviors and outcomes, and when these behaviors and outcomes occur, we are likely to perceive good leadership (Lord, 1985; Lord & Maher, 1991; Phillips & Lord, 1981).

THE PRESENT STUDY

The study presented in this chapter investigated the effects of these recognition-based and inference-based processes on perceptions of leaders, focusing primarily on the role that individual differences in prototype matching may play in the recognition-based processes, and the moderating effect of discounting and augmentation on inference-based processes. Moreover, the present study was conducted on actual group members in an experimental setting. Although Lord's theory has received substantial empirical support, most experimental investigations have addressed the perceptions of observers who responded to hypothetical group situations, rather than actual followers (Larson, 1982; Larson et al., 1984; Nye & Forsyth, 1991; Nye & Simonetta, 1996, Study 1; Phillips, 1984; Phillips & Lord, 1981). Moreover, past studies that have addressed the leadership perceptions of actual followers have been primarily nonexperimental (Brown & Lord, 2001; Hall & Lord, 1998; Foti, Fraser, & Lord, 1982; Lord et al., 1984), and therefore limited in their ability to yield cause and effect conclusions. Participants were first pretested for their leadership prototypes, then brought into the laboratory in small groups to interact during a problem solving exercise. Trained confederates served as group leaders. The groups were led to believe that they were competing against each other, and some groups later learned that they had won while others learned that they had lost. In addition, the materials for half of the groups were sabotaged, making their work more difficult to complete. At the close of the study, group members' reactions to their leaders were measured.

Several hypotheses were proposed. First, consistent with Lord's assumptions regarding recognition-based processes (Lord & Maher, 1991), it was predicted that leaders who matched participants' leadership prototypes would be rated more positively than leaders who did not match participants' prototypes would. Second, due to inference-based processes (performance cue effect; Binning et al., 1986; Larson et al., 1984), it was hypothesized that leaders whose groups won would be rated more positively than leaders whose groups lost. Third, it was hypothesized that these performance cue effects would be moderated by material sabotage because material sabotage would serve as a particularly salient discounting cue (Kelley, 1971, 1973). Specifically, participants whose groups lost after materials were sabotaged would still rate their leaders quite positively, due to discounting; consistent with the performance cue effect, however, participants in the two winning conditions (sabotaged and no sabotage) would also rate their leaders more positively; participants in the losing, no sabotage condition would rate their leaders more negatively. Fourth, consistent with Lord's assertions that both inference-based and recognition-based processes affect leadership processes, it was hypothesized that prototype matching would interact with performance information. The rationale behind this prediction was that participants would find it difficult to argue with outcome information (inference-based) when forming their leadership perceptions, however, they would also display a tendency to defend the leaders who matched their leadership prototypes (recognition-based). Specifically, leaders whose groups won (regardless of prototype match) would be rated more positively than leaders whose groups lost and did not match leadership prototypes, with ratings for matching leaders whose groups lost falling between. Finally, the present study addressed the combined effects of all three factors on leadership perceptions. For participants whose materials were sabotaged, it was hypothesized that losing leaders who matched participants' prototypes would be rated very positively (as positively as leaders whose groups won), and leaders who did not match participants' prototypes would be rated less positive. Thus, participants in the sabotaged conditions were provided with a ready excuse with which to defend their leaders (Kelley, 1971, 1973), however, they were only expected to do so if the leader matched their leadership prototype (Lord & Maher, 1991). Participants whose materials were not sabotaged were expected to react in the patterns outlined in hypothesis four.

METHOD

Participants

Participants were 80 females and 29 males from several sophomore-level social psychology classes who participated as part of a class exercise. Participants were tested in small groups of between three and seven individuals (mean group size 6.04) who were led by confederate leaders. Data were collected over two semesters from a total of 20 groups.

Materials

Participants' leadership prototypes were assessed using the SYstematic Multiple Level Observation of Groups (SYMLOG) "General Behavior Descriptions" checklist developed by Bales (Bales, Cohen, & Williamson, 1979; http://www.symlog.com). This 26-item measure taps into three dimensions of interpersonal behavior on the part of group members: dominance/submission, friendly/unfriendly, and instrumentally controlled/ emotionally expressive (as prescribed by Bales et al., 1979, nine items were used to construct each dimension; some items were used several times). Scores on each dimension can range from +18 to –18. For example, a score of +18 on the dominance/submission scale would suggest extreme dominance, whereas a score of –18 would suggest extreme submission.

Instructions on this measure required participants to "try to create an image of good student leadership qualities, then answer this questionnaire with that image in mind." In accordance with Bales et al. (1979), participants responded to each item on a 3-point scale: "not often" (1), "sometimes" (2), and "often" (3). Their responses on the measure yielded dominance/submission scores ranging from 0 to 10 ($M = 4.4$, slightly dominant), friendly/unfriendly scores ranging from –5 to 18 ($M = 12.5$, very friendly), and instrumentally controlled/emotionally expressive scores ranging from –3 to 11 ($M = 3.9$, slightly controlled). Participants were asked to complete this premeasure one week before data collection.

For the group interaction task, a two-page handout of problems was designed to require the group's full attention and collaborative efforts for completion. A variety of problems were presented, including logic puzzles, remote associates questions, math problems, and estimating the current room temperature. For example, one item read, "What is the next letter in the following sequence? O T T F F S S" (The answer is E, for eight. The sequence is the first letter of the first eight digits: One, Two, Three, Four, Five, Six, Seven, and Eight.) The problems were sufficiently difficult to engage the groups for at least 20 minutes, and the answers were ambiguous enough that participants would not be able to guess their group's score. The second page of the exercise was missing for groups in the material sabotage conditions.

Participants' perceptions of their group leaders were recorded on three measures. First, they responded to an item meant to tap into their global leadership impression, "How much leadership was exhibited by your group's leader?" Participants responded on a 5-point scale ranging from 1 ("none") to 5 ("extreme amount of leadership"; Phillips & Lord, 1981). Given that participants were responding to actual group leaders, two subscales of the Leadership Behavior Description Questionnaire (LBDQ; Stogdill, 1963) were also used to assess reactions to leaders. Both the consideration ("regards the comfort, well being, status, and contributions of followers"; Stogdill, 1963, p. 3) and initiation of structure ("clearly defines own role, and lets followers know what is expected"; Stogdill, 1963, p. 3) subscales were used because they were most relevant to the present study.[1] Each subscale included 10 items, and participants were asked to record "how frequently the leader engaged in the behavior" using a five-point scale ranging from 1 ("always") to 5 ("never"). Thus, their scores could range from 10 to 50. Participants' responses to each subscale were reverse-scored to simplify interpretation (higher scores indicate more consideration and initiation of structure; i.e., better leadership), and the sum score for each subscale was submitted to the analyses.

Leader Training/Prototype Matching

Two female and one male student confederates were carefully trained to lead their groups during the problem solving exercise (sex of leader was balanced across experimental conditions). On the day of the study, participants were told that these confederates were members of the author's upper level leadership course, who were brought into their groups to serve as leaders for added interest. The leaders were trained to behave in a somewhat dominant and instrumentally controlled manner, while being rather friendly toward their group members. Thus, confederate leaders were trained to coordinate their group's attempts to solve the problems while encouraging all group members to participate. Their script called for them to contribute several solutions to the group exercises, however, care was taken to keep leaders from appearing to already know the answers to the problems.

Despite their training, the confederates were not entirely consistent in their behaviors. That is, one leader was not as friendly as she was trained to be. However, the reader should recall that the present study addressed *prototype matching*, that is, the correspondence between a participant's leadership prototype and the actual leader behavior. Therefore, even though confederate leaders occasionally varied in their behavior, the degree of prototype matching was still able to be pinpointed for each participant.

To determine the actual behavior of each confederate, all group sessions were videotaped, and independent judges coded confederate behaviors. Individual confederate behavior between sessions was quite consistent, so rather than coding every videotape (coding all 20 group interactions would have been prohibitive), one tape was selected for each confederate leader. Tapes were selected based upon video and audio quality to allow coders the best opportunity to observe and hear the leader.

Judges were trained to code the videotapes using only half of the SYMLOG measure (to reduce fatigue). Thus, two groups of raters coded each tape. Training included going over the SYMLOG measure item-by-item, providing definitions for each item, and putting the item into context in a paragraph. Judges were instructed to "answer how often you believe the leader showed each of the following behaviors." Consistent with the scoring guidelines for the SYMLOG questionnaire, judges responded on 3-point scales: "not often" (1), "sometimes" (2), and "often" (3). They viewed the videotapes, then documented the stimulus leader's actual behavior on SYMLOG. Three judges responded to each SYMLOG item for each confederate leader, for a total of six judges coding each tape. Because judges answered using an ordinal scale, modal scores were used to determine their estimation of the stimulus leader's behavior. Judges agreed completely 51% of the time (40 of 78 total ratings), two judges agreed 46% (36 of 78 total ratings), and no one agreed in only two instances (in these cases the middle score of 2 was assigned because exclusion would have damaged the subscales).

The judges' average responses were combined to yield separate scores on the three SYMLOG dimensions for each confederate leader. Dominance/submission scores for the leaders ranged from 5 to 8 (dominant); friendly/unfriendly scores ranged from 1 to 14 (friendly; one leader was coded as not particularly friendly, but the other two were coded as very friendly at 11 and 14); instrumentally controlled/emotionally expressive scores ranged from 5 to 10 (instrumentally controlled). Based upon his or her specific scores determined by the judges, each confederate leader's behavior was pinpointed in the three-dimensional space conceptualized by Bales (Bales et al., 1979). The continuous factor, *prototype matching*, was created then by comparing participants' scores on the SYMLOG premeasure against the behavior of their actual group leader (as determined by the judges) via Euclidean distance.[2] As with any measure of distance, lower numbers on the prototype matching variable indicated closer matches.

Design and Procedure

The present study employed a 2 (group performance information: win vs. lose) × 2 (material sabotage: sabotage vs. no sabotage) between-subjects factorial design. Groups were randomly assigned within constraints to the group performance and material sabotage conditions. Every research session included one winning and one losing group, and one sabotaged and one no sabotage group.[3] A third predictor, prototype matching, was also included in the analyses to test the hypotheses. The confederate leaders were blind to experimental conditions, only learning their conditions as the sessions unfolded.

Participants were tested in small groups during a class period. All groups within one semester were tested within the same week (class did not meet that week) to reduce discussion among participants. Two groups competed against each other in each experimental session. Participants were brought into a reception area and separated into their groups. After informed consent was obtained, the groups were introduced to their leaders and the purpose of the study was explained. Participants were told that the two groups would be competing against each other, and to increase the sense of competition between the groups, they were told that the winning group would be entered into a $50 raffle. The groups were then led to their separate laboratory rooms. Each room contained a conference table, chairs, a video camera, a large envelope containing the group materials, and an electronic timer set to 20 minutes. The group leader sat at the head of the table, directly facing the video camera.

The groups were instructed to work for 20 minutes on the 2-page problem solving exercise. They expected to complete their work with only one interruption, when the experimenter entered the room briefly to oversee one component of the exercise. Groups in the no sabotage condition were treated in this manner, however, groups in the sabotage condition had more contact with the experimenter. Halfway into the exercise, when they turned to the second page of the handout, they discovered that the second page was a duplicate of the first. Unable to proceed with the exercise, they were forced to go back to the first page to reexamine their original responses. The experimenter soon entered the room, as promised, and the group leader immediately informed her of the flawed materials. The experimenter feigned surprise and dismay, left the laboratory briefly, then returned with copies of the second page. These copies, however, were of very poor quality and difficult to read. The experimenter explained that she was having trouble with the copy machine, and that these copies were all she could provide. Thus, the sabotage of group materials was particularly disruptive to group progress. At this point, the leader "persuaded" the experimenter to add five minutes to the timer, to give the group more time to complete their task. The experimenter agreed, added the five minutes, and left the room.[4]

When the timer sounded, the experimenter immediately entered the room to stop the group interaction. She gathered up the materials, and gave the group a short questionnaire to complete while she supposedly tallied their group's score. After a short period of time, the experimenter slipped a package containing the groups' performance information under the laboratory door. The leader opened this package and related the performance feedback to the group. He or she then distributed the dependent measure, and participants completed it. Once everyone was finished, the experimenter reentered the room, thanked participants for their help, answered their questions, and asked them not to discuss the study with anyone until the following week.

Participants were fully debriefed during their next class meeting. They were introduced to the confederate leaders and encouraged to ask questions. They were also told that every group (winning and losing) had been entered into the raffle, and the $50 prize was awarded. (A total of $100 was awarded over the two semesters of data collection.) Participants were encouraged to report whether they had been suspicious of their leader during their group interaction and thought that their suspicions affected their responses. It was made clear that this disclosure would have no bearing on their grades, and that no questions would be asked about the source of their suspicions. Data for three participants were excluded from analyses due to self-reported suspicion. Data for two participants were excluded because they did not properly complete the dependent measures. The final analyses included data for 109 participants.

RESULTS

Three measures tapped into participants' leadership perceptions, the global leadership impression item and the initiating structure and consideration subscales of the LBDQ. On the LBDQ subscales, scores ranged from 10 to 50, with higher scores indicating higher LBDQ ratings (Cronbach alphas were .75 for initiating structure and .73 for consideration). Table 1.1 presents a complete intercorrelation matrix of predictors and dependent variables. Participants' responses on the three dependent measures were subjected to separate hierarchical multiple regression analyses. Predictors were group performance information, material sabotage, prototype matching, and their interactions. As recommended by Cohen, Cohen, Aiken, and West (2003), contrast coding was used for categorical predictors (−1 vs. +1; see Table 1.1).

Table 1.1.   Intercorrelations Among Dependent Variables and Predictors

	1	2	3	4	5	6	7	8	9
Dependent Variables									
1. Global Leadership Impression	—								
2. Initiating Structure	.24*	—							
3. Consideration	.48**	.39**	—						
Predictors									
4. Performance (A)^a	.24*	.09	.17	—					
5. Sabotage (B)^b	−.07	−.03	−.13	.10	—				
6. Matching (C)^c	−.02	.03	−.20*	−.13	−.10	—			
7. A × B	−.04	−.05	.17	−.06	−.003	−.05	—		
8. A × C	.09	.05	.23*	.69**	.01	−.19	−.11	—	
9. B × C	−.14	−.18	−.28**	.01	.69**	−.25**	−.09	−.02	—
10. A × B × C	.02	−.05	.20*	−.11	−.09	−.02	.69**	−.26**	−.20*

^{a} lose = −1, win = 1; ^{b} sabotaged materials = −1, no sabotage = 1; ^{c} lower numbers indicated better prototype matching
** $p < .01$; * $p < .05$

Turning first to prototype matching (Hypothesis 1), participants' consideration ratings of their leaders were significantly influenced by this predictor, with leaders who matched better being rated higher in consideration than leaders who were not good matches, $t(93) = −2.93$, $p = .004$, $\beta = −.28$. Although not statistically significant, participants' initiating structure ratings [$t(94) = −.38$, ns, $\beta = −.04$] and global leadership ratings [$t(94) = −.46$, ns, $\beta = −.05$] were in the predicted direction.

Group performance information (Hypothesis 2) exerted a significant effect on participants' global leadership impressions, $t(94) = 2.50$, $p = .01$, $\beta = .34$. Participants in winning groups ($M = 4.5$) reported that their leaders exhibited significantly more leadership than did participants in the losing groups ($M = 4.1$). This difference in ratings of winning and losing leaders, however, was not revealed in either the initiating structure [$t(94) = .52$, *ns*, $\beta = .07$] or consideration [$t(93) = -.41$, *ns*, $\beta = -.05$] analyses.

Prototype matching and group performance information (Hypothesis 4) interacted significantly in participants' responses to the consideration subscale, $t(93) = 2.40$, $p = .02$, $\beta = .31$. To interpret this effect, Cohen et al.'s (2003) recommendation regarding interactions between dichotomous and continuous variables was followed. That is, separate regression lines were plotted for participants whose groups won and those whose groups lost. As shown in Figure 1.1, participants in the winning condition were consistent in their leadership ratings, regardless of prototype matching. Prototype matching, however, appeared to influence participants in the losing group condition, with their ratings dropping off as leaders matched their prototypes less and less. This interaction did not achieve significance on either the initiating structure [$t(94) = -.17$, *ns*, $\beta = -.03$] or global leadership impression [$t(94) = -1.10$, *ns*, $\beta = -.16$] ratings.

An unexpected interaction between prototype matching and group material sabotage achieved significance on both of the LBDQ subscales. This interaction was most pronounced in participants' consideration ratings of their leaders $t(93) = -3.24$, $p = .002$, $\beta = -.42$. As shown in Figure 1.2, participants in the no sabotage conditions responded based upon how well their leaders matched their leadership prototypes, with better-matching leaders being rated as more considerate. Participants in the sabotaged conditions, however, were consistently high in their leadership ratings, regardless of prototype matching. A similar pattern of responses was

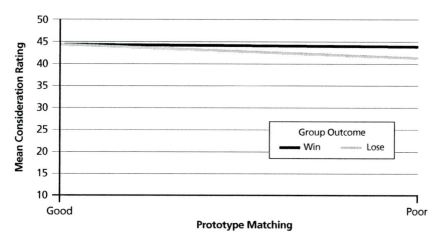

Figure 1.1.   Consideration ratings as a function of prototype matching and group outcome.

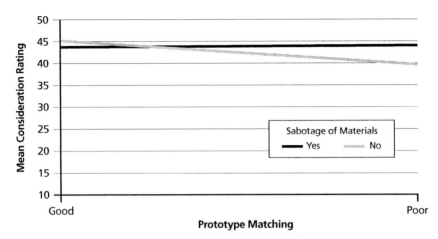

Figure 1.2.   Consideration ratings as a function of prototype matching and sabotage of group materials.

revealed in the analysis of initiating structure ratings [$t(94) = -2.05$, $p = .04$,
$\beta = -.30$], although in this analysis all leaders who were good matches with
followers' prototypes were rated similarly, regardless of the material sabotage condition. Participants' responses to the global leadership measure
were similar in pattern to this interaction, although the effect was not significant [$t(94) = -1.15$, ns, $\beta = -.17$].

A three-way interaction (Hypothesis 5) in the analysis of participants'
consideration ratings, although not quite significant, deserves mention
here, $t(93) = 1.77$, $p = .08$, $\beta = .23$. As shown in Figure 1.3 (top graph), participants in the no sabotage conditions clearly judged leaders based upon
their match with leadership prototypes. Regardless of whether their groups
won or lost, participants rated matching leaders quite highly in consideration. Ratings dropped off as leaders matched participants' prototypes less
and less. This drop was particularly pronounced among participants in the
losing groups. In the sabotaged conditions (bottom graph), however, prototype matching effects were clearly not evident. Instead, all leaders were
rated very positively. In fact, participants in the winning condition whose
leaders were poor matches with their prototypes rated their leaders the
most considerate of all conditions.

Unexpectedly, no interaction of performance information and material
sabotage (Hypothesis 3) was revealed in participants' global leadership
impressions [$t(94) = -.37$, ns, $\beta = -.05$] or initiating structure [$t(94) = -.05$,
ns, $\beta = -.01$] and consideration [$t(93) = .11$, ns, $\beta = .01$] ratings of their
leaders.

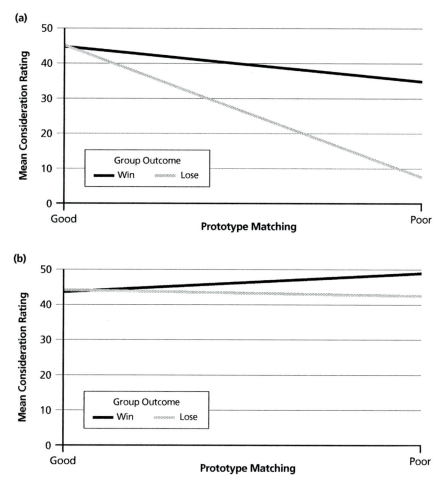

Figure 1.3.   Consideration ratings as a function of prototype matching and sabotage of group materials. Figure 1.3a depicts responses of participants in the no sabotage conditions and Figure 1.3b depicts responses of participants in the sabotaged conditions.

DISCUSSION

The second hypothesis, regarding the effects of group performance information on leadership perceptions, was only partially supported. That is, participants' global impressions of their leaders were clearly influenced by performance information, with winning leaders receiving higher ratings on this measure than losing leaders; participants' LBDQ ratings of their leaders, although in the expected directions, were not significantly affected by this manipulation. The partial support of this hypothesis is somewhat surprising, given the robust nature of the performance cue effect in the past literature (Binning et al., 1986; Larson et al., 1984). This discrepancy, however, is consistent with past findings that performance information has less importance when the focus shifts from impressions to ratings of actual leader behaviors (Binning & Lord, 1980). These findings suggest that specific behavioral measures may be less susceptible to the biasing effects of performance information than are more global evaluations. Moreover, the present participants were actual group members, sharing success or failure with their leaders, and may therefore have responded differently than observers would (Hall & Lord, 1995).

The prototype matching hypothesis (Hypothesis 1) was partially supported in that participants' consideration ratings increased as their leaders came closer to matching their leadership prototypes. However, participants' responses to the two other measures were not significantly influenced by their leadership prototypes. A significant interaction between matching and performance information in the analysis of consideration responses served to qualify this result. As predicted in Hypothesis 4, ratings of winning leaders were quite positive and remained stable regardless of prototype. Also as expected, losing leaders were judged in a way consistent with their match to follower prototypes; in fact, losing leaders who were good matches with participants' prototypes fared better than expected. However, this interaction was only revealed in the consideration analysis.

The potential interaction of these variables was of particular interest in the present study. Which process, inference-based or recognition-based, exerts the most influence over our perceptions of leaders? Lord and Maher (1990, 1991) suggested that both processes affect leadership perceptions. However, to date, Lord and his associates have not addressed what happens when the two processes conflict. What happens when a leader whom we believe should be a poor leader actually wins? Do we ignore our prototype and base our judgments purely on performance? The present findings suggest that we may do so in some cases. Perhaps more important, however, what happens when the leader of our dreams fails? Do we defend him or her in spite of the failure? The present data suggest that we may also do so in some cases. In short, the evidence from participants' consideration ratings of their leaders suggests that the two processes trade off in their influence over leader perceptions. Inference-based processes appeared to prevail in cases of winning group performance (participants may have felt they could not argue with success); and recognition-based processes appeared to prevail in cases of losing group performance (participants appeared to defend the leaders who matched their prototypes). This tendency is provocative, and a potentially fruitful direction for future research would be to continue to address this apparent tradeoff between recognition-based and inference-based processes.

Turning to the manipulation of material sabotage, the hypothesis regarding the effects of this variable in combination with performance information (Hypothesis 3) was not supported. It was predicted that, due to discounting (Kelley, 1971, 1973), losing leaders whose materials had been sabotaged would still be rated as highly as were winning leaders. Unexpectedly, no significant interaction between these variables was revealed, a finding that is inconsistent with past research (Nye, 2002; Phillips & Lord, 1981). Material sabotage did interact with prototype matching, however, which was an unanticipated finding. In this case, there was a drop in both LBDQ subscale ratings as leaders matched prototypes less and less—but only in the no sabotage conditions. Participants whose group materials were sabotaged tended to rate all of their leaders highly, regardless of prototype matching. One explanation for this finding would be that participants were simply more lenient in their ratings of these leaders in the sabotage conditions because they were friendly and likeable leaders. An alternative explanation for this effect would be that followers may have felt closer to their leaders as a result of the shared crisis created when group materials were sabotaged, and recalled more leadership than may have actually occurred. That is, under conditions of sabotage, leadership prototypes may have simply become less relevant in the minds of followers. Emrich (1999) found evidence that observers react in a similar way to leaders during crises. One way to test the relative merits of both explanations would be to replicate this study with unfriendly leaders. Should similar patterns emerge, the latter explanation would be supported. However, should this tendency to rate leaders highly in the sabotage condition disappear, the former explanation would be supported.

Finally, Hypothesis 5, regarding a three-way interaction between predictors, was not supported. However, a near significant three-way interaction in the consideration analysis was revealed. In the no sabotage conditions, the data support the original interaction hypothesis regarding performance information and prototype matching. The sabotage of group materials, however, appears to have changed the rules completely, with all leaders being rated quite highly. Performance cues still seem to be a factor, but prototype matching is no longer a factor when materials are sabotaged. This interaction, although not statistically significant, suggests the potentially important effects of situational variables such as material sabotage on followers' perceptions of their leaders, and deserves further investigation in future research.

Overall, the LBDQ consideration subscale appeared to be the most affected by the predictors in the present study. This finding is not surprising, considering that the prototype matching predictor played such a prominent role, and that participants' reported prototypes tended to emphasize leader friendliness. However, the reader should remember that participants' prototypes were made up of more than friendliness, with issues of dominance and control also considered. In short, leaders had to exhibit more than friendliness to match participants' prototypes; those who did match were regarded as more considerate (i.e., better leaders), a finding consistent with past research (Bass, 1990).

Some limitations in the present study should be noted. Perhaps most important was that the present study employed ad hoc groups who met for 20 minutes, rather than ongoing groups, and the confederate leaders were not known to their groups before the interaction. Although this methodology led to groups that would be less "real" in the minds of followers, it was used to maintain greater control over extraneous variables. Studying ongoing groups would have introduced history threats (prior group successes and failures; the leaders would have already had the opportunity to shape followers' prototypes). In short, internal validity concerns won out over generalizability concerns in the present study. Retrospectively, participants may have also experienced greater investment in their groups, overall, if a reward of more than $50 had been offered. However, one cannot underestimate the motivational power of a few dollars over the average college student.

The confederate leaders themselves are a concern in that they may have aroused the suspicions of group members. I would have preferred to bring the leaders into the groups in a more subtle manner. However, doing so was not feasible in the present study. To reduce disruption of the leader's script, I wished to use participants who were a bit older (and perhaps more serious about psychology) than the traditional Introduction to Psychology participant pool would have provided. For this reason, students who had already completed an introductory psychology course were used. During the debriefing, participants were asked to report any suspicions they had about the study, and the data of suspicious participants were excluded from the analyses.

The present data provide support for Lord's (1985; Lord & Maher, 1991) theory, revealing evidence of both recognition-based and inference-based processes in followers' leadership perceptions in short-term small groups. Leaders enjoyed more positive ratings when their behaviors tended to meet participants' prior expectations and when their groups won. These findings reveal the complex patterns of thinking going on in the minds of followers. Nye (2002) found that followers are keenly aware of their own roles in the group, but the present data suggest as well that followers are still able to step back to judge their group leaders. They appear to draw upon their prototypes, but are also willing to consider situational evidence (e.g., group outcomes, flawed materials) in their leadership appraisals.

The important role played by prototype matching as a predictor in the present findings suggests that tapping into individual differences in participants' leadership prototypes can provide important predictive power. Prototypes may be fleeting cognitive structures (Read & Miller, 1998; Smith, 1996, 1998), and therefore difficult to measure. However, we should not assume that everyone holds the same leadership prototype. In the future, researchers may wish to address not only the *degree* of prototype matching (how closely a leader matches) but the *direction* of the matching as well. That is, we may be more accepting of a poor match with our prototype if the leader's behavior is at least in the "right" direction.

The present findings also reinforce the importance of studying the leadership perceptions of actual group members. When group members react to leaders, they have to take into account their own role in the group, accepting some responsibility for group outcomes (Nye, 2002). Moreover, because they were members of the group rather than outside observers, participants may have not been as inclined as observers to blame leaders for poor performance (Hall & Lord, 1998; Jones & Nisbett, 1987). Still, the present study revealed that followers are not immune to the biasing effects of performance information.

In conclusion, future research should continue to tap into the incredibly complex patterns of thinking that go on in the minds of followers when they interpret leader behavior and group outcomes. Followers are no different than anyone else in thinking they know what good leadership is. Although followers may be susceptible to bias, their perceptions ultimately play a key role in group and organizational success (Chemers, 2001; Dansereau & Yammarino, 1998; Hollander, 1992).

AUTHOR NOTE

Special thanks to Anna Aldoy, Karen Burger, Thomas McCarthy, Dina Muraco, and Debra Stueber for their assistance with data collection. Address correspondence to Department of Psychology, Monmouth University, West Long Branch, NJ 07764, phone 732-571-3683, fax 732-263-5159, email nye@monmouth.edu.

NOTES

1. The complete LBDQ Form XII includes 12 subscales (including representation, demand reconciliation, tolerance for uncertainty, persuasiveness, tol-

erance of freedom, role assumption, production emphasis, predictive accuracy, integration, and superior orientation). For the most part, consideration and initiation of structure are the subscales most often addressed in the literature. Bass (1990) notes that these two subscales have often been linked to subordinate satisfaction and effectiveness.

2.   Euclidean distance is a standard measure of distance between two points (e.g., the Pythagorean theorem is a measure of Euclidean distance, used to address distance between two points in a plane; Weisstein, n.d.). The distance between two points in Euclidean three-dimensional space is

$$d = \sqrt{(x_2 - x_1)^2 + (y_2 - y_1)^2 + (z_2 - z_1)^2}$$

3.   Cell sizes were as follows: sabotaged/win 26, sabotaged/lose 32, no sabotage/win 28, no sabotage/lose 23.

4.   This persuasion was included to add face validity to the win/lose manipulation, as I was concerned that without it participants in the sabotaged conditions would not believe that they could win.

REFERENCES

Bales, R.F., Cohen, S.F., & Williamson, S.A. (1979). *SYMLOG: A system for the multiple level observation of groups.* New York: The Free Press.

Bartol, K.M., & Butterfield, D.A. (1976). Sex effects in evaluating leaders. *Journal of Applied Psychology, 61,* 446–454.

Bass, B.M. (1990). *Bass and Stogdill's handbook of leadership: Theory, research, and managerial applications* (3rd ed.). New York: The Free Press.

Binning, J.F., & Lord, R.G. (1980). Boundary conditions for performance cue effects on group process ratings: Familiarity versus type of feedback. *Organizational Behavior and Human Performance, 26,* 115–130.

Binning, J.F., Zaba, A.J., & Whattam, J.C. (1986). Explaining the biasing effects of performance cues in terms of cognitive categorization. *Academy of Management Journal, 29,* 521–535.

Brown, D.J., & Lord, R.G. (2001). Leadership and perceiver cognition: Moving beyond the first order constructs. In M. London (Ed.), *How people evaluate others in organizations* (pp. 181–202). Mahwah, NJ: Erlbaum.

Burns, J.M. (1978). *Leadership.* New York: Harper.

Calder, B.J. (1977). An attribution theory of leadership. In B.M. Staw & G.R. Salancik (Eds.), *New directions in organizational behavior* (pp. 179–204). Chicago: St. Claire Press.

Chemers, M.M. (1997). *An integrative theory of leadership.* Mahwah, NJ: Erlbaum.

Cohen, J.C., Cohen, P., Aiken, L.S., & West, S.G. (2003). *Applied multiple regression/ correlation analysis for the behavioral sciences* (3rd ed.). Mahwah, NJ: Lawrence Erlbaum Associates.

Dansereau, F., & Yammarino, F.J. (Eds.). (1998). *Leadership: The multiple-level approaches.* Stamford, CT: JAI Press.

Den Hartog, D.N., House, R.G., Hanges, P.J., Ruiz-Quintanilla, S.A., & Dorfman, P.W. (1999). Culture specific and cross-culturally generalizable implicit leadership theories: Are the attributes of charismatic/transformational leadership universally endorsed? *Leadership Quarterly, 10*, 219–258.

Eden, D., & Leviatan, V. (1975). Implicit leadership theory as a determinant of the factor structure underlying supervisory behavior scales. *Journal of Applied Psychology, 60*, 736–741.

Emrich, C.G., (1999). Context effects in leadership perception [Electronic version]. *Personality and Social Psychology Bulletin, 25*, 991–1006.

Forgas J.P. (Ed.) (2000). *Feeling and thinking: The role of affect in social cognition.* Cambridge: Cambridge University Press.

Foti, R.J., Fraser, S.L., & Lord, R.G. (1982). Effects of leadership labels and prototypes on perceptions of political leaders. *Journal of Applied Psychology, 67*, 326–333.

Fraser, S.L., & Lord, R.G. (1988). Stimulus prototypicality and general leadership impressions: Their role in leadership and behavioral ratings. *The Journal of Psychology, 122*, 291–303.

Hall, R.J., & Lord, R.G. (1998). Multi-level information processing explanations of followers' leadership perceptions. In F. Dansereau & F.J. Yammarino (Eds.), *Leadership: The multiple-level approaches* (pp. 159–183). Stamford, CT: JAI Press.

Hollander, E.P. (1992). Leadership, followership, self, and others. *Leadership Quarterly, 3*, 43–55.

Hollander, E.P. & Julian, J.W. (1969). Contemporary trends in the analysis of leadership processes. *Psychological Bulletin, 71*, 387–397.

Jones, E.E., & Nisbett, R. (1987). The actor and the observer: Divergent perceptions of the causes of behavior. In E.E. Jones, D.E. Kanouse, H.H. Kelley, R.E., Nisbett, S. Valins, & B. Weiner (Eds.), *Attribution: Perceiving the causes of behavior* (pp. 79–94). Hillsdale, NJ: Erlbaum.

Keller, T. (1999). Images of the familiar: Individual differences and implicit leadership theories [Electronic version]. *Leadership Quarterly, 10*, 589–607.

Kelley, H.H. (1971). Causal schemata and the attribution process. In E.E. Jones, D.E. Kanouse, H.H. Kelley, R.E. Nisbett, S. Valins, & B. Weiner (Eds.), *Attribution: Perceiving the causes of behavior* (pp. 151–174). Morristown, NJ: General Learning Press.

Kelley, H.H. (1973). The processes of causal attribution. *American Psychologist, 28*, 107–127.

Kenney, R.A., Schwartz-Kenney, B.M., & Blascovich, J. (1996). Implicit leadership theories: Defining leaders described as worthy of influence. *Personality and Social Psychology Bulletin, 22*, 1128–1143.

Kouzes, J.M., & Posner, B.Z. (1990, January). The credibility factor: What followers expect from their leaders. *Management Review*, 29–33.

Kouzes, J.M., & Posner, B.Z. (1993). *Credibility: How leaders gain and lose it, why people demand it.* San Francisco: Jossey-Bass.

Larson, J.R., Jr. (1982). Cognitive mechanisms mediating the impact of implicit leadership theories of leader behavior on leader behavior ratings. *Organizational Behavior and Human Performance, 29*, 129–140.

Larson, J.R., Jr., Lingle, J.H., & Scerbo, M.M. (1984). The impact of performance cues on leader-behavior ratings: The role of selective information availability and probabilistic response bias. *Organizational Behavior and Human Performance, 33*, 323–349.

Lord, R.G. (1985). An information processing approach to social perceptions, leadership and behavioral measurement in organizations. In B.M. Staw & L.L. Cummings (Ed.), *Research in organizational behavior* (Vol. 7, pp. 87–128). Greenwich, CT: JAI Press.

Lord, R.G., Brown, D.J., & Freiberg, S.J. (1999). Understanding the dynamics of leadership: The role of follower self-concepts in the leader/follower relationship [Electronic version]. *Organizational Behavior and Human Decision Processes, 78*, 167–203.

Lord, R.G., Brown, D.J., & Harvey, J.L. (2001). System constraints on leadership perceptions, behavior and influence: An example of connectionist level processes. In M.A. Hogg & R.S. Tindale (Eds.), *Blackwell handbook of social psychology: Group processes* (pp. 283–310). Oxford: Blackwell.

Lord, R.G., Brown, D.J., Harvey, J.L., & Hall, R.J. (2001). Contextual constraints on prototype generation and their multilevel consequences for leadership perceptions [Electronic version]. *The Leadership Quarterly, 12*, 311–338.

Lord, R.G., De Vader, C., & Alliger, G. (1986). A meta-analysis of the relation between personality traits and leadership perceptions: An application of validity generalization procedures. *Journal of Applied Psychology, 71*, 402–410.

Lord, R.G., & Emrich, C.G. (2001). Thinking outside the box by looking inside the box: Extending the cognitive revolution in leadership research [Electronic version]. *Leadership Quarterly, 11*, 551–579.

Lord, R.G., Foti, R.J., & De Vader, C.L. (1984). A test of leadership categorization theory: Internal structure, information processing, and leadership perceptions. *Organizational Behavior and Human Performance, 34*, 343–378.

Lord, R.G., Foti, R.J., & Phillips, J.S. (1982). A theory of leadership categorization. In H.G. Hunt, U. Sekaran, & C. Schriescheim (Eds.), *Leadership: Beyond establishment views.* Carbondale: Southern Illinois University Press.

Lord, R.G., & Maher, K.J. (1990). Perceptions of leadership and their implications in organizations. In J. Carroll (Ed.), *Applied social psychology and organizational settings* (pp. 129–154). Hillsdale,NJ: Lawrence Erlbaum Associates.

Lord, R.G., & Maher, K.J. (1991). *Leadership and information processing: Linking perceptions and performance.* Boston: Unwin Hyman.

Meindl, J.R. (1995). The romance of leadership as a follower-centric theory: A social constructionist approach. *Leadership Quarterly, 6*, 329–341.

Mischel, W. (1973). Toward a cognitive social learning reconceptualization of personality. *Psychological Review, 80*, 252–283.

Nye, J.L.(2002). The eye of the follower: Information processing effects on attributions regarding leaders of small groups. *Small Group Research, 33*, 337–360.

Nye, J.L., & Forsyth, D.R. (1991). The effects of prototype-based biases on leadership appraisals: A test of leadership categorization theory. *Small Group Research, 22*, 360–379.

Nye, J.L., & Simonetta, L.G. (1996). Followers' perceptions of group leaders: The impact of recognition-based and inference-based processes. In J.L. Nye & A.M.

Brower (Eds.) *What's social about social cognition? Research on socially shared cognition in small groups.* Thousand Oaks, CA: Sage Publications.

Offerman, L.R., Kennedy, J.K., Jr., & Wirtz, P.W. (1994) Implicit leadership theories: Content, structure, and generalizability. *Leadership Quarterly, 5*, 43–58.

Pfeffer, J. (1977). The ambiguity of leadership. *Academy of Management Review, 12*, 104–112.

Phillips, J.S. (1984). The accuracy of leadership ratings: A cognitive categorization perspective. *Organizational Behavior and Human Performance, 33*, 125–138.

Phillips, J.S., & Lord, R.G. (1981). Causal attributions and perceptions of leadership. *Organizational Behavior and Human Performance, 28*, 143–163.

Phillips, J.S., & Lord, R.G. (1982). Schematic information processing and perceptions of leadership in problem-solving groups. *Journal of Applied Psychology, 67*, 486–492.

Read, S.J., & Miller, L.C. (Eds.). (1998). *Connectionist models of social reasoning and social behavior.* Mahwah, NJ: Lawrence Erlbaum Associates.

Smith, E.R. (1996). What do connectionism and social psychology offer each other? *Journal of Personality and Social Psychology, 70*, 893–912.

Smith, E.R. (1998). Mental representation and memory. In D.T. Gilbert, S.T. Fiske, & G. Lindzey (Eds.), *The handbook of social psychology* (Vol. 1, pp. 391–445). Boston: McGraw-Hill.

Stogdill, R.M. (1963). *Manual for the leader behavior description questionnaire—Form XII.* Columbus: Ohio State University, Bureau of Business Research.

Weisstein, E.W. (n.d.). *Distance.* Retrieved January 10, 2005, from http://mathworld.wolfram.com/Distance.html

CHAPTER 2

COGNITION MATTERS

Leader Images and Their Implications for Organizational Life

Tiffany Hansbrough (Keller)

ABSTRACT

This chapter considers how implicit leadership theories may develop and the resulting organizational implications when individual leadership models differ from organizational reality. In particular, an exploratory study is presented that examines the relationship between congruence of ideal leader images and organizational reality and job satisfaction. Individuals whose descriptions of ideal leaders differed from their perceptions of actual leaders reported lower levels of job satisfaction as did individuals whose ideal leader images differed from those of their superiors. The results indicate that the implicit leadership theory dimensions that support followers' sense of worth are more important for follower job satisfaction than are the other dimensions. The theoretical and practical implications are discussed.

Implicit Leadership Theories: Essays and Explorations, pages 63–77

INTRODUCTION

Implicit leadership theory origins are based in cognitive social psychology. Accordingly, the label "leader" serves as a schema, or mental model, that contains all relevant information, such as personality traits, thought to be representative of leaders. Observers classify individuals as either "leaders" or "non leaders" depending on how well they fit the ideal prototype. Once activated, the leadership schema employs the same cognitive shortcuts as other schemas; such as selective attention, encoding, and retrieval of schema-consistent information as well as cuing schema-consistent information where such information does not exist (Lord & Maher, 1991; Lord, Foti, & De Vader, 1984; Phillips & Lord, 1982).

Research has found that the content of the leadership schema is widely shared thus providing individuals with a common frame of reference (Lord et al., 1984; Pavitt & Sackaroff, 1990; Kenney, Blascovich, & Shaver, 1994). Specifically eight traits have been associated with the word "leader" including sensitivity, dedication, tyranny, charisma, attractiveness, masculinity, intelligence, and strength (Offerman, Kennedy, & Wirtz, 1994). Although the schema consists largely of socially desirable characteristics, it also allows for the possibility that leaders may have undesirable traits.

Evidence also exists for individual level variation within this prototype. Personality traits such as agreeableness, conscientiousness, extroversion, openness, and self-monitoring influence implicit leadership theories (Keller, 1999). Specifically individuals characterize a leader similar to self as ideal. Keller (1999) suggests that since becoming a leader and leadership is construed as socially desirable (e.g., Meindl, Ehrlich, & Dukerich, 1985); individuals may view themselves as potential leaders and thus project their own traits onto idealized leadership images. In other words, the ideal leader is analogous to self. The tendency to prefer familiar leadership images is also evidenced in the relationship between parental traits and implicit leadership theories whereby idealized leadership images mirror descriptions of parental traits (Keller, 1999). Ideal leader images mirrored descriptions of parental traits regardless of whether parents were characterized as dedicated or tyrannical. These findings suggest that both personality traits and previous interactions with parents play a role in shaping leadership expectations.

The Development of Implicit Leadership Theories

Hunt, Boal, and Sorenson (1990) posit that individual differences in implicit leadership theories may be the result of early childhood experiences. Parental models of leadership may play a pivotal role in shaping leadership schemas as they represent a primary encounter with leadership figures, are based on tangible, repetitive interactions, and may accordingly shape expectations for future exchanges with authority figures. Both social learning and psychoanalytic frameworks suggest that parents shape individuals' ideas about leadership. First, social learning holds that individuals acquire much of their behavior by imitating others observed in a social context (Kreitner & Luthans, 1984). Jablin and Krone (1987) note that parents provide anticipatory socialization about work, leadership, and communication and so doing impart the primary model of the leader-follower relationship to children.

According to psychoanalytic theory, authority figures in the workplace are symbolically equated with parents as individuals re-enact, and attempt to rework, childhood scenarios (Kout, 1977; Oglensky, 1995). Since all social interaction results from a mixture of realistic reactions based on the present and transferential reactions based upon imagery and emotions rooted in the past (Greenberg & Mitchell, 1983), individuals may attempt to apply previously learned patterns of interactions to those with superiors. Therefore existing leadership schemas may be utilized as a heuristic device to understand a new situation.

Implicit Leadership Theories and Organizational Life: The Importance of Congruence

The importance of implicit leadership theories in dyadic functioning is highlighted in Lord and Maher's (1991) reciprocal influence model. Social perception is conceptualized as a sensemaking process that mediates between the behavior of one dyadic partner and the response of the other. It is the *interpretation* of the behavior, not the behavior per se that impacts leadership relationships (Gioia, Thomas, Clark, & Chittipeddi, 1994). Likewise, according to the Lord and Maher model, people use implicit leadership theories both as a basis for interpreting the behavior of their dyadic partners and as a foundation for generating their own behavior.

Congruence between leader and follower implicit leadership theories may be important since congruence may foster perceived similarity and identification with the dyadic partner, provide a basis for common understanding, and permit more automatic, intuitive social interactions (Engle & Lord, 1997). In this manner the actual behavior of both members is likely to align with expectations and both parties are likely to interpret behavior similarly. In combination these processes should produce greater liking and high quality relationships as assessed by LMX (Engle & Lord, 1997) as well as influence follower satisfaction with the leader (Hunt et al., 1990).

This notion of congruence, or fit, extends the central premise of the unmet expectations literature whereby newcomers to the organization encounter discrepancies between expectations of organizational life and reality. The discrepancy between expectations and reality determines whether expectations are met (Major et al., 1995). Met expectations are traditionally associated with job satisfaction (Greenhaus, Seidel, & Marinis, 1983; Wanous et al., 1992). This study explores whether met expectations in the form of congruence between followers' ideal leader images and subsequent perceptions of actual leaders impact job satisfaction. Accordingly, the notion that congruence between implicit leadership theories and organizational reality impacts job satisfaction is consistent with and extends previous research on unmet expectations. Implicit leadership theories, with their focus on personality traits associated with leadership, may be categorized as weak scripts. Weak scripts serve to organize expectations about the behavior of people in certain situations (Abelson, 1981). Thus a focus on implicit leadership theories may further elucidate the leadership expectations followers bring to organizations.

EXPLORATORY STUDY

The literature suggests two different variations of the fit hypothesis, one based on congruence between followers' leadership expectations and subsequent organizational reality and the other based on follower-leader cognitive congruence. First, Hunt et al., (1990) suggest that congruence between implicit leadership theories and perceptions of actual leaders may influence job satisfaction. One purpose of this study is to test this hypothesis. Second, a cognitive version of the fit hypothesis is articulated by Engle and Lord (1997). If superiors' and subordinates' implicit leadership theories are similar, such congruence may foster perceived similarity and identification as well as provide a basis for common understanding. Thus it seems likely that fit between leader and follower implicit leadership theories may also impact job satisfaction. However since congruence in implicit leadership theories can be a cause and a result of dyadic processes (Engle & Lord, 1997), this study employs a longitudinal design.

H1:   *Discrepancies between ideal leader images and perceived leader behavior will negatively relate to follower job satisfaction.*

H2:   *Discrepancies between superior and subordinate ideal leader images will negatively relate to follower job satisfaction.*

Some Dimensions Are More Important than Others

Although implicit leadership theories have been conceptualized as multidimensional, speculation about the congruence of implicit leadership theories with organizational reality has focused primarily on the overall fit (e.g., Hunt et al., 1990; Engle & Lord, 1997). Such conceptualizations assign equal weight to each dimension, yet it is possible that not all dimensions are key factors in newcomer satisfaction. Here, I propose that leader sensitivity, or lack thereof, will predict follower job satisfaction better than will the other implicit leadership theory dimensions.

Leader sensitivity may be particularly crucial to followers since it may support a positive view of self. According to self-verification theory (e.g., Swann, 1984), individuals choose opportunities structures, such as organizations and jobs, that will confirm their self-concepts. Most individuals hold a positive self-concept (Markus & Wurf, 1987) as well as harbor overly positive self-evaluations (e.g., positive illusions) characteristic of normal human thought (Taylor & Brown, 1988). Accordingly, most followers will likely seek feedback that corroborates such images. For example, if followers perceptions of supervisor sensitivity suggests previous interactions during which supervisors were perceived as warm, sympathetic, and understanding (leader sensitivity). Similar interactions may serve to sustain followers' positive view of self, as individuals deserving, and worthy of, sensitivity from others. Conversely, leaders perceived as domineering and pushy (leader tyranny) may convey a lack of respect to followers and thus fail to nourish their sense of worth. In this manner, perceptions of leader sensitivity and actual leader sensitivity may facilitate job satisfaction while perceptions of leader tyranny and actual leader tyranny may impede job satisfaction.

Attachment dynamics in the workplace also indicate the importance of leader sensitivity. According to attachment theory, during childhood individuals form strong emotional bonds with caregivers that promote survival of the species (Bowlby, 1977). Since infants cannot survive on their own, they are motivated to obtain proximity and protection from caregivers. Caregivers that are readily available, sensitive to children's signals and lovingly responsive when they seek comfort and protection, provide children with both a safe haven as well as a secure base from which they may confidently explore their environment.

Popper and Mayless (2003) argue that attachment dynamics are relevant in every day organizational situations as leaders fulfill followers' attachment needs by offering a secure base. Moreover, feeling safe and secure is required for daily functioning as the provision of security may foster followers' capacity to learn, take risks and be creative (Popper & Mayless, 2003).

The definitions of "good" parenting in the attachment literature are remarkably similar to the implicit leadership theory factor of leader sensitivity identified by Offerman et al. (1994) (see Table 2.1). Leader sensitivity includes characteristics such as sympathetic, sensitive, compassionate, and understanding. Likewise, a good parent is sensitive, available, and responsive to the child's needs, and adapts his/her responses to those needs (Ainsworth et al., 1978; De-Wolff & Van Ijzendoorn, 1997). Moreover, a good parent does not criticize, domineer, pressure or forbid without a reason (Baumrind, 1978; Barber & Harmon, 2002). Thus from an attachment perspective, the dimension of leader sensitivity may facilitate the establishment of a secure base while leader tyranny, including characteristics such as domineering, pushy, and demanding, may interfere with such goals.

Table 2.1.   Comparison of Definitions of the "Good" Parent and Leader Sensitivity

Dimensions of leader sensitivity (Offerman et al., 1994)	The "good parent"
Sympathetic, sensitive, compassionate, understanding, sincere, warm, forgiving, helpful.	Is sensitive, available, and responsive to the child's needs, understands the child's needs, and adapts his/responses to those needs (Ainsworth et al., 1978; De-Wolff & Van IJzendoorn, 1997).
	Is emotionally open and expressive. Engages in warm, loving, and accepting emotional communication (Cassidy, 1994).

H3:   *For both fit hypotheses (H1 and H2), discrepancies between the implicit leadership theory dimensions of leader sensitivity and leader tyranny will better predict follower job satisfaction than will the other dimensions.*

METHOD

Subjects and Setting

At Time 1, surveys were mailed to 680 graduating seniors from a small, private university. One hundred-sixty surveys were returned, yielding a response rate of 24%. Six months later, a second survey was mailed to responding alumni, including an additional survey to be completed by their supervisor. Fifty-two subordinate surveys and 25 superior surveys were returned, yielding response rates of 33 and 16% respectively. Data were collected from newcomers to control for organizational cultural dynamics.

The average subject was 22 years old. Sixty-three percent of the respondents were female. Subjects reported a wide range of majors at Time 1, including business, biology, psychology, English and political science. A total of 20 majors were reported; accordingly one major did not dominate responses.

Measures

Implicit leadership theory.   Offerman et al.'s (1994) typology of 41 prototypical leadership traits includes eight different dimensions associated with the word "leader." These dimensions include sensitivity, dedication, tyranny, charisma, attractiveness, masculinity, intelligence, and strength. This particular taxonomy was selected since it allows for the possibility that leaders may possess socially undesirable traits, such as tyranny. At Time 1, subjects indicated, on a five-point scale, the extent that each trait described their ideal leader. At Time 2, subjects rated their actual supervisor on those same traits. Finally, subjects' supervisors indicated the extent that each trait described their ideal leader. Thus, both subordinate and superior reports of ideal leaders were obtained. Due to the low reliability of leader strength, it was omitted from further analyses.

Job satisfaction.   Job satisfaction was assessed at Time 2 by a three-item, five-point scale (Cammann et al., 1983). Items include (1) All in all, I am satisfied with my job, (2) In general, I don't like my job (reverse scored), and (3) In general, I like working here. (Descriptive statistics and correlations among variables are presented in Tables 2.2 and 2.3 for subordinate and superior reports respectively.)

Table 2.2.   Correlations among Subordinate Implicit Leadership Theories, Job Satisfaction, and Descriptive Statistics

	M	*SD*	*1*	*2*	*3*	*4*	*5*	*6*	*7*	*8*
Job satisfaction	10.75	2.12	(.85)							
Sensitivity	32.16	4.61	.16	(.86)						
Dedication	19.10	1.25	−.01	.07	(.88)					
Tyranny	18.48	5.79	−.15	−.43**	.10	(.84)				
Charisma	22.29	2.28	.25	.11	.23	.22	(.74)			
Attractiveness	12.46	3.81	.17	.08	.08	.13	.24	(.86)		
Masculinity	4.16	1.94	.03	−.27	−.23	.35*	.22	.24	(.86)	
Intelligence	25.79	2.82	.07	.38**	.16	.26	.33	.34*	.09	(.75)

*$p < .05$, **$p < .01$, n = 52

Table 2.3.   Correlations among Superior Implicit Leadership Theories and Descriptive Statistics

	M	SD	1	2	3	4	5	6	7
Sensitivity	32.50	3.40	(.81)						
Dedication	19.04	1.20	.23	(.70)					
Tyranny	14.92	4.13	−.46*	.28	(.76)				
Charisma	21.58	2.84	.44*	.18	−.38	(.76)			
Attractiveness	13.58	3.20	−.04	.53**	.45*	.25	(.82)		
Masculinity	2.76	1.76	−.10	.28	.61**	−.30	.48*	(.97)	
Intelligence	25.46	2.70	.29	.34	−.09	.47*	.20	−.11	(.87)

$*p < .05$, $**p < .01$, n = 25

RESULTS

Fit Hypothesis 1: Ideal Leader and Actual Leader

First, difference scores, resulting in absolute values, were computed between subordinate reports of ideal leader images (at Time 1) and subordinate reports of actual supervisors (at Time 2) for each of the seven implicit leadership theory dimensions. Next, stepwise regression analysis was used to test the hypothesis that discrepancies between ideal leader images and perceptions of actual leaders are negatively related to follower job satisfaction. Leader sensitivity significantly entered into the equation to predict job satisfaction ($\beta = -.30$, $p < .05$), although in the predicted direction ($\beta = -.21$), leader tyranny failed to reach statistical significance. Consistent with Hypothesis 3, none of the other dimensions significantly entered into the equation to predict follower job satisfaction (Table 2.4).

Fit Hypothesis 2: Superior/Subordinate Ideal Leader Images

First, difference scores were computed resulting in absolute values, between subordinate reports of ideal leader images (at Time 1) and superior reports of ideal leader images (at Time 2) for each of the implicit leadership theory dimensions. Next, stepwise regression analysis was used to test the hypothesis that discrepancies between superior and subordinate ideal leader images negatively relate to follower job satisfaction. Discrepancies between superior and subordinate ideal leader images of tyranny significantly entered into the equation to predict subordinate job satisfaction

Table 2.4.   Fit Hypothesis 1: Prediction of Job Satisfaction from Subordinate Ideal Leader Traits and Actual Leader Traits

	Beta
Sensitivity	$-.30^{*}$
Dedication	.09
Tyranny	$-.21$
Charisma	.07
Attractiveness	$-.17$
Intelligence	$-.01$
Masculinity	.17
Adjusted R^2	.07

$^{*}p < .05$, n = 52

Table 2.5.   Fit Hypothesis 1: Prediction of Job Satisfaction from Superior and Subordinate Ideal Leader Images

	Beta
Sensitivity	.12
Dedication	$-.25$
Tyranny	$-.47^{**}$
Charisma	.35
Attractiveness	$-.42^{**}$
Intelligence	.10
Masculinity	.02
Adjusted R^2	.28

$^{**}p < .01$

($\beta = -.47$, $p < .01$). Additionally, discrepancies between superior and subordinate ideal images of leader attractiveness also significantly predicted subordinate job satisfaction ($\beta = -.42$, $p < .05$). None of the other dimensions significantly predicted subordinate job satisfaction (Table 2.5).

DISCUSSION

This study found support for two different fit hypotheses. Individuals whose descriptions of ideal leaders differed from their perceptions of actual leaders reported lower levels of job satisfaction as did individuals

whose ideal leader images differed from those of their superiors. Moreover, the results suggest a modified fit hypothesis: Congruence between
implicit leadership theories and organizational reality, based on leader sensitivity and leader tyranny, impacts subordinate job satisfaction.

Individuals who encountered discrepancies between ideal leader images
of sensitivity and actual leader sensitivity reported lower levels of job satisfaction. Attributions of leader warmth and sympathy (sensitivity) may be
particularly crucial since they may facilitate a positive view of self (e.g.,
Swann, 1984).

Likewise, discrepancies between superior and subordinate ideal leader
images of tyranny were associated with lower levels of subordinate job satisfaction. This may represent a tension regarding acceptable limits of supervisory behavior. For example, superiors and subordinates may disagree
about the extent to which superiors may engage in pushy, manipulative,
and domineering (tyranny) behavior. Such behaviors may lead followers to
conclude that superiors do not support or value them as individuals nor do
leaders nourish their sense of self-worth. In this manner, discrepancies
between superior and subordinate ideal leader images of tyranny may negatively impact job satisfaction. These findings add emphasis to Engle and
Lord's (1997) assertion that a schematic match may have direct implications for the quality of the superior/subordinate relationship.

Interestingly, discrepancies in superior and subordinate ideal leader
images of attractiveness also significantly predicted subordinate job satisfaction. Attractiveness includes such traits as classy and well-dressed. This
definition seems more akin to professionalism rather than physical attractiveness. Accordingly, it is possible that individuals who are perceived as
loud, pushy, and selfish (tyranny) may also be deemed unprofessional.

Limitations

There was little variability in the sample. Ideal leader images were
largely consistent with descriptions of actual leaders. However, even with
such limited range, discrepancies between ideal leader images and organizational reality impacted job satisfaction. Moreover, the response rate for
supervisors was rather low (16%, n = 25) thus impacting the statistical
power of the analyses using superior and subordinate reports. Future studies, using a sample with greater variability as well as a larger sample size
may find more statistically significant results.

The magnitude of the results was rather small. However, they are in line
with other research on met expectations whereby the mean correlation for
job satisfaction is .39 (e.g., Wanous et al., 1992). Here, subordinate job satisfaction served as the dependent variable. Future research, using a more

proximal variable such as subordinate satisfaction with the leader, may find results of a greater magnitude.

Theoretical Implications and Future Research

It is likely that individuals hold scripts about ideal leader behavior. The results suggest that newcomers enter organizations with expectations that leaders will support their sense of worth. For example, sensitive leaders may facilitate the maintenance of a positive view of self. Alternatively, discrepancies between expected leader sensitivity and actual leader sensitivity might represent a threat to self. As noted by Swann (1984) when an opportunity structure, such an organization or job, fails to provide confirmation of self, individuals may seek change rather than change their view of self. Ultimately, turnover may result when individuals encounter leaders who fail to meet their expectations and in doing so fail to confirm their view of self.

Followers may vary in the support desired from leaders or their need for leadership (e.g., De Vries & van Gelder, 2005). For example, De Vries et al. (2004) found that emotional stability is among the most important predictors of need for leadership. Such findings are compatible with an attachment perspective on implicit leadership theories (e.g., Keller, 2003) where individual differences in leadership schemas may be the result of early childhood experiences. In particular, anxious-ambivalent individuals seem particularly predisposed to view work as an opportunity to satisfy their unmet attachment needs (Hazan & Shaver, 1990). As children, anxious-ambivalent individuals held onto inconsistent caregivers by maintaining close proximity to caregivers (Shaver, Collins, & Clark, 1996). In this manner, vigilance toward the attachment figure was positively reinforced. Accordingly, the ideal follower may be characterized as dependent.

Transferring this behavior to the work place, anxious-ambivalent followers may "cling" to superiors, needing continual reassurance about their performance. However help-seeking entails costs (Lee, 1997). By acknowledging incompetence and dependence, the help seeker creates a negative public impression of himself or herself that undermines the help seeker's desire to create positive public impressions (Gerstein, Ginter, & Graziano, 1985: Leary & Kowalski, 1990; Sclenker & Weigold, 1992; Wolfe, Lennox, & Cutler, 1986). Thus, leaders, possessing a schema that characterizes followers as independent, may interpret this incessant need for reassurance as lack of ability. Leaders may become overwhelmed by the intense demands of anxious-ambivalent followers, come to view them as burden, and actually withdraw support and attention. Thus, discrepancies between superior and subordinate ideal follower images could result in lower subordinate performance evaluations.

Future research may also address whether ideal leader images represent fundamental or superfluous expectations of leaders. In particular, it may be crucial that expectations about leader sensitivity and tyranny are met as they may sustain a positive view of self. On the other hand, it may be less important that expectations regarding the other dimensions of implicit leadership theories be met as they seem less central to followers' view of self. As proposed by Engle and Lord (1997), subordinates may use implicit leadership theories to evaluate their superiors. This exploratory study suggests that expectations of leaders, and whether they are met, have tangible consequences for subsequent job satisfaction.

The context and cues from the environment may also impact the extent to which followers need leaders to function as a secure base. Specifically, the terror management literature, based on Ernest Becker's work (e.g., Greenberg and his colleagues), alludes to a link between crisis and the need for the leader to provide a secure base in the form of a heroic protector. According to Becker (1973), the most unique aspect of human beings is their awareness of their own morality. Awareness of the inevitability of death in a species programmed for self-preservation creates the potential for paralyzing terror. Yet in order to go on with our lives we must push aside this fear. Lipman-Blumen (1996) contends that perhaps the most common method to deal with this existential dread is to seek protectors outside ourselves. Specifically, godlike heroic leaders help us maintain the illusion that someone more powerful than ourselves can protect us from the whims of fate. In times of crisis we seek powerful leaders who promise to take charge and set things right (Lipman-Blumen, 1996). The resulting belief that the leader is "on top of things" permits us to set aside our deep anxiety and go about our daily lives. Accordingly, it is plausible that crisis may intensify followers' need for leader sensitivity as they search for a heroic protector.

Follower expectations about what type of leader best provides a secure base may be influenced by leader gender. Although women may have the perceived edge in terms of stereotypically being emotionally available and supportive (e.g., Ridgeway, 1988), men, holding a disproportionate number of positions of status and authority in organizations (e.g., Ridgeway, 1988; Kanter, 1977), may be perceived as better connected and thus better able to offer protection and/or information. Further, of all the leadership functions, subordinates appear to most need the ones related to upward influence and provision of information (De Vries et al., 2004). Thus followers may anticipate that in organizational settings male leaders are more likely to provide a secure base.

In conclusion, the organizational significance of implicit leadership theories is wide-ranging and may impact leader-follower interactions, follower job satisfaction and performance evaluations. Future research may further specify what leadership expectations followers bring to the organization, how they differ, and what happens when those expectations meet organizational reality. Leader images do not reside only in the head as they are cognitions that have direct implications for action and behavior in organizations.

REFERENCES

Abelson, R.P. (1981). Psychological status of the script concept. *American Psychologist, 36*, 715–729.

Ainsworth, M.D.S., Blehar, M., Waters, E., & Wall, S. (1978). *Patterns of attachment: A psychological study of strange situations.* Hillsdale, NJ: Erlbaum.

Barber, B.K., & Harmon, E.L. (2002). Violating the self: Parental psychological control of children and adolescents. In B.K. Barber (Ed.), *Intrusive parenting* (pp.15–52). Washington, DC: American Psychological Association.

Baumrind, D. (1978). Parental disciplinary patterns and social competence in children. *Youth and Society, 9*, 239–275.

Becker, E. (1973). *Denial of death.* New York: Free Press.

Bowlby, J. (1977). The making and breaking of affectional bonds. *British Journal of Psychiatry, 130*, 201–210.

Cammann, C., Fichman, M., Jenkins, D., & Klesh, J.R. (1983). Assessing the attitudes and perceptions of organizational members. In S.E. Seashore, E.E. Lawler, III., P.H. Mirvis, & C. Cammann (Eds.), *Assessing organizational change: A guide to methods, measures, and practices* (pp. 71–138). New York: Wiley.

Cassidy, J. (1994). Emotion regulation: Influences of attachment relationships. In N.A. Fox (Ed.) The development of emotion regulation: Biological and behavioral considerations. Monographs of the Society for Research in Child Development, vol. 59 (pp. 228–249).

De Vries, R.E., Roes, R.A., Taillieu, T.C.B., & Nelissen, N.J.M. (2004). Behoefte aan leiderschap in organisaties: Wie heft het en waarom? [Who needs leadership in organizations and why?]. *Gedrag en Organisatie, 17*(4), 204–226.

De Vries, R.E., & Van Gelder, J.L. (2005). Leadership and need for leadership: An implicit followership theory. In B. Schyns & J.R. Meindl (Eds.), *Implicit leadership theories: Essays and explorations.* Greenwich, CT: Information Age Publishing.

De-Wolff, M., & Van Ijendoorn, M.H. (1997). Sensitivity and attachment: A meta-analysis on parental antecedents of infant attachment. *Child Development 68*, 571–591.

Engle, E.M., & Lord, R.G. (1997). Implicit theories, self-schemas, and leader-member exchange. *Academy of Management Journal, 40*, 988–1010.

Gerstein, L., Ginter, E., & Graziano, W. (1985). Self monitoring, impression management, and interpersonal evaluations. *The Journal of Social Psychology, 125*(3) 379–389.

Gioia, D.A., Thomas, J.B., Clark, S.M., & Chittipeddi. K. (1994). Symbolism and strategic change in academia: The dynamics of sensemaking and influence. *Organization Science, 5,* 363–383.

Greenberg, J., & Mitchell, S.A. (1983). *Object relations in psychoanalytic theory.* Cambridge, MA: Harvard University Press.

Greenhaus, J.H., Seidel, C., & Marinis, M. (1983). The impact of expectations and values and job attitudes. *Organizational Behavior and Human Performance, 31,* 394–417.

Hazan, C., & Shaver, P.R. (1990). Love and work: An attachment-theoretical perspective. *Journal of Personality and Social Psychology, 59,* 270–280.

Hunt, J.G., Boal, K.B., & Sorenson, R.L. (1990). Top management leadership: Inside the black box. *The Leadership Quarterly, 1*(1), 41–65.

Jablin, F.M., & Krone, K.J. (1987). Organizational assimilation. In C.R. Berger & S.H. Caffee (Eds), *Handbook of communication science* (pp. 711–746). Newbury Park, CA: Sage.

Kanter, R.M. (1977). *Men and women of the corporation.* New York: Basic Books.

Keller, T. (1999). Images of the familiar: Individual differences and implicit leadership theories. *The Leadership Quarterly, 10*(4), 589–607.

Keller, T. (2003). Parental images as a guide to leadership sensemaking: An attachment perspective on implicit leadership theories. *Leadership Quarterly, 14,* 141–160.

Kenney, R.A., Blascovich, J., & Shaver, P.R. (1994). Implicit leadership theories: Prototypes for new leaders. *Basic and Applied Social Psychology, 15*(4), 409–437.

Kout, H. (1977). *The restoration of self.* New York: International University Press.

Kreitner, R., & Luthans, F. (1984). A social learning approach to behavioral management: racial behaviorists "mellowing out." *Organizational Dynamics, 13*(2), 47–65.

Leary, M., & Kowalski, R. (1990). Impression management: A literature review and two-component model. *Psychological Bulletin, 107,* 34–47.

Lee, F. (1997). When the going gets tough, do the tough ask for help? Help seeking and power motivation in organizations. *Organizational Behavior and Human Decision Processes, 72,* 336–363.

Lipman-Blumen, J. (1996). *The connective edge: Leading in an interdependent world.* San Francisco: Jossey-Bass.

Lord, R.G., Foti, R.J., & De Vader, C.L. (1984). A test of leadership categorization theory: Internal structure, information processing, and leadership perceptions. *Organizational Behavior and Human Performance, 34,* 343–378.

Lord, R.G., & Maher, K.J. (1991). *Leadership and information processing: Linking perceptions and performance.* Cambridge: Unwin Hyman Ltd.

Major, D.A., Kozlowski, S.W.J., Chao, G.T., & Gardner, P.D. (1995). A longitudinal investigation of newcomer expectations, early socialization outcomes, and the moderating effects of role development factors. *Journal of Applied Psychology, 80,* 418–431.

Markus, H., & Wurf, E. (1987). The dynamic self concept: A social psychological perspective. *Annual Review of Psychology, 38,* 299–337.

Meindl, J.R., Ehrlich, S.B., & Dukerich, J.M., (1985). The romance of leadership. *Administrative Science Quarterly, 30,* 78–102.

Offerman, L.R., Kennedy, J.K., & Wirtz, P.W., (1994). Implicit leadership theories: Content, structure, and generalizability. *The Leadership Quarterly, 5*(1), 43–58.

Oglensky, B.D. (1995). Socio-psychoanalytic perspective on the subordinate. *Human Relations, 48,* 1029–1054.

Pavitt, C., & Sackaroff, P. (1990). Implicit leadership theories of leadership and judgments among group members. *Small Group Research, 21*(3), 374–392.

Phillips, J.S., & Lord, R.G. (1982). Schematic information processing and perception of leadership in problem solving groups. *Journal of Applied Psychology, 67,* 486–492.

Popper, M., & Mayseless, O. (2003). Back to basics: Applying a parenting perspective to transformational leadership. *Leadership Quarterly, 14,* 41–65.

Ridgeway, C.L. (1988). Gender differences in task groups: A status and legitimacy account. In M. Webster & M. Foschi (Eds.), *Status generalization: New theory and research.* Stanford, CA: Stanford University Press.

Sclenker, B., & Weigold, M. (1992). Interpersonal processes involving impression regulation and management. *Annual Review of Psychology, 43,* 133–168.

Shaver, P.R., Collins, N., & Clark, C.L. (1996). Attachment styles and internal working models. In G. Fletcher & J. Fitness (Eds.), *Knowledge structures in close relationships: A social psychological approach* (pp. 25–61). Hillsdale, NJ: Erlbaum.

Swann, W.B., Jr. (1984). Self-verification: Bringing social reality into harmony with the self. In J. Suls & A.G. Greenwald (Eds.), *Social psychological perspectives* (Vol. 2, pp. 33–36). Hillsdale, NJ: Erlbaum.

Taylor, S.E., & Brown, J.D. (1988). Illusion and well-being: A social psychological perspective on mental health. *Psychological Bulletin, 103,* 193–210.

Wanous, J.P., Poland, T.D., Premack, S.L., & Davis, K.S. (1992). The effects of met expectations on newcomer attitudes and behaviors: A review and meta-analysis. *Journal of Applied Psychology, 77,* 288–297.

Wolfe, R., Lennox, R., & Cutler, B. (1986). Getting along and getting ahead: Empirical support for a theory of protective and acquisitive self-presentation. *Journal of Personality and Social Psychology, 50,* 356–361.

PART II

CONTENTS AND GENERALIZABILITY
OF IMPLICIT LEADERSHIP THEORIES

CHAPTER 3

THE PERCEPTION
OF LEADERSHIP—
LEADERSHIP AS PERCEPTION

An Exploration Using the Repertory
Grid-Technique

Andreas Müller and Birgit Schyns

ABSTRACT

Cognitive and social-constructivist leadership theories postulate that it is not what the leader *does* that is crucial for the understanding of leadership processes, but it is what *perceptions* followers have of what the leader does. This conceptualization of leadership must also have consequences for the methodological operationalization of leadership. We used the Repertory Grid Technique (Kelly, 1991) to assess the Implicit Leadership Theories (ILTs, cf. Eden & Leviatan, 1975) of 13 followers. The Repertory Grid Technique can be very well adapted to the specifics of cognitive leadership theories. One main advantage is that it is possible to acquire data concerning the content of an individual's ILTs. Our results suggest that the perception of leadership is highly dependent on follower's self-perceptions. In addition, a leader's social

Implicit Leadership Theories: Essays and Explorations, pages 81–101
Copyright © 2005 by Information Age Publishing

competencies appear to play a crucial role in followers' perceptions. Furthermore, our results point out that if leadership-irrelevant information,.such as the gender of the leader, no matter if male or female, becomes salient in the perception process a less positive evaluation of leaders is more likely.

INTRODUCTION

In a classic experiment, Eden and Leviatan (1973) found that followers make use of *Implicit Leadership Theories (ILTs)* when interpreting leader behavior. This is to say that expectations or already existing ideas concerning leadership build the basis for follower's interpretation of leader's behavior and have an important impact on leadership processes. Eden and Leviathan's study encouraged a wide range of leadership research, which opposed the then traditional leader-centered concepts. Similarly to everyday concepts of leadership, traditional leadership research was almost exclusively focused on the leader. It tended to "romanticize" leaders (more or less implicitly) as "larger-than-life" persons who possess extraordinary abilities and personal characteristics that render them distinct from ordinary people (Meindl, 1990, 1993, 1998; Meindl & Ehrlich, 1987; Meindl, Ehrlich, & Dukerich, 1985). Such a conceptualization neglected the most apparent aspect of leadership, namely: "Without followers there can be no leader" (Katz & Kahn, 1966, p. 301). Therefore traditional leader-centered concepts merely attempted to scientifically replicate everyday concepts of leadership (Calder, 1977). Thus: "A more viable reorientation for scientific inquiry is to make the everyday constructs and hypotheses of leadership an *object* of study" (Calder, 1977, p. 186).

In this chapter we want to emphasize that the conceptualization of leadership as a perception of followers should also include alternative research methodologies. In doing so, we pay particular attention to the criticism directed toward traditional questionnaires—the classic instrument in leadership research—that force people to adapt to the researcher's leadership categories. Thus, the analysis of questionnaires only rearranges already given contents (cf. Neuberger, 2002, p. 396) and makes it impossible to acquire information concerning the individual content of ILTs. With Kelly's (1991) Repertory Grid Technique (Repgrid), we applied a very flexible instrument that can be adapted in a theoretically-founded way to the purposes of this field of research.

We first put some of the main assumptions in Kelly's Psychology of Personal Constructs (PCP, 1991)—the theory underlying the Repgrid technique—in the context of theories about leadership perception (e.g., Lord & Maher, 1993). In doing so, we want to illustrate the usefulness of Repgrid in the field of leadership research. Moreover, we show that the discussion about the perception of leadership is not merely of academic importance: Prejudices toward female leaders and their practical consequences can be best described by the lack of fit between followers "think manager—think male expectations" (cf. Schein, 1975) and perceived characteristics of female leaders. Thus, we will supplement our theoretical considerations with practical issues concentrating on the aspect of gender in connection with leadership. Subsequently, we present an example of a Repgrid application, which explores the ILTs of followers and their evaluation of common leadership roles.

THEORETICAL CONSIDERATIONS

The Psychology of Personal Constructs and the Perception of Leadership

Because of the restrictions of the human sensorial and memory system, people are forced to categorize and systematize their perceptions in order to manage the complexity and constant change in their surroundings. In terms of Kelly's Psychology of Personal Constructs such categorization processes are the key for an understanding of human experience and behavior.

> "[...] a person's processes are psychologically channelized by the ways in which he anticipates events." (Kelly, 1991, p. 32)

According to Rosch's (1978) principles of categorization, we can say that persons will be perceived as leaders when at least some of the typical leader-characteristics can be ascribed to them. Sensitivity, dedication, tyranny, charisma, attractiveness, masculinity, intelligence and strength can be regarded as characteristics commonly expected of leaders (Offermann, Kennedy, & Wirtz, 1994). We can therefore say that certain characteristics of a person are more ore less likely to be associated with the concept of leadership and therefore more or less suitable for characterizing the person as a leader. The degree to which a given characteristic is associated with a certain category is called the *cue validity* of a characteristic (Rosch, 1978).

> "[...] a construct is convenient for the anticipation of a finite range of events only." (Kelly, 1991, p. 48)

Those characteristics of a stimulus which are unexpected for a certain category become particularly salient in perception processes (Crocker & McGraw, 1984). We will discuss the practical relevance of this aspect later.

Lord and his colleagues suppose that categories about leadership are organized in a hierarchically structured system of categories (Lord, Foti, & De Vader, 1984; Lord, Foti, & Phillips, 1982).

> Kelly hypothesizes a similar hierarchical system of constructs, which he regards as the tool to carry out psychological processes. "[...] each person characteristically evolves, for his convenience in anticipating events, a construction system embracing ordinal relationships between constructs." (Kelly, 1991, p. 39)

Lord and Maher (1993) distinguish between *recognition-based* and *inferential* modes of leadership perception.

Recognition-based modes can be described as *dichotomous* prototype matching processes: The observed behavior of a potential leader will be compared with existing beliefs about what the observing person regards as typical for a leader. In the case of concordance between the observed behavior on the one hand, and implicit beliefs on the other hand, the person observed will be seen by the observer as a leader.

> Compared to Lord and Maher, Kelly attaches more importance to the content of both poles of a dichotomous construct. "[...] a person's construction system is composed of a finite number of dichotomous constructs" (Kelly, 1991, p.41). "[...] a person chose for himself that alternative in a dichotomized construct through which he anticipates greater possibility for extension and definition of his system" (Kelly, 1991, p. 45). An attribution concerning leaders, such as "being authoritarian," gets therefore another connotation depending if the antonym of this attribution is for instance "being slack" or "being socially competent." This fact poses problems for the interpretation of traditional research results. First of all, we do not usually have access to information concerning the subject's dichotomous constructs when we rely on traditional questionnaires. Furthermore, a participant of a questionnaire-study is also always speculating about what meaning the creator of the questionnaire had in mind when using particular descriptive words. Thus, if we really want to know what people mean when they think and talk about leadership, we also need to know what they do *not* mean.

Inferentially based modes concerning the perception of leadership focus on the causal attribution of events. From this perspective, leadership can be regarded as a concept used to explain causes for complex organizational events, irrespective of whether or not a direct effect of leader behavior is observable (Calder, 1977; Meindl et al., 1985; Pfeffer, 1977). But *why* will organizational events be likely attributed toward leadership rather than to various other external or internal influential factors, such as market conditions or organizational structure? Keller (1999) found that individual expectations toward leadership mirror early experiences of parental behavior, which can be seen as the first representatives of leadership. Thus thinking in terms of leadership is possibly based on primary experiences in childhood and seems to be a deeply ingrained social categorization. Perhaps this can explain why complex organizational events are often attributed to the acting of one single person, the leader.

> Similarly, Kelly assumes that persons always try to recognize past experiences in present processes of perception or construction. Or in Kelly's own words: "[...] a person's construction system varies as he successively construes the replications of events." (Kelly, 1991, p. 50)

Keller (1999) also emphasizes another aspect: She argues that every person views him/ herself as a potential leader and projects his/her own traits on an idealized leader. Thus we can see that the perceiver's characteristics, more than the leader's, serve as the bases for the evaluation of leaders. An individual's early expectations and personal characteristics seem to channel his/her cognition and lead to the selection of certain stimuli—out of an enormous array of perceivable stimuli—as well as to their classification into certain categories.

Person-based, as well as inferential-based, modes are carried out by means of automatic or controlled processes:

As has already been mentioned, one of the most important points of Lord's and Maher's theory is that leadership will be perceived only when certain kinds of events or behaviors can be interpreted in terms of followers ILTs. In other words, observed behavior of a stimulus person will be compared with existing beliefs about what the perceiver regards as a typical leader. Only in the case of concordance between actual behavior and expectations will leadership be seen to have occurred. Lord and Maher (1993) call these kinds of processes *automatic* processes. These processes only require a minimum amount of cognitive resources and effectively ensure that existing experiences about past events can be used to understand and handle current situations. But this effectiveness does negatively affect the accuracy and flexibility of cognitive processes, which means that the kind of judgment about a current event depends on the kind of actual activated cognitive category. Thus, one and the same leader-behavior can be interpreted in quite different ways depending on the content of the activated category of the perceiver.

However, an adaptive and flexible cognitive system implicates that environmental stimuli can also be perceived much more precisely and that the stimuli's characteristics can be integrated in the cognitive system. *Controlled* processes allow for this and thus guarantee a gradual adjustment between cognitive categories and the stimuli's characteristics. But these kinds of processes are much more demanding than automatic processes. Because a majority of daily demands can be managed with "convenient" automatic processes, they dominate over controlled processes.

> Kelly does not speak of perception *processes*, which differ in their ability to adapt to the characteristics of an external stimulus, but rather ascribes more or less flexibility to the *constructs* themselves. "[...] the variation in a person's construction system is limited by the permeability of the constructs within whose range of convenience the variants lie" (Kelly, 1991, p. 54). In other words, the more permeable one's individual construct "leadership" is, the more new, incongruent experiences can be integrated.

The occurrence of automatic processes is more likely in situations in which insufficient information is available (cf. Eagly & Johnson, 1990), leading to the situation that new leaders in particular will be evaluated on the basis of existing stereotypes (Kenney, Blascovich, & Shaver, 1994). Because controlled processes require a great deal of cognitive effort, Lord and Maher (1993) suggest that such processes also need a high level of intrinsic motivation to be carried out. Unfortunately, the human ability to reduce own stereotyping must be judged rather pessimistically (Emrich, 1999). Studies show that, despite pervious information about such effects, the amount of stereotyping in evaluation-processes cannot be reduced (e.g., Bernardin & Pence, 1980).

So far we have not explicitly mentioned the social perspective of leadership perception. Meindl (1990) assumes that followers create leadership in a process of *social contagion*. This process can be understood as an almost irrational and affective arousal process in which the leaders presence is not necessary. Pastor (1998) showed that individual representations of leaders are to some extent determined by social networks of the organization. He found that close group-relationships are associated with more similar group ILTs and that group members with higher social status may have particular influence on the group representation of leadership. In a common sense, this process can be understood as the constructivist creation of reality.

> Regarding the social perspective of cognitive processes Kelly pointed out that our own social interaction will be influenced by our expectations about the motives and needs of other persons even if we do not know anything about them. "[...] to the extent that one person construes the construction processes of another, he may play a role in social processes involving the other person" (Kelly, 1991, p. 66). He presents the following example: When we are driving on a highway, our own safety depends on our ability to anticipate the behavior of the other drivers. By anticipating the behavior of other persons, we are at the same time affected in our own behavior even if we cannot directly communicate our anticipations.

Thus, shared expectations are the inalienable precondition of social processes like leadership. Hall and Lord (1998) assume that expectations about leadership differ depending on the social level (individual-, dyadic-, group-, and collective level) on which they are operationalized. Higher-level cognitions are *not* to be seen as one's own creation or possession, but rather as "knots" of a network of social perception (Lord & Emrich, 2001). However, the scientific assessment of perception processes requires cuts through this complex system. Therefore, if we talk about the perception of leadership, we have to refer explicitly to level we are focusing on when we assess these perceptions.

One Practical Issue: "Think Manager-think Male" and the Perception of Leadership

When we replace terms like *effectiveness* (of automatic processes) and *accuracy* (of controlled processes) with terms like *stereotypes* or *prejudices* on the one hand and *openness* or *fairness* on the other hand, the practical relevance of the aforementioned issues becomes much clearer: Findings by Offermann et al. (1994) show that prototypical leaders are still regarded as male leaders. Consequently, the characteristic "female" has rather low cue validity for the category "leadership" (see above). The negative effects of this "think manager-think male" phenomenon (e.g., Schein, 1975; Schein, Mueller, Lituchy, & Liu, 1996) are discussed manifold: Because of their minority status in the outmost branches, the aspect of gender will more likely be activated in the perception of *female* leaders (Eagly & Karau, 2002). This saliency of the characteristic gender hinders the perception of *occupationally relevant* information, which can be regarded as the only kind of information in professional contexts that can lead to a less stereotyped evaluation of female leaders (Heilman, 1984). Moreover, the minority status of female leaders alone often leads to a more negative evaluation (Ayman, 1993; Heilman, 1995). The vicious circle closes.

Regarding the influence of *followers'* gender on leadership perception, the image of a prototypical leader seems to be very consistent over different demographic groups (Ayman, 1993; Schyns, 2002). However, male followers show a stronger tendency toward a devaluation of female leaders (Eagly, Makhijani, & Klonsky, 1992) whereas women generally give higher leadership ratings (Lord, Phillips, & Rush, 1980).

Of course, it would be a gross overgeneralization to say automatic processes are "bad" and controlled processes are "good." Both kinds of processes are indispensable for the human capacity to act. But the quality of leadership relationships seems to depend highly on the ability and willingness of all participants to be open with respect to their beliefs about leadership.

In summary, we see a large concordance between the basic assumptions of theories about leadership perception and Kelly's (1991) theory of the PCP. Leadership can be regarded as a hierarchical system of constructs (*Implicit Leadership Theories*, Eden & Leviatan, 1975). This construct system has a powerful impact on the interpretation and evaluation of leader-behavior or leader-characteristics (*person-based modes*) and organizational events (*inferential modes*). In most cases, the perception of leadership can be regarded in terms of dichotomous prototype matching processes between individually activated cognitions and perceived stimuli (*automatic processes*). The same leader-behavior can be interpreted in a quite different way depending on the individual content of the perceiver's activated category. Differences between own expectations concerning leadership and perceived reality can lead to the devaluation of leaders. Because of the common "think manager—think male" phenomenon, such negative effects can especially be expected in the evaluation of female leaders.

Although ILTs have their origin in early individual experiences about leadership, this learning process took place in a societal framework. We can therefore expect both highly individualized as well as commonly shared aspects of ILTs. The projection of individual characteristics on idealized leadership may serve as an example of the aforementioned individualized perspective. Traditional questionnaires do not enable us to deduce the individual aspects of ILTs. Thus, we should apply alternative research methods to gain both kinds of information. To prevent misinterpretations on the side of the respondents as well as on the researchers side, it seems especially important not only to present the attributes of leadership but also its antonyms. In the following exploration, we tried to consider all of these assumptions. We consequently focused on the following research questions:

1. Which constructs can describe leadership in general?
2. How are common leadership roles described and evaluated?
3. Are there any gender differences (regarding perceivers and perceived persons) in the description and evaluation of leadership roles?

METHOD

We explored the Implicit Leadership Theories (ILTs) of 13 employed followers (female = 7, mean of age of the total sample = 33 years, $SD = 11.24$) with the Repertory Grid Technique (Repgrid, Kelly, 1991). Female and male participants have comparable characteristics regarding age, education level, and own leadership experiences. Following Lord and Maher (1993), we operationalized ILTs as person-based automatic processes which have been aggregated on a group-level. The setting of the exploration was a one-to-one interview. The approximate duration per session amounted to 45–60 minutes. In spite of the variety of possibilities in the design of a Repgrid analysis, it basically consists of three steps: The choice of so-called elements, the generation of constructs, and the forming of the grid. In our survey these three steps were designed as follows.

The choice of elements. In terms of Kelly (1991), elements can be regarded as cognitive representations of objectively existing things or events. The participants in our analyses were provided with five general leadership roles ("A Female Leader," "A Male Leader," "A Liked Leader," "An Efficient Leader," and "An Ideal Leader") as well as two self-related roles ("Me as a Leader," and "Me as a Follower"). This choice of elements can be reasoned in the following way: First of all, we aimed at a neutral connotation of elements to allow the participants a wide range of interpretation and to prevent pushing them in a certain direction or providing them with stimuli that are actually meaningless for them. Secondly, because the participants were occupied in quite different branches (public services, IT-branch, retail, education, . . .), we had to choose roles of inter-branch relevancy.

Self-related elements are basic components of many Repgrid analyses because they can offer the participants a better access to the survey. In our analyses, the inclusion of these elements allowed for some interesting questions, for instance: Are there different expectations between the sexes concerning own leadership qualities (cf. the "think manager-think male" phenomenon)? Are there any similarities between the perceptions of leadership roles and self-perceptions.

Ideal elements serve as important benchmarks for the evaluation of all elements because ideal elements will almost always be evaluated very distinctly.

We have already discussed the importance of the *aspect gender* in relation to leadership. So the choice of the roles of "A Female Leader" and "A Male Leader" was essential for our analyses.

Last but not least, the elements of "A Liked Leader" and "A Efficient Leader" refer to the two *basic dimensions of leader-behavior*—consideration and initiating structure (e.g., Fleishman, 1973). To allow the participants a better access to the meaning of these elements, they were first asked to allocate an existing person out of their professional biography to every leadership role.

The generation of constructs is usually the second step of a Repgrid survey. In terms of Kelly (1991), constructs are the patterns by which elements are abstracted. In other words they are the "building blocks" which we use to "create" the things of our reality (the elements). The generation of constructs in our analysis results from paired comparisons between the above named elements. In preparation for the study, we systematically built up 21 pairs out of the seven elements. Every pair was noted on a card. During the inquiry, the examiner chose one of these cards at random and presented it to the participant. It was the task of the participant to name personal attributes (constructs) that either are able to discriminate between both presented roles or which the roles have in common. (For instance: "What do you think is the difference or the accordance between "A Liked Leader" and "An Ideal Leader?" Answer: "Both are always friendly.") Afterward he or she was asked to name the antonym to the just named attribute. ("What is in your opinion the antonym for to be always friendly?" Answer: "To be unkind.") The so generated dichotomous construct was written down. The participants were further asked to label the positive pole of the dichotomous construct. The chosen card of paired elements was separated and the next card was drawn. This procedure was repeated. By the end of this part of the Repgrid analyses, every participant had created his/her own personal leadership questionnaire with 12 bipolar items. (Originally we had planned to impose 21 dichotomous constructs, in other words, to present all pairs of elements to the participants. But in the first sessions, we noticed that the participants had difficulty creating more than 10 to 14 dichotomous constructs.)

The forming of the grid: The dichotomous constructs were scaled with a bipolar seven-point scale (–3 to +3) where the positive values represent the positive and negative values represent the negative pole of the constructs. The participants were requested to evaluate all of the seven elements on the basis of the twelve dichotomous constructs.

The described Repgrid procedure allowed for the qualitative content analysis of the dichotomous constructs as well as for quantitative analyses of the evaluation of elements.

Qualitative analysis of dichotomous constructs: Aim of this analysis was the aggregation of the construct-content without losing the essential aspects contained in the raw data. For this purpose, the two most *salient* dichotomous constructs of every grid were included. In the sense of Kelly (1991), salient constructs are constructs that best allow for the distinction between elements. In statistical terminology, these are the constructs with the highest variance. Overall, 27 constructs were chosen because in one grid two constructs possessed the same high variance. These 27 constructs were inductively aggregated due to their textual accordance into new higher-level categories. These new categories were then presented to 10 experts (psychologists and psychology students). These experts were requested to reassign the constructs to the categories to validate these new categories. The procedure of category formation and reassignment was repeated until all constructs were respectively assigned with 70%-accordance between the experts.

Quantitative analyses of elements.   The first aim was to explore which kind of leadership role the participants liked best. Here the mean of every leadership role (every element) was computed for every grid. We have to stress that a qualitative element comparison over the different grids on the *construct-level* wasn't possible, because—like mentioned above—each participant created the constructs individually. Consequently, the analyses we carried out can only be interpreted on a very global level of "liking or disliking" a certain leadership role. The second aim was the analysis of similarity between the roles. As the measure of similarity, we computed Euclid distances between the roles as well as hierarchical cluster analysis.

RESULTS

Qualitative Analysis of Attributes

Overall Sample

The following seven categories resulted from the above described qualitative analysis of the constructs: structured, progressive, ambitious, assertive, confident, open, and fair. Thus, these seven categories describe the main aspects of the ILTs in our sample.

Structured is understood in the broadest sense and describes constructs about the management abilities of the leader, his or her effectiveness or organizing ability. *Progressive* labels the ability and willingness to overcome established structures. *Ambitious* describes the will to success. The four categories *assertive, confident, open, and fair* can all be subsumed under the category social competence. The category *open* describes the communicative aspect of leadership. It refers to the leader's ability to integrate incitements or information offered by the followers to some extent but in our case it refers primarily to the ability of the leader to make organizational demands transparent and understandable. *Confidence,* the last aspect within social competence, subsumes in particular the leader's ability to handle things calmly and to believe in him/herself.

We also analyzed differences in the textual construction between the two gender related leadership roles as well as between the task-related leadership roles. For that purpose we chose all the constructs of all grids in which the participants differentiated with more than one scale point between the respective pair of roles. Again we systematized the constructs with the seven above named categories. The role of "A Female Leader" was more frequently ascribed to be ambitious (4:1), in turn "A Male Leader" was much more frequently described to be confident, thus informal, relaxed, calm (9:1). On the basis of the five other categories, no differences were found. "An Efficient Leader" and "A Liked Leader" were most frequently differentiated on the ambitious and the assertive category, with more frequent ascriptions for "An Efficient Leader" (7:1, resp. 6:2). In turn, "A Liked Leader" was described to be more fair (8:2).

Exploration of Differences Between Male and Female Participants

We explored typical differences between male and female participants in terms of the most salient attributes used to describe leadership. Here we chose again the two most salient constructs (see above) of every grid and assigned them to the above described seven categories. In our analyses, no typical differences between the sexes were found. We conclude therefore that the attributes of all categories describing leadership were applicable both for women and men in our sample.

Evaluation of Elements

Overall Sample

Like already mentioned, the leadership roles were evaluated on the basis of the −3 to +3 scaled constructs. We used these values to compute the mean evaluation of every single leadership role in every grid. Figure 3.1 shows the average evaluations of all roles over all grids. It can be seen that the overall construct leadership, operationalized with the above named leadership roles, was evaluated in a positive way because none of the roles received negative average evaluations (cf. Figure 3.1). Beside the role "An Ideal Leader," the role of "An Efficient Leader" followed by the self-related leadership role obtained the highest evaluations.

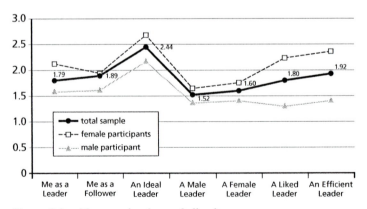

Figure 3.1.   Mean evaluations of all roles.

A paired post-hoc analysis showed that the evaluation of "An Ideal Leader" was significantly higher than all of the other roles ($Z = 2.17$ to 3.12; $p < .001$ to .05; Wilcoxon Test). The two gender-related leadership roles "A Female Leader" and "A Male Leader" received the less positive evaluations. The post-hoc analysis revealed that—beside the comparison with the ideal leadership role—the evaluation of the two gender related roles were in further two cases significantly lower than the evaluations of the other roles ("A Male Leader": "An Efficient Leader": $Z = -2.13$, $p < .05$; "A Female Leader": "An Efficient Leader": $Z = -1.96$, $p < .05$; Wilcoxon Test).

We also wanted to know if some of the respondents evaluated *all* roles consistently higher or lower compared to the other participants. Such differences would indicate, on the one hand, different response styles of the participants, and on the other hand, the existence of different attitudes toward leadership in general. In any case, it would affect the comparability of the role-evaluation between all participants. As a measure, we used the mean evaluations of every role respectively in every grid. These analyses revealed significant differences of the evaluation levels between the participants ($\chi^2 = 27. 82$, $df = 6$, $p < .001$; Friedman-Test), which means that at least one of the respondents tended to evaluate all of the roles higher/lower compared to the other persons. A paired post hoc-analysis showed that three of the grids differed from the other grids in their evaluation of the leadership roles in more than half of the cases ($7/12$ up to $9/12$). To account for this aspect, we also analyzed the frequencies of every leadership role getting the highest respectively the lowest evaluation in every grid (see Figure 3.2). Analogue to the analyses of means, this figure shows that aside from "An Ideal leader" (which in fact except in one case was always

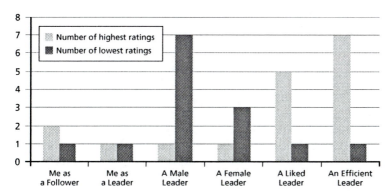

Figure 3.2.   Frequencies of highest and lowest evaluations of all presented roles (except " An Ideal Leader")
Note: The amount of highest resp. lowest evaluations exceeds the total number of participants because sometimes more than one role got the same evaluation from one participant.

evaluated the best), the "task-related" leadership roles ("A Liked Leader" and "An Efficient Leader") in 5 respectively 7 cases got the best evaluation, whereas the leaders on the gender dimension "A Female Leader" and "A Male Leader") were evaluated worst in 3 respectively 7 of the cases.

Exploration of Differences Between Male and Female Participants

We also analyzed gender differences in the respondents' evaluations of all roles. Figure 3.1 illustrates that male participants, unlike female participants, evaluated nearly all leadership roles except "An Ideal leader" on almost the same level.

The results also show that women evaluated all roles higher than men. However, in a post-hoc analysis *significant* differences between men and women were only found for the evaluations of the roles "A Liked Leader" ($Z = -1.94$) and an "An Efficient Leader" ($Z = -2.01$; resp. $p < .05$; Mann-Whitney-U-Test). It has to be mentioned that from the above named three participants with the extreme response styles, two of the men showed the significant lower and one of the women the significant higher evaluations than all of the other participants. After exclusion of these three grids, all gender related differences vanished.

Figure 3.3 shows the frequencies of every leadership role receiving the highest respectively the lowest evaluation in every grid, separated for men and women. The two charts reveal that the above mentioned low ratings in respect to the gender-related leadership roles can almost exclusively be ascribed to the comparatively low evaluations of the role of "A Male Leader" by female participants.

Similarity Between Elements

Overall Sample

The perceived similarity between elements was analyzed with a hierarchical cluster analysis (see Figure 3.4).

The dendrogram in Figure 3.4 shows that the two self-related roles were perceived most alike. "An Efficient Leader" is perceived most similarly to the "An Ideal Leader," which can be regarded again as evidence of the positive evaluation of this element. This couple of leadership roles in turn was seen akin to the two self-related roles. The role of "A Liked Leader" can be regarded as the most "non-resembling" (dissimilar) representative of the whole construct leadership. However, the (dis-) similarity indexes of the cluster analysis show no erratic increase between any of the single steps of the cluster combination. Thus, all roles can be regarded as reasonable components of the *same* cluster solution.

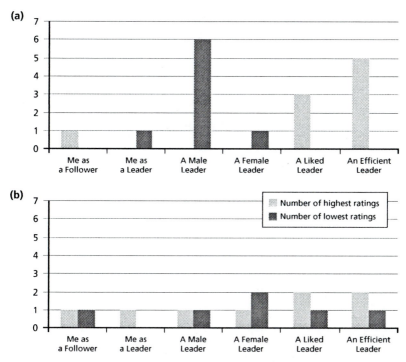

Figure 3.3. Frequencies of highest and lowest evaluations of all presented roles (except " An Ideal Leader") separated for female (Figure 3.3a) and male (Figure 3.3b) respondents.

Note: The amount of highest resp. lowest evaluations exceeds the total number of participants because sometimes more than one role got the same evaluation from one participant.

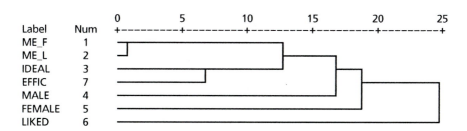

Figure 3.4.   The similarity between roles.

Note: Rescaled distance cluster combine. ME_F = "Me as a Follower", ME_L = "Me as a Leader", IDEAL = "An Ideal Leader", EFFIC = "An Efficient Leader", MALE = "A Male Leader", FEMALE = "A Female Leader", LIKED = "A Liked Leader".

Table 3.1 outlines the descending Euclid distances between the roles. The results affirm and differentiate the results of the cluster analysis. The lowest distances throughout were observed between the role "Me as a Leader" and all the other presented roles (the only exception is the distance between "An Ideal-" and "An Efficient Leader").

Table 3.1.   Mean Standardized Euclid Distances between All Pairs of Elements

Pair of Elements	Mean standardized Euclid Distance
A Liked Leader: An Efficient Leader	.66
A Liked Leader: A Male Leader	.62
A Liked Leader: A Female Leader	.61
Me as a Follower: A Male Leader	.58
A Female Leader: An Efficient Leader	.55
Me as a Follower: An Ideal Leader	.52
An Ideal Leader: A Female Leader	.51
Me as a Follower: An Efficient Leader	.51
Me as a Follower: A Liked Leader	.50
Me as a Follower: A Female Leader	.50
An Ideal Leader: A Male Leader	.48
A Male Leader: A Female Leader	.48
An Ideal Leader: A Liked Leader	.47
A Male Leader: An Efficient Leader	.47
Me as a Leader: A Male Leader	.42
An Ideal Leader: An Efficient Leader	.40
Me as a Leader: A Liked Leader	.38
Me as a Leader: An Efficient Leader	.38
Me as a Leader: Me as a Follower	.36
Me as a Leader: A Female Leader	.35
Me as a Leader: An Ideal Leader	.23

Note: The computed distances were scaled from 0 (lowest values) to 1 (highest values).

Exploration of Differences Between Male and Female Participants

With respect to the "think manager-think male" phenomenon, we were interested whether or not male participants differ in their self-description of having good leadership qualities compared to female participants. The gender-specific Euclid distances between the roles "Me as a Leader" and an "An Ideal Leader" can provide information about such possible gender-specific anticipations of one's own leadership qualities. However in our sample no differences between men and women were found ($Z = -.50$, $p = .62$; Mann-Whitney-U-Test).

DISCUSSION

Starting Point

The starting assumption of our study was that followers Implicit Leadership Theories (ILTs, Eden & Leviathan, 1975), or, in other words, individual perceptions or expectations about leadership, have a powerful influence on leadership processes (cf. Lord & Maher, 1993). As a consequence, we have to integrate methodologies that account for the individual content of ILTs. In our study, we therefore applied the Repertory Grid Technique (Repgrid, Kelly, 1991). We demonstrated the similarities between the Psychology of Personal Constructs (PCP, Kelly, 1991)—the underlying theory of the technique—and common assumptions about leadership perception.

Previous studies point to the impact of person-based automatic processes especially in the evaluation of female leaders: A lack of concordance between perceiver's think manager—think male expectations on the one hand, and characteristics and behavior of a potential female leader on the other hand, can lead to a devaluation of women in leadership positions (e.g., Ayman, 1993; Eagly et al., 1992). Such evaluations seem especially to occur when men evaluate women (Eagly et al., 1992). Therefore, in our study, we concentrated particularly on the influence of followers' gender as well as gender-related leadership roles on the perception of leadership.

Summary and Discussion of Results

We explored the ILTs of 13 followers. All of the participants in our study had fundamental occupational experiences allowing us to expect much more elaborated, and reliable constructions of leadership, compared to studies working with student samples (cf. Eagly & Johnson, 1990). ILTs were operationalized in terms of *individual* constructs that build the basis for person-based automatic perception-processes (cf. Lord & Maher, 1993). These individual constructs were aggregated to higher-level social perceptions (cf. Hall & Lord, 1998) in terms of *followers'* expectations about leadership.

In addition to the two self-related roles ("Me as a Leader," and "Me as a Follower"), we presented five common leadership roles ("A Female

Leader," "A Male Leader," "A Liked Leader," "An Efficient Leader," and "An Ideal Leader"), which are regarded to represent a wide range of leadership prototypes on a very common and understandable level. The attributes or ILTs by which these roles were construed in our sample can best be described with the seven categories *structured, progressive, ambitious, assertive, confident, open, and fair.* In line with scientific theories about the distinction between management and leadership or between "the leading of things" and "the leading of people" (Kotter, 1998; Lord & Maher, 1993; Zaleznik, 1977), social competences played the most important role in the ILTs of the respondents. Followers do indeed seem to evaluate their leaders with particular emphasis on how they handle social situations. However, social competences were not exclusively understood in terms of reponding to followers needs. Aspects such as assertiveness outline that leaders are also evaluated in terms of how they succeed in getting an organizational task done.

Consequently, we find that the role of "An Efficient Leader," which was described with attributes such as ambitious, structure, and assertiveness, corresponds much more with the idealized expectations of leadership than the role of the "A Liked Leader," which was attributed with categories like fair and open. The latter were shown to be the most untypical representative of the overall construct leadership.

The activation of the cognitive category gender, operationalized with the presentation of the two gender-related leadership roles, led to the tendentious decrease in the leader evaluation. Until now, this phenomenon has only been discussed in relation to female leaders (e.g., Eagly & Karau, 2002). In our study, female followers in particular evaluated typical male leaders less positively than other leadership roles. It seems that the surface associations of men with concepts such as power or authority and leadership does make it easier for men to attain leadership positions, but "to be solely a man" is not enough to be perceived as a good leader. The evaluation of leaders seems to relate much more to the actual leadership tasks, and consequently to associated organizational success. These results are conform to theories that describe leadership in terms of simplifying causal explanations of complex organizational outcomes (Calder, 1977, Lord & Maher, 1993; Meindl, et al., 1985; Pfeffer, 1977). We can suggest therefore an extension of Eagly´s and Karaus (2002) theory concerning the role congruity of prejudice toward female leaders and suggest the hypothesis that only task- or behavior-related information leads to a positive evaluation of leaders, whereas the activation of irrelevant categories like gender, *no matter if male or female,* promotes a less positive evaluation of leaders.

From all analyzed roles, both self-related roles "Me as a Leader" and "Me as a Follower" showed the closest relation to idealized leadership. This result is congruent with the assumption that constructs about leadership mirror projections of the perceivers own personal traits (cf. Keller, 1999).

In line with previous findings (e.g., Ayman, 1993; Schyns, 2002) no *textual* differences in the construction of leadership were found between male and female participants. The predominant "think manager-think male" phenomenon also did not lead to gender-related differences in the self-description of one's own leadership qualities in our study. The consistent higher evaluation of all leadership roles by women can be attributed to the extreme response styles of merely three of the 13 participants (two men with extremely low and one woman with extremely high evaluations) and should not be over-interpreted.

Methodological Considerations

Repgrid features some critical issues: The comparatively high effort of Repgrid inquiries makes it difficult to collect a high amount of data. The face-to-face setting of Repgrid cannot provide anonymity to the same extent as questionnaire studies, which may increase social desirable constructions of the participants. Researchers have also to pay high attention to rule out an interviewer bias. The flexibility of the technique limits the comparability of results.

However, the close relationship between Kelly's (1991) Psychology of Personal Constructs and the theories of leadership perception allows for a theoretical founded access to individual ILTs. It provides the possibility to operationalize specific perception processes, like automatic processes or person-based processes (cf. Lord & Maher, 1993). Moreover, the technique offers a wide range of qualitative and quantitative analyses. Therefore we feel confident that Repgrid can be regarded as a valuable enrichment in the research of leadership perception.

REFERENCES

Ayman, R. (1993). Leadership perception: The role of gender and culture. In R. Ayman (Ed.), *Leadership theory and research: Perspectives and directions* (pp. 137–165). San Diego, CA: Academic Press.

Bernardin, H.J., & Pence, E.C. (1980). Effects of rater training. Creating new response sets and decreasing accuracy. *Journal of Applied Psychology, 65*(1), 60–66.

Calder, B.J. (1977). An attribution theory of leadership. In G.R. Salancik (Ed.), *New direction in organizational behavior* (Vol. 179–204). Chicago: St. Clair.

Crocker, J., & McGraw, K.M. (1984). What´s good for the goose is not good for the gander. Solo status as an obstacle to occupational achievement for males and females. *American Behavioral Scientist, 27*(3), 357–369.

Eagly, A.H., & Johnson, B.T. (1990). Gender and leadership style: A meta-analysis. *Psychological Bulletin, 108*(2), 233–256.

Eagly, A.H., & Karau, S.J. (2002). Role congruity theory of prejustice toward female leaders. *Psychological Review, 109*(3), 573–598.

Eagly, A.H., Makhijani, M.G., & Klonsky, B.G. (1992). Gender and the evaluation of leaders. A meta-analysis. *Psychological Bulletin, 111*(1), 3–22.

Eden, D., & Leviatan, U. (1973). Implicit leadership theory as a determinant of the factor structure underlying supervisory behavior scales. *Journal of Applied Psychology, 60*(6), 736–741.

Emrich, C. (1999). Context effects in leadership perception. *Personality and Social Psychology Bulletin, 25*(8), 991–1006.

Fleishman, E.A. (1973). Twenty years of consideration and structure. In J.G. Hunt (Ed.), *Current developements in the study of leadership*. Carbondale & Edvardsville: Southern Illinois University Press.

Hall, R.L., & Lord, R.G. (1998). Multi-level information processing explanations of followers´ leadership perceptions. In F.J. Yammarino (Ed.), *Leaderhip: The multiple-level approaches*. Stamford, CT: JAI Press.

Heilman, M.E. (1984). Information as a deterrent against sex discrimination: The effects of applicant sex and information type on preliminary employment decisions. *Organizational Behvior and Human Performance, 33*(174–186).

Heilman, M.E. (1995). Sex stereotypes and their effects in the workplace: What we know and what we don´t know. *Journal of Social Behavior and Personality, 10*(6), 3–26.

Katz, D., & Kahn, R.L. (1966). *The social psychology of organizations*. New York: Wiley.

Keller, T. (1999). Images of the familiar. Individual differences and implicit leadership theories. *Leadership Quarterly, 10*(4), 589–607.

Kelly, G.A. (1991). *The psychology of personal constructs* (Vol. 1, 2nd ed.). London: Routledge.

Kenney, R.A., Blascovich, J., & Shaver, P.R. (1994). Implicit leadership theories. Prototypes for new leaders. *Basic and Applied Social Psychology, 15*(4), 409–437.

Kotter, J.P. (1998). What leaders really do. In R.L. Taylor (Ed.), *Contemporary issues in leadership* (4th ed., pp. 198–207). Boulder, CO: Westview Press.

Lord, R.G., & Emrich, C. (2001). Thinking outside the box by looking inside the box. Extending the cognitive revolution in leadership research. *Leadership Quarterly, 11*(4), 551–579.

Lord, R.G., Foti, R.J., & De Vader, C. (1984). A test of leadership categorization theory: Internal structure, information processing, and leadership perceptions. *Organizational Behavior and Human Performance, 34*(343–378).

Lord, R.G., Foti, R.J., & Phillips, J.S. (1982). A theory of leadership categorization. In C. Schriesheim (Ed.), *Leadership: Beyond established views*. Carbondale: Southern Illinois University Press.

Lord, R.G., & Maher, K.J. (1993). *Leadership and information processing*. London: Routledge.

Lord, R.G., Phillips, J.S., & Rush, M.C. (1980). Effects of sex and personality on perceptions of emergent leadership, influence, and social power. *Journal of Applied Psychology, 65*(2), 176–182.

Meindl, J.R. (1990). On leadership: An alternative to the conventional wisdom. In B.M. Staw & L.L. Cummings (Eds.), *Research in organizational behavior* (Vol. 12, pp.159–203). Greenwich, CT: JAI Press.

Meindl, J.R. (1993). Reinventing leadership: A radical, social psychological approach. In J.K. Murnighan (Ed.), *Social psychology in organizations* (pp. 89–118). Englewood Cliff, NJ: Prentice-Hall.

Meindl, J.R. (1998). The romance of leadership as a follower-centric theory: A social constructionist approach. In F.J. Yammarino (Ed.), *Leadership: The multiple-level approaches* (pp. 285–298). Stamford, CT: JAI Press.

Meindl, J.R., & Ehrlich, S. (1987). The romance of leadership and the evaluation of organizational performance. *Academy of Management Journal, 30*(91–109).

Meindl, J.R., Ehrlich, S., & Dukerich, J.M. (1985). The romance of leadership. *Administrative of Science Quarterly, 30,* 78–102.

Neuberger, O. (2002). *Führen und führen lassen.* Stuttgart: Lucius & Lucius.

Offermann, L.R., Kennedy, J.K., & Wirtz, P.W. (1994). Implicit leadership theories. Content, structure, and generalizability. *Leadership Quarterly, 5*(1), 43–58.

Pastor, J.C. (1998). *The social construction of leadership: A semantic and social network analysis of social representations of leadership.* Unpublished dissertation, State University of New York at Buffalo.

Pfeffer, J. (1977). The ambiguity of leadership. *Academy of Management Journal, 2,* 104–112.

Rosch, E. (1978). Prinziples of categorization. In B.B. Lloyd (Ed.), *Cognition and categorization.* Hillsdale, NJ: Lawrence Erlbaum.

Schein, V.E. (1975). Relationships between sex role stereotypes and requisite management characteristics among female managers. *Journal of Applied Psychology, 60*(3), 340–344.

Schein, V.E., Mueller, R., Lituchy, T., & Liu, J. (1996). Think manager—think male: A global phenomenon? *Journal of Organizational Behavior, 17*(1), 33–41.

Schyns, B. (2002). Geschlecht und die Differenzierung von Führung. *Wirtschaftspsychologie, 1,* 45–49.

Zaleznik, A. (1977). Managers and leaders: Are they different? *Harvard Business Review, 55*(5), 67–78.

CHAPTER 4

IMPLICIT THEORIES
OF RELATIONSHIPS IN THE
WORKPLACE

Mary Uhl-Bien

ABSTRACT

New models of leadership are beginning to shift the focus away from individual, "heroic" leaders to leadership as shared and social, and emerging
through networks of interactions and relationships in the workplace
(Fletcher, 2004; Gronn, 2002; Marion & Uhl-Bien, 2001; Murrell, 1997).
Because of this, it is becoming increasingly important to understand interpersonal relationships and how they develop in the workplace. To address
this, the present paper provides a framework for investigating work relationships through exploration of *implicit theories of relationships* in the workplace.
This framework builds on research on implicit theories developed by Dweck
and colleagues (Dweck, 1996) and implicit theories of relationships from
the personal relationships literature (Knee, 1998; Franiuk, Cohen, &
Pomerantz, 2002). It uses the distinction between *entity* theorists (e.g., trait/
destiny theories) and *incremental* theorists (e.g., growth/work-it-out theories) to develop propositions regarding how one's implicit theory will influence the way one perceives and reacts to relational partners in different
relational contexts (e.g., initial impressions, relationship development and

Implicit Leadership Theories: Essays and Explorations, pages 103–133

maintenance, conflict, etc.). These propositions are offered as a starting point for exploring implicit theories of relationships in the workplace, and directions for future research are suggested.

INTRODUCTION

With the ... recreating of organizational forms, even into virtual forms of networks and associations, it is important to have a leadership theory capable of both leading and tracking the new means of human organizing and social relationships. (Murrell, 1997, p. 39)

As indicated in the quote above, the nature of organizational forms are changing, with emphasis on interconnectivity, interaction, networks, and relationships (Lipman-Blumen, 1996; Shockley-Zalabak, 2002; Uhl-Bien, Marion, & McKelvey, 2004; Volberda, 1996). To address these changes, new paradigms are beginning to emerge in leadership theory and the organizational sciences that shift our focus from individual leaders operating in the context of hierarchy and authority, to leadership as the process by which social systems change through the structuring of roles and relationships (Fletcher, 2004; Pearce & Sims, 2000; Seers, 2004; Senge & Kaeufer, 2001; Uhl-Bien, 2003). Leadership is seen as an interactive dynamic that includes more parties than just the leader, and more than the "leader-follower" exchange relationship (Gronn, 1999; Marion & Uhl-Bien, 2005; Murrell, 1997). This new discourse is so significant that some are suggesting it may require a language system beyond traditional leadership terminology of "leaders" and "followers," which limits us to perspectives of leadership as leader-centric, hierarchical, formalized roles and authoritarian relationships (Alvesson & Sveningsson, 2003; Gronn, 2002; Marion & Uhl-Bien, 2005; Murrell, 1997).

In the present paper I focus on one element of these new views of leadership—relational dynamics that are involved in the generation and emergence of leadership. Murrell (1997) labels these dynamics *relational leadership*. "Relational leadership puts the emphasis of study squarely on the human processes of how people decide, act, and present themselves to each other" (p. 39). From a relational leadership perspective, "it is possible to see relationships other than those built from hierarchy ... and to envision transformational phenomenon where the social change process occurs well outside the normal assumptions of command and control" (Murrell, 1997, p. 39). Non-hierarchical relationships that are nurturing and supporting could be legitimized as means of influence, and thus forms of leadership (Gronn, 2002; Murrell, 1997; Uhl-Bien, 2003). This focus breaks away from the prevailing socially constructed notion that position in an organization is necessarily a reflection of leadership. It allows us to account for more of the social forces working to influence group leadership (Gronn, 1999), and to view leadership responsibility as lying with the collective and not just the individual leader (Marion & Uhl-Bien, 2001; Murrell, 1997).

All of this points to the growing importance of relationships in the workplace. However, despite the fact that relationship behavior has been acknowledged in the leadership literature since its inception (Blau, 1964; Follett, 1941), we still know very little about how work relationships develop and grow. Leader-member exchange (LMX) theory (Graen & Uhl-Bien) has done an excellent job of highlighting the need for effective relationships in leadership, but key questions remain about how LMX relationships are formed and maintained (Uhl-Bien, 2003; Uhl-Bien & Maslyn, 2003). Moreover, though research is beginning to identify the need to consider other forms of exchanges (Graen & Uhl-Bien, 1995; Seers, 1989, 2004; Sherony & Green, 2002; Uhl-Bien, Graen & Scandura, 2000), LMX theory has focused primarily on manager-subordinate dyads rather than other types of relationships. As noted by Murrell (1997), the breakthrough in the LMX literature is in legitimizing a question of how the relationships of leaders and followers better explain or help direct leadership research. LMX theory has the capacity to evolve into more sociological or social-psychology orientations if it goes beyond the limited focus on dyadic or leader-follower singular relationships (Murrell, 1997). To do this, I believe LMX theory has to evolve into a relational leadership theory. This can happen by focusing LMX scholars on relational leadership beyond the manager-subordinate dyad and on the question of, what are the relational dynamics by which leadership is developed throughout the workplace?

Therefore, the focus of the present paper is on relational leadership, and specifically the human processes of how people decide, act and present themselves to each other (Murrell, 1997). Drawing from work on implicit theories (Dweck, 1996; Levy, Plaks, & Dweck, 1999), leader-member exchange theory (Graen & Scandura, 1987; Graen & Uhl-Bien, 1995), implicit theories of relationships (Knee, 1998; Franiuk et al., 2002), and the personal relationships literature (Fletcher & Kininmonth, 1992; Fletcher & Thomas, 1996), I develop and present an initial framework for theorizing about implicit relational theories. This concept, introduced in Uhl-Bien (2003), was offered as a way to help understand the cognitive processes involved in development of leadership relationships (including, but not limited to, manager-subordinate relationships). Specifically, Uhl-Bien (2003) described implicit relational theories (IRTs) as prototypes that individuals hold regarding work relationships. They represent the beliefs and assumptions about the characteristics of effective work relationships and the prototypical behaviors they expect relational partners to demonstrate. When dyad partners exhibit these prototypes, *relational favorability* is higher, and relationship development to more advanced stages of relationship-building is facilitated. When prototypes are not met, or when anti-prototypical behaviors are present, relational favorability is lower, and advancement to higher levels of relationship development is inhibited *unless* individuals recognize the nature of the mismatch and take steps to manage the relationship development process more carefully.

While I originally conceived of implicit relational theories (IRTs) in the context of leader-member exchange relationships, and the concept certainly has applicability to those relationships, consistent with new paradigmatic approaches described earlier, I will not limit the framework of IRTs presented here to "leader-follower" or "manager-subordinate" relationships. Rather, I will talk about implicit theories of relationships in the workplace. I assume that leadership is not limited to hierarchical relationships or formalized roles—and therefore the model of IRTs should extend beyond this as well to consider work relationships more broadly.

To explain this, I begin with a discussion of relational leadership theory. While relational leadership can be interpreted in multiple ways (e.g., Hunt, 2004; Murrell, 1997), for this paper I adopt the framework of relational leadership that represents a paradigm shift to leadership research (Fletcher, 2004). Rather than viewing relational leadership as simply a shared influence model in the traditional hierarchical leadership paradigm (e.g., views that extend power beyond the leader to also consider the reciprocal/mutual influence of followers, Pearce & Conger, 2003), I describe relational leadership as an emergent process that emanates from interactions and exchanges among organizational members (Gronn, 1999; Marion & Uhl-Bien, 2005). After reviewing what this paradigm shift means for leadership theory and research, I use this as the context for developing the framework for implicit relational theories. I conclude by offering propositions and directions for future research on implicit relational theories in the workplace.

RELATIONAL LEADERSHIP THEORY

By looking more deeply into the relational dynamics of organizations, we may be on the verge of a completely new view of leadership (Murrell, 1997). This new view moves away from assumptions that leadership is about the formal leader and toward views of leadership as connective (Lipman-Blumen, 1996), distributed (Gronn, 2002), dispersed (Bryman, 1996), relational (Drath, 2001; Murrell, 1997; Hosking, Dachler, & Gergen, 1995), shared (Pearce & Conger, 2003), or emergent (Marion & Uhl-Bien, 2001). Relational leadership assumes that organizations are complex social entities that cannot be led through the acts and will of a single individual (Stacey, 2001; Streatfield, 2001). It does not view leadership as the source where significant rewards and punishments are parceled out in order to get people to do what is good for them (Murrell, 1997) or that leadership is the acts of individual, heroic leaders who inspire or lead society organizations, or groups to be different (Hargadon, 2003; McKelvey, 2004).

The view of relational leadership provided by Murrell (1997) contrasts with the relational models identified in Hunt (2004). Hunt (2004) described relational leadership as approaches that see leadership as shared influence. These approaches include social network analysis (Burt, 1992), leader-member exchange (Graen & Uhl-Bien, 1995), lateral and distributive approaches (Sayles, 1993; Osborn, Hunt, & Jauch, 1980), social construction views (Dachler, 1988), and self-managing teams (Manz & Sims, 1987). The difference between these approaches and the view presented by Murrell (1997) is in the extent to which the theories move beyond traditional assumptions about leadership. While, many of the relational approaches described by Hunt (2004) appear to operate within the context of traditional (hierarchical, power-based) leadership structures (e.g., Industrial Age paradigms) (cf. Brower, Schoorman, & Tan, 2000), Murrell (1997) sees relational leadership as an entirely new way to view structure in the post-industrial world.

This distinction is important because the new view Murrell (1997) describes represents a paradigm shift in leadership theorizing. In this approach leadership and structure become very similar concepts, and both are produced from the same relational process:

> As leadership is shared and created jointly, so is the responsibility for structuring the organization ... What this means is that people work together to define and develop their relationships not just as questions of influence and leadership, but also as questions of how to keep all of this moving and working together. How to ... [work] becomes a question not just of technology or work design but very much of how we relate to each other and work together. In answering this we lay out a structure ... this structure becomes a product of the leadership relationships we envision as appropriate to our condition ... [In this way] we become more consciously influencing the structure rather than only it influencing us. (Murrell, 1997, p. 40)

Murrell's (1997) view of relational leadership is consistent with other leadership scholars who are suggesting a paradigm shift in leadership research. For example, Seers (2004) describes leadership in organizational forms in which people need to lead without a stable foundation of supervisory authority on which to build. "What is needed at this juncture is a better understanding of what is 'usual' in the interaction of people. A better analysis of the influence inherent in interactions among individuals should provide a basis ... for explaining leadership in flexible organizational forms ... and flexible leadership structures" (Seers, 2004, p. 26). Hunt and Dodge (2000) describe a relational focus as one that "moves beyond unidirectional or even reciprocal leader/follower relationships to one that recognizes leadership wherever it occurs, is not restricted to a single or even small set of formal or informal leaders, and in its strongest form, functions as a dynamic system embedding leadership, environmental, and organizational aspects" (p. 448).

Similarly, Drath (2001) presents a model of relational leadership that goes beyond personal dominance (more traditional models) or interpersonal influence (shared influence perspectives) to leadership as the capacity of a system to accomplish leadership tasks at various levels of complexity. According to Drath (2001), in this interconnected and interdependent world, "the very idea of leadership—what it is and how it works and even how people even know it when they see it—is in the process of changing.... Nothing less than a revolution of mind is required, a shift in order of thought, a reformation of how leadership is known" (Drath, 2001, p. 124). In his framework, leadership is generated by bringing in increasing numbers of increasingly responsible people to produce an unfolding of ever more involving and complex knowledge principles, which are produced through relational dialogue. Leadership development, according to Drath (2001), involves not simply training people in positions of authority but rather recognizing that leadership relies on and is generated by the whole system of relationships.

Gronn's (2002) work on distributed leadership represents another call for such a shift in theorizing. He suggests that distributed leadership should become a new "unit of analysis" in the study of leadership. Distributed leadership does not require an individual who can perform all the essential leadership functions but rather people who collectively perform them (Yukl, 1999). Gronn's approach dispenses with the category of followership, such that "organization becomes a process of negotiation between leaders" (Miller, 1998, p. 18, in Gronn, 2002, p. 427). According to Gronn (2002), in distributed leadership the problem of coordination is less one of hierarchical consolidation of knowledge than one of those lower down finding more and more ways of getting connected and interrelating the knowledge they have (Tsoukas, 1996).

In perhaps the most extensive theoretical description of this, Marion and Uhl-Bien (2001, 2005) present a model of Complexity Leadership that is consistent with Murrell's (1997) depiction of relational leadership. In their model, systems emerge through correlation (e.g., relationship-building) and aggregation (e.g., networks, structure), concepts they draw from Complexity Theory (Mainzer, 1997). According to Complexity Theory, micro-level processes in a complex system refer to the dynamics of proximal relationships among the basic agents in a network (Marion & Uhl-

Bien, 2005). Micro dynamics enable agents (individuals or groups) to exhibit or experience what Poincaré (1957; Prigogine, 1997) has called correlation. When randomly resonating particles interact, they "correlate" their resonances; that is, each transfers a little of their resonant pattern to the other. After interaction, the resonant pattern of each is modified and each resonates a bit like the other. Transferring this principle metaphorically to humans, when two, independently "resonating" humans (each with individualistic patterns of beliefs, worldviews, etc.) interact, they share some amount of that resonance (Marion, 1999). If they interact over an extended period of time, those individuals will begin to think and act increasingly alike (e.g., they become part of a relational context). Because resonances are individualistic and random, outcomes in complex systems are often unpredictable. Something similar can be said of social correlation; a relationship that might otherwise be "made in heaven," for example, might abort prematurely because of random events that happen early in that relationship (Marion, 1999).

Random resonance, and sensitive dependence (i.e., sensitivity to initial conditions) conspire to create "surprise"—they are the underlying sources of dynamic creativity in a complex network. As systems of agents stabilize (high degree of correlation), they become somewhat predictable (they carry information better), less prone to surprise, and less sensitively dependent (Kauffman, 1993, borrowing from biology, calls this an Environmentally Stable State); however, even then the system is susceptible to unforeseen changes simply because of the very dynamism that defines such systems (Marion & Uhl-Bien, 2005).

Therefore, Complexity Leadership describes a model in which leadership is not top-down or power-driven, but rather bottom-up, emergent, evolving (unpredictably), and driven by interactive dynamics of heterogeneous agents. In relational leadership terms (Murrell, 1997; Seers, 2004), leadership lies in the relational dynamics among organizational members, and structure emerges nonlinearly from these dynamics (Marion & Uhl-Bien, 2001). Therefore, managerial leadership in complex systems does not involve directing, "leading," or controlling, but rather facilitating and enabling. Managers in complex systems should not try to lead the way, but instead should work to create the conditions conducive to the bottom-up emergence of innovation and surprise that generate from interactions among "agents" (a term used because it does not involve hierarchical connotations) (Marion & Uhl-Bien, 2005).

In an interesting empirical investigation that has implications for the theoretical arguments just described, Alvesson and Sveningsson (2003) examined leadership of an international biotech company operating in a highly complex and ambiguous knowledge-intensive context. Using interviews, they asked managers to report on the leadership that occurred in the organization. They found that as managers continued to describe their activities relative to leadership, after exhausting their initial recitation of "contemporary fashionable scripts" concerning how one should conduct leadership, their ability to convey the leadership that occurs in their setting became muddled, to the point that by the end of the interviews, it pretty much broke down and "there was not much leadership left intact" (p. 374). Alvesson and Sveningsson (2003) described this as "the disappearance of leadership ... At least, in our study it seems very difficult to identify any specific relationships, behavioral styles, a coherent set of values, or an integrated, coherent set of actions that correspond to or meaningfully can be construed as leadership as important and intended" (p. 376). They concluded that, by any traditional conceptualizations about what leadership is, they did not find support for the "existence" of leadership. The authors then suggest that mainstream ideas about leadership—as expressed in the leadership literature and among practitioners—may assume too much.

I would argue that perhaps it is not that leadership "assumes too much" so much as that our traditional paradigms of leadership *view too little:* that leadership is occurring in this organization, but that it is in a form that is not familiar to us and does not fit within our language systems. Similar to Murrell (1997) and others, perhaps we need a new language system, a new way to think about leadership in 21st century organizations. It seems that the firm studied by Alvesson and Sveningsson (1997) is leadership in a "new organizational form" (Pettigrew et al., 2003)—a picture of 21st century leadership (Bennis, Spreitzer, & Cumings, 2001)—but that our 20th century lenses of leadership are not adequate to capture it.

This new leadership does not lie solely with the manager but in the interactions (and relationships) of the "knowledge workers" (Drucker, 1993). By looking only at the managerial *leader* we may be missing the leader*ship*. Managerial leaders can influence the conditions in which these workers function to facilitate leadership and emergent outcomes, but as illustrated by the managers' descriptions, they really do not see their roles as leading or directing in any traditional sense of the word. Instead, it seems they do everything they can to be non-directive and non-decisive so as not to stifle innovation or creativity of the team.

Given this, leadership in these contexts lies in the collective, and more specifically, in the interactive dynamics of the teams (units, groups, aggregates). It is the "agents" (individuals or groups) who decide directions to take, determine the "meaning" for the work, and generate the ideas, knowledge, and innovation that lead to productive outcomes. Managers, if anything, seem to clear the way for the teams, and even *stay out of the way.* The managers "foster the energy," but the energy—the leadership—lies in the group. In this way, leadership is bottom-up and not just top-down; it is based on interactive processes among organizational members, operating within relational contexts.

Therefore, to understand leadership in the new era, we need to better understand relational dynamics that occur among organizational members. However, as I said earlier, we still know very little about how relationships develop and grow in the workplace. While organizational behaviorists have intensively studied group processes, and leadership researchers have explored considerate or supportive (i.e., relationship-oriented) leadership styles, what is missing in the managerial literature is the study of work *relationships*. LMX has told us that effective work relationships produce leadership, but we still don't know much about how these relationships function. Moreover, we do not know what the relational dynamics are by which leadership is constructed in the workplace. Therefore, I turn next to a discussion of development of work relationships, and offer implicit relational theories as a potential vehicle for exploring the landscape of relational dynamics in the workplace.

IMPLICIT RELATIONAL THEORIES

In an attempt to bring attention to relationship development in leadership research, Uhl-Bien (2003) presented an initial framework for thinking about cognitive processes in the development of work relationships. When considered relative to relational leadership, that framework might help us begin to help explore "the human processes of how people decide, act, and present themselves to each other" (Murrell, 1997).

Uhl-Bien (2003) suggested that exploration of why some relationships develop well and others develop poorly may depend on *relational favorability* (i.e., the extent to which conditions are favorable or unfavorable for the development of the relationship) and *implicit relational theories*. For example, some relationships may be easier, more "natural" to form than others (e.g., individuals "hit it off" right away and the relationship develops positively and stays that way). In these relationships, conditions are favorable for relationship development, individuals do not feel they have to work at the relationship, and perhaps are not even conscious of the relationship development process. On the other hand, some relationships may be much harder to develop, due to personality differences, style differences, incongruent values, demographic similarity/dissimilarity, etc., that make it more difficult for dyad members to build the relational components necessary for effective relationship development. In these situations, individuals are highly conscious of these differences, and if they desire to develop the relationship, they must work hard to get past the obstacles to relationship development (i.e., situations with low relational favorability).

Extending this concept, it is possible that relational favorability may be associated with *implicit relational theories*. This construct was adapted from implicit leadership theories (Eden & Leviatan, 1975; Lord & Maher, 1990, 1991; Offermann, Kennedy, & Wirtz, 1994). Implicit Leadership Theories (ILTs) represent cognitive structures or schemas specifying traits and behaviors that followers expect from leaders. Such schemas provide people with an underlying structure of meaning that persists over time, shaping their perception, interpretation, and behavior (Epitropaki & Martin, 2004; Jelinek, Smircich, & Hirsch, 1983). From a cognitive categorization standpoint (Lord, Foti, & DeVader, 1984; Phillips, 1984; Phillips & Lord, 1986), schemas are hierarchically organized cognitive categories, each of which is represented by a set of prototypes, or "abstract conception(s) of the most representative member or most widely shared features of a given cognitive category" (Phillips, 1984, p. 126, in Epitropaki & Martin, 2004, p. 293). Leadership prototypes are developed through socialization and past experiences with leaders, stored in memory and activated when followers interact with a person in a leadership position (Lord & Maher, 1993). Subsequently, people are categorized as leaders on the basis of the perceived match between their behavior or character and the prototypic attributes of a preexisting leader category (Epitropaki & Martin, 2004; Rush & Russell, 1988).

Adapting ILTs to relationships, implicit relational theories (IRTs) would be schematic knowledge structures individuals hold regarding work relationships. They represent the beliefs and assumptions about work relationships and the characteristics they expect relational partners to demonstrate. When dyad partners exhibit qualities consistent with these knowledge structures, *relational favorability* is higher, and relationship development to more advanced stages of relationship-building is facilitated. When schemas are not met, or when anti-prototypical behaviors are present, relational favorability is lower, and advancement to higher levels of relationship development may be inhibited (Uhl-Bien, 2003).

In sum, based on Uhl-Bien (2003), it appears useful to explore the concept of implicit relational theories in the workplace. The concept of "implicit theories" has been an important topic in psychology for quite some time (Dweck, 1996; Eden & Leviatan, 1975; Heider, 1958; Kelly, 1955; Thompson & Phillips, 1977) as well as in leadership research (Lord et al., 1984; Lord & Maher, 1991). It has also received significant attention in the achievement and social judgment literatures (Dweck & Leggett, 1988; Levy et al., 1999). However, while the earliest references to implicit theories of relationships (ITRs) were made by Thompson and Phillips (1977) (e.g., "implicit theories of interpersonal relations," the set of assumptions or expectations a person has about interpersonal interaction) and Rands and Levinger (1979) (e.g., "implicit theories of relationships," people share notions about what characteristics of relationships should co-occur), it was not until very recently that this area began to develop as a stream of research. Because research on implicit theories of relationships can help inform a discussion of relational leadership, I turn next to a review of work in this area, and then discuss how it can be applied to relationships in work settings.

Implicit Theories of Relationships

In the personal relationships literature, a body of research is very recently emerging that examines implicit theories of relationships (ITRs) (Knee, Patrick, Vietor, & Neighbors, 2004; Franiuk et al., 2002). This research assumes that individuals have different belief systems about what makes for a good relationship (Knee, 1998). These beliefs, or implicit theories, determine, in part, one's goals and motivations in relationships (Knee, Patrick, & Lonsbary, 2003).

This work builds on the large body of research on implicit theories in the achievement and social judgment literature. For example, Dweck and colleagues, examining issues of achievement, morality, and social understanding, suggested that people hold implicit theories about themselves and the world, and that these theories guide their social behavior (Dweck & Elliott, 1983; Dweck & Leggett, 1988; Erdley & Dweck, 1993; Hong, Chiu, & Dweck, 1995). Dweck and Leggett (1988) distinguished between people who believe personal attributes are fixed and unchanging (entity theory) and people who believe these attributes are developed (incremental theory). They found that such theories have important consequences for cognition, affect, and behavior (Dweck, Chiu, & Hong, 1995a,b; Plaks, Stroessner, Dweck, & Sherman, 2001). Someone holding an entity theory of intelligence would believe that intelligence is a fixed trait—a personal quality that cannot be changed. On the other hand, someone holding an incremental theory of intelligence would conceive of intelligence as cultivatable (Chiu, Hong, & Dweck, 1994). This work has been helpful in understanding how and why individuals give up or persist in the face of challenges and setbacks (Dweck et al., 1995a,b).

Recognizing that these concepts could have applicability to interpersonal relations, recent research has begun to explore the role of such theories in romantic relationships (Ruvolo & Rotondo, 1998; Franiuk, 2003; Franiuk et al., 2002; Knee, 1998; Knee et al., 2003; Patrick, 2003). For example, Ruvolo and Rotondo (1998) examined ratings of romantic partners and reports of well-being relative to an individual's implicit theory, and found a stronger relation between ratings of partner characteristics and relationship well-being for entity theorists than for incremental theorists (i.e., ratings of partners were more salient to feelings of well-being if one holds an entity, or "trait," theory). Knee (1998) applied the concept of entity and incremental theories to beliefs about the nature of romantic relationships. He differentiated between the extent to which individuals believed that their partner was immediately compatible (an entity theory) and the extent to which they believed that relationships can change over time (an incremental theory), labeling these two views a "destiny" theory and a "growth" theory, respectively. According to Knee (1998), a belief in destiny holds that potential relationship partners are either meant for each other or not; a belief in growth holds that successful relationships are culti- vated and developed.

Extending this logic further, individuals who believe that relationships are destined would view the early stages of relationships as tests of their potential success—they may be sensitive to early indications that they can- not succeed at the relationship, and thus, would give up easily (Knee, 1998). Individuals who believe in growth would hold that successful rela- tionships are constructed and developed by conquering obstacles and growing closer. Therefore, they would weigh initial impressions of compat- ibility less heavily, emphasizing the more dynamic facets of understanding, development, and closeness. The latter are consistent with work showing that successful relationships evolve from the resolution of risks, challenges, and difficulties (Holmes & Rempel, 1989; Lydon, 1999).

Franiuk et al. (2002) extended the work of Knee and colleagues (Knee, 1998; Knee, Nanayakkara, Vietor, Neighbors, & Patrick, 2001), which focused on the compatibility of one's partner and the ability of a relation- ship to change, to consider whether people may hold a *constellation* of beliefs that are related to this central idea (Franiuk, 2003). "Some people may enter a romantic relationship expecting the most important thing is to find the 'right' person with whom one is passionately in love, and then one must simply let the relationship unfold. In contrast, others may view a rela- tionship as something that is constantly shaped and actively maintained by the relationship partners and do not believe that perfect compatibility is necessarily the key to a successful relationship" (Franiuk et al., 2002, p. 346). They called the former a "soulmate" theory (e.g., destiny/entity the- ory) and the latter a "work-it-out" theory (e.g., incremental/growth the- ory). The soulmate theory reflects the belief that finding the right person is critical for relationship success; there is only one or a select few people in the world with whom a person is meant to have a satisfying relationship. The work-it-out theory reflects one's belief that he or she could have a suc- cessful relationship with most people, and that relationships take effort to grow over time (Franiuk, 2003).

Taken together, this work may have implications for relationship devel- opment in the workplace. ITRs set in motion a process that guides the perception, interpretation, attribution, and resolution of events relative to relationships (Knee et al., 2004). Moreover, given that ITRs describe not only specific relationships but approaches to relationships more broadly (Fletcher & Thomas, 1996; Patrick, 2003), it is reasonable to assume that concepts that individuals have about personal relationships may carry over to how they view relationships in the workplace. Therefore, I turn next to a more detailed discussion of ITRs and work relationships.

Implicit Relational Theories in the Workplace

Levy et al. (1999) offered a detailed discussion of how implicit theories relate to social understanding, and particularly, how individuals perceive and judge others' behavior. When combined with the work already mentioned, their description of implicit theories and social cognition offers potentially useful applications to relationships in the workplace.

Levy et al. (1999) report on a series of studies investigating implicit theories and different modes of social understanding. These studies differ from the relational theories described above (e.g., Knee, 1998; Franiuk, 2003) in that they were not focused on romantic relationships, making their applicability to work settings more straightforward. According to Levy et al. (1999), implicit theories can help explain different modes of social thought. One mode (entity theory), which believes in a more static social reality, is organized around traits: seeking trait information, viewing traits as causes of behavior, drawing trait-centered inferences, and categorizing people by traits. The other mode (incremental theory) is organized around more dynamic psychological mediators (e.g., people's goals, needs, states of mind). People who operate according to this mode tend to analyze and understand others in terms of dynamic psychological processes. Dweck and colleagues (Dweck et al., 1995a,b; Dweck, 1996) have provided extensive support for this distinction and how it applies in social contexts (Levy et al., 1999) that is consistent with findings regarding Knee's "destiny" and "growth" theories (Knee et al., 2001, 2002) and Franiuk's "soulmate" and "work-it-out" theories (Franiuk et al., 2002; Franiuk, 2003).

Applying these concepts to work settings, we could expect that implicit theories will influence how individuals approach work relationships. In particular, we can propose that individuals with an *entity* implicit relational theory will approach work relationships differently from individuals with an *incremental* implicit relational theory. From what we know about entity theories, individuals holding such a view will focus on traits. Their approach in social situations will be to seek trait information, view traits as causes of behavior, draw trait-centered inferences, and categorize people by traits (Levy et al., 1999). They are more likely to make more rapid judgments about whether a partner is compatible based on quick assessments of the other's traits. Incremental theorists, on the other hand, interpret social situations relative to a more dynamic psychological process, and as such, work to analyze and understand people in terms of these processes (Levy et al., 1999). Rather than seeing relational partners as immediately compatible (or not), incremental theorists believe that relationships can be cultivated and developed over time (i.e., "growth" theory, Knee, 1998). Incremental, or growth, theorists are primarily interested in developing the relationship, and believe that relationships grow not despite the obstacles but rather because of them (Knee et al., 2003).

For entity theorists, traits seem to reflect enduring dispositional labels, whereas for incremental theorists, traits seem to reflect more temporary, descriptive labels (Levy et al., 1999). In this way, entity theories are consistent with destiny (Knee, 1998) or "soulmate" (Franiuk, 2003) views of relationships, in which if the proper traits are identified, the individuals are perceived to be a right fit and the individuals must simply let the relationship unfold. Those who believe more strongly in destiny attempt to determine the compatibility of their partner and the viability of the relationship based on minimal information. They place a high value on whether a relationship is meant to be, and tend to diagnose the potential of the relationship based on specific events (Knee et al., 2003). Alternatively, incremental theory is compatible with a "work-it-out" theory (Franiuk, 2003), which reflects one's belief that he or she could have a successful relationship with most people and that relationships take effort to grow over time (Franiuk, 2003). Whereas an entity belief about personality has been associated with making global trait inferences from brief samples of behavior, perceiving behavior as stable, and showing an increased likelihood to blame and punish others for undesirable behavior (Erdley & Dweck, 1993; Knee et al., 2003), an incremental belief about personality is associated with seeing traits as reflecting more temporary, descriptive labels, such that individuals make fewer dispositional and more provisional inferences (Dweck, 1996; Knee et al., 2003; Levy et al., 1999). Based on this, we can propose the following:

Proposition 1:   *Individuals will approach work relationships differently depending on whether they hold an entity implicit relational theory or an incremental implicit relational theory.*

ITRs and Initial Impressions

Work on implicit theories of relationships also suggest that initial impressions will matter, more so for entity theorists than incremental theorists.

Theory on social cognition in relationships developed out of early research on attraction and initial impressions (Patrick, 2003). Investigation of initial impressions suggested that expectations about a relationship's future often stem from first interactions. These expectations form quickly and spontaneously, often without the individual's awareness (Uleman, Hon, Roman, & Moskowitz, 1996) and in turn affect subsequent interaction behaviors (Fiske, 1998; Patrick, 2003).

With regard to implicit theories, these initial impressions may influence relationship progress differently for entity theorists than for incremental theorists. Levy et al. (1999) reported that entity theorists were more willing to make strong trait inferences about others in the face of limited information than incremental theorists, and that they formed these judgments very quickly. Knee (1998) suggested and found that individuals who believe that relationships are destined would view the early stages of relationships as tests of their potential success. They may be sensitive to early indications that they cannot succeed at the relationship, and thus, would give up easily, whereas individuals who believe in growth would hold that successful relationships are constructed and developed by conquering obstacles and growing closer, and would therefore weigh initial impressions of compatibility less heavily (Knee et al., 2003). This is because a stronger belief in destiny is associated with a more judgmental approach to relationships and a focus on fixed aspects of the relationship or partner. For destiny theorists, however, if initial satisfaction is higher, their relationships tended to last particularly long (Knee et al., 2001).

This is consistent with Franiuk's (2003) findings. According to Franiuk et al. (2002), for soulmate theorists, finding the "right" person is central to their beliefs about how their relationships should be. Franiuk and colleagues' (2002) longitudinal research revealed that soulmate theorists were less likely to remain in their relationships than work-it-out theorists if they did not believe their partner was a perfect match. However, if they believed a partner was a right fit, they may be more likely than work-it-out theorists to use certain tactics to maintain the *perception* the person is right. Thus, once past the initial impression, destiny/soulmate theorists' relationships lasted particularly long; for growth/work-it-out theorists, negative initial impressions would not be a deterrent to relationship development. Therefore, with respect to work relationships, we can propose that:

Proposition 2: *Initial impressions will be more strongly linked to failure to develop work relationships for entity theorists than for incremental theorists, such that if initial impressions in a relationship are negative, an individual holding an entity theory will be less likely to work to develop the relationship further than an individual who holds an incremental theory.*

ITRs, Perceived Similarity, and Maintenance Behaviors

As noted by Franiuk et al. (2002), there is a wealth of research demonstrating the importance of perceived similarity of another's view to one's own in attraction and relationship success (e.g., Houts, Robins, & Huston, 1996; Marks & Miller, 1982). However, whether perceived similarity influences relationship development and maintenance behaviors may depend again on one's implicit relational theory. For soulmate theorists, given the importance of being with the right person, an important indicator of whether or not a relationship is worth continuing may be the perception of one's partner as similar to oneself (Franiuk, 2003). According to Franiuk et al. (2002), "to a soulmate theorist, agreement with his or her partner on various issues could offer valuable information about whether or not the person is the right person. Similarly, researchers have shown that dissimilarity between partners' views can take away from attraction (Rosenbaum, 1986). Dissimilarity may be a warning signal to soulmate theorists, but work-it-out theorists may place less importance on this information because of their belief that dissimilarity can either be changed to similarity or worked through" (p. 348). Because not agreeing could signal the end of a relationship, a soulmate theorist might convince him or herself that the partner is more similar than he or she actually is, distorting their perception to make it appear that the partner agrees, particularly when the relationship has a longer duration. This would allow continuation when a lot of time and energy have been invested (Franiuk et al., 2002).

Perceptions of similarity may be influenced by the extent to which individuals are aware of discrepancies among the relational partners. Knee et al. (2001) found that entity theorists reacted more negatively to relational discrepancies (i.e., differences in views about the relationship) than incremental theorists. Entity theorists see discrepancies such as perceived lack of agreement in views as a threat to the relationship or a sign that it may be doomed to fail. Incremental theorists reacted with more positive affect, believing that discrepancies can be worked through effectively. These findings suggest that incremental, or work-it-out, theorists do not seem threatened by relationship discrepancies and may even be happily challenged by them (Franiuk et al., 2002; Knee et al., 2003).

In terms of relationship maintenance, Knee (1998) found that entity theorists are more likely to engage in avoidance coping in response to a stressful relationship event. As found by Knee (1998), a destiny theory of relationships may be tantamount to the belief that relationship outcomes are beyond one's control, and this rigid belief may lead one to judge negative relationship events particularly strongly and thus withdraw from the relationship. Destiny beliefs can lead individuals to infer grand meaning from relatively minor events or feel threatened by even minor discrepancies in how they and their partner perceive their relationship (Knee et al.,

2003). When problems arise early on, or when initial satisfaction is low, belief in destiny is associated with disengaging from the relationship (Knee et al., 2004). Growth theory, however, was generally associated with relationship-maintenance strategies, since maintenance and development are core principles of belief in growth.

In sum, entity (destiny) implicit theory is linked to attempts to diagnose the status and potential success of the relationships, and incremental (growth) implicit theory is linked to attempts to maintain the relationship. Therefore, with regard to work relationships, we could expect that entity theorists would place more importance on perceived similarity than incremental theorists, and that when faced with discrepancies in the relationship or negative relational events, entity theorists are less likely to engage in maintenance behaviors than incremental theorists.

Proposition 3: *Individuals holding an entity theory will place more importance on perceived similarity than incremental theorists for development of work relationships, and when faced with discrepancies or negative relational events, entity theorists are less likely to engage in maintenance behaviors than incremental theorists.*

ITRs and Conflict

Research on implicit theories of relationships has also addressed the association between ITRs and conflict. In particular, recent work has examined the moderating role of ITRs in the link between relational stressors such as conflict and relationship satisfaction (Franiuk et al., 2002) and commitment (Knee et al., 2004). This work considers the emotional reactions engendered by viewing conflict as something that can or cannot be overcome. For example, some people may see confronting or working through problems as one way that they become more invested in a relationship, whereas others may see confrontations as an indication that the relationship is not worth continuing (Knee et al., 2004).

Knee et al. (2004) suggested that conflict is a potentially negative factor in relationships that may either bring partners closer or force them apart, depending on one's ITR. Their findings supported this by showing that when individuals were *lower* in growth belief, they felt less committed when the conflict remained unresolved and when they already had a less favorable view of the partner. However, when individuals were *higher* in growth belief, these otherwise adverse circumstances were not associated with how committed individuals felt after the conflict. Growth belief served as a "buffer" of circumstances becoming more negative after a conflict (destiny belief did not yield an analogous buffering effect). They also found that if individuals were higher in growth belief it did not matter if the conflict was resolved, and this was especially true if the individual already had a less favorable view of the partner (Knee et al., 2004). They concluded that when one endorses a belief that relationships require maintenance and problems can be resolved, disagreements become opportunities for better understanding one's partner, improving the relationship, and becoming more interdependent. Individuals higher in growth may see the experience of making it through a conflict as an investment in the relationship, which could lead to increased commitment (Rusbult, 1980, 1983).

For others (who are lower in growth belief) conflict may seem unsettling and not beneficial to the development of the relationship. For a destiny theorist, the presence of conflict could be perceived as a sign that the relationship is not meant to be. However, in established and satisfying relationships, destiny beliefs also may indicate the relationship is unique and valuable and lead to the individual potentially overlooking or denying the impact of conflict (Knee et al., 2004). This is consistent with Franiuk et al.'s (2002) description of soulmate theorists. Franiuk et al. (2002) described soulmate theorists as individuals who, because they believe they are with the right person, perceived the partner to be more similar to oneself than they actually may be. Moreover, when conflicts arise, soulmate theorists are more likely to react passively to arguments in their relationships than work-it-out theorists. They speculate that giving in may be the easiest answer for a soulmate theorist, who wants to protect the image of the relationship, and who might see the need to put effort into resolving conflict as a relationship stressor and indication of serious trouble in the relationship. To maintain relationship satisfaction when problems arise, soulmate theorists may overlook the problem or try to assuage it. Work-it-out theorists, on the other hand, should be less concerned with avoiding conflicts because they are not as threatened by them, and may even see them as a way to strengthen the relationship (Franiuk et al., 2002). Therefore, based on the above, we can propose that:

Proposition 4:   *When faced with relational conflict, individuals holding a stronger incremental theory (i.e., individuals who are higher in growth or work-it-out beliefs) will be more willing to address the conflict and grow from it than individuals who are weaker in incremental theory (i.e., individuals who are lower in growth or work-it-out beliefs).*

Note that this proposition does not address entity theorists, primarily because the empirical findings for entity or soulmate theorists are not as apparent with conflict, likely due to the reasons mentioned above (the distortion of perceptions, etc.) (Franiuk et al., 2002; Knee et al., 2004). However, it is possible we could make a proposition that entity theorists may be more conflict avoidant, either because they see conflict as a threat to the relationship and they are unsettled by it, or because they distort their perceptions, overlook the problem, or try to quickly assuage it (e.g., Franiuk et al., 2002). This is an area that will need further consideration when examined in the context of ITRs in the workplace. Given the growing importance of conflict in the leadership (Gronn, 1999, 2002; Heifetz & Laurie, 2001; Marion & Uhl-Bien, 2005) and organizational behavior literatures, examining how ITRs relate to conflict could be extremely helpful in advancing understanding regarding conflict in the workplace. This work should also consider how the handling of conflict varies depending on type of work relationship examined, since individuals in manager-subordinate relationships, which are grounded in hierarchy, may react to conflict differently from individuals in peer exchanges (this would be more consistent with the personal relationships literature, which did not involve explicit hierarchy).

ITRs and Prototypes for Work Relationships

While the majority of this discussion has focused on the general distinction between entity and incremental implicit theories and how they link to relationships (e.g., destiny/growth v. soulmate/work-it-out), examination of ITRs in the workplace can also address more specific cognitive prototypes of work relationships. As mentioned earlier regarding implicit leadership theories, ILTs represent cognitive structures or schemas specifying traits and behaviors that followers expect from leaders. They are represented by a set of prototypes, which are abstract conceptions of the most representative member or most widely shared features of a given cognitive category. Examples of leadership prototypes include intelligent, honest, educated, and dedicated (Lord et al., 1984) and sensitivity, charisma, attractiveness, and strength (Offermann et al., 1994). Therefore, in addition to the general discussion of entity and incremental implicit theories, it may also be worthwhile to explore prototypes of ITRs for work relationships. In the present section I discuss some possible avenues for research regarding workplace ITRs and prototypes, but do not develop specific propositions, as this is an area that requires empirical investigation to be able to develop it further.

In discussing ITRs for romantic relationships, Knee et al. (2004) suggested that while people may have a global set of beliefs about what makes for good relationships, there may also be particular aspects of relationships that they believe are especially fixed or especially malleable. For example, they may view certain factors as crucial to relationship success (e.g., for romantic relationships these may include trust, respect, sex, and love) and other factors as nice but not necessarily crucial (e.g., friendly, honest, sensitive). In other words, people may put different levels of importance on certain characteristics of a relationship. Therefore, more specified measures of ITRs may provide a more sophisticated model that takes into account specific aspects of relationships (Knee et al., 2004). It may even be that

ITRs of specific relationship aspects would mediate the association between general ITRs and various relationship phenomena. If this were the case, then more global ITRs may be related to ITRs about specific aspects of relationships, which in turn predict or moderate relationship phenomena.

For work relationships, research could consider what these characteristics are and how they vary depending on the type of relationship. For example, LMX theory has identified several variables as important for leader-member exchanges, including trust, respect, and obligation (Graen & Uhl-Bien, 1995) and affect, loyalty, contribution, and respect (Liden & Maslyn's "MDM dimensions," 1998). While these dimensions have been considered in the LMX literature, however, we still do not know the extent to which these are important to *all* participants in LMXs or whether they would vary depending on one's relational prototypes. Using the MDM dimensions, it may be that individuals vary in the extent to which these dimensions are a fixed part of their LMX relational prototype (i.e., it is necessary for the relationship to advance) or are more malleable. As noted by Liden and Maslyn (1998), any particular relationship could be based on one, two, three, or all four of the dimensions. For example, some individuals might hold affect as an important characteristic of their LMX relationship prototype, while others may not consider affect (i.e., liking) to be important at all. This is an especially relevant topic for investigation, as affect is an area that has been disputed in the LMX literature, with Graen and Uhl-Bien (1995; Uhl-Bien et al., 2000) arguing that affect (or liking) is not critical to LMX relationships since they are *work* relationships (not friendship or personal relationships), and others suggesting that affect is an important dimension of LMX (Dienesch & Liden, 1986; Liden, Sparrowe, & Wayne, 1997) or that friendship is an important element of leadership relationships (Boyd & Taylor, 1998).

On the other hand, an area that may be a "fixed" characteristic of an LMX relationship may be trust. Trust has been a defining element of LMX throughout the history of the theory (Graen & Uhl-Bien, 1995). In fact, trust is so core to LMX that there has been little empirical work because multicollinearity issues make distinguishing between the two concepts difficult (Wech, 2002; Mitchell & Uhl-Bien, 2004). Because of the importance of this topic, Brower et al. (2000) present a paper devoted to developing a conceptual framework that offers an integrated model of trust and LMX. Therefore, trust may be a prototypical characteristic of LMX relationships, and more likely, of work relationships in general.

On a related note, Brower et al. (2000) suggest that future research on relational leadership examine the concept of "propensity to relate," which they introduce to the LMX literature. This concept is adapted from "propensity to trust" (Mayer, Davis, & Schoorman, 1995), and describes an individual difference variable in which leaders (their focal unit of analysis) are predisposed to develop more high LMX relationships than other leaders. Leader propensity to relate is a characteristic that *the leader brings to the relationship before the dyad members engage in exchanges* or begin to evaluate specific characteristics of one another. They suggest that this propensity is likely to be different from the generalized propensity to relate due to specific experiences the leader has with respect to other subordinates. This concept sounds very much like relationship schemas. Relationship schemas are pre-existing and influence subsequent processing of events and behavior (Knee et al., 2004). These schemas, or knowledge structures, become more complex as individuals experience continuing streams of relationship experiences and are exposed to observations of others' relationship experiences (Berscheid, 1994). Therefore, propensity to relate may be very similar to relationship schemas; as such, research on ITRs and relationship schemas and prototypes may be one way to help explore the kinds of issues raised as important by Brower et al. (2000) for relational leadership research.

DISCUSSION

As we move deeper into the "Age of Connectionism" (McKelvey, 2004), the need for effective relationships in the workplace becomes increasingly important. As social systems, organizations are enacted through the networks and patterns of interactions among organizational members. Relationships provide the context that determines whether these interactions are productive, neutral, or even destructive (Uhl-Bien et al., 2000).

Even more important, relationships may provide a mechanism through which leadership is generated and maintained. Emerging models of leadership are beginning to describe leadership as distributed throughout the organization rather than lying with particular individuals (Gronn, 2002). These models argue that leadership occurs in the emergent dynamics of aggregates (e.g., teams, work units, groups, networks) that include interacting "agents" (individuals or groups) who decide directions to take, determine the "meaning" for the work, and generate the ideas, knowledge, and innovation that lead to productive outcomes (Uhl-Bien et al., 2004). This perspective, which I refer to in the present paper as *relational leadership* (Murrell, 1997), views leadership as a bottom-up process that emerges from interactive dynamics among organizational members operating within relational contexts (Marion & Uhl-Bien, 2001, 2005).

Because these relational contexts can influence the types of leadership processes that are generated (e.g., more or less productive), it is important that we understand how these dynamics occur within organizations. As noted by Murrell (1997), deep examination of relational dynamics may lead us to an entirely new way to view leadership. One way to approach such investigation is to explore social cognitive processes of relational dynamics. Therefore, in the present paper I presented a framework of implicit theories of relationships in the workplace. I do not limit these theories to hierarchical relationships, but rather consider that individuals hold implicit theories that influence how they approach work relationships in general. I allow that they may also have more specified theories that address different types of relationships more specifically.

This framework uses Dweck's distinction between entity theorists and incremental theorists, also applied by Knee and colleagues (Knee et al., 2004) and Franiuk et al. (2002) to personal relationships, to develop propositions regarding how one's implicit theory will influence the way they perceive and react to relational partners in different relational contexts (e.g., initial impressions, relationship development and maintenance, relational stressors such as conflict or perceived discrepancies). While I lay out the basic framework for such an approach to exploring relational dynamics, I have only scratched the surface; there is a wide open field for future lines of investigation to examine these issues more explicitly in organizational contexts and relative to relational leadership.

For example, future research is needed to engage in basic empirical investigation to identify the relational schemas and prototypes individuals hold for work relationships and to test the types of propositions I laid out in this paper. This work could also examine how these schemas and prototypes differ across various types of work relationships (e.g., manager-subordinate, coworker, network, peer, etc.). In the personal relationships literature, Fletcher and Kininmonth (1992) offered general beliefs about what makes for successful relationships (intimacy, external factors, passion, and individuality) and then more specific characteristics that represent these beliefs, e.g., intimacy (trust, respect, love, and communication), external factors (personal security, finances and children), passion (sex and vitality), and individuality (independence and equity). Such a framework of broader and more specific belief structures may be useful for relational leadership theory. It might be that certain individuals have knowledge structures around more *relational* variables, such as affect/liking, friendship, interpersonal trust, interpersonal identification, perceived similarities, support, and consideration. Others might hold a more *instrumental*, task-based knowledge structure, emphasizing characteristics such as self-interest, competence and professional respect, which does not require personal liking or "feel-good" types of characteristics (Gronn, 1999). The organizational literature on leadership, teamwork, group processes, etc. may offer suggestions for variables that would be potential candidates to consider as parts of such relational schemas.

Exploration of ITRs and relational schemas could also consider how prototypes change over time. For example, Fletcher and Thomas (1996) suggested that individuals' relational working models (in their case attachment styles) begin with a focus on a particular relationship and then broaden to encompass how the individual views relationships more generally. There has also been some speculation about the reciprocal link between relationships in general and a particular relationship with regard to internal working models. Specifically, as individuals move in and out of relationships, there is a continual interchange between the general and specific such that specific salient experiences may affect more general internal working models (e.g., attachment styles) (Patrick, 2003). Therefore, research will need to consider the dynamic and interactive nature of these prototypes. This is an issue that is gaining increased attention in the Implicit Leadership Theory literature (e.g., Brown & Lord's 2001, "connectionist models," Epitropaki & Martin, 2004) and one that will need to be considered here as well.

This leads to a related question as to whether these theories can be manipulated. It seems from the descriptions that entity theories have more drawbacks for effective and widespread relationship development than incremental theories. In fact, Dweck et al. (1995a,b) addressed this issue specifically in their response to comments on their approach—"we have thus far tended to find fewer benefits for the entity view" than the incremental view (p. 324). Because of this, it is important to know whether these theories are fixed or whether they can be influenced (Patrick, 2003). Both Dweck et al. (1995a,b; Levy et al., 1999) and Knee et al. (2003) report that implicit theories can be measured overtly but can also be induced situationally to influence attributions and perceptions of self and others. Therefore, another line of research could examine how fixed or malleable implicit relational theories are in the workplace and the consequences of holding one or the other for both the individuals and the organization. It is possible that people may have tendencies toward one implicit theory or another, but that most are not locked into one worldview. Research could examine whether there is "backtracking" if one learns he or she is wrong in their thinking about a relational partner.

Recent work on ITRs (Knee et al., 2003) is considering potential interactive effects of entity and incremental theories. These have been shown to be independent dimensions; thus, it is conceivable to hold both beliefs simultaneously. This suggests that each dimension can contribute uniquely to predicting and explaining relationship perceptions, cognitions, and behaviors (Knee et al., 2003). Knee et al. (2003) are building on this to consider combinations of high and low destiny and growth beliefs to see how they would relate to outcomes of interest. They develop a typology of these combinations to highlight two primary orientations to relationships:

a cultivation orientation and evaluation orientation, each with different attributions and behavioral outcomes. Hence, research on ITRs in the workplace should also examine such combinations and their potential applications in work relationships.

Moreover, research on ITRs has interesting implications regarding "dysfunctional" relationships in the workplace that can result from people "trusting too much." Uhl-Bien et al. (2000), drawing from the mentoring literature, raised the possibility in discussing trust that some relationships can be harmed when individuals trust too much (and are blinded to another's faults). Research on ITRs may provide an "answer" for why this happens. As discussed earlier, both Knee and colleagues (Knee et al., 2003) and Franiuk et al. (2002) describe that destiny or soulmate theorists may distort perceptions of a relational partner because they do not want to consider counteracting information to their belief that the partner is the right one. Therefore, it may be that this also occurs in the workplace, such that individuals with entity theories are more likely to get into situations of being blinded to relational partners' faults because they do not want to admit the relationship may not be what they thought it was going to be.

Finally, the changing work context presents challenges to development of relationships. New psychological contracts, temporary employment relationships/contract workers, greater job mobility, and work-at-home translate to challenges for relationship development. It is important to point out that even though work contexts may change, the development of effective work relationships is still critical for organizational functioning, as relationships may offer key sources of social capital and competitive advantage for the firm (Uhl-Bien et al., 2000). Therefore, it is important to understand how implicit theories can help relationships go beyond transactional to more relational types of social exchanges. The real challenge today is to build deeper relationships in spite of work contexts that create less deep structural ties.

CONCLUSION

The world is changing, and a focus on relationships is becoming essential to understanding how new organizational forms are functioning in the dynamic, hypercompetitive contexts they face. A serious paradigm shift is needed in leadership research to keep up with this change. A focus on relational leadership—a deep examination of relational dynamics and how they influence the structure rather than only be influenced by it—may lead to entirely new ways to view leadership. In the present paper I begin to present a framework for exploring relational dynamics in the workplace. This framework, grounded in implicit theories and personal relationships literature, addresses "the human processes of how people decide, act, and present themselves to each other" (Murrell, 1997, p. 39). However, this framework is only a start, and much more work is needed to begin to more fully understand the nature of work relationships and how they operate within a system of relational leadership.

ACKNOWLEDGMENT

I would like to thank John Maslyn, Julie Sharek, and Russ Marion for their comments on this manuscript.

REFERENCES

Alvesson, M., & Sveningsson, S. (2003). The great disappearing act: Difficulties in doing "leadership." *Leadership Quarterly, 14*, 359.

Baldwin, M.W. (1992). Relational schemas and the processing of social information. *Psychological Bulletin, 112*, 461–484.

Bennis, W., Spreitzer, G.M., & Cummings, T. (Eds.). (2001). *The future of leadership: Today's top leadership thinkers speak to tomorrow's leaders.* San Francisco: Jossey-Bass.

Berscheid, E. (1994). Interpersonal relationships. *Annual Review of Psychology, 45*, 79–129.

Blau, P. (1964). *Exchange and power in social life.* New York: Wiley.

Boyd, N.G., & Taylor, R.R. (1998). A developmental approach to the examination of friendship in leader-follower relationships. *Leadership Quarterly, 9*, 1–25.

Brower, H.H., Schoorman, F.D., & Tan, H.H. (2000). A model of relational leadership: The integration of trust and leader-member exchange. *The Leadership Quarterly, 11*(2), 227–250.

Brown, D.J., & Lord, R.G. (2001). Leadership and perceiver cognition: Moving beyond first order constructs. In M. London (Ed.), *How people evaluate others in groups* (pp. 181–202). London: Earlbaum.

Bryman, A. (1996). Leadership in organizations. In S.R. Clegg, C. Hardy, & W. Nord (Eds.), *Handbook of organization studies* (pp. 276–292). London: Sage.

Burt, R.S. (1992). *Structural holes: The social structure of competition.* Cambridge, MA: Harvard University Press.

Chiu, C.-y., Hong, Y.-y., & Dweck, C.S. (1994). Toward an integrative model of personality and intelligence: A general framework and some preliminary steps. In R.J. Sternberg & P. Ruzgis (Eds.), *Personality and intelligence* (pp. 104–134). New York: Cambridge University Press.

Dachler, H.P. (1988). Constraints on the emergence of new vistas in leadership and management science: An epistemological overview. In J.G. Hunt, B.R. Baliga, H.P. Dachler, & C.A. Schriesheim (Eds.), *Emerging leadership vistas* (pp. 261–285). Lexington, MA: Lexington Books.

Dienesch, R.M., & Liden, R.C. (1986). Leader-member exchange model of leadership: A critique and further development. *Academy of Management Review, 11,* 618–634.

Drath, W. (2001). *The deep blue sea: Rethinking the source of leadership.* San Francisco: Jossey-Bass & Center for Creative Leadership.

Drucker, P. (1993). *Post-capitalist society.* Oxford: Butterworth-Heinemann.

Dweck, C.S. (1996). Implicit theories as organizers of goals and behaviors. In P.M. Gollwitzer & J.A. Bargh (Eds.), *The psychology of action* (pp. 69–90). New York: Guilford Press.

Dweck, C.S., Chiu, C., & Hong, Y. (1995a). Implicit theories and their role in judgments and reactions: A world from two perspectives. In *Psychological inquiry* (Vol. 6, pp. 267–285). Mahwah, NJ: Lawrence Erlbaum.

Dweck, C.S., Chiu, C.-y., & Hong, Y.-y. (1995b). Implicit theories: Elaboration and extension of the model. In *Psychological inquiry* (Vol. 6, pp. 322–333). Mahwah, NJ: Lawrence Erlbaum.

Dweck, C.S., & Elliott, E.S. (1983). Achievement motivation. In P.H. Mussen & E.M. Hetherington (Eds.), *Handbook of child psychology, Vol IV: Social and personality development* (pp. 643–691). New York: Wiley.

Dweck, C.S., & Leggett, E.L. (1988). A social-cognitive approach to motivation and personality. *Psychological Review, 25,* 109–116.

Eden, D., & Leviatan, U. (1975). Implicit leadership theory as a determinant of the factor structure underlying supervisory behavior scales. *Journal of Applied Psychology, 60,* 736–741.

Epitropaki, O., & Martin, R. (2004). Implicit leadership theories in applied settings: Factor structure, generalizability, and stability over time. *Journal of Applied Psychology, 89,* 293–310.

Erdley, C.A., & Dweck, C.S. (1993). Children's implicit personality theories as predictors of their social judgments. *Child Development, 64,* 863–878.

Fiske, S.T. (1998). Stereotyping, prejudice, and discrimination. In D.T. Gilbert & S.T. Fiske (Eds.), *Handbook of social psychology* (Vol. 2, 4th ed., pp. 357–411. New York: McGraw-Hill.

Fletcher, G.J.O., & Kininmonth, L. (1992). Measuring relationship beliefs: An individual differences measure. *Journal of Research in Personality, 26,* 371–397.

Fletcher, G.J.O., & Thomas, G. (1996). Close relationship lay theories: Their structure and function. In G.J.O. Fletcher & J. Fitness (Eds.), *Knowledge structures and interaction in close relationships: A social psychological approach* (pp. 3–24). Mahwah, NJ: Lawrence Earlbaum Associates Inc.

Fletcher, J.K. (2004). The paradox of postheroic leadership: An essay on gender, power, and transformational change. *Leadership Quarterly, 15,* 647–661.

Follett, M.P. (1941). In H.S. Metcalf & L. Urwick (Eds.), *Dynamic administration: The collected papers of Mary Parker Follett.* New York: Harper & Row.

Franiuk, R. (2003). Theories of relationships and their influence on relationship satisfaction and relationship processes. *Dissertation Abstracts International: Section B: The Sciences & Engineering* (Vol. 63, pp. 5567). Ann Arbor, MI: University Microfilms International.

Franiuk, R., Cohen, D., & Pomerantz, E.M. (2002). Implicit theories of relationships: Implications for relationship satisfaction and longevity. *Personal Relationships* (Vol. 9, pp. 345–367). Oxford: Blackwell Publishing Limited.

Franiuk, R., Pomerantz, E.M., & Cohen, D. (2004). The causal role of theories of relationships: Consequences for satisfaction and cognitive strategies. *Personality & Social Psychology Bulletin, 30*, 1494–1507).

Graen, G.B., & Scandura, T. (1987). Toward a psychology of dyadic organizing. In B.M. Staw & L.L. Cummings (Eds.), *Research in organizational behavior* (Vol. 9, pp. 175–208). Greenwich, CT: JAI Press.

Graen, G.B., & Uhl-Bien, M. (1995). Relationship-based approach to leadership: Development of leader-member exchange (LMX) theory of leadership over 25 years: Applying a multi-level multi-domain perspective. *Leadership Quarterly, 6*, 219–247.

Gronn, P. (1999). *A realist view of leadership.* Paper presented at the Educational leaders for the new millenium—leaders with soul, ELO-AusAsia On-line Conference.

Gronn, P. (2002). Distributed leadership as a unit of analysis. *Leadership Quarterly, 13*, 423.

Hargadon, A. (2003). *How breakthroughs happen.* Cambridge, MA: Harvard Business School Press.

Heider, F. (1958). *The psychology of interpersonal relations.* New York: Wiley.

Heifetz, R.A., & Laurie, D.L. (2001). The work of leadership. *Harvard Business Review, 79*(11), 131–141.

Holmes, J.G., & Rempel, J.K. (1989). Trust in close relationships. In C. Hendrick (Ed.), *Close relationships* (pp. 187–220). Beverly Hills, CA: Sage.

Hong, Y.-y., Chiu, C.-y., & Dweck, C.S. (1995). Implicit theories of intelligence: Reconsidering the role of confidence in achievement motivation. In M.H. Kernis (Ed.), *Efficacy, agency, and self-esteem* (pp. 197–216). New York: Plenum Press.

Hosking, D.M., Dachler, H.P., & Gergen, K.J. (Eds.). (1995). *Management and organization: Relational alternatives to individualism.* Brookfield, MA: Avebury.

Houts, R.M., Robins, E., & Huston, T.L. (1996). Compatibility and the development of premarital relationships. *Journal of Marriage & the Family, 58*, 7–20.

Hunt, J.G. (2004). What is leadership? In J. Antonakis, A.T. Cianciolo, & R.J. Sternberg, (Eds.), *The nature of leadership* (pp. 19–48). Beverly Hills, CA: Sage.

Hunt, J.G., & Dodge, G. (2000). Leadership deja vu all over again. *Leadership Quarterly, 11*, 435–458.

Jelinek, M., Smircich, L., & Hirsch, P. (1983). Introduction: A code of many colors. *Administrative Science Quarterly, 28*, 331.

Kauffman, S.A. (1993). *The origins of order.* New York: Oxford University Press.

Kelly, G.A. (1955). *The psychology of personal constructs.* New York: Norton.

Knee, C.R. (1998). Implicit theories of relationships: Assessment and prediction of romantic relationship initiation, coping, and longevity. *Journal of Personality and Social Psychology, 74*, 360–370.

Knee, C.R., Nanayakkara, A., Vietor, N.A., Neighbors, C., & Patrick, H. (2001). Implicit theories of relationships: Who cares if romantic partners are less than ideal? *Personality & Social Psychology Bulletin, 27*, 808–819.

Knee, C.R., Patrick, H., & Lonsbary, C. (2003). Implicit theories of relationships: Orientations toward evaluation and cultivation. *Personality & Social Psychology Review, 7*, 41–55.

Knee, C.R., Patrick, H., Vietor, N.A., Nanayakkara, A., & Neighbors, C. (2002). Self-determination as growth motivation in romantic relationships. *Personality & Social Psychology Bulletin, 28*, 609–619.

Knee, C.R., Patrick, H., Vietor, N.A., & Neighbors, C. (2004). Implicit theories of relationships: Moderators of the link between conflict and commitment. *Personality & Social Psychology Bulletin, 30*, 617–628.

Levy, S.R., Plaks, J.E., & Dweck, C.S. (1999). Modes of social thought: Implicit theories and social understanding. In S. Chaiken & Y. Trope (Eds.), *Dual-process theories in social psychology* (pp. 179–202). New York: Guilford.

Liden, R.C., & Maslyn, J.M. (1998). Multidimensionality of leader-member exchange: An empirical assessment through scale development. *Journal of Management, 24*(1), 43–72.

Liden, R.C., Sparrowe, R.T., & Wayne, S.J. (1997). Leader-member exchange theory: The past and potential for the future. In G.R. Ferris (Ed.), *Research in personnel and human resources management* (Vol. 15, pp. 47–119). Greenwich, CT: JAI Press.

Lipman-Blumen, J. (1996). *Connective leadership: Managing in a changing world.* New York: Oxford University Press.

Lord, R.G., Foti, R.J., & de Vader, C.L. (1984). A test of leadership categorization theory: Internal structure, information processing, and leadership perceptions. *Organizational Behavior & Human Performance, 34*, 343–378.

Lord, R.G., & Maher, K.J. (1990). Alternative information-processing models and their implications for theory, research, and practice. *Academy of Management Review, 15*, 9.

Lord, R.G., & Maher, K.J. (1991). Cognitive theory in industrial and organizational psychology. In M.D. Dunnette & L.M. Hough (Eds.), *Handbook of industrial and organizational psychology* (Vol. 2, 2nd ed., pp. 1–62). Consulting Psychologists Press, Inc.

Lord, R.G., & Maher, K.J. (1993). *Leadership and information processing: Linking perceptions and performance.* London: Routledge.

Lydon, J. (1999). Commitment and adversity: A reciprocal relation. In J.M. Adams & W.H. Jones (Eds.), *Handbook on interpersonal commitment and relationship stability* (pp. 193–203). New York: Plenum.

Mainzer, K. (1997). *Thinking in complexity* (3rd ed.). New York: Springer-Verlag.

Manz, C.C., & Sims Jr., H.P. (1987). Leading workers to lead themselves: The external leadership of self-managing work teams. *Administrative Science Quarterly, 32*, 106.

Marion, R. (1999). *The edge of organization: Chaos and complexity theories of formal social organization.* Newbury Park, CA: Sage.

Marion, R., & Uhl-Bien, M. (2001). Leadership in complex organizations. *Leadership Quarterly, 12*, 389–418.

Marion, R., & Uhl-Bien, M. (2005). A model of complex leadership. *Working Paper.*

Marks, G., & Miller, N. (1982). Target attractiveness as a mediator of assumed attitude similarity. *Personality & Social Psychology Bulletin, 8*, 728–735.

Mayer, R.C., Davis, J.H., & Schoorman, F.D. (1995). An integrative model of organizational trust. *Academy of Management Review, 20,* 709–734.

McKelvey, B. (2004). MicroStrategy from MacroLeadership: Distributed intelligence via new science. In A.Y. Lewin & H. Volberda (Eds.), *Mobilizing the self-renewing organization.* Armonk, NY: M. E. Sharp.

Miller, E.J. (1998). The leader with the vision: Is time running out? In E.B. Klein, F. Gabelnick, & P. Herr (Eds.), *The psychodynamics of leadership* (pp. 3–25). Madison, CT: Psychosocial Press.

Mitchell, M., & Uhl-Bien, M. (2004). *Exploring the relationship of trust and leader-member exchange: A social exchange perspective.* Paper presented at the Annual Meeting of the Academy of Management, New Orleans.

Murrell, K.L. (1997). Emergent theories of leadership for the next century: Towards relational concepts. *Organization Development Journal, 15*(3), 35–42.

Offermann, L.R., Kennedy, J.K., & Wirtz, P.W. (1994). Implicit leadership theories: Content, structure, and generalizability. *Leadership Quarterly, 5,* 43–58.

Osborn, R.N., Hunt, J.G., & Jauch, L.R. (1980). *Organization theory.* New York: John Wiley.

Patrick, H.A. (2003). The domain-specificity of implicit theories of relationships: Toward a more comprehensive model of relationship beliefs., *Dissertation Abstracts International: Section B: The Sciences & Engineering* (Vol. 64, pp. 2443). Ann Arbor, MI: University Microfilms International.

Pearce, C., & Sims, H. (2000). Shared leadership: Toward a multi-level theory of leadership. In M. Beyerlein, D. Johnson & S. Beyerlein (Eds.), *Advances in interdisciplinary studies of work teams* (Vol. 7, pp. 115–139). New York: JAI Press.

Pettigrew, A., Whittington, R., Melin, L., Sanchez-Runde, C., Van Den Bosch, F.A.J., Ruigrok, W., et al. (Eds.). (2003). *Innovative forms of organizing: International perspectives.* London: Sage.

Phillips, J.S. (1984). The accuracy of leadership ratings: A cognitive categorization perspective. *Organizational Behavior & Human Performance, 33,* 125–138).

Phillips, J.S., & Lord, R.G. (1986). Notes on the practical and theoretical consequences of implicit leadership theories for the future of leadership measurement. *Journal of Management, 12*(1), 31–41.

Poincaré, H. (1957). *Les méthodes nouvelles de la mécanique céleste.* New York: Dover Publications.

Prigogine, I. (1997). *The end of certainty.* New York: The Free Press.

Rands, M., & Levinger, G. (1979). Implicit theories of relationship: An intergenerational study. *Journal of Personality & Social Psychology, 37,* 645–661.

Rosenbaum, M.E. (1986). The repulsion hypothesis: On the nondevelopment of relationships. *Journal of personality and social psychology, 51,* 1156–1166.

Rusbult, C.E. (1980). Commitment and satisfaction in romantic associations: A test of the investment model. *Journal of Experimental Social Psychology, 16,* 172–186.

Rusbult, C.E. (1983). A longitudinal test of the investment model: The development (and deterioration) of satisfaction and commitment in heterosexual involvements. *Journal of Personality & Social Psychology, 45,* 101–117.

Rush, M.C., & Russell, J.E. (1988). Leader prototypes and prototype-contingent consensus in leader behavior descriptions. *Journal of Experimental Social Psychology, 24,* 88–104.

Ruvolo, A.P., & Rotondo, J.L. (1998). Diamonds in the rough: Implicit personality theories and views of partner and self. *Personality & Social Psychology Bulletin, 24*, 750–758.

Sayles, L.R. (1993). *The working leader.* New York: Free Press.

Seers, A. (1989). Team-member exchange quality: A new construct for role-making research. *Organizational Behavior & Human Decision Processes, 43*, 118.

Seers, A. (2004). Interpersonal workplace theory at a crossroads. In G.B. Graen (Ed.), *New frontiers of leadership* (LMX Leadership: The Series, Vol. 2, pp. 1–31). Greenwich, CT: Information Age.

Senge, P., & Kaeufer, K. (2001). Communities of leadership or no leadership at all. In S. Chowdhury (Ed.), *Management 21C* (pp. 186–204). New York: Prentice-Hall.

Sherony, K.M., & Green, S.G. (2002). Coworker exchange: Relationships between coworkers, leader-member exchange, and attitudes. *Journal of Applied Psychology, 87*, 542–548.

Shockley-Zalabak, P. (2002). Protean places: Teams across time and space. *Journal of Applied Communication Research, 30*, 231.

Stacey, R.D. (2001). *Complex responsive processes in organizations: Learning and knowledge creation.* London: Routledge.

Stacey, R.D., Griffin, D., & Shaw, P. (2000). *Complexity and management: Fad or radical challenge to systems thinking.* London and New York: Routledge.

Streatfield, P.J. (2001). *The paradox of control in organizations.* London: Routledge.

Thompson, E.G., & Phillips, J.L. (1977). The effects of asymmetric liking on the attribution of dominance in dyads. *Bulletin of the Psychonomic Society, 9*, 449–451.

Tsoukas, H. (1996). The firm as a distributed knowledge system: A constructionist approach. *Strategic Management Journal, 17*(Winter, Special Issue), 11–25.

Uhl-Bien, M. (2003). Relationship development as a key ingredient for leadership development. In S. Murphy & R. Riggio (Eds.), *The future of leadership development* (pp. 129–147). Mahwah, NJ: Lawrence Erlbaum Associates Inc.

Uhl-Bien, M., Graen, G., & Scandura, T. (2000). Implications of leader-member exchange (LMX) for strategic human resource management systems: Relationships as social capital for competitive advantage. In G.R. Ferris (Ed.), *Research in personnel and human resource management* (Vol. 18, pp. 137–185). Stamford, CT: JAI Press.

Uhl-Bien, M., Marion, R.A., & McKelvey, B. (2004). *Complex leadership: Shifting leadership from the industrial age to the knowledge era.* Paper presented at the National Academy of Management Meeting, New Orleans, LA.

Uhl-Bien, M., & Maslyn, J.M. (2003). Reciprocity in manager-subordinate relationships: Components, configurations, and outcomes. *Journal of Management, 29*, 511.

Uleman, J.S., Hon, A., Roman, R.J., & Moskowitz, G.B. (1996). On-line evidence for spontaneous trait inferences at encoding. *Personality & Social Psychology Bulletin, 22*, 377–394.

Volberda, H.W. (1996). Toward the flexible form: How to remain vital in hypercompetitive environments. *Organization Science, 7*(4), 359.

Wech, B.A. (2002). Team-member exchange and trust contexts: Effects on individual level outcome variables beyond the influence of leader-member exchange., *Dissertation Abstracts International Section A: Humanities & Social Sciences* (Vol. 62, pp. 2486). Ann Arbor, MI: University Microfilms International.

Yukl, G. (1999). An evaluation of conceptual weaknesses in transformational and charismatic leadership theories. *Leadership Quarterly, 10*(2), 285–305.

CHAPTER 5

IMPLICIT THEORIES OF LEADERSHIP AT DIFFERENT HIERARCHICAL LEVELS

Deanne N. Den Hartog and Paul L. Koopman

ABSTRACT

This chapter focuses on the context dependency of implicit leadership theories. We address two aspect of the context that may play a role, namely the type of leader considered and the background of the rater. Specifically, the chapter explores implicit theories of leadership for leaders at different hierarchical levels of the organization and looks at differences between male and female raters. We present a study among 2161 respondents (1198 males; 963 females), who rated the importance of 22 characteristics for being a good top manager and for being a good lower level manager or supervisor. Results show that charismatic characteristics (e.g., inspirational, visionary, innovative, persuasive) are considered more important for top managers, whereas supportive and people oriented characteristics (e.g., concern for subordinates' interests, compassionate, participative) are considered more important for lower level managers. Female raters consider dominance less desirable and people oriented characteristics, a long term orientation and diplomacy more important for leaders than males, whereas male raters consider the characteristics inspirational, rational and persuasive more important than female raters.

Implicit Leadership Theories: Essays and Explorations, pages 135–158
Copyright © 2005 by Information Age Publishing

INTRODUCTION

Some thirty years ago, Eden and Leviathan (1975) first studied implicit leadership theories (ILTs), or in other words the beliefs held by individuals about how leaders behave in general and what is expected of them. Their conclusion was that leadership factors, at least in part, are in the mind of the respondent. As Lord and Emrich (2001, p. 551) note: "If leadership resides, at least in part, in the minds of followers, then it is imperative to discover what followers are thinking." What followers think depends (at least in part) on the context, for instance, and this chapter addresses contextual factors that shape followers' leadership beliefs and perceptions. Relevant contextual influences can relate both to the type of leader followers thinking about and to the background of the follower. As Offermann, Kennedy, and Wirtz (1994) state, there has been a lack of attention to systematic variation of implicit theories across different leader stimuli and perceiver characteristics. This chapter addresses these points. It presents theory and a study aiming to highlight the differences in preferred leadership attributes for top-managers versus lower level managers and assesses potential gender differences in such perceptions or ILTs.

CONTEXT DEPENDENCY OF ILTS

As stated, ILTs refer to beliefs held about how leaders ought to behave and the characteristics leaders typically have. ILTs can be seen as personal constructs used to make judgments about leadership (Korukonda & Hunt, 1989). As is described in the introduction to this volume, leadership perceptions involve cognitive categorization processes in which perceivers match the perceived attributes of potential leaders they observe to an internal prototype of leadership categories (e.g., Foti & Luch, 1992). This internal prototype of leadership can be conceived as a collection of traits or attributes the perceiver sees as highly characteristic of leadership. The better the fit between the perceived individual (i.e., the leader) and the leadership prototype, the more likely this person will be seen as a leader (e.g., Epitropaki & Martin, 2004; Foti & Luch, 1992; Gerstner & Day, 1994; Offermann et al., 1994), For example, Bass and Avolio (1989) related leadership prototypes to ratings of transformational and transactional leadership. They showed that attributes respondents associated with their prototypical or "ideal" leader were much more highly correlated with transformational than with transactional leadership scales. Thus, prototypical leaders are characterized by visioning, charisma and intellectual stimulation and people showing such characteristics and behaviors are more likely to be perceived as leaders. Other studies have also tried to find factors representing ILTs across different organizational settings (e.g., Epitropaki & Martin, 2004).

This chapter specifically focuses on the context dependency of ILTs. Context profoundly affects perceptions of leaders. Emrich (1999) demonstrates that context can even affect perceptions of potential leaders. She found that a crisis context magnifies qualities that are consistent with individuals' ILTs. Participants perceived the same job candidate to display more leader qualities when his potential group was a troubled one rather than a tranquil one and described the candidate more favorably as a leader and in a test of recognition memory falsely recognized this person as having performed more leadership-consistent and fewer leadership-irrelevant behaviors.

There are different ways in which context plays a role in leadership perception. The first relates to the type of leader perceivers have in mind. In their work on categorization, Lord et al. (1982, 1984) propose a hierarchical organization of leadership categories with three levels that relates to context. The most general category of "leaders" (superordinate level) holds attributes common to most leaders that should overlap little with those of the contrasting category of "non-leaders." The middle-range (or basic) level categories are less inclusive and refine the notion of leadership by including situational or contextual information. This implies leaders are differentiated into specific types of leaders based on context, such as religious, military, political or business leaders. The attributes associated with religious leaders may differ (to some extent) from those associated with military leaders. At the lowest (subordinate) level, types of leaders within a context are differentiated (e.g., left or right wing political leaders). These subordinate categories are the least inclusive. One general distinction made within contexts is that between lower- and upper-level leaders, i.e., the inclusion of hierarchical information as well as contextual information. Examples are the differentiation by rank for military leaders or by position in the organizational hierarchy for business leaders (Lord & Maher, 1991). Here, we focus on this differentiation. Specifically, we compare preferred characteristics for leaders at different hierarchical levels of organizations (upper echelon versus lower level leaders).

A different way in which the context may play a role is that contextual influences may shape individual perception. Here we focus on gender differences in ILTs. Both individual and shared (elements of) ILTs exist and the ILTs of members of a group may be similar due to shared values or experiences. Shared ILTs are related to culture. In categorization terms, leadership can be seen as a so-called "fuzzy category" (Cantor & Mischel, 1979). A category is "fuzzy" when there are no signs that differentiate *all* members from *all* nonmembers. In such cases, people use abstract categorizations learned from others and transmitted through culture (Rosch,

1978; Lord et al., 1982). Thus, differences between perceivers in cultural background or socialization experiences could lead to differences in categorization and ILTs that are, to some extent, shared. Thus, to the extent they have different socialization experiences, men and women may have different ILTs (e.g., Ayman, 1993). Also, societal culture may shape the content of ILTs. For example, people from a culture valuing assertiveness may value dominance and toughness in leaders more than people from more passive cultures.

This chapter will address gender differences in leadership perception and ILTs in relation to hierarchical levels of the organization and present a study looking at these two points. However, before we go into more detail on gender and hierarchical level, we will illustrate the role of context in ILTs through the findings of the cross-cultural GLOBE study.

Cross-cultural Differences in ILTs: The GLOBE Study

The GLOBE research project provides more insight in cross-cultural differences in the content of ILTs. The GLOBE study was done among more than 15,000 middle managers from 60 countries from all major regions of the world, who indicated which leader attributes and behaviors they thought would enhance or impede outstanding leadership in their context (House et al., 1999, 2002, 2004). This study found that several leader characteristics were universally valued. These include several attributes reflecting transformational or charismatic leadership. For instance, in all countries involved in the study, an outstanding leader is expected to be encouraging, positive, motivational, a confidence builder, dynamic, and to have foresight. Such a leader is decisive, excellence oriented, and intelligent. Around the world, an outstanding leader is expected to be trustworthy, just, and honest. A team orientation is also universally seen as important for outstanding leaders. They need to be good at team building, communicating and coordinating. Also, several attributes were universally viewed as ineffective, including being non-cooperative, ruthless, non-explicit, a loner, irritable, and dictatorial (Den Hartog et al., 1999; Dorfman et al., 2004).

Although some characteristics were universally valued or disliked, the importance of many leader attributes varied across cultures. For instance, characteristics such as cautious, elitist or unique are considered desirable for leaders in some cultures, but undesirable in others. Cultural differences play a role here (for large scale studies on national culture dimensions, see, e.g., Hofstede, 2001 or House et al., 2004). Several of the leader attributes that were found to vary across cultures reflect preferences for high power distance versus egalitarianism in society. For example, status and class-conscious, elitist, and domineering are attributes that are appreciated for leaders in some but not in other cultures. Also, being perceived as a risk taker, habitual, procedural, able to anticipate, formal, cautious, and orderly impede outstanding leadership in some countries and enhance it in others. These leader characteristics seem to reflect differences in cultural uncertainty avoidance, which as a culture dimension refers to the tolerance for ambiguity. Also, being autonomous, unique, and independent contribute to outstanding leadership in some cultures and form a barrier in others. This is linked to different cultural preferences for individualism or collectivism. Finally, differences were found in appreciation of characteristics such as subdued and enthusiastic that seem to reflect differences in cultural rules regarding the appropriate expression of emotion. In some cultures, a display of emotion is interpreted as a lack of self-control, a sign of weakness. In others, it is hard to be seen as an effective leader and communicator without vividly expressing emotions (Den Hartog et al., 1999).

The GLOBE study illustrates how the cultural background of the perceiver may shape leadership perceptions. In this chapter, we also address whether gender plays such a role. Do the ILTs of men and women differ?

GENDER DIFFERENCES IN ILTS

Most studies have focused on communalities in implicit theories, whereas relatively few studies have focused on possible individual or group level differences. However, some exceptions exist (e.g., Keller, 1999). In her work on individual differences, Keller found that individuals' idealized leadership images in part reflect their personality traits. For example, agreeable individuals characterized their ideal leader as sensitive, and dedication was valued by conscientious individuals. Other perceiver characteristics may also be relevant. For example, Ayman (1993) suggests that gender might affect expectations of leaders. Gender differences in the structure of perceptions of leadership might result from differences in socialization history and experiences with leaders (Offermann et al., 1994). Such differences may lead women to value different behaviors and characteristics in leaders than men.

There are different streams of research on gender differences in leadership. Much research in this area focuses on whether there are differences in leader behavior between men and women. Recent studies on gender differences in leader behavior focus on ratings of transformational and transactional leadership behavior (see, for instance, the meta-analytical review by Eagly, Johansen-Schmidt, & Van Engen, 2003, or studies by Bass, Avolio, & Atwater, 1996; Maher, 1997; Yammarino et al., 1997). Although some studies do not find differences between men and women, the meta-analysis on gender and transformational leadership does suggest that women tend to display somewhat more transformational leader behavior than men. An interesting question in this type of research would be how women's leader behavior is rated in predominantly or traditionally male environments (e.g., Boyce & Herd, 2003). Here we focus on perceptions of leadership rather than ratings of actual leader behavior.

An influential line of research on gender and leadership perception addresses which leadership characteristics are associated more with men than with women. Research shows that individuals hold a stereotype of the successful manager that is more like their stereotype of men in general than of women in general (e.g., Brenner, Tomkiewicz & Schein, 1989; Schein, 2001). Successful managers are viewed as more similar to men than to women on attributes considered critical to effective work performance, such as leadership ability, self-confidence, ambition, assertiveness, and forcefulness (Heilman, Block, Martell, & Simon, 1989; Schein, 1973). Although these studies were done some time ago, more recently, Schein (2001) found that this pattern still held and replicated it in several countries (China, Japan, UK, Germany, United States). Descriptions of women in general were still less congruent with descriptions of successful managers than those of men in general. These stereotypes hold for male and female perceivers; however, evidence suggests the effect is stronger for men. Thus, men are often seen as more assertive, achieving, and dominant and women as more socially responsive, passive, and submissive, especially by men (Den Hartog, 2004). Such characteristics refer to sex-trait *stereotypes*. The *real* differences in behavior between the sexes are far less pronounced than the *beliefs* about those differences (Segall, Dasen, Berry, & Poortinga, 1990). Also, these views may be changing as more women enter the managerial ranks and are seen to successfully perform leadership roles. For example, somewhat less traditional views of leadership were found in a recent study on managerial gender typing among management students in Australia, Germany and India, especially among female participants (Sczesny, Bosak, Neff, & Schyns, 2004). Nevertheless, they found an interculturally shared view of a female-specific leadership competence according to which women are seen as more person-oriented than men.

Male and Female ILTs: Similar or Different?

In the study we report in this chapter, we took yet another approach to studying gender and leadership. We explore whether men and women differ in their implicit theories or prototypes of good leaders. Do males and females see the same characteristics as important? Such possible gender differences in ILTs have not received much attention so far. Notable exceptions include the work by Graves and Powell (1982) and Offermann et al. (1994). Offermann and her colleagues looked at the content and factor structure variations in ILTs for male and female perceivers across three stimuli: leaders, effective leaders, and supervisors and found that implicit theories of leaders as well as effective leaders were generally more favorable than implicit theories of supervisors. They did not find systematic gender differences in the prototypicality ratings or factor structure of the implicit theories they measured. However, the aforementioned research on perceptions of men and women suggests differences in how men and women in the leadership role are perceived. Such differences might extend to the ILTs held by men and women, so that women may value social, person-oriented and transformational characteristics more than men, who may place more emphasis on task-oriented, assertive and dominant characteristics of leaders.

In the study we present below, we build on previous research in two ways. First, we readdress the question of possible gender differences in perceptions and test whether they are found in the study, and second, we look at the content of prototypes of effective leaders at different hierarchical levels. Thus, besides looking at gender differences in characteristics associated with successful leaders, we compare whether both men and women rate the importance of characteristics differently for different types of leaders. Specifically, we compare preferred characteristics for leaders at different hierarchical levels (upper echelon versus lower level leaders). Before we turn to the study we address the perception of leaders at different hierarchical levels in more detail.

ILTs and Hierarchical Level

As stated, regarding ILTs, an important distinction is that between lower- and upper-level leaders, i.e., the inclusion of hierarchical information as well as contextual information in ILTs. As Lord and Maher note, "perceptual processes that operate with respect to leaders are very likely to involve quite different considerations at upper versus lower hierarchical levels" (1991, p. 97). As demands, tasks and responsibilities at different hierarchical levels are quite different, it seems likely that preferred leader attributes also differ for the different levels. In other words the implicit theory people hold regarding an effective top-manager or CEO is likely to differ from the implicit theory they hold for an effective supervisor or lower level manager.

Effectiveness of a pattern of behavior is in part dependent on the hierarchical level of leaders. At upper levels of organizations (the strategic echelon) the work of leaders is quite different than at lower levels (see, e.g., Waldman & Yammarino, 1999). According to Antonakis and Atwater (2002), research shows that high-level leaders show qualitatively different behaviors than low-level leaders. In Etzioni's (1961) view, top-management is concerned with ends rather than means; middle management with means more than ends and lower level management or supervisors are instrumental performers. Katz and Kahn (1978, p.539) present a model in which top echelons of the organization are concerned with "origination" (change, creation and elimination of structure). At this level charismatic leadership and a system perspective are needed. Intermediate levels are concerned with "interpolation" (supplementing and piecing out structure) and need human relations skills and a two-way perspective. Lower levels are concerned with "administration" (use of the existing structure), requiring a concern with equity in use of rewards and sanctions as well as technical knowledge and an understanding of rules. Followers expect different behaviors and characteristics from top echelon leaders than from intermediate or lower level leaders, thus, to be considered effective, top managers might need to display different characteristics than supervisors.

At upper levels in the organization influence is often indirect. There is usually less face-to-face contact with shop-floor workers and more indirect influence through association with significant organizational events and the development of norms and values in the organization. Due to the nature of the work which involves effectively communicating with different audiences through varied means, developing a broad systems perspective and accurately perceiving both internal and external environments, top management leadership is much more cognitively demanding than lower level leadership (Lord & Maher, 1991). Hunt, Boal, and Sorensen (1990) distinguish between top level leader's direct effects, for instance their choice of markets or design of organizational structure and their indirect effects. The indirect effects involve operating in the symbolic domain, for instance, by articulating values. Yammarino (1994) focuses on the distinction between direct and indirect leadership in a somewhat different sense. Rather than referring to direct or indirect effects, he uses the term direct leadership to describe the relationships between focal leaders and their immediate followers or direct reports. This type of direct leadership has been the subject of extensive research for leaders at various levels and in many settings, whereas our understanding of indirect leadership, i.e., the influence of leaders on those not directly reporting to them, is more limited (Yukl, 1999).

Besides differences between leadership prototypes, perceptions and behaviors due to hierarchical level or focusing on direct or indirect leadership there is a third distinction made in this regard which refers to a large or small (social) distance between leader and followers (see Antonakis &

Atwater, 2002, for an overview). Social distance refers to the psychological distance between the top-echelon and the rank-and-file memberships of an organization (Katz & Kahn, 1978). Thus, social distance has to do with the intimacy of the relationship between leaders and followers. Katz and Kahn see charisma as important for top echelon leaders and state that charisma requires some psychological distance between leader and follower. As such, charisma is less likely in close leadership situations according to them, because day-to-day intimacy would destroy the illusion needed for charisma. A leader in the top echelon would be sufficiently distant from most organization members to make a simplified and almost magical image possible (Katz & Kahn, 1978).

ILTs and Social Distance

In an article on the relationship between social distance and charismatic leadership, Shamir (1995) proposes that the perception of distant charismatic leaders is more prototypical than the perception of close charismatic leaders. He bases this proposition on the fact that in most situations people receive only scant and indirect information about leaders at a large social distance. In a close leadership situation subordinates interact with a leader directly. They are exposed to much richer and more varied information. Among other things this would mean that perceptions of distant charismatic leaders should be more similar to each other than perceptions of close charismatic leaders (Shamir, 1995). Yagil (1998) examined the attribution of charisma to socially close and distant leaders. Yagil found that the attribution of charisma to socially close leaders is related to the ascription of extraordinary traits to the leader and to the perception both of the leader as a behavioral model and of his/her confidence in the individual. The attribution of charisma to distant leaders was related to a willingness to accept the leader's ideas, the perceived confidence of the leader in the group, the ascription of extraordinary traits to the leader, and a general positive impression of the leader.

Shamir (1995) notes that the ideas underlying studies of charismatic leadership are often derived from theories assuming distant leadership. However, the empirical tests are usually conducted in situations of close leadership. In his study, Shamir assessed which behaviors, characteristics and effects are more associated with close, distant or both types of charismatic leadership. He found that rhetorical skills, persistence, courage and an ideological orientation were more often attributed to distant charismatic leaders. Sociability, consideration, openness, a sense of humor, expertise, competence, setting high standards, energy, dynamism and originality were more frequently attributed to close charismatic leaders.

Self-confidence, dominance, sacrifice, personal example, honesty and negative traits and behaviors were attributed equally to close and distant charismatic leaders. From these results it seems likely that charismatic leadership is indeed found both at a large and small social distance but that the behaviors and characteristics inducing the attribution of charisma are different for these two types of leadership. Close charismatic leadership entails personal contact on a frequent basis, ensuring that subordinates have more information about the leader's personal behavior, probably resulting in a more realistic picture of the leader. Also, subordinates can rely on what leaders do instead of just what they say, increasing the importance of role modeling and decreasing the importance of, for instance, a leader's rhetoric.

GENDER, HIERARCHY AND ILTS: A STUDY

The study presented in this chapter focuses on what perceivers consider successful leaders at upper or lower levels in the organization and whether there are gender differences in these perceptions. In other words, we studied implicit theories of effective top-level and lower level leadership for men and women.

Expectations

In the study, respondents are asked to rate how important a number of characteristics are to be a good top-level and lower-level leader. As stated, the development and communication of an attractive vision were associated more with distant leadership (Shamir, 1995). Realization of goals ensuing from the vision calls for a long-term perspective and redistribution of resources (Hunt, 1991; Mintzberg, 1989). Power and influence regarding long-term policies as well as distribution of resources is usually located at the upper levels of organizations. Thus, it seems likely that perceivers rate characteristics that have to do with the aforementioned, such as long-term orientation, an eye for innovation and vision as more important for top-managers than for lower-level managers. The more political nature of the job probably also leads to valuing characteristics such as diplomacy and persuasiveness as more important for top-level leaders. On the other hand, lower-level managers are usually responsible for daily operations and interact closely and often with their subordinates. As compared with top-managers an increased emphasis of operational skills and social interaction seem likely. Thus, the expectation is that the importance for being a good leader of characteristics such as compassionate, attention for the needs of subordinates and orderly should be rated higher for lower-level managers than for top-level managers. We expect that for both levels women will emphasize the importance of person-oriented characteristics and social competence more than men, whereas men value task oriented attributes and dominance more than women.

Methodology of the Study

To test these ideas, we conducted a study among 2161 respondents who are part of a computerized panel in the Netherlands. The panel members are sent questionnaires about diverse topics on a regular basis and fill out the questionnaires in their own home at a moment of their own choice. The sample for the current study consists of all members of the households who were at least 19 years of age and had at least one year of current or previous work experience. In total, 1198 men and 963 women participated. Their ages varied between 19 and 90, with an average age of 49 years old. Respondents' highest level of education varied widely (ranging from no or only primary education to college/university degrees).

In this study we measured leadership perceptions through questionnaires. Respondents were first asked to rate the importance of a list of 22 characteristics for being a good or outstanding top-manager (manager of a company), and next to rate the importance of the same characteristics for being a good or outstanding lower level manager (a department manager or supervisor). Thus, the manipulation of rating high versus low level managers was done within-subjects. Importance of the 22 characteristics was rated on a 5-point Likert type scale ranging from a low of "hardly important" to a high of "essential" (see also Den Hartog et al., 1999). As the chosen method is rather costly, no more than 44 items could be presented, thus, 22 items reflecting a wide range of characteristics possibly associated with leaders were chosen. An overview of the items used in this study and the instruction is presented in Figure 5.1.

Results of the Study

Before looking at item level comparisons, we first conducted a multivariate analysis of variance was performed to assess overall differences for top and lower level. The within-subjects effect indicating overall differences was significant at the .00 level (Hotellings T = 1.24, F-value = 120.45).

Next, we performed univariate paired samples T-tests comparing the importance ratings of the 22 characteristics for top and lower level leadership. These item level comparisons were performed in order to assess

The instruction given to respondents was as follows:

Below you will find a list of characteristics of leaders/managers in organizations. Could you identify which of these characteristics are important to be a good leader? In judging the importance of the characteristics two types of leaders are distinguished. First we ask you to rate the importance of these characteristics for being a good top manager, that is a leader of an organization. Second we would like you to rate the importance of the same characteristics for being a leader lower in the organization, a departmental manager or supervisor. Which characteristics are important to being a good leader of an organization a good top manager? (or "a good leader of a department or supervisor?" in the second part). Items were judged on a five point scale ranging from 1—hardly important to 5—essential. The characteristics that were used are:

Inspirational	Orderly
Innovative	Compassionate
Formal	Long term oriented
Trustworthy	Team builder
Communicative	Integrating (viewpoints and interests)
Dominant	Participative, allowing room for subordinate's
Vision	opinions
Concern for subordinate's	Confidence builder
interests	Calm
Modest	Courageous, not afraid to risk his/her neck
Rational	Diplomatic
Persuasive/Convincing	Self-knowledge

Figure 5.1.   The items and instruction used in this study.

whether certain characteristics are judged more important at certain hierarchical levels (see also Den Hartog et al., 1999). In other words, do respondents judge certain characteristics as more important for good top level leaders and others as more important for lower level leaders? Table 5.1 presents the results of T-tests comparing the perceived importance of each characteristic for top and lower level leaders. In general, the characteristics dominant, formal and modest score low for both top and lower level managers. These characteristics could be considered undesirable for managers. Modesty, however, is considered less negative for lower than for higher level managers and dominance is considered less negative for higher than for lower level managers. For three characteristics (trustworthy, communicative and calm), the differences are not significant. These characteristics are considered equally important for both types of managers. For several other characteristics the difference is significant but small (namely formal, inspirational, rational and confidence builder). The differences on the remaining items are larger. Characteristics such as innovative, visionary, persuasive, long-term oriented, diplomatic and courageous are considered more important for good top managers than for lower level managers. Lower-level managers score higher on characteristics such as attention for subordinates, team building, compassionate, and participative. Such social and participative characteristics are deemed more important for lower level managers than for top managers to be successful.

Table 5.1. T-tests on Differences in Rated Importance for Being a Good Top Manager or Lower-level Manager of 22 Characteristics

Characteristic	Top	Low	T-value	Characteristic	Top	Low	T-value
Inspirational	3.73	3.81	-3.48^{**}	Orderly	3.17	3.60	-20.92^{**}
Innovative	4.09	3.61	23.20^{**}	Compassionate	3.02	3.73	-32.75^{**}
Formal	2.64	2.50	6.23^{**}	Long-term oriented	4.10	3.35	31.15^{**}
Trustworthy	4.35	4.31	2.26^{ns}	Team builder	3.71	4.18	-20.12^{**}
Communicative	4.00	4.02	$-.83^{ns}$	Integrating	3.77	3.55	10.89^{**}
Dominant	2.46	2.19	12.13^{**}	Participative	3.66	4.13	-21.92^{**}
Visionary	4.15	3.49	30.73^{**}	Builds confidence	4.00	4.13	-7.27^{**}
Concern for subord.'s interests	3.81	4.36	-24.56^{**}	Calm	3.60	3.59	$.52^{ns}$
Modest	2.26	2.69	-20.27^{**}	Courageous	3.98	3.74	12.29^{**}
Rational	3.41	3.26	8.27^{**}	Diplomatic	3.78	3.44	16.33^{**}
Persuasive	4.14	3.90	13.79^{**}	Self-knowledge	3.87	3.72	8.53^{**}

n = 2161, ns = not significant, *difference significant at .01, ** difference significant at .001

Further item level independent sample T-tests were performed to test for possible gender differences in valuing characteristics. In other words, do men value certain characteristics more or less than women do? For independent sample T-tests the Levene statistic was used to determine whether variances were equal and the appropriate T-value (either for equal or unequal variances) was chosen accordingly. The mean rating for each characteristic was computed by averaging the rating for top and lower managers. Table 5.2 presents these average scores on the characteristics and T-tests showing differences in means for male and female raters on several characteristics. Highest mean scores are found for characteristics trustworthy, building confidence, concern for subordinate's interests, persuasive and communicative. Female respondents rate the importance of concern for subordinates' interest higher than men, whereas men consider persuasive more important than women. Male raters consider inspirational more important than female raters, whereas female raters consider compassionate and participative more important than male raters. Also, women consider diplomatic and long-term oriented more important than men,

Table 5.2. Mean Scores and T-tests for Differences for Male and Female Raters on the 22 Averaged Scores on the Characteristics

Characteristic	mean	male	female	T-value	Characteristic	mean	male	female	T-value
Inspirational	3.77	3.83	3.71	3.48**	Orderly	3.38	3.35	3.42	-1.79ns
Innovative	3.85	3.85	3.85	-.09ns	Compassionate	3.37	3.28	3.48	-5.99**
Formal	2.57	2.54	2.60	-1.34ns	Long-term oriented	3.72	3.68	3.78	-3.39**
Trustworthy	4.33	4.32	4.36	-1.38ns	Team builder	3.94	3.97	3.91	2.04ns
Communicative	4.01	4.00	4.02	-.86ns	Integrating	3.66	3.65	3.69	-1.31ns
Dominant	2.33	2.43	2.20	5.88**	Participive	3.90	3.85	3.95	-3.49*
Visionary	3.82	3.84	3.80	1.14ns	Builds confidence	4.06	4.03	4.10	-2.30ns
Concern for subordinate's interests	4.08	3.99	4.19	-6.64**	Calm	3.60	3.60	3.60	-.04ns
Modest	2.47	2.45	2.49	-1.11ns	Courageous	3.86	3.86	3.87	-.37ns
Rational	3.34	3.39	3.27	3.74**	Diplomatic	3.61	3.55	3.69	-3.94*
Persuasive	4.02	4.06	3.97	3.07*	Self-knowledge	3.79	3.76	3.84	-2.16ns

total sample n = 2161, male respondents n = 1198, female respondents n = 963, ns = not significant, *difference significant at .01, **difference significant at .001

whereas men consider rational more important than women. Dominance, formal and modesty score low (mean < 3). Female respondents score dominant as even less desirable for managers than male respondents.

Besides item level comparisons, a more general factor structure underlying these perceptions for leaders at both levels is also of interest. It could well be that besides mean differences for certain characteristics, respondents perceive different "clusters" as important at different levels or items take on a different meaning in different contexts. In other words, is the factor structure the same when focusing on top-level leaders as it is for lower-level leaders or are different structures found? Before assuming that one factor structure represents perceptions of both preferred top and lower management without too much loss of information, the correlation matrices between the items for top and lower level were compared. We found that the correlation matrix of the items for top managers was highly similar to that of items for lower level management, and concluded that the underlying structure was similar enough to identify one factor structure.

Next, we did a principal component factor analyses with rotation on the averaged scores using a randomly selected half of the respondents (n = 1080). The results indicate that a three factor structure reflects the data best. The first factor (12 items) represents charismatic leadership, with items such as visionary, innovative, inspirational, convincing and courageous. The second factor only has 2 items (dominant and formal) and seems to represent a distancing and aloof manager. The third factor (5 items) presents a people oriented manager, the items compassionate, participative, concern for subordinates as well as orderly and modest load on this factor. Three items loaded on two factors (1 and 3). To minimize overlap they were not included in further analyses, namely trustworthy, calm and self-knowledge. Table 5.3 presents the loadings of the items on the factors. Loadings for the items used in further analyses are printed in bold. For one of the scales the reliability was low and care is needed in interpreting that factor (see Table 5.3). The stability of the found factor structure was assessed through a confirmatory factor analysis on the remaining random half of the sample (using EQS; Bentler & Wu, 1995). The results showed that the fit of the model needed improvement. This was achieved by having items load on two factors. The items orderly and modest were allowed to load on both factors 2 and 3 and item 18, confidence builder was allowed to load both factors 1 and 3 (final fit statistics were .90 NNFI and .90 CFI; see Table 5.4 for a summary of the changes and reliability analyses).

Thus, again, three main factors were found: Charismatic/Inspirational leadership; Supportive/Managerial leadership and Distancing/Aloof leadership. For the total sample, charismatic/inspirational is rated highest (3.81) and distancing/aloof leadership lowest (2.69). In other words, in

Table 5.3.   Factor loadings of items on the three factors of the exploratory factor analysis and Cronbach α's for the resulting scales

Items	Factor 1 Charismatic α = .91	Factor 2 Distant/aloof α = .59	Factor 3 Support/ managerial α = .78
Inspirational	.64	−.03	−.07
Innovative	.62	.05	.01
Formal	−.01	**.60**	.29
Trustworthy	.44	−.23	.28
Communicative	**.70**	−.12	−.06
Dominant	.22	**.59**	−.12
Visionary	**.76**	−.02	−.14
Concern for s interests	.17	−.21	**.59**
Modest	−.12	.26	.58
Rational	**.58**	.22	−.02
Persuasive/Convincing	.66	.14	−.01
Orderly	.21	.19	**.44**
Compassionate	.09	−.04	.69
Long-term oriented team builder	**.55**	.07	.12
Integrating	.64	.07	.08
Participative	.66	.00	.07
Builds confidence	.29	−.24	**.49**
Calm	.52	−.14	.32
Courageous	.33	.17	.37
Diplomatic	.51	.05	.19
Self-knowledge	.50	.19	.12

Table 5.4.   Reliability Analyses for the Factors After Confirmatory Factor Analyses

Factor	Number of items	Mean score	α	Average (range) of intercorrelations among items	Range of item–rest correlations	Changes after confirmatory analyses
1. Charismatic	12	3.81	.91	.44 (.31–.57)	.34–.53	none
2. Distancing/ Aloof	4	2.69	.63	.30 (.17–.42)	.33–.56	items orderly; modest added
3. Supportive/ Operational	5	3.44	.83	.43 (.27–.59)	.41–.60	item confidence builder added

general the charismatic/inspirational attributes are valued most. T-tests for gender differences on the three mean factor scores show that only the difference on the third factor (supportive/ managerial) is significant. Women score significantly higher on this factor than men. Scale scores for both top and lower leadership were calculated by taking the corresponding items referring to the two levels and calculating the mean. A mean score for top level charisma, for instance, is calculated by averaging the ratings for top level leaders on the 12 items in this scale. These mean scores for the two levels were then compared using T-tests. Table 5.5 presents the differences in means for top and lower level both for the total sample and separately for male and female respondents.

Table 5.5. Differences of Importance of Characteristics for Top and Lower Levels for the Total Sample and for Male and Female Raters

	Total sample (n = 2161)			Male raters (n = 1198)			Female raters (n = 963)		
	Top	Low	T-value	Top	Low	T-value	Top	Low	T-value
1. Charismatic	3.91	3.71	23.24^{**}	3.93	3.68	21.06^{**}	3.87	3.73	11.29^{**}
2. Distancing/ aloof	2.63	2.74	-9.96^{**}	2.62	2.76	-8.80^{**}	2.64	2.72	-5.06^{**}
3. Support/ managerial	3.32	3.77	-35.76^{**}	3.25	3.73	-27.68^{**}	3.40	3.81	-22.73^{**}

**difference significant at .001

Table 5.6. Differences between Male and Female Raters on Rated Importance of Factors for Top and Lower Levels of Leadership

	Male raters (n = 1198)	Female raters (n = 963)	T-value
1a. Charismatic top	3.93	3.87	2.67^{**}
1b. Charismatic low	3.68	3.73	-2.26^{*}
2a. Distancing top	2.62	2.64	$-.31^{ns}$
2b. Distancing low	2.76	2.72	1.55^{ns}
3a. Support top	3.25	3.40	-5.15^{**}
3b. Support low	3.73	3.81	-3.19^{**}

ns = not significant, *difference significant at .05, **difference significant at .01

Many of the differences in means between male and female raters are also significant, see Table 5.6. For charismatic leadership, males rate the importance higher than female raters for top level leaders. However, in contrast, for lower level leaders women rate charisma as more important than men. This difference is very small though ($t = -2.26$, $p = .02$). Differences between male and female raters for factor 2 are not significant. For factor 3 (support) both at top and lower level female raters score the importance significantly higher.

DISCUSSION OF THE FINDINGS OF THE STUDY AND IMPLICATIONS

This study aimed to highlight the differences in what respondents perceive as important to successful top-level and lower-level leadership, i.e., their implicit theories of what good leadership at these levels entails, and to explore possible gender differences in these perceptions. Both differences between ILTs for these two levels and gender differences were found.

The results of the detailed item-level analyses show that characteristics such as being trustworthy, inspirational and communicative are considered important for both types of managers. Good top managers should also be innovative, visionary, persuasive, long-term oriented, diplomatic and courageous. Dominant and formal are less desirable characteristics, which also goes for modesty. Modesty, however, is considered less negative for lower than for top level managers and dominance less negative for top than for lower level managers. Good lower-level managers should be more social and participation oriented; characteristics such as attention for subordinates, team building and participative are judged more important for these managers than for top managers. Thus, the expectation that charismatic components, long-term orientation and innovativeness would be valued more for top level leaders and supportive, managerial and people oriented characteristics more for lower level leaders was confirmed.

Averaging the scores on characteristics for top and lower level shows how important the characteristics are for managers more in general in the eyes of the respondents. Highest mean scores are found for characteristics trustworthy, building confidence, concern for subordinate's interests, persuasive and communicative. These elements are seen as important for leaders in general. Testing differences between male and female raters shows that women consider concern for subordinates interest more important than men, whereas men find persuasive more important than women. Also, high are means for the characteristics team builder, participative, courageous, innovative, visionary, self-knowledge, and inspirational. Men consider inspirational more important than women, whereas female raters consider participative more important than male raters. Considered relatively important are: long-term oriented, integrating, diplomatic, calm, rational, and orderly. Women consider diplomatic and long-term oriented more important than men, whereas men consider rational more important than women. Less desirable for leaders are the characteristics formal, modest and dominant. Interestingly, females rate dominance to be even less desirable than men.

Three interpretable factors were also found. The first factor, combining characteristics such as inspirational, innovative, visionary, communicative, persuasive, and courageous, seems to reflect charismatic leadership. Charismatic leadership is considered more important for top level leaders than for lower level leaders. Interestingly, although both men and women rate charisma to be more important at the top than at the lower level, men rate the importance of charisma higher for top level leaders than women but women rate it more important than men at the lower level. The second factor, combining formal, dominant, orderly and modest reflects an aloof and emotionally uninvolved leader, who keeps contact formal and to a minimum. The factor has two characteristics (orderly and modest) in common with the third factor. This last factor combines participative, concern for subordinates interests and compassionate with orderly and modesty and seems to reflect a supportive, people oriented leader with managerial skills. This factor scores higher for lower level than for top level leaders and women rate the importance of this factor higher at both the top and lower level.

One limitation of the current study is the relatively small number of characteristics rated. Future research could involve a broader set of characteristics, perhaps more attuned to the different leadership contexts. Further research into both the effects of context and the effects of rater characteristics on leadership perceptions seems important. A very important context factor in this regard is societal culture. For instance, as suggested by the aforementioned GLOBE study, attributes that are seen as characteristic, desirable or prototypical for leaders may vary in different cultures. The current study took place in the Netherlands, it may well be that the emphasis on certain characteristics rather than others or even the entire factor structure is different in other societies. Further research on differences between prototypes of leaders in different leadership roles or contexts and how they come about is of interest.

Other lines of cross-cultural research are also of interest. For example, research could address whether the protoypicality of leaders within given cultures is important for the attribution of charisma. Do leaders need to match the prototypes of effective leadership held in a given society to be seen as charismatic? In a first vignette study on this topic performed in two cultures, Ensari and Murphy (2003) show that the attribution of charisma to leaders is based both on high performance outcomes and leader prototypicality ratings. Prototypicality was more important for the attribution of charisma in the US than in Turkey. Future research could further address the role of prototypicality in attribution of charisma in different cultures. In different types of cross-cultural studies in this area, De Voe and Iyengaar (2003) address managers theories held about subordinates, which also seems like an interesting area to explore further when it comes to the role of perception in the leadership process.

The current study shows gender differences in the appreciation of certain leader characteristics. Such gender differences concerning leadership preferences may be universal, but more likely they exist in some cultures but not in others. The fact that Offermann et al. (1994) did not find gender differences whereas this study did, may be due to methodological differences (design, sampling) or differences in the content of items. However, it is also possible that there are stronger gender differences concerning preferred leadership in the Netherlands than in the United States. Further research into how and why rater characteristics associated with different socialization experiences (e.g., gender, generation, level or type of education, profession) could lead to different leader prototypes is important. Besides gender, other rater characteristics may also be of interest.

The findings in this study suggest that level of the leader is an important characteristic to consider when researching the effectiveness of leaders of or within the organization. Behavior and effectiveness are influenced by differential expectations of subordinates at these levels which should be taken into account when researching and drawing conclusions about the effects of leader behavior. Another interesting line of research which is not addressed in the current study concerns possible differential implicit theories for male and female leaders. Do people (or maybe only men or women) expect different behavior from women as they take on the leadership role? And, are these expectations changing as more women are entering the managerial ranks? Only partial and incomplete conclusions can be drawn on basis of the existing literature. Both the issue of implicit theories especially across cultures and the relation of implicit theories to gender of both rater and leader deserve further attention.

In the study, we focused on perceptions of good or effective leadership at the different levels, not about leadership in general. It may well be that different images would come to mind had respondents been asked to indicate what they saw as typical leader behavior at that level. Such images of typical leadership may also change more over time than those of good or successful leadership. For example, the ethical scandals involving top managers of highly reputable firms were covered extensively in the media and may have made people more cynical about the typical behavior of top managers.

In sum, the study presented in this chapter shows differences in characteristics that are considered important for top-level versus lower level leaders in organizations. The expectation that charismatic leadership, long-term orientation and innovativeness would be valued more for top level leaders and supportive, managerial and people oriented characteristics more for lower level leaders was confirmed both through item-level and factor analyses. Also, gender differences were found. Women place a stronger emphasis on supportive and participative characteristics as well as diplomacy and long term orientation and women have a more negative attitude to dominance than men. Men rate the importance of persuasiveness, rationality and being inspirational higher for good leadership. The study presented in this chapter illustrates the context dependency of ILTs. People may hold different ILTs for different types of leaders based on the demands of the context and ILTs are influenced by characteristics of the perceiver and the groups they belong to. Thus, in order to increase our understanding of perceptions of leadership, we will need to take different aspects of the context into account.

REFERENCES

Antonakis, J., & Atwater, L. (2002). Leader distance: A review and a proposed theory. *Leadership Quarterly, 13,* 673–704.

Ayman, R. (1993). Leadership perception: The role of gender and culture. In M.M. Chemers & R. Ayman (Eds.), *Leadership theory and research: Perspectives and directions.* New York: Academic Press.

Bass, B.M., & Avolio, B.J. (1989). Potential biases in leadership measures: How prototypes, leniency and general satisfaction relate to ratings and rankings of transformational and transactional leadership constructs. *Educational and Psychological Measurement, 49,* 509–527.

Bass, B.M., Avolio, B.J., & Atwater, L. (1996). The transformational and transactional leadership of men and women. *Applied Psychology: An International Review, 45*(1), 5–34.

Bentler, P.M., & Wu, E.J.C. (1995). *EQS for Windows User's Guide.* Encino, CA: Multivariate Software, Inc.

Boyce, L.A., & Herd, A.M. (2003). The relationship between gender role stereotypes and requisite military leadership characteristics. *Sex Roles, 49,* 365–378.

Brenner, O.C., Tomkiewicz, J., & Schein, V.E. (1989). The relationship between sex role stereotypes and requisite management characteristics revisited. *Academy of Management Journal, 32,* 662–669.

Cantor, N., & Mischel, W. (1979). Prototypes in person perception. In L. Berkowitz (Ed.), *Advances in experimental social psychology.* New York: Academic Press.

Den Hartog, D.N., House, R.J., Hanges, P., Dorfman, P., Ruiz-Quintanilla, A., & 159 co-authors. (1999). Culture specific and cross-culturally endorsed implicit leadership theories: Are attributes of charismatic/transformational leadership universally endorsed? *Leadership Quarterly, 10*(2), 219–256.

Den Hartog, D.N. (2004). Leadership in a global context. In H. Lane, M. Maznevski, M. Mendenhall, & J. McNett (Eds.), *Blackwell handbook of global management* (pp. 175–198). Oxford: Blackwell Publishers.

DeVoe, S.E., & Iyengaar, S.S. (2003). Managers' theories of subordinates: A cross-cultural examination of manager perceptions of motivation and appraisal of performance. *Organizational Behavior and Human Decision Processes, 93*, 47–61.

Dorfman, P.W., Hanges, P., & Brodbeck, F. (2004) Leadership and cultural variation: The identification of culturally endorsed leadership profiles. In R.J. House, P.J. Hanges, M. Javidan, P.W. Dorfman, V. Gupta, & GLOBE associates (Eds.), *Cultures, leadership, and organizations: A 62 nation GLOBE study.* Thousand Oaks, CA: Sage.

Eagly, A.H., Johannesen-Schmidt, M., & Engen, M.L. van (2003). Transformational, transactional, and laissez-faire leadership styles: A meta-analysis comparing women and men. *Psychological Bulletin, 129*(4), 569–591.

Eden, D., & Leviathan, U. (1975). Implicit leadership theory as a determinant of the factor structure underlying supervisory behavior scales. *Journal of Applied Psychology, 60*, 736–741.

Emrich, C.G. (1999). Context effects in leadership perception. *Personality and Social Psychology Bulletin, 25*(8), 991–1006.

Ensari, N., & Murphy, S.E. (2003). Cross-cultural variations in leadership perceptions and attribution of charisma to the leader. *Organizational Behavior and Human Decision Processes, 92*, 52–66.

Epitropaki, O., & Martin, R. (2004). Implicit leadership theories in applied settings: factor structure, generalizability, and stability over time. *Journal of Applied Psychology, 89*(2), 293–310.

Etzioni, A. (1961). *A comparative analysis of complex organisations.* New York: Free Press.

Foti, R.J., & Luch, C.H. (1992). The influence of individual differences on the perception and categorization of leaders. *Leadership Quarterly, 3*, 55–66.

Gerstner, C.R., & Day, D.V. (1994). Cross-cultural comparison of leadership prototypes. *Leadership Quarterly, 5*, 121–134.

Graves, L. M., & Powell, G. N. (1982). Sex differences in implicit theories of leadership: An initial investigation. *Psychological Reports, 50*, 689–690.

Heilman, M.E., Block, Martell, R.F., & Simon, M.C. (1989). Has anything changed? Current characterizations of men, women, and managers. *Journal of Applied Psychology, 74*, 935–942.

Hofstede, G. (2001). *Culture's consequences: Comparing values, behaviors, institutions, and organizations across nations* (2nd ed.). Newbury Park, CA: Sage.

House, R.J., Hanges, P.J., Ruiz-Quintanilla, S.A., Dorfman, P.W., Javidan, M., Dickson, M., et al. (1999). Cultural influences on leadership and organizations: Project GLOBE. In W.H. Mobley (Ed.), *Advances in global leadership* (Vol. 1, pp. 171–233). Stamford, CT: JAI Press.

House, R., Javidan, M, Hanges, P., & Dorfman, P. (2002). Understanding cultures and implicit leadership theories across the globe: An introduction to project GLOBE. *Journal of World Business, 37*(1), 3–10.

House, R.J., Hanges, P.J., Javidan, M., Dorfman, P.W., Gupta, V., & Globe Associates (Eds.). (2004). *Cultures, leadership, and organizations: Globe: A 62 nation study.* Thousand Oaks, CA: Sage.

Hunt, J.G. (1991). *Leadership: A new synthesis.* London: Sage.

Hunt, J.G., Boal, K.B., & Sorensen, R.L. (1990). Top management leadership: Inside the black box. *Leadership Quarterly, 1,* 41–65.

Katz, D., & Kahn, R.L. (1978). *The social psychology of organizations* (2nd ed.). New York: John Wiley.

Keller, T. (1999). Images of the familiar: Individual differences and implicit leadership theories. *Leadership Quarterly, 10*(4), 589–607.

Lord, R.G., & Emrich, C.G. (2001). Thinking outside the box by looking inside the box: Extending the cognitive revolution in leadership research. *Leadership Quarterly, 11*(4), 551–579.

Lord, R.G., Foti, R., & De Vader, C. (1984). A test of leadership categorization theory: Internal structure, information processing, and leadership perceptions. *Organizational Behavior and Human Performance, 34,* 343–378.

Lord, R.G., Foti, R.J., & Philips, J. (1982). A theory of leadership categorization. In J.G. Hunt, U. Sekaran, & C.A. Schriesheim (Eds.), *Leadership: Beyond establishment views* (pp. 104–121). Carbondale: Southern Illinois University Press.

Korukonda, A.R., & Hunt, J.G. (1989). Pat on the back vs kick in the pants: An application of cognitive inference to the study of leader reward and punishment behaviors. *Group and Organization Studies, 14,* 299–334.

Lord R.G., & Maher, K.J. (1991). *Leadership & information processing.* London: Routledge.

Maher, K.J. (1997). Gender-related stereotypes of transformational and transactional leadership. *Sex Roles, 37,* 209–225.

Mintzberg, H. (1989). *Mintzberg on management.* New York: Free Press.

Offermann, L.R., Kennedy, J.K., & Wirtz, P.W. (1994). Implicit leadership theories: content structure, and generalizability. *Leadership Quarterly, 5,* 43–55.

Rosch, E. (1978). Principles of categorization. In E. Rosch & B.B. Lloyd (Eds.), *Cognition and categorization.* Hillsdale, NJ: Erlbaum.

Schein, V.E. (1973). The relationship between sex role stereotypes and requisite management characteristics. *Journal of Applied Psychology, 57,* 330–335.

Schein, V.E. (2001). A global look at psychological barriers to women's progress in management. *Journal of Social Issues, 57,* 675–688.

Sczesny, S., Bosak, J., Neff, D., & Schyns, B. (2004). Gender stereotypes and the attribution of leadership traits: A cross-cultural comparison. *Sex Roles,* 631–645.

Segall, M.H., Dasen, P.R., Berry, J.W., & Poortinga, Y.H. (1990). *Human behavior in global perspective: An introduction to cross-cultural psychology.* New York: Pergamon Press.

Shamir, B. (1995). Social distance and charisma: Theoretical notes and an exploratory study. *Leadership Quarterly, 6,* 19–47.

Waldman, D.A., & Yammarino, F.J. (1999). CEO charismatic leadership: Levels-of-management and levels-of-analysis effects. *Academy of Management Review, 24,* 266–285.

Yagil, D. (1998). Charismatic leadership and organizational hierarchy: Attribution of charisma to close and distant leaders. *Leadership Quarterly, 9*(2), 161–176.

Yammarino, F.J. (1994). Indirect leadership: Transformational leadership at a distance. In: B.M. Bass & B.J. Avolio (Eds.), *Improving organizational effectiveness through transformational leadership* (pp. 26–47). Thousand Oaks, CA: Sage.

Yammarino, F.J. Dubinsky, A.J. Comer L.B., & Jolson, M.A. (1997) Women and transformational and contingent reward leadership: A multiple levels of analysis perspective. *Academy of Management Journal, 40,* 205–222.

Yukl, G.A. (1999). *Leadership in organizations.* Englewood Cliffs, NJ: Prentice-Hall.

CHAPTER 6

GENDER STEREOTYPES AND IMPLICIT LEADERSHIP THEORIES

Sabine Sczesny

ABSTRACT

Previous research indicates that the social image of a successful manager shows a higher correlation to characteristics of a typical man than to those of a typical woman. Managers are perceived as possessing traits that are part of the male stereotype, the so-called think-manager-think-male stereotype (for an overview, see, Schein, 2001). Eagly and Karau (2002) assumed that changes in the descriptive contents of gender and occupational roles require a general change in the distribution of men and women into social roles. Therefore, a greater fit of female role and leader role should be observed in cultures in which the actual participation of women in leadership is higher compared to cultures in which their participation in leadership is still low. The present overview describes three studies in which the perception of leadership traits in others or in themselves was analyzed (Sczesny, 2003a,b; Sczesny, Bosak, Neff, & Schyns, 2004). Management students from three different countries—Australia, Germany, and India—and German executives estimated the percentage to which one of three stimulus groups possesses person-oriented and task-oriented leadership traits (descriptive norms).

Implicit Leadership Theories: Essays and Explorations, pages 159–172
Copyright © 2005 by Information Age Publishing

They evaluated executives-in-general (no gender specification), male executives, or female executives. Participants also rated the importance of these characteristics for the respective group (prescriptive norms). Furthermore, other groups of participants described themselves regarding the two types of traits and their importance for themselves. The results indicate a less gender-sterotypic view of leadership than expected. Nevertheless, there exists an interculturally shared view of a female-specific leadership competence according to which women are assumed to possess a higher person orientation than men. In their self-descriptions male and female participants described themselves as similarly person- and task-oriented.

INTRODUCTION

Recent research has indicated that women have been moving up the hierarchical ladder of organizations (see Eagly, 2003; Wirth, 2001). Nevertheless, all over the world women are still under-represented in management positions compared to men (Powell, 1999; for an overview, see Schein, 2001). Some examples: in the United States women currently represent 15.7% of corporate officers in the largest companies of the country, the "Fortune 500" (Catalyst, 2002); in Australia's 300 largest companies, only 10.7% of board seats are held by women (Corporate Women Directors International, 1999); in Germany women represent only 1% of the executive board members and 8% of the supervisory board members in the largest companies of the country, i.e., in 87 Old Economy companies (Handelsblatt, 2005). The under-representation of women in management positions is described as the "glass ceiling," a barrier so subtle that it is transparent but simultaneously so strong that it prevents women and ethnic minorities from moving up in the management hierarchy (Morrison & Von Glinow, 1990).

Gender stereotypes can be seen as one possible explanation for this phenomenon, resulting in a perceived incongruity between the feminine role and the leader role (Eagly & Karau, 2002). Stereotypes about women and men are based on observations of their behavior in gender-typical social roles (e.g., breadwinner, homemaker), and contain consensual beliefs about the attributes of women and men (Eagly, 1987; see also the implicit personality theory: Ashmore & Del Boca, 1979). Men in general are consistently seen as more agentic (e.g., assertive, individualistic) than women, whereas women are seen as more communal (e.g., gentle, child-loving) than men (e.g., Diekman & Eagly, 2000; Williams & Best, 1990). Analogously, leadership characteristics can at least be described on two dimensions, both of which are associated with gender stereotypes: a "masculine typed" task-oriented dimension (initiating structure) and a "feminine typed" person-oriented dimension (consideration) (for an overview, see

Schriesheim, Cogliser, Neider, Fleishman, & James, 1998; see also Maher, 1997, for gender stereotypes regarding transformational and transactional leadership). Cann and Siegfried (1990) examined the relationship between those two types of leadership styles on the one hand and feminine and masculine behaviors on the other, showing that consideration is perceived as more feminine and initiating structure is perceived as more masculine. Furthermore, person-oriented characteristics were considered as more important for lower level managers than for top managers (see Den Hartog & Koopman, this volume, Ch. 5).

In implicit leadership theories the influence of beliefs and expectations on the evaluation of leaders is emphasized. Implicit leadership theories can be understood as cognitive schemata or prototypes allowing the perceiver to categorize traits and behaviors of a person with respect to leadership (e.g., Kenney, Blascovich, & Shaver, 1994). The social perception of leadership is influenced by gender stereotypes. In the following I will review my own research on the perceived incongruity between the feminine and leader roles as well as on self-descriptions regarding leadership traits among women and men (Sczesny, 2003a,b; Sczesny et al., 2004). It examines leadership-specific gender stereotypes (i.e., of female and male leaders) by assessing two different managerial qualities (i.e., person- and task orientation). Moreover, descriptive and prescriptive aspects of stereotyping, and the impact of cultural background on stereotyping were investigated. At first, I will review research on gender stereotypes and leadership attribution, and research on self-description of leadership traits by women and men.

GENDER STEREOTYPES AND LEADERSHIP ATTRIBUTION

The attribution of leadership abilities is one area in which gender stereotypes manifest themselves (Heilman, 2001). Schein (1973, 1975) investigated the social image of successful middle managers in U.S. samples. She found that the attributes ascribed to managers elicited a significantly higher correlation with the description of a typical man than with the description of a typical woman. This phenomenon of *think-manager-think male* was confirmed in many subsequent studies indicating that management is still associated with being male (e.g., Heilman, Block, & Martell, 1995; Powell, Butterfield, & Parent, 2002; Willemsen, 2002). Schein and colleagues also conducted cross-cultural comparisons by which the impact of gender stereotypes on the perception of leadership was observed in different countries: in Germany, the United Kingdom (Schein & Mueller, 1992), China, and Japan (Schein, Mueller, Lituchy, & Liu, 1996). Usually the social image had been assessed by using items of general personality

traits. These instruments mainly contain global traits of the masculine stereotype, i.e., instrumentality, and of the feminine stereotype, i.e., expres-
siveness (see Bem, 1974; Schein, 1973).

Perceivers' gender seems to be an important factor in the evaluation of
men's and women's leadership abilities. Male participants evaluated
women more negatively relative to men than female participants did (e.g.,
Eagly, Makhijani, & Klonsky, 1992). Male and female college students had
similar perceptions both of prototypical managers and male managers,
whereas male students were more likely to have negative views of female
managers than female students (Deal & Stevenson, 1998): Men in comparison to women described female managers less likely as ambitious, competent, intelligent, objective, well-informed, etc., and more likely as easily
influenced, nervous, passive, having a strong need for social acceptance,
uncertain, etc. In her recent research, Schein (2001) observed a less gender-stereotypic perception of leadership among women than among men
in the United States. This shift among women was not found in several
other countries (China, Germany, Japan, and the United Kingdom). Following Schein (2001) such "variations in the degree of managerial sex typing, however, may reflect the females' view of opportunities for and actual
participation of women in management in their respective countries" (p.
680). The responses of women may serve as a "barometer of change."

In addition, two *types of expectations or norms* can be differentiated:
descriptive and prescriptive norms (e.g., Burgess & Borgida, 1999).
Descriptive norms contain beliefs about what people actually do, whereas
prescriptive norms contain beliefs about what people ought to do. Most
previous research on the think-manager-think-male stereotype has focused
on descriptive norms, i.e., what leaders do and how they are. Since both
types of norms have different implications for the development of prejudice toward female leaders, Eagly and Karau (2002) suggested that both
ought to be taken into consideration.

Heilman (1983) assumed that expectations about the success of an individual are determined by the fit between the perception of an individual's
attributes and the perception of job requirements. A divergence was
described by Heilman as a *lack of fit,* which was held to be responsible for
sex-biased judgments or behaviors: The perceived requirements of masculine-typed jobs such as leadership positions did not fit with the traits typically attributed to women as a group. Prejudice against female leaders
occurs especially in situations that intensify perceptions of incongruity
between the feminine gender role and leadership roles. In their *role congruity theory,* Eagly and Karau (2002) assumed two forms of prejudice toward
female leaders: The less favorable evaluation of women's *potential for leadership* compared to men's potential, can be explained by the activation of
descriptive norms about women's characteristics and the consequent

ascription of feminine-stereotypic qualities to women, which are not the qualities expected or desired in leaders. The less favorable evaluation of the *actual leadership behavior* of women compared to men can be due to prescriptive norms. By occupying leadership roles, women are subjected to biased evaluations that originate from their nonconformity to the cultural definitions of femininity. Therefore, women's violation of their traditional gender role results in the dilemma of either being "too feminine or too masculine" in the context of leadership. Women who break through the glass ceiling are subjected to diverse obstacles such as the "glass cliff" meaning that their position of leadership is risky or precarious (see Ryan & Haslam, this volume, Ch. 7).

SELF-DESCRIPTION OF LEADERSHIP TRAITS

Besides the perception by others, gender differences in traits, skills, and behavior also exist in self-description (e.g., Costa, Terracciano, & McCrae, 2001). Eagly and Wood (Eagly, 1987; Wood & Eagly, 2002) explained existing differences with reference to the distribution of women and men into social roles within society. Since role behavior shapes the contents of gender stereotypes, they represent "dynamic constructs." The feminine stereotype was found to be particularly dynamic, due to greater changes in the recent past in the roles of women than men (Diekman & Eagly, 2000). For example, a decrease in gender differences in self-description of masculine and feminine traits over a twenty-year period (1973–1993) was observed by Twenge (1997): Whereas women increasingly reported possessing masculine-stereotyped traits, men showed no changes regarding feminine-stereotyped traits. Also recent meta-analytical research by Twenge (2001) on self-reported assertiveness indicated an increasing similarity between women and men. She deduced that assertiveness varies with status and roles and, therefore, social change is internalized in form of a personality trait.

THE PRESENT RESEARCH: AIM AND RESEARCH QUESTIONS

The aim of the present research was to analyze variations of managerial sex typing (Sczesny, 2003a,b; Sczesny et al., 2004). Compared to earlier work the present research represents a multifaceted analysis of the think-manager think-male stereotype by taking the following aspects into consideration.

First, most personality traits in general can be seen as irrelevant or even misleading in the context of leadership (e.g., individualistic, child-loving).

As an alternative to commonly used gender-role-oriented inventories, the influence of gender stereotypes on *leadership specific traits* such as assertive and cooperative was analyzed in the present studies.

Second, previous research has focused on the comparison of global gender stereotypes (women and men as stimulus groups) with the perception of leaders in general, i.e., without gender specification. In the present studies, *gender-specific leadership roles* (female and male executives as stimulus groups) were analyzed, assuming that traditional global gender stereotypes are also effective here.

Third, most previous research on the think-manager-think-male stereotype has focused on descriptive norms regarding leadership characteristics. In the present studies, *descriptive as well as prescriptive kinds of expectations* were analyzed.

Fourth, on the basis of the idea of gender stereotypes as dynamic constructs and the recently observed changes in the self-images of women in global personality traits and assertiveness, the *self-description* of leadership traits among women and men was investigated.

Finally, the *cultural background* was taken into consideration. There exists a broad consensus across cultures about the contents of gender stereotypes, i.e., the attribution of personality traits (see Williams & Best, 1990; Williams, Satterwhite, & Best, 1999) as well as a high global resemblance with respect to leadership roles, i.e., what kind of characteristics a leader should possess (e.g., communicative skills, trustworthiness, and dynamism; Den Hartog et al., 1999). Eagly and Karau (2002) suggested that changes in descriptive contents of gender and occupational roles require a "general change in the distribution of men and women into social roles" (p. 590). Furthermore, societies differ in their work-related values. Hofstede's (1980,1998) masculinity-femininity dimension distinguishes societies with masculine work-related values focusing on performance, assertiveness, and material success from societies with feminine work-related values in which people focus on relationships, modesty, and quality of life. This raises the question of whether the cultural background influences the perceived incongruity between the female role and leader role as well as the self-descriptions of women and men regarding their own leadership traits.

Hypotheses

The gender-stereotypic *perception of leadership traits* is expected to depend on the cultural background: When the distribution of women and men into social roles is less different in the respective country, participants should perceive no or small/modest differences between *female executives and executives-in-general* (no gender specification) at all. Whereas when the distribution is more different in the respective country, participants should perceive larger differences between female executives and executives-in-general. Since some cultural variations in the degree of managerial sex typing among women and men had been observed in previous research, the assumed impact of culture and leaders' sex on the perception of leadership traits is expected to be moderated by perceiver's sex. For example, in the United States women reported a less gender-stereotypic view of leadership than men (see Schein, 2001). Such variations among women of different cultures can be due to their different opportunities for and actual participation in management in the respective country. Therefore, in countries with a less different distribution of women and men into social roles, a less gender stereotypic view of leadership among women than men is expected. Women in such countries are expected to perceive no differences regarding the leadership traits of female executives and executives-in-general, whereas men are expected to still perceive differences. In contrast, in countries with a more different distribution, both sexes should hold a comparable traditional view of leadership. Independent of their cultural background and their sex, participants should not differ in their perception of male executives and executives-in-general.

The cultural background described above should also influence the *self-description of women and men* as follows: Independent of their cultural background, men should report possessing or a desire to possess *person-oriented leadership traits* to a lesser extent than women, since no change in men's self-view of feminine-typed traits in general has been observed in previous research. In contrast, sex differences in the self-view of *task-oriented leadership traits* should depend on the respective cultural background, since changes in the self-images of women in masculine-typed global personality traits and assertiveness have recently been observed indicating that women increasingly described themselves as instrumental and assertive (Diekman & Eagly, 2000; Twenge, 1997, 2001). Women in comparison to men should report possessing or a desire to possess task-oriented leadership traits to a similar extent in cultures in which the actual participation of women in leadership is higher and/or the work-related values are more masculine-typed. In cultures in which the women's participation in leadership is lower, sex differences should be observed.

Method

Three studies were accomplished to analyze cultural variations of managerial sex typing. Participants estimated the percentage to which one of three stimulus groups, i.e., executives-in-general (no gender specification), male executives, or female executives, possesses person- and task-oriented leadership traits. Person-oriented traits were, for example, dependable, just, intuitive, cooperative, and motivational. Task-oriented traits were, for example, decisive, career-oriented, effective bargainer, and planning ahead. The descriptive norms were measured by asking to which percentage in their opinion all executives-in-general (female executives/male executives) possess this characteristic (*percentage estimates*). Participants also rated the importance of these characteristics for the respective stimulus group. The prescriptive norms were measured by the question of how important they estimate the respective characteristic to be for an executive (female executive/male executive; *importance ratings*). Furthermore, other groups of participants described themselves regarding the two types of traits and their importance for themselves. In these self-description groups, participants indicated whether they possessed the given characteristics or not and to what extent they considered the respective characteristics to be important for themselves.

Participants were management students of both sexes from Australia ($N = 130$ in Sczesny et al., 2004), Germany ($N = 215$ in Sczesny, 2003a; $N = 253$ in Sczesny et al., 2004), and India *($N = 127$ in Sczesny et al., 2004)* and executives from Germany *($N = 177$; Sczesny, 2003b)*. The selection of these three countries was based on several indicators (for details see Sczesny et al., 2004). Australia and Germany seem to be quite similar regarding their achieved high gender equality compared to India (see the gender-related development index and the gender empowerment measure; Wirth, 2001, reporting data of the Human Development Report of the United Nations of 1999). Despite this fact, Australia and Germany differ with respect to values relevant in the context of work (see Hofstede, 1980, 1998). Following these indicators, Germany and Australia are similar regarding gender equality and leadership participation: Both countries show a less different distribution of women and men into social roles than India. Australia and India are similar in their lesser masculinity of work-related values compared to Germany.

EMPIRICAL FINDINGS

Perception of leadership traits.   The results of the three studies indicated that women and men of all investigated cultures ascribed *person-oriented traits* to a greater extent to *female executives* than to executives-in-general (descriptive norms). With respect to the comparison of *male executives* and executives-in-general, men from all three countries and German women did not differentiate in the attribution of person-oriented traits. Australian and Indian women even ascribed a lesser person-orientation to male executives compared to executives-in-general. The attribution of *task-oriented traits* showed the following pattern: The Australian men made no difference *between female executives* and executives-in-general The Australian women not only made no such differences, they even described female executives as possessing these traits more often than executives-in-general. In one German sample (students in Sczesny, 2003a) participants of both sexes ascribed task-oriented traits less often to female executives than to executives-in-general. In the two other German samples (executives in Sczesny, 2003b; students in Sczesny et al., 2004), women and men perceived no such differences. In India both sexes did not differentiate between female executives and executives-in-general. *Male executives* and executives-in-general were ascribed with task-oriented traits to a similar degree by women and men of all three cultures, except for Indian women. These attributed male executives with task-oriented traits less often than executives-in-general. Furthermore, the results of the importance ratings (prescriptive norms) indicated that women and men of all three cultures valued *person- and task-oriented traits* to a similar degree as important for *female executives* and executives-in-general. Also, women and men of all three cultures did not differentiate in the importance of person- and task-oriented traits to *male executives* and executives-in general.

Self-description of women and men.   Women and men of all three cultures reported possessing *person- and task-oriented traits* to a similar degree. Furthermore, men of all three cultures favored possessing *person-oriented traits* to a lesser extent than women in the respective country. Whereas German women and men favored possessing *task-oriented traits* to a similar extent, in Australia, women reported even a higher importance of task-oriented traits for themselves than the men. In India women as well as men also favored possessing task-oriented traits to a similar extent.

DISCUSSION

In previous research the perception of leadership was found to be predominately associated with being male, the think-manager-think-male stereotype. The present research allows a closer look beneath the surface of this stereotype by investigating the managerial sex typing in a context-specific way (i.e., analyzing leadership-specific gender roles rather than global gender roles), by assessing the influence of these roles on leadership-specific traits (rather than on global personality traits), by analyzing the perception by others as well as the self-perception, and by taking descriptive as well as prescriptive norms into account. By using this different approach, the reliability of the findings was increased and certain limitations of previous studies were overcome.

A better fit of male executives with "executives in general" than of female executives was found in one of five samples (among German management students of both sexes; Sczesny, 2003a). Only this finding is in line with results of previous research, again confirming the think-manager-think-male stereotype (see Schein, 2001). German executives (Sczesny, 2003b) and Australian, German, and Indian students (Sczesny et al., 2004) as well showed a less gender-stereotypic view of leadership compared to previous findings. Nevertheless, an interculturally shared view of a feminine-specific leadership competence (Friedel-Howe, 1993) was observed: Women were assumed to possess a higher social competence (person orientation) than men (contrary to the similar self-views of women and men with respect to person-oriented traits). To sum up, neither the descriptive nor prescriptive norms among women and men seem to be influenced by the think-manager-think-male stereotype.

One cultural variation is worth mentioning: Australian women attributed task-oriented traits to a greater extent to female executives and they valued this specific competence as especially important for female executives. Can such cultural variation in the degree of managerial sex typing among women be due to their different opportunities for and actual participation in management in the respective countries as suggested by Schein (2001)? So far, no systematic empirical analyses of this explanation exist and, therefore, some questions remain still open. For example, is the counter-stereotypic effect shown by the Australian women related to disadvantageous or preferential treatment of women in their country (see "reversed discrimination effect," Branscombe & Smith, 1990; "women-are-wonderful effect," Eagly & Mladinic, 1994)? The further investigation of such culture-specific findings might be an interesting issue for future research contributing to the question how diverse sociocultural indicators, e.g., promotion opportunities or demand for professionals with higher education, are related to perceiver's mental representations of gender and leadership in different cultures.

In the previous research the *self-description of women and men* indicates that women and men in all three countries reported to possess and desire to possess task- and person-oriented traits to a similar extent. Only German female students had reported to possess more person-oriented traits than male students (Sczesny, 2003a) and German female executives emphasized the importance of person-oriented characteristics for themselves (Sczesny, 2003b). Probably these German women try to handle the dilemma of either "being too feminine or too masculine" (Eagly & Karau, 2002) by fulfilling gender-stereotypic expectancies at least partly. Altogether the findings on the self-description reflect the recently observed changes in the self-images of women in masculine-typed global personality traits and assertiveness (Twenge, 1997, 2001). The observed change in men's self-view of person-oriented traits was not expected. One possible explanation can be seen in the fact that not only task-orientation, but also person-orientation was valued as important for leadership in all three countries. About 50% of executives-in-general were assumed to possess person-oriented traits, and in Australia and India person-oriented traits were assessed even as more important for leadership than were task-oriented traits (reflecting work cultures less pronounced in masculinity in both countries; Hofstede, 1980, 1998). To sum up, the self-description of women and men in all three countries corresponds to social expectations relevant in leadership context.

CONCLUSION

The present findings indicate a less traditional gender-stereotypic view of leadership in the investigated countries. This view was observed not only among women (as in Schein, 2001), but also among men. The many cultural similarities probably indicate a homogeneity of the management context in countries with free-market economies. Thus, female management students in India may be similarly socialized as female management students in other countries and may differ to a greater extent from other female subgroups within their own country. Furthermore, in previous research (see Schein, 2001) and in the present findings management students and executives showed a similar pattern of attitudes. Nevertheless, it would also be interesting to investigate managerial sex typing among executives cross-culturally. By such research our understanding of socialization or selection processes (e.g., London, 2002; Wigfield, Battle, Keller, & Eccles, 2002) and their impact on the social perception of gender and leadership could be increased. To conclude, gender stereotypes still influence the perception of leadership, albeit to a much lesser degree than in previous research. Therefore, gender stereotypes with respect to leadership still have to be taken into account as one possible source for biases in social judgment and interactions.

REFERENCES

Ashmore, R.D., & Del Boca, F.K. (1979). Sex stereotypes and implicit personality theory: Toward a cognitive-social psychological conceptualization. *Sex Roles, 5,* 219–248.

Bem, S.L. (1974). The measurement of psychological androgyny. *Journal of Consulting and Clinical Psychology, 31,* 634–643.

Branscombe, N.R., & Smith, E.R. (1990). Gender and racial stereotypes in impression formation and social decision-making processes. *Sex Roles, 22,* 627–647.

Burgess, D., & Borgida, E. (1999). Who women are, who women should be: Descriptive and prescriptive gender stereotyping in sex discrimination. *Psychology, Public Policy, and Law, 5,* 665–692.

Cann, A., & Siegfried W.D. (1990). Gender stereotypes and dimensions of effective leader behavior. *Sex Roles, 23,* 413–419.

Catalyst. (2002, November 19). *Catalyst census marks gains in numbers of women corporate officers in America's largest 500 companies* [press release]. Retrieved December 12, 2003, from http://www.catalystwomen.org/press_room/press_releases/2002_cote.htm.

Corporate Women Directors International. (1999). *CWDI Report: Women board directors of Australia's top companies* [press release]. Retrieved February 6, 2005, from http://www.globewomen.com/cwdi/country_rep/australia_report.asp.

Costa, P.T., Terracciano, A., & McCrae, R.R. (2001). Gender differences in personality traits across cultures: Robust and surprising findings. *Journal of Personality and Social Psychology, 81,* 322–331.

Deal, J.J., & Stevenson, M.A. (1998). Perceptions of female and male managers in the 1990s: Plus a change.... *Sex Roles, 38,* 287–300.

Den Hartog, D.N., House, R.J., Hanges, P.J., Ruiz-Quintanilla, S.A., Dorfman, P.W., et al. (1999). Culture specific and cross-culturally generalizable implicit leadership theories: Are attributes of charismatic/transformational leadership universally endorsed? *Leadership Quarterly, 10,* 219–256.

Den Hartog, D., Koopman, P. (this volume). Implicit theories of leadership at different hierarchical levels.

Diekman, A.B., & Eagly, A.H. (2000). Stereotypes as dynamic constructs: Women and men of the past, present, and future. *Personality and Social Psychology Bulletin, 26,* 1171–1181.

Eagly, A.H. (1987). *Sex differences in social behavior: A social role interpretation.* Hillsdale, NJ: Erlbaum.

Eagly, A.H. (2003). The rise of female leaders. *Zeitschrift für Sozialpsychologie, 34,* 123–132.

Eagly, A.H., & Karau, S.J. (2002). Role congruity theory of prejudice toward female leaders. *Psychological Review, 109,* 573–598.

Eagly, A.H., Makhijani, M.G., & Klonsky, B.G. (1992). Gender and the evaluation of leaders: A meta-analysis. *Psychological Bulletin, 111,* 3–22.

Eagly, A.H., & Mladinic, A.(1994). Are people prejudiced against women? Some answers from research on attitudes, gender stereotypes, and judgments of competence. *European Review of Social Psychology, 5,* 1–35.

Friedel-Howe, H. (1993). Frauen und Führung: Mythen und Fakten. In L.V. Rosenstiel (Ed.), *Führung von Mitarbeitern: Handbuch für erfolgreiches Personalmanagement* (Vol. 2, pp. 455–467). Stuttgart: Schaffer-Poeschel.

Handelsblatt, (2005, January 19). Italien ist Schlusslicht. Deutschland nur Mittelmaß bei Frauen in Chefetagen [article]. Retrieved February 6, 2005, from http://www.handelsblatt.de/pshb/fn/relhbi/sfn/buildhbi/cn/GoArt!200014,200812,848576/SH/0/depot/0/.

Heilman, M.E. (1983). Sex bias in work settings: The lack of fit model. In B.M. Staw & L.L. Cummings (Eds.), *Research in organizational behavior* (Vol. 5, pp. 269–298). Greenwich, CT: JAI Press.

Heilman, M.E. (2001). Description and prescription: How gender stereotypes prevent women's ascent up the organizational ladder. *Journal of Social Issues, 57,* 657–674.

Heilman, M.E., Block, C.J., & Martell, R.F. (1995). Sex stereotypes: Do they influence perception of managers? *Journal of Social Behavior and Personality, 10,* 237–252.

Hofstede, G. (1980). *Culture consequences: International differences in work-related values.* Beverly Hills, CA: Sage.

Hofstede, G. (1998). *Masculinity and femininity: The taboo dimension of national cultures.* Thousand Oaks: CA: Sage.

Kenney, R.A., Blascovich, J., & Shaver, P.R. (1994). Implicit leadership theories: Prototypes for new leaders. *Basic and Applied Social Psychology, 15,* 409–443.

London, M. (2002). *Leadership development: Paths to self-insight and professional growth.* Mahwah, NJ: Lawrence Erlbaum.

Maher, K.J. (1997). Gender-related stereotypes of transformational and transactional leadership. *Sex Roles, 37,* 209–225.

Morrison, A.M., & von Glinow, M.A. (1990). Women and minorities in management. *American Psychologist, 45,* 200–208.

Powell, G.N. (1999). Reflections on the glass ceiling. Recent trends and future prospects. In G.N. Powell (Ed.), *Handbook of gender and work* (pp. 325–345). Thousand Oaks, CA: Sage.

Powell, G.N., Butterfield, D.A., & Parent, J.D. (2002). Gender and managerial stereotypes: Have the times changed? *Journal of Management, 28,* 177–193.

Ryan, M., & Haslam, S. A. (this volume). The glass cliff: Implicit theories of leadership and the precariousness of women's leadership positions.

Schein, V.E. (1973). The relationship between sex-role stereotypes and requisite management characteristics. *Journal of Applied Psychology, 57,* 95–100.

Schein, V.E. (1975). Relations between sex-role stereotypes and requisite management characteristics among female managers. *Journal of Applied Psychology, 60,* 340–344.

Schein, V.E. (2001). A global look at psychological barriers to women's progress in management. *Journal of Social Issues, 57,* 675–688.

Schein, V.E., & Mueller, R. (1992). Sex role stereotyping and requisite management characteristics: A cross cultural look. *Journal of Organizational Behavior, 13,* 439–447.

Schein, V.E., Mueller, R., Lituchy, T., & Liu, J. (1996). Think manager-think male: A global phenomenon? *Journal of Organizational Behavior, 17,* 33–41.

Schriesheim, C.A., Cogliser, C.C., Neider, L.L., Fleishman, B.A., & James, L. (1998). The Ohio State model. In F. Dansereau & F.J. Yamniarino (Eds.), *Leadership: The multiple-level approaches: Classical and new wave* (pp. 3–72). Stamford, CT: JAI Press.

Sczesny, S. (2003a). A closer look beneath the surface: Various facets of the think-manager-think-male stereotype. *Sex Roles, 49,* 353–363.

Sczesny, S. (2003b). Führungskompetenz: Selbst- und Fremdwahrnehmung weiblicher und männlicher Führungskrafte. *Zeitschrift für Sozialpsychologie, 34,* 133–145.

Sczesny, S., Bosak, J., Neff, D., & Schyns, B. (2004). Gender stereotypes and the attribution of leadership traits: A cross-cultural comparison. *Sex Roles, 51,* 631–645.

Twenge, J.M. (1997). Changes in masculine and feminine traits over time: A meta-analysis. *Sex Roles, 36,* 305–325.

Twenge, J.M. (2001). Changes in women's assertiveness in response to status and roles: A cross-temporal meta-analysis, 1931–1993. *Journal of Personality and Social Psychology, 81,* 133–145.

Wigfield, A., Battle, A., Keller, L.B., & Eccles, J.S. (2002). Sex differences in motivation, self-concept, career aspiration, and career choice: Implications for cognitive development. ill A. McGillicuddy-De Lisi & R. De Lisi (Eds.), *Biology, society, and behavior: The development of sex differences in cognition* (pp. 93–124). Westport, CT: Ablex Publishing.

Willemsen, T.M. (2002). Gender typing of the successful manager: A stereotype reconsidered. *Sex Roles, 46,* 385–391.

Williams, J.E., & Best, D.L. (1990). *Measuring sex stereotypes: A multination study.* Newbury Park, CA: Sage.

Williams, J.E., Satterwhite, R.C., & Best, D.L. (1999). Pancultural gender stereotypes revisited: The five factor model. *Sex Roles, 40,* 513–525.

Wirth, L. (2001). *Breaking through the glass ceiling: Women in management.* Geneva: International Labor Office.

Wood, W., & Eagly, A.H. (2002). A cross-cultural analysis of the behavior of women and men: Implications for the origins of sex differences. *Psychological Bulletin, 128,* 699–727.

CHAPTER 7

THE GLASS CLIFF

Implicit Theories of Leadership and Gender and the Precariousness of Women's Leadership Positions

Michelle K. Ryan and S. Alexander Haslam

So much for smashing the glass ceiling and using their unique skills to enhance the performance of Britain's biggest companies. The triumphant march of women into the country's boardrooms has instead wreaked havoc on companies' performance and share prices. (Judge, 2003, p. 21)

In my previous company I was appointed to a position that sought to change the business focus. This had been declined by three male colleagues in my peer group on the management board. I was not told this. When I expressed reservations about the viability in the time frame given, I was told I always produced the results and nothing else was coming up so I would have to do it for the company. At the end of 12 months my reservations were shown to be accurate. The company decided to abandon the plans and I was given another equally risky project which I refused. I was made redundant in three weeks. Four other male colleagues who also refused the "offer" were not. (Female Executive, 45)

Implicit Leadership Theories: Essays and Explorations, pages 173–196
Copyright © 2005 by Information Age Publishing

AFTER THE GLASS CEILING: THE SECOND WAVE
OF GENDER DISCRIMINATION IN THE WORKPLACE

Women continue to be markedly under-represented in leadership positions. The most widely-documented explanations of this fact center (a) on the invisible barrier of the "glass ceiling" that prevents them gaining access to such positions (The Corporate Woman, 1986; Kanter, 1977; Morrison, White, & Van Velsor, 1987) and (b) on the corresponding phemomenon of the "glass escalator" by which means men are accelerated through the organizational ranks (especially in female-dominated professions; Williams, 1992). However, despite these barriers, the number of women who occupy management positions is greater than ever before (Equal Opportunities Commission, 2002). This increase in representation has focused both the media and the research spotlight on the way in which women leaders perform once placed in these leadership roles. As a result, commentators are continually asking a series of probing questions: How good are women managers? Are they as good as men? What happens to the companies that appoint women to senior positions? Indeed, it was questions of exactly this form that inspired Judge (2003) to write the scathing article from which the first of the above quotations was taken.

As Judge's comments indicate, women's march into senior positions has been far from smooth. In the first instance, women managers tend to receive greater scrutiny and criticism than do men, and they tend to be evaluated less favorably, even when performing exactly the same leadership roles as men (Eagly et al., 1992). Workers also express a tendency to prefer male supervisors to female ones (e.g., Simon & Landis, 1989), and, many men—particularly male managers—remain unconvinced about the effectiveness of women leaders (Sczesny, 2003). An obvious question here is whether this treatment is deserved or whether it is a consequence of additional barriers that women encounter once they have broken through the glass ceiling.

Evidence that companies which appoint women to their Board tend to perform worse than those which remain exclusively male might lead one to conclude, like Judge (2003), that female leaders deserve their frosty reception. However, in contrast to this analysis, in the present chapter we argue that the negative outcomes experienced by companies that appoint female leaders are the consequence of a "second-wave" of discrimination that women—like the female executive quoted above—must overcome in the workplace. Extending the metaphor of the glass ceiling and the glass elevator, we argue that such women are more likely than men to find themselves on a *"glass cliff,"* such that their positions of leadership are associated with greater risk and an increased possibility of failure (e.g., Ryan & Haslam,

2005a,2005b). If and when that failure occurs, it is then women (rather than men) who are singled out for criticism and blame.

In support of this analysis, the chapter presents a summary of initial research which provides evidence of the glass cliff and which provides preliminary insight into its causes and consequences. This evidence comes from archival studies in corporate and political settings and from a series of ongoing experimental studies. Qualitative data collected from on-line interviews also point to a multiplicity of processes—including implicit theories of leadership and gender—which potentially underlie glass cliff appointments.

IMPLICIT THEORIES OF GENDER AND LEADERSHIP

Think Manager-Think Male

Much of the evidence for gender differentiation in the workplace can be seen to reflect people's implicit theories about leadership and about gender. More specifically, they can be seen to arise from the perceived incompatibility between beliefs about what it means to be a good leader and what it means to be female (e.g., Agars, 2004; Eagly & Karau, 2002; Heilman, Block, Martell, & Simon, 1989; Schein, 1973, 1975, 2001). Along these lines, Berthoin Antal and Izreali (1993, p. 63) suggest that "probably the single most important hurdle for women in management . . . is the persistent stereotype that associates management with being male."

Early work into the stereotypes of managers, of men and of women, and the relationships between these stereotypes, was conducted by Schein (1973, 1975). This reported data based on a Descriptive Index in which participants were given a list of 92 descriptive terms and asked to indicate how characteristic each term was of either women in general, men in general, or successful middle managers. Results demonstrated that both male (Schein, 1973) and female (Schein, 1975) managers believed that men were more likely than women to posses the characteristics associated with managerial success. Indeed, of the 92 descriptors used, 60 were seen to be characteristic of both managers and men, including: emotionally stable, aggressive, (has) leadership ability, self-reliant, competitive, self-confident, objective, ambitious, well informed, and forceful.

Furthermore, this perceived relationship between what is managerial and what is male appears to be remarkably durable and global (Deal, 1998). Thus more recent replications of Schein's original studies demonstrate that these implicit theories are still endorsed today. In the last decade or so the think manager-think male effect has been reproduced in the United States (e.g., Brenner, Tomkiewicz, & Schein, 1989; Heilman,

Block, & Martell, 1995), the United Kingdom and Germany (Schein & Mueller, 1992), Japan and China (Schein, Mueller, Lituchy, & Liu, 1996), as well as in military settings (Boyce & Herd, 2003).

Importantly, people's implicit theories of management and gender are not only descriptive, but also powerfully prescriptive (Heilman, 2001; Rudman & Glick, 2001). They guide both how we act ourselves and our expectations about how others should act. As a result, these stereotypes have the potential to have an enormous impact on the way in which women (and men) are treated in the workplace. For example, in a recent review, Eagly and Karau (2002) argue that the incongruity between what it means to be female and what is seen to be managerial can produce two forms of prejudice: (a) less favorable evaluation of the potential for women to take on leadership roles compared to men, and (b) less favorable evaluations of the actual behavior of female leaders.

In the first instance, then, implicit theories have the potential to affect women's perceived suitability for management roles. This arises from a perceived *lack of fit* (e.g., Heilman, 1983) and expectations of failure. As Schein (2001) notes, if a management position is seen to be inherently masculine, then, all else being equal, a male candidate will appear to be more qualified than a female one. In addition, Eagly and Karau (2002) note that the repeated pairing of notions of masculinity and notions of management means that observers are less likely to "spontaneously categorize" women as leaders or potential leaders. In this way, men's advantage over women may be twofold, since they are seen to have both (a) the traits associated with leadership and (b) greater potential to be a leader.

Implicit theories are also implicated in the subsequent evaluation of individuals as leaders. Here, evidence suggests that women leaders are evaluated less favorably than their male counterparts, even when behaving in exactly the same manner (e.g., Agars, 2004; Eagly et al., 1992). In a meta-analysis of studies investigating gender differences in leader evaluation, Eagly et al. (1992) demonstrated that this tendency is particularly pronounced when leadership behaviors are stereotypically masculine in nature. Thus a male manager who acts in a forceful or assertive way is seen to be behaving appropriately and displaying leadership, while a female leader who behaves in the same way is considered to be unacceptably pushy (see, e.g., Fiske, Bersoff, Borgida, Deaux, & Heilman, 1991). In this way, women leaders are often in a lose-lose situation. If their behavior confirms the gender stereotype they are not thought to be acting like a proper leader, but if their behavior is consistent with the leader stereotype they are not thought to be acting as a proper woman. Violating either of these stereotypes can then lead to negative evaluations (e.g., Eagly & Karau, 2002; Eagly et al., 1992; Heilman, Wallen, Fuchs, & Tamkins, 2004; Rudman & Glick, 2001).

The Importance of Context

It is apparent from the previous section that implicit theories about gender and leadership are an important basis for, and reflection of, women's experiences in the workplace. However, by focusing on the *content* of people's theories about leaders and about gender, much research and analysis fails to take into account *contextual variation* in these stereotypes. A key question here concerns the flexibility in those theories: is it the case that implicit theories of leadership and gender are the same across time and across context?

Consistent with the idea that theories are more flexible than commonly supposed, there is some evidence to suggest that there is no single prototype of a good leader that observers (whether leadership theorists or lay followers) endorse in all situations (e.g., Haslam, 2001; Lord, Brown, Harvey, & Hall, 2001). As a basic illustration of this point, it is apparent that contingency models of leadership are founded on an assumption that the appropriateness of particular leadership styles varies with context. For example, Fiedler's (1964, 1978) contingency model suggests that successful leadership depends on a match between leader characteristics and features of the situation that any leader confronts. Distinguishing between different types of leaders, the model suggests that task-orientated leaders perform best when things are either (a) going particularly well (e.g., they have a strong leadership position, relations with followers are good, and the task at hand is structured) or (b) going particularly badly (leadership position is weak, relations with followers are poor, and the task is lacking in structure). On the other hand, a relationship-orientated leader will be most effective when conditions are mixed, for example, when leader power is lacking, relationships are strained, but the task is well-structured. In this way, particular types of leaders are seen as more suited to some types of tasks than to others.

Beyond this, more recent approaches to leadership suggest not only that evaluations of leadership effectiveness vary across situations, but also that perceptions of what it means to be a good leader are dynamic and context-dependent. In particular, this is true of leadership categorization theory (e.g., Lord, Foti, & DeVader, 1984; Lord & Maher, 1990, 1991; see also Lord & Smith, 1999; Lord et al., 2001) and the social identity approach to leadership (e.g., Haslam, 2001; Hogg, 2001; Turner & Haslam, 2001).

Leadership categorization theory emphasizes the importance of followers' perceptions of leaders, suggesting that leadership perceptions are based largely on leadership prototypes (Lord & Maher, 1990). Here, leadership success is predicted to follow from a leader's ability to meet the expectations of his or her followers. Importantly, these prototypes are often specific to a particular context or domain (e.g., business, sport, the military), and thus a leader who is perceived to be effective in one domain may not be seen as effective in another (e.g., Lord & Maher, 1990). Applying this to gender, the leadership categorization approach would suggest that women are under-represented in leadership roles (and are perceived an unsuccessful when they hold them) because they are not perceived to possess the traits required for, and expected of, a managerial role. However, the fact that this match varies across situations might explain why there are more women managers in service sectors (e.g., in healthcare or retail) than in industrial sectors (e.g., manufacturing or mining; Singh & Vinnicombe, 2003).

In contrast, the social identity approach to leadership moves away from a simple matching of leaders' abilities to the appropriate situation, and instead looks at the way in which perceptions of leadership emerge as a result of the shared social identity of group members and the needs and interests that arise from that identity (e.g., Haslam, 2001; Hogg, 2001; Turner & Haslam, 2001). According to this analysis, a leader must be seen to epitomize what it means to be an ingroup member, and only a prototypical group member (i.e., one that maximizes both intragroup similarity *and* intergroup difference; self-categorization theory's principle of *meta-contrast*, Turner, 1985) is likely to be able to influence and lead the group (Turner, 1991).

As a result, it is more important for leaders to be prototypical group members than it is for them to have the traits of a prototypical leader in the abstract (e.g., Haslam & Platow, 2001; Hogg & Terry, 2000). This means, for example, that if a group consisting of people of average intelligence contrasts itself from an outgroup consisting of people who are highly intelligent, then that group may preferentially select a leader who is of moderate intelligence rather than one who is highly intelligent—because the former person epitomizes what it means to be "one of us" rather than "one of them" (Turner & Haslam, 2001; see also Duck & Fielding, 1999; Haslam et al., 2001; Jetten, Duck, Terry, & O'Brien, 2002; Reicher & Hopkins, 1996). Among other things, this helps explains why groups sometimes prefer leaders who *violate* stereotypic assumptions of what a good leader should be (e.g., intelligent, articulate, well informed; Hollander, 1985). Indeed, such dynamics can been used to explain the popularity of a tongue-tied political leader like George Bush over his more eloquent counterparts. In social identity terms, Bush's success derives in part from his ability to define himself as a representative of down-to-earth "middle-America" set in opposition to an intellectual elite of professional politicians and bureaucrats.

Importantly, though, this group prototypicality is not fixed or static, but varies as a function of social context and the nature of intergroup relations (e.g., Haslam & Turner, 1992, 1995; Turner & Oakes, 1989). The group that prefers a moderately intelligent person in the context of competition with a highly intelligent outgroup, may thus opt for a highly intelligent leader when in competition with a group perceived to be of inferior intelligence.

Applied to gender, the social identity approach would suggest that inequalities in the number of male and female leaders could arise from the fact that women are seen by those who appoint them (mainly men) to be less prototypical than men of the groups they are expected to lead. Indeed, the fact that the upper echelons of management are dominated by men means that this outcome is doubly-determined since women are (a) less likely to define the leader prototype (because they do not maximize intragroup similarity) and (b) less likely to be doing the defining.

Again, though, such outcomes should be seen as context-dependent rather than set in stone. Most obviously, this is because demographics characteristics such as gender are not the only way of representing a group, and those attributes that are valued by a group may be unrelated to gender or may explicitly counter gender discrimination. Thus if a group's norms value equality or diversity, a woman may be seen to be an appropriate leader for a group, even if that group is male-dominated.

Think Crisis: Think Female?

The literature reviewed in the previous section suggests that there is no simple or universal implicit theory of what it means to be a leader that is likely to be inform perception and action across all situations. Indeed, Schein's (1973, 1975, 2001) work into perceptions of what it means to be a manager and what it means to be a man or a woman has looked solely at perceptions of *successful* managers. There is, however, some evidence that what is needed from a leader when all is going smoothly might be very different from what is required or expected in times of crisis or risk (Bligh, Kohles, & Meindl, 2004; Haslam et al., 2001; Hunt, Boal, & Dodge, 1999; Meindl, 1993; Pillai & Meindl, 1998).

For example, Pillai and Meindl (1998) identified a negative relationship between evaluations of leaders and perceptions of crisis, such that those who held the reins through a time of crisis were more likely to be seen as poor leaders and to be blamed for being "part of the problem" (Emrich, 1999). In this way, when one thinks of leaders in a crisis situation, one may not expect them to have, or attribute to them, the same traits as successful managers. Accordingly, in such situations, individuals may not automatically "think manager-think male," they may in fact "think crisis–think female."

Consistent with this analysis, in Schein's (1973, 1975) original studies there were a small number of traits associated with managerial success that participants believed women were more likely to posses than men. These included being understanding, helpful, sophisticated, aware of the feelings of others, intuitive, creative, and cheerful. It seems plausible that some of these traits, (e.g., being understanding, intuitive, and creative) are ones which are seen be particularly useful in times of crisis.

Empirical support for this analysis comes from a preliminary study (Ryan, Haslam, Hersby, & Bongiorno, 2005) in which participants were asked to identify those traits from a list of 14 which were most useful for the leader of a company that was doing (a) well or (b) badly. Seven of the traits were those associated with managerial success that men are typically believed to be more likely to posses than women ("male manager" traits; e.g., self-reliant, aggressive), and seven were those associated with managerial success that women are typically believed to be more likely to posses than men ("female manager" traits; e.g., intuitive, understanding). As predicted, and as can be seen in Table 7.1, "male manager" traits were more likely to be seen as useful in a company that was performing well, but "female manager" traits were more likely to be seen as useful in a company that was performing badly.

Table 7.1.   The Association between "Male" and "Female" Manager Traits and Successful and Poorly Performing Companies

	Proportion associated with leadership of a successful company	Proportion associated with leadership of a failing company
"Male" manager traits (e.g., self-reliant, aggressive)	.60	.40
"Female" manager traits (e.g., intuitive, understanding)	.35	.65

Women in A Time of Risk: the Glass Cliff

Building on the observations in the previous section, the notion that women may be seen as more suitable for managerial positions in a time of crisis is consistent with a program of research investigating the contexts in which women are appointed into leadership positions (Ashby, Ryan, & Haslam, 2005; Ryan & Haslam, 2005a, 2005b; Ryan, Haslam, & Kulich, 2005). This research suggests that women tend to be appointed to leadership positions under very different circumstances than men. More specifically, as intimated above, this research suggests that women are more likely to be appointed to leadership positions that are associated with an increased risk of criticism and failure. Women's leadership positions can thus be seen as more precarious than those of men. Extending the metaphor of the "glass ceiling" and the "glass elevator," we have dubbed this phenomenon "the glass cliff" (Ryan & Haslam, 2005a). The following sections summarize archival and experimental investigations into the glass cliff phenomenon to date.

Archival Studies

The comments by Judge (2003) that prefaced this chapter vividly illustrate the fact that one way of making sense of the tendency for companies with women on their boards to perform less well than those that have all-male boards, is to see women leaders as "wreaking havoc" in the workplace. Judge's conclusions were based on simple correlational analysis of the performance of FTSE 100 companies (an index of the 100 largest companies on the London Stock Exchange) with and without women on their boards in the UK throughout 2003. However, to make the case for a glass cliff-based reinterpretation of this data, Ryan and Haslam (2005a) conducted a more detailed analysis of the performance of these same companies, both before and after the appointment of a male or female board member.

Putting paid to the argument that women directors are bad for business, the analyses revealed that the appointment of a woman director was *not* associated with a subsequent drop in company performance. Indeed, in a time of a general financial downturn, companies that appointed a woman actually experienced a marked *increase* in share price after the appointment. On the other hand, those appointments that were made in less unsettled times tended to be followed by a period of share price stability. In contrast, those companies that appointed men to their boards displayed no such pattern.

Yet this study did more than simply refute claims that women were unable to cut it in the corporate world. More noteworthy, there were fluctuations in company performance *leading up* to the appointment of women to boards of directors. As can be seen in Figure 7.1, in a time of a general downturn in the stock market, companies that appointed a woman to their board had experienced consistently poor performance in the months preceding the appointment. Thus *women were more likely than men to be placed in positions already associated with poor company performance.* In this way, female directors were more likely than male directors to find themselves on a glass cliff, such that their positions of leadership were more risky and precarious than those in which men found themselves.

Importantly, these glass cliff positions do not seem to be restricted to large businesses and corporations. Ryan, Haslam, and Kulich (2005) also identified the existence of glass cliff positions in the 2003 Scottish Parliamentary

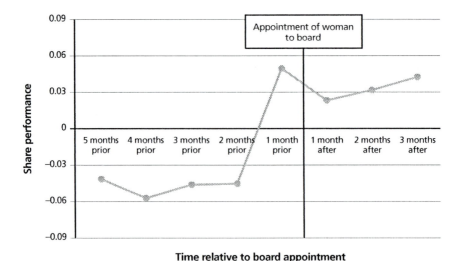

Figure 7.1.   FTSE 100 Companies' relative monthly performance in the 5 months prior to and 3 months post appointment of a female board member during a period of poor stock market performance (from Ryan & Haslam, 2005a).

Elections. Here there was evidence that, in more conservative parties, women were required to run in more difficult seats than were men. More specifically, analysis demonstrated that the Scottish Conservative and Unionist Party stood significantly less women candidates than men in the election, with only 18% of candidates being female. Moreover, those women who were put forward as candidates were preselected in seats that were less winnable in the sense that they were held by an opposition candidate with a significantly larger margin (34%) than were the seats in which men ran (28%).

Experimental Studies

One potential objection to the above studies is that they are archival and hence could arise from any number of processes over which the researchers have no control. Certainly, evidence that such effects could be reproduced in experimental contexts where key variables (e.g., leader competence, confidence, experience) are held constant and others (in particular, gender) are manipulated would lend stronger support to the causal reanalysis for which we have argued. For this reason, we recently embarked on a series of experimental laboratory studies designed to replicate and extend these archival studies (Ashby et al., 2005; Ryan & Haslam, 2005b).

In a first study (Ryan & Haslam, 2005b, Study 1) participants (graduate business students) were asked to indicate whom they thought should fill a vacant executive board position in a company that was described as having either increasingly good or increasingly bad performance. Participants were given descriptions of three candidates for the position, a male and a female candidate who were equally well qualified, and a third male candidate who was clearly not suitable for the job. Consistent with findings from archival studies, participants saw the female candidate as significantly more appointable when the company's performance was said to be decreasing, than when it was increasing.

These findings were also replicated in a study conducted with high-school students (Ryan & Haslam, 2005b, Study 2). Here, adolescent participants were more likely to choose a female candidate to be a youth representative for a local music festival when they were led to believe that the festival's popularity was declining over time than when it was thought to be improving. In addition, Ashby et al. (2005) also reproduced a pattern of glass cliff appointments in a legal context. In this study law students were more likely to select a female lawyer to take a lead role in a case when that case was described as associated with negative publicity and criticism than when it was described as easy and trouble-free.

These empirical studies suggest that the glass cliff is a robust phenomenon that is not isolated to a particular context or participant group. Importantly too, the fact that the studies allow us to hold constant key factors that might otherwise contribute to gender inequalities in the workplace (e.g. ability and past experience), increases our confidence that gender has a causal role to play in the appointment of women to class cliff positions.

Why Do Glass Cliffs Exist? Issues of Process

Taken together, our archival and empirical studies provide a substantial body of evidence that speaks to the existence the glass cliff phenomenon and reiterates the importance of context in determining the perceived suitability of men and women for positions of leadership. As we have noted, these glass cliff positions hold a greater element of danger for those who occupy them, because companies that have experienced consistently bad performance are likely to attract negative publicity and attention of the "wrong sort" (e.g., in the media, on the stock market). In such cases too, explanations for poor performance are more likely to focus on the individual abilities of the leaders involved than on situational and contextual factors that affect the company (e.g., Meindl, Ehrlich, & Dukerich, 1985). In this way, compared to men, women leaders may be in greater danger of being subjected to unfair criticism and being blamed for negative outcomes.

Yet while the glass cliff phenomenon is itself becoming increasingly well documented, it is less clear at this stage what social-psychological or other processes are responsible for its emergence. For this reason, the question of *why* it is that women are more likely than men to be placed in risky leadership positions is a major focus of our current research.

As with other forms of gender inequity in the work place, glass cliff appointments are likely to be due to a number of factors including: (a) overt sexism in the workplace, (b) women's competing responsibilities in the home (Equal Pay Task Force, 2001), and, as discussed in the previous section, (c) the perceived mismatch between women's abilities and the requirements of leadership (e.g., Agars, 2004; Eagly & Karau, 2002; Heilman et al., 1989; Schein, 1973, 1975, 2001).

In order to investigate these possibilities further, a large scale on-line study was conducted in which people were given the opportunity both to describe their own experiences of glass cliffs and to identify the factors that they thought were responsible for them (Ryan, Haslam & Postmes, 2005). Amongst other things, this allowed us (a) to gather qualitative data related to the subjective experience of being on a glass cliff, (b) to identify the range of factors which employees themselves consider responsible for the phenomenon, (c) to gauge the relative popularity of these accounts, and (d) to gain some insight into the relative popularity of accounts among both men and women.

Just under 300 people from around the world (in particular, from Britain, the United States, Canada, and Australia) participated in the study. Of these nearly 75% identified themselves as women. All had read a BBC-online news story about the glass cliff phenomenon (Ryan & Haslam, 2004) and, after this, had been given the opportunity to complete a questionnaire and to provide open-ended accounts of their experiences and explanations of the glass cliff phenomenon. In total, 250 separate qualitative responses were collected, including 130 comments on the likely causes of glass cliff appointments and 120 descriptions of glass cliff experiences.

Participants' observations supported the notion that the glass cliff phenomenon is multiply-determined, with a number of discrete themes emerging from the various responses. These explanations are summarized in Table 7.2, and each is discussed in more detail in the following sections.

Table 7.2.   Candidate Explanations for the Glass Cliff

Explanation	Form taken	*Proportion of women who generate this explanation (w)*	*Proportion of men who generate this explanation (m)*
Sexism	Women are singled out for inferior positions	20.4%	4.2%
Group dynamics/ ingroup bias	Those in senior positions (men) prefer to hire ingroup members (men) for 'cushy' jobs	17.5%	0%
	Women are seen as more expendable than men and make better potential scapegoats	16.5%	0%
	Lack of support	8.7%	4.2%
Social-structural factors	Women have fewer opportunities than men and therefore accept risk-ier positions	31.1%	8.3%
	Appointment of a woman is a powerful signal of change	14.6%	8.3%
	Try something different	8.7%	12.5%
Implicit theories (task–ability fit)	Women are more suited to dealing with a crisis	16.5%	16.7%
Scientific error	Women are *not* differentially placed in precarious leadership positions	2.9%	50%

Note: Responses to the question 'What do you think leads women to be appointed to 'Glass Cliff' positions? (N = 130, 103 female, 24 male, 3 undisclosed gender)

Overt Sexism

One of the most straightforward explanations for the tendency to place women in precarious leadership positions might suggest that it is a basic manifestation of sexism in the workplace. Indeed, when asked to choose from a list of possible explanations, outright sexism was favored by almost 20% of respondents to the survey, but women were almost five times more likely to favor this explanation than men. Furthermore, qualitative responses frequently referred to what one respondent termed the "blatantly sexist motives" of men in the workplace.

However, our experimental research suggests that glass cliffs cannot simply be explained by out-and-out sexism. In particular, this is because negative attitudes towards gender equality—as measured by support for feminist ideals—were not predictive of the tendency to appoint women to risky leadership positions (Ryan & Haslam, 2005b). In other words, people who espoused sexist views were no more likely to appoint women to glass cliffs than those who rejected those views. Accordingly, it would appear that the phenomenon needs to be interpreted in terms of processes that are more subtle (e.g., subconscious) and less overtly malign.

Group Dynamics and Ingroup Bias

Along the lines of our discussion above, one alternative account is to see glass cliffs as an expression of intergroup discrimination by decision-makers who are predominantly male. This discrimination would take the form of ingroup favoritism on the part of those males (i.e., "jobs for the boys"), such that more attractive positions are reserved for fellow ingroup members (e.g., Tajfel & Turner, 1979). As one respondent commented:

> I think when a cushy job comes up, the old boys' network set-up means that men select their friends for the position. When none of their chums want the job, it gets given to the woman. (Female professional, 28)

Such discrimination can also be seen as a means of reducing the threat to the status quo and men's positions of status superiority that is posed by women who seek to climb the corporate ladder (Schmitt, Ellemers, & Branscombe, 2003). In one respondent's words:

> I think the glass cliff is another form of the glass ceiling, intended to block women's passage up the ranks. Women will be put in glass cliff positions because there is a resentment of ambitious women who are often seen as threatening or difficult (not just by men) and also because it gives those who appoint them the excuse that they do allow women (superficially) equal

opportunities and therefore allows them to avoid any charge of sexism. (Female student, 28)

Related to explanations based on discrimination, it can be argued that women are appointed to glass cliff positions because company decision makers (reflecting widely-held societal views) see women as more expendable and are thus more willing to put them forward for leadership positions of dubious status. Moreover, in such positions women may be more attractive as potential scapegoats who can be shouldered with blame should things go wrong. As one middle-manager suggested:

> Women will be placed in glass cliff situations because women are expendable. A glass cliff requires a competent individual so senior managers will figure which candidates can handle the role. Then they will take out any candidates that they are grooming or care about in order to protect them. Those will often be men, because senior managers are men and are more likely to mentor younger men than they are women. So the candidate pool they are left with will have a large percentage of women—women who are capable, yet expendable because no one is really rooting for their success. (Female middle-manager, 35)

In this way, women often lack the support networks, infrastructure, and resources that are provided to male leaders.

However, while explanations based on these various forms of group dynamics are popular with respondents (particularly women), they are not lent strong support by findings from our experimental studies. In particular, there was no evidence that participants saw leadership positions in poorly performing companies to be any less desirable than positions in more successful one (Ryan & Haslam, 2005b).

On the other hand, more subtle measures of desirability used by Ashby et al. (2005) *did* indicate that participants were less likely to recommend a risky position to a friend than a non-risky position. This suggests that men may be less likely to find themselves on glass cliffs than women because members of their gender-based ingroup direct them away from them.

Implicit Theories

Another recurring theme in participants' qualitative responses was the suggestion that people's implicit theories about gender and leadership play an important role in women's appointment to glass cliffs. These observations support a number of the predictions made by leadership categorization and social identity theories. Consistent with leadership categorization theory, there was some evidence that glass cliff appointments were seen to be associated with perceptions of a match between stereotypic beliefs about women's abilities and the requirements of management in poorly performing companies—that is, a belief that women possess traits that may be useful in a struggling company.

Along these lines, respondents repeatedly suggested that women were chosen over men because of their "special" abilities, including an ability to remain calm in a crisis and to manage difficult situations. Illustrative of such statements, one female respondent observed:

> Women have a different way of approaching a problem to men which might contribute to their being asked to address such a situation. (Female professional, 35)

In this vein, respondents identified many concrete abilities which women are perceived to possess that may be useful for poorly performing companies. These included observations that "women always want to help, and often help the underdog," and that women "have more skills to balance risk," and that they "tend to cope with failure more pragmatically than men." These perceived abilities are epitomized in the comments of one respondent when describing the reasons why she thought her mother had been placed in a glass cliff situation:

> In certain cases, women are thought to inherently possess "soft" skills that make them part manager-part human resource director. My mother was given a department of viciously feuding staff members to oversee—a job that no-one in their right mind would take—because, aside from her managerial skills, they felt that she could "smooth things over." Not something a man would be expected to do. (Female professional, 35)

However, some respondents were more skeptical, suggesting that women are given glass cliff positions not because their traits or abilities were seen to match the concrete managerial tasks they faced, but instead because they are *not* men. If a company is performing poorly, this may indicate that the "think manager-think male" approach to management is not working, and hence that a change from the traditional, prototypical male leader is called for. In one respondent's words:

> I think many companies are willing to continue with the status quo if everything is running successfully. This is because they use the theory that they've always done it this way and it's worked so why change it? This at the moment normally means a male-dominated managerial system. When companies or other institutions suffer problems they are much more likely to try and change their operating methods. One of the obvious things to change about a group of managerial staff is the male/female ratio as the rationale is it can't hurt to try. (Female student, 21)

And those of another:

> I think women often get appointed to these positions following a period of poor business performance because there is a feeling that trying something different is better than trying nothing at all. I suspect companies sometimes also feel that they are unlikely to be criticized for appointing a female, even if she fails to turn round the business, because it would not be seen to be politically correct to relate performance to gender. (Female senior manager, 35)

Respondents also noted that such strategies present themselves as "win-win" options for those who seek to preserve the gender-based status quo. If women succeed after having been placed in difficult positions, then the organization is better off, and if they fail then women can be blamed and the prior practice of appointing men can be justified. Moreover, in either event, equal opportunities policy can be seen to have been enacted and the organization is given the opportunity to present itself as enlightened and progressive.

Signaling Change

Related to this last explanation, respondents also noted that appointing a woman to a leadership role is often a "last-ditch effort" that is attempted only when the situation "is really dire." In this way, it may be the case that women are appointed to glass cliff positions not simply for their ability to perform the role, but because their appointment will attract favorable attention (Kanter, 1977)—signaling to both internal and external audiences that the company is embracing change (Lee & James, 2004).

Consistent with this idea, there is evidence to suggest that, at least in Japan, poor company performance is associated with the appointment of highly visible "outsiders" to boards of directors (Kaplan & Minton, 1994). By this means, the appointment itself can be used as an opportunity to engage in favorable impression management. As one suggested:

> If a woman is appointed following public scandal . . . it may be to "soften" the company's image or change the public image of the company. (Female middle manager, 35)

The appointment of women was also seen as a way of signaling that a company values gender equality, with one respondent suggesting that companies have a "sense of need to show willingness to be equity-minded" and another that companies had a "need to be seen to promote women." Glass cliff positions can thus be seen as a consequence of (misguided) attempts to enact equal opportunity norms by appointing women to any vacant position that becomes available:

> To address issues of equality at upper levels of management there has been a trend to fill open positions with women or minorities. High risk positions have higher turnover rates in general so these positions open up more often and provide opportunities in which to place women into upper levels and thus show that there is not a glass ceiling. It may be more of a coincidence than any deliberate attempt to correct a wrong or see women fail. (Female middle manager, 35)

OVERVIEW

The foregoing sections provide some insight into the key theories that people spontaneously invoke in order to explain the occurrence of glass cliffs. Clearly there are significant problems associated with any attempt to use this as a basis for providing definite answers to the question of which theory is "correct" (even if one were to assume that this is a meaningful question). Most obviously, the sample of respondents here is self-selected and there is no sense in which it can be seen as representative of the broader population. This is clearly indicated by the disproportionately large number of women who participated.

Related to this fact, it can also be argued that the motivations of this sample of respondents are likely to have been very different from those of the population at large and led them to favor certain explanations and deny others. In particular, this is because it is apparent that those women who responded were predominantly those who had first-hand experience of glass cliffs and hence who had "a story to tell" (or in the terms of some male respondents "an axe to grind"). At the same time, it is apparent that many of the men who responded (in fact half of them) were keen to downplay the significance of glass cliffs and the processes that lead to them (Branscombe, 1998). In the most extreme cases this took the form of direct attacks on the scientific validity of the research, as in the following response:

> Speaking as a research scientist, I am disgusted with the way in which you have attempted to select a very limited group of participants and ask them extremely leading questions. Your approach is entirely unscientific. (Male professional, 21)

While not wanting to make statements about the extent to which these different theories would be endorsed by men and women in the population at large, it is noteworthy that the differential patterns of theorizing displayed by men and women mirror those observed in other research (including experimental studies; see Schmitt, Branscombe, Kobrynowicz, & Owen, 2002; Schmitt, Branscombe, & Postmes, 2003). Thus women tended to explain the glass cliff in terms of pernicious processes (e.g., sexism, discrimination) while men favored more benign interpretations or denied the existence of glass cliffs altogether.

In this respect, we also believe that participants' responses provide valuable insight into the *range* of theories that can be generated in order to explain glass cliffs. Not least, this is because the sample included participants of all age groups, with a broad range of leadership experiences, and from countries all round the world. Certainly too, we believe the taxonomy of accounts that this helps to generate (as in Table 7.2) provides a useful framework for future research.

CONCLUSION

In this chapter we have provided an overview of a novel program of research into the processes that lead to women being placed in more precarious leadership positions than men. In the first instance our efforts have focused on attempting to uncover instances of the effect and to delineate the subtle and not-so-subtle forms in which it manifests itself. In this regard, a range of field and experimental studies convince us that the phenomenon is both robust and pervasive. Indeed, it is worth noting that although the size of glass cliff effects is variable, and although there is more research that we intend to conduct, to date, we have failed to conduct a study in which there is not some evidence of its existence.

Having established this, a second goal of our research has been to identify those social psychological and social-structural processes that might underpin the differential placement of women and men on glass cliffs. Here a number of candidate explanations can be proposed. These range from overt sexism to scientific error, but they can also be couched in terms of group dynamics, implicit leadership theories, and social structural factors.

It is apparent that, in their own analyses, men and women tend to endorse these theories to differing degrees—a pattern of attribution that can be seen as functional from the standpoint of their own gender-based ingroup (Hewstone, 1990). It seems highly likely too that understandings of the process vary as a function of the form and extent of participants' identification with that ingroup and their ideological analysis of the nature of status relations between men and women (e.g., whether it is legitimate or illegitimate, stable or unstable; Tajfel & Turner, 1979; see Schmitt et al., 2003, for an excellent discussion).

For this reason alone, we believe that attempts to discover the "one true" basis of the glass cliff phenomenon are likely to prove fruitless. This would also seem foolhardy, however, in light of evidence (a) that the various theories we have identified are not mutually exclusive and (b) that each of the processes postulated by the theories has some role to play in the creation and maintenance of glass cliffs (with the exception of scientific error—which hopefully our research has minimized). If one considers the implicit leadership theory that underpins the "think crisis–think female" effect, for example, it is clear that it can (a) derive from, and reinforce, sexism, (b) be created by, and contribute to, group dynamics (including communication and interaction), and (c) flow from and promote structural inequalities.

In future research, it would therefore seem to be important to explore the dynamic interplay between these various elements in order to develop and test a more thoroughgoing theoretical understanding of the phenomenon. While helping us to answer the fascinating intellectual questions that the existence of glass cliffs raises, we also hope that this research will provide much-needed insight into the social psychological and structural conditions that can help to eliminate discriminatory appointment practices. By this means we should be in a better position to ensure that society is able to harness the leadership potential of *all* its constituent groups—not just some.

ACKNOWLEDGMENT

Thanks to Tom Postmes and Giles Wilson for their contribution to the online components of the research reported in this chapter. This research was jointly funded by a grant from the Leverhulme Trust (Grant F.00144.V) and by the European Social Fund (Project Reference 4130).

REFERENCES

Ashby, J., Ryan, M.K., & Haslam, S.A. (2005). *Legal work and the glass cliff: Evidence that women are preferentially selected to lead problematic cases.* Manuscript under review, University of Exeter.

Agars, M.D. (2004). Reconsidering the impact of gender stereotypes on the advancement of women in organizations. *Psychology of Women Quarterly, 28,* 103–111.

Berthoin Antal, A., & Izreali, D.N. (1993). A global comparison of women in management: Women managers in their homelands and as expatriates. In E. Fagenson (Ed.), *Women in management: Trends, issues, and challenges in managerial diversity* (pp. 52–96). Newbury Park, CA: Sage.

Bligh, M.C., Kohles, J.C., & Meindl, J.R. (2004). Charisma under crisis: Presidential leadership, rhetoric, and media responses before and after the September 11th terrorist attacks. *The Leadership Quarterly, 15,* 211–239.

Boyce, L.A., & Herd, A.M. (2003). The relationship between gender role stereotypes and requisite military characteristics. *Sex Roles, 49,* 365–379.

Branscombe, N.R. (1998). Thinking about one's gender group's privileges or disadvantages: Consequences for well-being in women and men. *British Journal of Social Psychology, 37,* 167–184.

Brenner, O.C., Tomkiewicz, J., & Schein, V.E. (1989). The relationship between sex-role stereotypes and requisite management characteristics revisited. *Academy of Management Journal, 32,* 662–669.

The corporate woman: A special report. (1986, March 24). *Wall Street Journal,* 32 page supplement.

Deal, J.J. (1998). Perceptions of female and male managers in the 1990s: plu ça change.... *Sex Roles, 38,* 287–300.

Duck, J.M., & Fielding, K.S. (1999). Leaders and subgroups: One of us or one of them? *Group Processes and Intergroup Relations, 2,* 203–230.

Eagly, A.H., & Karau, S.J. (2002). Role congruity theory of prejudice toward female leaders. *Psychological Review, 109,* 573–598.

Eagly, A.H., Karau, S.J., & Makhijani, M.G. (1995). Gender and leader effectiveness: A meta-analysis. *Psychological Bulletin, 117,* 125–145.

Eagly, A.H., Makhijani, M.G., & Klonsky, B.G. (1992). Gender and the evaluation of leaders: A meta-analysis. *Psychological Bulletin, 111,* 3–22.

Emrich, C.G. (1999). Context effects in leadership perception. *Personality and Social Psychology Bulletin, 25,* 991–1006.

Equal Opportunities Commission (EOC). (2002). *Women and men in Britain: Management.* Manchester: Equal Opportunities Commission.

Equal Pay Task Force. (2001). *Just Pay.* Manchester: Author.

Fiedler, F.E. (1964). A contingency model of leadership effectiveness. In L. Berkowitz (Ed.), *Advances in experimental social psychology* (Vol. 1, pp. 149–190). New York: Academic Press.

Fiedler, F.E. (1978). The contingency model and the dynamics of the leadership process. In L. Berkowitz (Ed.), *Advances in experimental social psychology* (Vol. 11, pp. 59–112). New York: Academic Press.

Fiske, S.T., Bersoff, D.N., Borgida, E., Deaux, K., & Heilman, M.E. (1991). Social science research on trial: Use of sex stereotyping research in Price Waterhouse v. Hopkins. *American Psychologist, 46,* 1049–1060.

Haslam. S.A. (2001). *Psychology in organizations: The social identity approach.* London: Sage.

Haslam, S.A., & Platow, M.J. (2001). The link between leadership and followership: How affirming social identity translates vision into action. *Personality and Social Psychology Bulletin, 2,* 1469–1479.

Haslam, S.A., Platow, M.J., Turner, J.C, Reynolds, K.J., McGarty, C., Oakes, P.J., Johnson, S., Ryan, M.K., & Veenstra, K. (2001). Social identity and the romance of leadership: The importance of being seen to be "doing it for us." *Group Processes and Intergroup Relations, 4,* 191–205.

Haslam, S.A., & Turner, J.C. (1992). Context-dependent variation in social stereotyping 2: The relationship between frame of reference, self-categorization and accentuation. *European Journal of Social Psychology, 22,* 251–277.

Haslam, S.A., & Turner, J.C. (1995). Context-dependent variation in social stereotyping 3: Extremism as a self-categorical basis for polarized judgment. *European Journal of Social Psychology, 25,* 341–371.

Heilman, M.E. (1983). Sex bias in work settings: The lack of fit model. In B. Staw & L. Cummings (Eds.), *Research in organizational behavior* (Vol. 5, pp. 269–298). Greenwich, CT: JAI Press.

Heilman, M.E. (2001). Description and prescription: How gender stereotypes prevent women's ascent up the organizational ladder. *Journal of Social Issues, 57,* 657–674.

Heilman, M.E., Block, C.J., & Martell, R.F. (1995). Sex stereotypes: Do they influence perceptions of managers? *Journal of Social Behavior and Personality, 10,* 237–252.

Heilman, M.E., Block, C.J., Martell, R.F., & Simon, M.C. (1989). Has anything changed? Current characterizations of men, women, and managers. *Journal of Applied Psychology, 74,* 935–942.

Heilman, M.E., Wallen, A.S., Fuchs, D., & Tamkins, M.M. (2004). Penalties for success: Reactions to women who succeed at male gender-typed tasks. *Journal of Applied Psychology, 89,* 416–427.

Hewstone, M. (1990). The ultimate attribution error: A review of the literature on intergroup causal attribution. *European Journal of Social Psychology, 20,* 311–355.

Hogg, M.A. (2001). Social identification, group prototypicality, and emergent leadership. In M.A. Hogg & D.J. Terry (Eds.), *Social identity processes in organizational contexts* (pp. 197–213). Philadelphia: Taylor & Francis.

Hogg, M.A., & Terry, D.J. (2000). Social identity and self-categorization processes in organizational contexts. *Academy of Management Review, 25,* 121–140.

Hollander, E.P. (1985). Leadership and power. In G. Lindzey & E. Aronson (Eds.), *Handbook of social psychology* (Vol. 2, pp. 485–537). New York: Random House.

Hunt, J.G., Boal, K.B., & Dodge, G.E. (1999). The effects of visionary and crisis-responsive charisma on followers: An experimental examination of two kinds of charismatic leadership. *The Leadership Quarterly, 10,* 423–448.

Jetten, J., Duck, J., Terry, D., & O'Brien, A. (2002). Being attuned to intergroup differences in mergers: The role of aligned leaders for low status groups. *Personality and Social Psychology Bulletin, 28,* 1194–1201.

Judge, E. (2003, November 11). Women on board: Help or hindrance? *The Times,* p. 21.

Kanter, R.M. (1977). *Men and women of the corporation.* New York: Basic Books.

Kaplan, S. & Minton, B. (1994). Appointments of outsiders to Japanese boards: Determinants and implications for managers. *Journal of Financial Economics, 36,* 225–257.

Lee, P.M., & James, E.H. (2003). *'She'-E-Os: Gender effects and stock price reactions to the announcements of top executive appointments.* Darden Graduate School of Business Administration. Working paper 02-11.

Lord, R.G., Brown, D.J., Harvey, J.L., & Hall, R.J. (2001). Contextual constraints on prototype generation and their multi-level consequences for leadership perceptions. *Leadership Quarterly, 12*, 311–338.

Lord, R.G., Foti, R., & DeVader, C.L. (1984). A test of leadership categorization theory: Internal structure, information processing, and leadership perceptions. *Organizational Behavior and Human Performance, 34*, 343–78.

Lord, R.G., & Maher, K.J. (1990). Perceptions of leadership and their implications in organizations. In J.S. Carrol (Ed.), *Applied social psychology and organizational settings* (pp. 129–154). Hillsdale, NJ: Erlbaum.

Lord, R.G., & Maher, K.J. (1991). *Leadership and information processing: Linking perceptions and performance.* Boston: Unwin Hyman.

Lord, R.G., & Smith, W.G. (1999). Leadership and the changing nature of work performance. In D.R. Ilgin & E.D. Pulakos (Eds.), *The changing nature of work: Implications for staffing, personnel actions, and development* (pp. 192–239). Santa Barbara, CA: New Lexington Press.

Meindl, J.R. (1993). Reinventing leadership: A radical social psychological approach. In J.K. Murnighan (Ed.), *Social psychology in organizations* (pp. 89–118). Englewood Cliffs, NJ: Prentice-Hall.

Meindl, J.R., Ehrlich, S.B., & Dukerich, J.M. (1985). The romance of leadership. *Administrative Science Quarterly, 30*, 78–102.

Morrison, A.M., & Von Glinow, M.A. (1990). Women and minorities in management. *American Psychologists, 45*, 200–208.

Morrison, A.M., White, R.P., & Van Velsor, E. (1987). *Breaking the glass ceiling: Can women reach the top of America's largest corporations?* Reading, MA: Addison-Wesley.

Pillai, R., & Meindl, J.R. (1998). Context and charisma: A meso level approach to the relationship of organic structure, collectivism and crisis to charismatic leadership. *Journal of Management, 24*, 643–671.

Reicher, S.D., & Hopkins, N. (1996). Self-category constructions in political rhetoric: An analysis of Thatcher's and Kinnock's speeches concerning the British Miners' Strike (1984–5). *European Journal of Social Psychology, 26*, 353–372.

Rudmen, L.A., & Glick, P. (2001). Prescriptive gender stereotypes and backlash toward agentic women. *Journal of Social Issues, 57*, 743–762.

Ryan, M.K., & Haslam, S.A. (2004, May 29) *Introducing the glass cliff.* Online BBC article: http://news.bbc.co.uk/1/hi/magazine/3755031.stm

Ryan, M.K., & Haslam, S.A. (2005a). The glass cliff: Evidence that women are over-represented in precarious leadership positions. *British Journal of Management, 16*, 81–90.

Ryan, M.K., & Haslam, S.A. (2005b). *The road to the glass cliff: Differences in the perceived suitability of men and women for leadership positions in succeeding and failing organizations.* Manuscript under review, University of Exeter.

Ryan, M.K., Haslam, S.A., Hersby, M.D., & Bongiorno, R. (2005). *Think crisis–think female: Using the glass cliff to reconsider the think manager–think male stereotype.* Manuscript under review, University of Exeter.

Ryan, M.K., Haslam, S.A., & Kulich, C. (2005). *Why women fail in politics: Further evidence for existence of the glass cliff.* Manuscript in preparation, University of Exeter.

Ryan, M.K., Haslam, S.A., & Postmes, T. (2005). *Reactions to the glass cliff phenomenon.* Manuscript in preparation: University of Exeter.

Schein, V.E. (1973). The relationship between sex role stereotypes and requisite management characteristics. *Journal of Applied Psychology,* 57, 95–105.

Schein, V.E. (1975). The relationship between sex role stereotypes and requisite management characteristics among female managers. *Journal of Applied Psychology,* 60, 340–344.

Schein, V.E. (2001). A global look at psychological barriers to women's progress in management. *Journal of Social Issues, 57,* 675–688.

Schein, V.E., & Mueller, R. (1992). Sex role stereotyping and requisite management characteristics: A cross cultural look. *Journal of Organizational Behavior, 13,* 439–447.

Schein, V.E., Mueller, R., Lituchy, T., & Liu, J. (1996). Think manager—think male: A global phenomenon? *Journal of Organizational Behavior, 17,* 33–41.

Schmitt, M.T., Branscombe, N.R., Kobrynowicz, D., & Owen, S. (2002). Perceiving discrimination against one's gender-group has different implications for well-being in women and men. *Personality and Social Psychology Bulletin, 28,* 197–210.

Schmitt, M.T., Branscombe, N.R., & Postmes, T. (2003). Women's emotional responses to the perception of pervasive gender discrimination. *European Journal of Social Psychology, 33,* 297–312.

Schmitt, M.T., Ellemers, N., & Branscombe, N.R. (2003). Perceiving and responding to gender discrimination in organizations. In S.A. Haslam, D. van Knippenberg, M.J. Platow, & N. Ellemers (Eds.), *Social identity at work: Developing theory for organizational practice* (pp. 277–292). Philadelphia, PA: Psychology Press.

Sczesny, S. (2003). A closer look beneath the surface: Various facets of the think-manager-think-male stereotype. *Sex Roles, 49,* 353–363

Simon, R.J., & Landis, J.M. (1989). Women's and men's attitudes about a woman's place and role. *Public Opinion Quarterly, 53,* 265–276.

Singh, V., & Vinnicombe, S. (2003). *The 2003 Female FTSE Index. Women Pass a Milestone: 101 Directorships on the FTSE 100 Boards.* Cranfield School of Management.

Tajfel, H., & Turner, J.C. (1979). An integrative theory of intergroup conflict. In W.G. Austin & S. Worchel (Eds.), *The social psychology of intergroup relations* (pp. 33–47). Monterey, CA: Brooks/Cole.

Turner, J.C. (1985). Social categorization and the self-concept: A social cognitive theory of group behaviour. In E.J. Lawler (Ed.), *Advances in group processes* (Vol. 2, pp. 77–122) Greenwich, CT: JAI Press.

Turner, J.C. (1991). *Social influence.* Milton Keynes: Open University Press and Pacific Grove, CA: Brooks/Cole.

Turner, J.C., & Haslam, S.A. (2001) Social identity, organizations and leadership. In M.E. Turner (Ed.), *Groups at Work: Advances in theory and research* (pp. 25–65). Hillsdale, NJ: Erlbaum.

Turner, J.C., & Oakes, P.J. (1989) Self-categorization theory and social influence. In P.B. Paulus (Ed.), *The psychology of group influence* (2nd ed., pp. 233–275). Hillsdale, NJ: Erlbaum.

Williams, C.L. (1992). The glass escalator: Hidden advantages for men in the "female" professions. *Social Problems, 39,* 253–267.

PART III

EXPLAINING IMPLICIT LEADERSHIP THEORIES

CHAPTER 8

PERSONALITY AND ROMANCE OF LEADERSHIP

Jörg Felfe

ABSTRACT

From a follower-centric point of view, several authors have raised the question as to what degree the emergence and evaluation of leadership is a result of followers' perceptions, attributions and social construction. These perceptions and attributions may be driven by followers' implicit theories on leadership. As many studies have shown, romance of leadership as an implicit leadership theory actually has an impact on the perception and evaluation of leadership (Ehrlich, Meindl, & Viellieu, 1990; Meindl & Ehrlich, 1988; Shamir, 1992). Particularly in cases of unexpected success or failure people tend to overestimate leaders' responsibilities and neglect external circumstances. However, little is known as to how far followers' personality influences the tendency to develop a romantic view of leaders in general. Therefore, in an empirical study the influence of personal characteristics of followers on the tendency to overestimate leaders' responsibility and influence is examined. Besides demographic variables, Big-five, measures for achievement, power and affiliation motives are considered. Furthermore, self-efficacy, need for structure, and need for leadership are included. The participants were 184 students from different subjects and universities in Germany who self-rated several personality scales and their romance of lead-

Implicit Leadership Theories: Essays and Explorations, pages 199–225
Copyright © 2005 by Information Age Publishing

ership. Results indicate that individuals' romance of leadership is related to personality. Participants' occupational self-efficacy, self-esteem, extraversion, conscientiousness and dominance are positively related to romance of leadership, whereas for neuroticism a negative correlation is found. No relationships occurred for uncertainty tolerance, need for structure and need for leadership. However, a positive relationship between need for leadership and romance of leadership was found for participants with low self-esteem. It is concluded that social construction of leadership such as romance of leadership is based on similarity to the self.

INTRODUCTION

Most research in the field of leadership can be considered as leader-centric, as it is focused on leaders' behavior and its effectiveness with regard to different outcomes. Meanwhile, there is also a growing interest in leaders' personality characteristics as predictors of leadership emergence and effectiveness. Besides this mainstream in leadership research an alternative approach has been established that puts emphasis on the role of the followers in an interactive, dyadic process of leadership. In recent years, research with a follower-centered perspective has received increased attention (e.g., Awamleh & Gardner, 1999; Ayman, 1993; Gardner & Avolio, 1998; Lord & Maher, 1993; Meindl, 1995; Nye, 2002).

From this point of view, there is evidence that the chance to become and to maintain being an effective leader does not solely depend on the leaders' own behavior but also on the social construction of followers. Expectancies of followers as to what a leader is like or how he or she should act influence perceptions and attributions in a particular leadership situation. Thus, the resulting evaluation and acceptance of a specific leader are determined by followers' mind-sets consisting of assumptions, beliefs, and expectations, regarding the causes, nature, and the consequences of leadership. These mind-sets are regarded as implicit leadership theories (ILT). The romance of leadership can be regarded as a specific ILT that emphasizes an outstanding influence of leaders for organizational success or failure. Before we take a closer look at this specific approach, the theoretical background of ILT is briefly outlined.

IMPLICIT LEADERSHIP THEORIES

According to Schneider's (1973) implicit personality theory, Eden and Leviathan (1975) consider implicit leadership theories as cognitive structures that contain typical traits and behaviors of leaders. These structures are made salient when followers are confronted with leaders. In a similar way, Lord, deVader, and Alliger (1986) refer to the term of cognitive schemata as a basis of implicit leadership theories (ILT). ILTs can be seen as cognitive frameworks and categorization systems that influence the perception and evaluation of leaders. Prototypes of leadership are a key concept for categorization. It is argued that people within one culture share a common set of categories that characterize a prototypical leader (House, Hanges, Javidan, Dorfman, & Gupta, 2004; Lord, 1985; Shamir, 1992).

From research on the emergence of leadership there is considerable evidence that potential leaders' characteristics such as sensitivity, dedication, tyranny, charisma, attractiveness, masculinity, intelligence, and strength are associated with leadership (Offermann, Kennedy, & Wirtz, 1994). Personality traits such as extraversion, conscientiousness and emotional stability (Judge, Bono, Ilies, & Gerhardt, 2002) are also important facets of implicit leadership theories. High performance and success as a result of leaders' behavior also seem to be embedded in implicit leadership theories. Followers' ratings of leaders are systematically influenced by information on the previous success of the leader (Rush, Phillips, & Lord, 1981; Nye, 2002). Both cognitive processes, categorization and causal attribution, are labeled recognition and inference (Lord & Maher, 1993; Nye, 2002). Recognition and inference explain the social construction of leadership. If a focal leader matches categories or cognitive schemata of leader prototypes, this leader will be recognized as a leader (Lord, Foti, & de Vader, 1984). Based on assumptions concerning organizational functioning, followers analyze cause and effect, and infer that an observed specific success can be attributed to leadership.

For a more differentiated perspective Social Identity Theory (Tajfel & Turner, 1986) proposes that the cognitive structures are not static, but will be continually rebuilt as new information is available or task and context change (Hogg, 2001; Lord, Brown, Harvey & Hall, 2001; Lord & Emrich, 2001). Studies conducted within the frame of Social Identity Theory were able to show that the emergence of a leader is based on her or his prototypicality for the characteristics of a group in a specific situation (Haslam & Platow, 2001; Nye, 2002). Besides changing goals or follower needs, followers' own self conceptions may, in part, exert influence on implicit leadership categories (Keller, 1999). However, current results from the GLOBE study show that beyond individual and situational variability there appear to be universal elements of implicit leadership theories. For example, visionary leadership is a worldwide prominent facet of implicit leadership theories (House et al., 1999; House et al., 2004).

Besides a better theoretical understanding of leadership processes there are also at least two practical reasons why implicit leadership theories should be considered. (1) In general, this follower oriented approach may help to better understand why leaders are evaluated differently by different followers. Although systematic differences exist between leaders, there may be considerable variation in the degree to which different followers perceive and evaluate a focal leader. If these differences are not simply random variation, systematic influences may be identified. For example, followers' individual implicit leadership theories may serve as an explanation for the individual bias in the response to leaders' behavior. It is an important empirical question as to what extent leadership ratings are due to leader behaviors and to what extent they are due to followers' implicit leadership theories. This is, for example, of practical importance for a better understanding and interpreting of results obtained from survey feedback procedures (e.g., 360-degree feedback). (2) Moreover, it can be assumed that followers influence their leaders' behavior by their feedback and behavior. Leaders who meet their followers' expectations and demands have a better chance of being effective as they can expect more motivation, cooperation, support, reinforcement, and less resistance (Lord & Emrich, 2001). Thus Lord et al. (1984) were able to show that leaders who match their followers' image are perceived to be more powerful and are given more credit for work outcomes. Nye and Forsyth (1991) found that the closer the match between the individual's prototype of an effective leader and the attributes of a presented leader was, the more favorable was the evaluation. Accordingly, Kenney, Schwartz-Kenney, and Blascovich (1996) identified followers' categories of appointed and elected leaders' worthy of influence (LWI). The categories are based on basic-level behaviors such as being determined, knowledgeable, caring etc. Once followers consider a person/leader as worthy of influence, they report that they will be more likely to allow that person to exert influence. To sum up, there is empirical evidence that leadership can be understood as a phenomenon of social construction (Nye, 2002), and effective leaders are made by their followers on the basis of their implicit theories.

Romance of Leadership can be regarded as a prominent implicit leadership theory. It was first introduced by Meindl, Ehrlich, and Dukerich (1985). It also puts emphasis on the social construction of leadership as a complement to leader-centric approaches (Meindl, 1998). Romance of leadership can be defined as the tendency to view leadership as the most important factor to the functioning and dysfunctioning of organizations. Whereas the influence of other factors is de-emphasized, the influence and role of leadership are overestimated. In the beginning (Meindl, 1995), the tendency to overestimate the role of leadership for organizations' success or failure was primarily explained by situational factors. Particularly in cases of unexpected success or failure people tend to overestimate leaders' responsibilities and neglect external circumstances.

Meanwhile, Romance of leadership is also considered as a characteristic of the individual that remains stable in all sorts of situations. As Meindl (1990) states, some persons may be especially prone to the romanticized leadership and thereby underestimate other factors. Actually, this general propensity affects the perceptions in a specific leadership situation (Meindl, 1998; Felfe & Schyns, 2004a; Shamir, 1992). However, little is known about what personal characteristics influence the tendency to develop a romantic view of leaders. It is of theoretical and practical interest to better understand how this implicit leadership theory develops. Who are the followers with a high tendency to overestimate leaders' power and how do they differ from subordinates who have a more realistic and differentiated view on leadership? Therefore, in this study the influence of followers' personal characteristics on the tendency to overestimate leaders is examined.

ROMANCE OF LEADERSHIP

When starting the romance of leadership approach Meindl et al. (1985) began by analyzing the Wall Street Journal and found an increasing number of business articles dealing with leadership in years of economic growth. In a second study they showed that academic publication rates on leadership issues were notably higher when the economic situation was less optimistic. From these findings the authors derived the idea that in cases of unexpected or outstanding success or failure there is a focus on leadership as the most important factor while other factors such as the economical context, market-forces, or governmental regulations seem to be ignored. In a subsequent set of experimental studies information on the economic performance of organizations were systematically varied (failure or success). In accordance with the authors' assumptions, the reasons of outstanding success and failure were attributed to leadership whereas performance on an average level that did not challenge expectations was not primarily attributed to leadership. Following studies have directly (Shamir, 1992) or indirectly (de Vries, 2000) confirmed, in particular, the finding that performance outcomes positively influence the attribution of causality to leaders, relative to other factors. In a recent study Felfe and Petersen (in review) could even show that persons high in romance of leadership emphasize information about a leader and neglect information about the situational context when making their decisions in a managerial context.

Within a general model, Meindl (1995, 1998) outlines that Romance of Leadership can be regarded as a social construction that is based on individual and group level processes. The individual level processes consist of input variables that are connected to different constructions of leadership including definitions, criteria for evaluation etc. These individual processes are influenced by group level processes that can be described with concepts such as social contagion and interaction networks. The social construction is a result of an intersubjective collaboration, and negotiation on the basis of a shared system of leadership concepts. Depending on a specific construction of leadership, persons engage in self-defined follower-ship and commitment to a leader. The result is follower-ship action.

To measure individual differences with regard to the tendency to view leadership as important to the functioning and dysfunctioning of organizations, the RLS scale (Romance of Leadership Scale) was developed (Meindl & Ehrlich, 1988) and later on modified (Meindl, 1998). The items focus on the perceived causal significance of leadership, the assignment of blame and responsibility to leaders for success or failure, and the value of investing in extensive and costly assessment procedures to select applicants for vacant leadership positions.

As pointed out above, several studies were able to show that contextual factors such as performance cues and the perception of crisis influence romance of leadership on an individual level (Meindl, 1995). Moreover, romance of leadership was found to be closely linked to the perception of charismatic or transformational leadership. Meindl and Ehrlich (1988) found that RLS was positively related to the charisma subscale of the Multifactor Leadership Questionnaire (Bass, 1985) and postulate that "Transformational leadership, with its emphasis on charisma and vision, is in part a matter of perception and attribution, myth and symbol, that is likely to a romanticized component to it" (p. 182). This finding has been confirmed by Shamir (1992), who replicated and extended Meindl et al.'s (1985) fourth study. Romance of leadership also increased subjects' tendency to attribute influence to the leader across different experimental conditions. Ehrlich et al. (1990) report a considerable correlation for charisma of $r = .32$ that did not reach significance due to the small sample size. These results are also supported by recent findings in experimental studies with German samples (Felfe & Schyns, 2004a). They found that romance of leadership as an implicit leadership theory positively influenced the perception and acceptance of transformational leadership. In contrast to these findings there was no support for the relationship between romance of leadership and the perception of transformational leadership in the study of Awamleh and Gardner (1999) and Schyns and Sanders (2004) with a Dutch sample. For an overview and meta-analytic results see Schyns, Felfe, and Blank (in review). However, with a few exceptions, there is not much research addressing the question as to what the individual determinants of generalized propensity to see leadership as extraordinarily important for the functioning of organizations are.

CHARACTERISTICS OF FOLLOWERS WHO ARE SUSCEPTIBLE TO ROMANCE OF LEADERSHIP

What are the characteristics, personality traits or need configurations of persons who romanticize leadership? This question can be located within

Meindl's (1998) general model mentioned above, and refers to the individual processes that lead to a specific construction of leadership. Meindl (1990) himself found no relationships between romance of leadership and followers' gender, education, tenure, size of work unit, authoritarianism, and social desirability but positive correlations with age, internal control and self-esteem.

However, there seem to be good reasons for the assumption that those who lack control, self-efficacy, competences and self-esteem have a high need to reduce complexity, and to find simple explanations as well as tending to overestimate the role of leadership. This compensating mechanism could help to reduce complexity and give a conviction of understanding and control (Shamir, 1992). Complexity and uncertainty are reduced when responsibility and control can be attributed to leaders: if I can't do—leaders will do it for me/us. From this point of view romance of leadership is an expression of dependency and powerlessness. This would also mean that followers with high self-efficacy expectations and self-esteem have a differentiated or even critical attitude toward the impact of leadership.

On the other hand, it also seems plausible that followers with a high self-esteem and internal control beliefs generalize this attitude with regard to leaders: if one can effectively influence and control one's own environment, leaders will be even more able to shape their environment. Vice versa, people with a lack of influence or control experience leaders to be in a similar situation of powerlessness. Empirical support for this similar attribution of influence is provided by an experimental study conducted by Nye (2002). She was able to demonstrate that subjects who attributed responsibility for success or failure in a group task to the leader also attributed high responsibility to the group members, including themselves. Even though followers tend to attribute success to the leader, it appears that they also feel involved and probably would claim that the leader depends on their contribution and effort. Identification, generalization, and the experience of similarity may be underlying processes. Another explanation is provided by Meindl (1990). He argues that through their attribution to leadership, such persons are able to confirm their own need for control and stabilize their self-concept by attributing their own qualities to their leaders. According to this argumentation, Keller (1999) points out that implicit leadership theories may be based on followers' self conceptions. Engle and Lord (1997) also emphasize the role of similarity between leader and follower. They postulated that congruence with regard to implicit leadership and performance theories is a predictor for liking and LMX quality. In their study they also examined the role of similar self-schemas as a moderator for this relationship. Derived from self-schema literature they assumed that people tend to use the same categories when describing others as they use when describing themselves.

With regard to these contrary assumptions a parallel discussion exists in the field of charismatic/transformational leadership (for a more detailed discussion, see Felfe & Schyns, in press). The perception of transformational leadership is related to the concept of romance of leadership as was pointed out above. Accordingly, Klein and House (1998) have distinguished contradicting assumptions concerning the relationship between transformational leadership and subordinates' characteristics: completion and similarity. Although results are somewhat mixed, there seems to be more empirical support for the assumption of similarity with regard to personality (extraversion, self-esteem etc.) and values (achievement orientation, congruence). For example, Keller (1999) found that followers' extraversion predicted the preference for charismatic leaders. Accordingly, results from Felfe and Schyns (in press) revealed a positive influence of extraversion and a negative impact of neuroticism as followers' characteristics on the perception of leadership. Moreover, Ehrhart and Klein (2001) could show a correlation between achievement orientation and high self-esteem of followers and the preference for a charismatic leader. In a recent study, also a slightly positive relationship between perceived transformational leadership and occupational self-efficacy occurred (Schyns, 2001). Kirkpatrick and Locke (1996) found a correlation between the congruence persons perceived between their values and the values communicated through a vision and the perception of charisma. To sum up, these results indicate that followers perceive a higher level of transformational leadership and leaders are more influential when subordinates are similar to their leaders.

Derived from Meindl's (1990) early studies, theoretical assumptions with regard to similar self schemas (Engle & Lord, 1997), and Keller's (1999) conclusion that "the ideal leader was construed as similar to self" (p. 600), as well as empirical research on charismatic/ transformational leadership, we expect persons to show more romance of leadership when they are similar to leaders in general. There are two lines of argumentation that may explain why followers' personality resembles their implicit leadership theory. It (1) can be assumed that persons extend their individual theory of personality and influence to leaders in general. This argument is in line with the idea that leadership is primarily a social construction of followers. In this case similarity is a result of followers' generalization. (2) Alternatively, followers compare themselves with their picture of a leader based on their implicit theory and find themselves to be more ore less similar. The more they feel like leaders the more prone they will be to being identified with the role of leadership. Identification may cause a more positive evaluation, including the attribution of influence and power. This explanation is closer to the similarity-attraction paradigm. However, both processes may occur at the same time.

To sum up, the hypotheses presented below are based both on the assumption that followers' implicit leadership theory is constructed similar to the self and on the assumption that followers' perception of similarity between self and leaders in general influences leaders' evaluation. Therefore, in order to set up hypotheses on the relationship between followers' personality and romance of leadership we focused on personality characteristics that have been found to be linked to leadership in general. However, it has to be stated that similarity serves as a theoretical frame to direct our hypothesis, but it is not similarity itself that is going to be tested. It should not be neglected that there remain alternative psychological mechanisms for explanation besides similarity, for example, identification, projection, and reduction of dissonance. Hence, the focus of this study is to examine in how far followers' characteristics influence the willingness to romanticize leadership and is thereby not an explanation of the underlying processes.

Self-efficacy and Self-esteem

Self-efficacy as a personal trait reflects on beliefs and convictions concerning one's competence and capabilities to cope actively with demands in life (Bandura, 1997). "Occupational self-efficacy" (OSE; Schyns & von Collani, 2002) is a specification of that general belief related to the work context. In general, self-efficacy and self-esteem are relevant predictors for job performance and job satisfaction (Judge & Bono, 2001). Compared to their followers leaders show slightly higher self-efficacy scores and older employees tend to have more self-efficacy than younger employees (Felfe, 2003). Moreover, Judge et al. (2002) could show in their meta-analysis that self-esteem and locus of control are related to leadership effectiveness. In particular transformational leaders are supposed to be high in self-esteem and self-efficacy (Crant & Bateman, 2000; House & Howell, 1992). As Paglis and Green (2002) could show, leaders' self rated self-efficacy in the field of leadership is related to self-esteem and control experience. Subordinates perceive leaders with a higher level of self-efficacy to be more active and engaged in their leadership. Based on the assumption of similarity, people with a high level of self-efficacy and self-esteem are prone to attribute a high degree of influence and control to leaders in general, which in turn leads to a higher romance of leadership. Moreover, followers' self-esteem is correlated to the preference for a charismatic leader (Ehrhart & Klein, 2001). In this line, Meindl (1990) already found slight but significant positive relationships between romance of leadership, internal locus of control ($r = .17$) and self-esteem ($r = .12$). Therefore, it is assumed:

H1.1:   *Followers self-esteem is positively related to romance of leadership.*

H1.2:   *Followers occupational self-efficacy is positively related to romance of leadership.*

Big Five

Several studies have shown that some of the Big-five dimensions are consistently related to leaders' emergence and performance (Barrick & Mount, 1993; Judge et al., 2002; Silverthorne, 2001). As Judge et al. (2002) state, in comparison to the other Big-five dimensions, extraversion emerged as the most consistent correlate of leadership. According to research on the five-factor model, people high in extraversion are sociable, energetic, and high in positive affect, whereas people low in extraversion are more inwardly oriented and low in positive affect (Watson, 2000). Whereas conscientiousness is also positively related to leadership emergence and performance, neuroticism, being the contrary of emotional stability, was found to be negatively related to leadership emergence and performance (Judge et al., 2002). In particular, transformational leaders are supposed to be high in emotional stability (i.e., low in neuroticism). People with higher extraversion and lower neuroticism experience higher control, particularly in social contexts. Based on the assumption of similarity, extraverted people are more likely to attribute influence to leaders, who in general are also supposed to be extraverted and less neurotic, and thus have more romance of leadership. As aforementioned, followers' extraversion is also related to the perception of charismatic/transformational leaders (Felfe & Schyns, in press; Keller, 1999). On the other hand, neuroticism means lower self-esteem, higher anxiety, and the experience of more insecurity. Those people may also have less confidence in the abilities of others, including leaders, and therefore have less romance of leadership. Thus, with regard to the Big-five dimensions it is expected:

H2.1:   *Followers' extraversion is positively related to romance of leadership.*

H2.2:   *Followers' conscientiousness is positively related to romance of leadership.*

H2.3:   *Followers' neuroticism is negatively related to romance of leadership.*

Motives

Leaders' motives are related to effectiveness of leadership. In their meta-analysis Judge et al. (2002) found that achievement motivation and power motivation (dominance) are relevant motives in the context of leadership. Individuals who strive for difficult and demanding goals and power over others want to accomplish their aims by individual efforts. To improve performance and to gain feedback they even seek competition and expect success. Accordingly, people high in achievement and power motivation are more willing to attribute power and influence to leaders, i.e., romance of leadership, who in general are also supposed to be dominant and achievement oriented. Vice versa, people low in achievement and power motivation avoid competition and challenging goals because they are afraid of failure. This perspective may be extended toward leadership. Moreover, with regard to transformational leadership, Ehrhart and Klein (2001) could show a correlation between followers' achievement orientation and the preference for charismatic leaders. Thus, it is expected:

H3.1:   *Followers' achievement motivation is positively related to romance of leadership.*

H3.2:   *Followers' power motivation (dominance) is positively related to romance of leadership.*

Uncertainty Tolerance

Romance of leadership can be viewed from an information processing perspective. It helps people to structure and to make sense of organizational phenomena that are complex, ambiguous and difficult to comprehend (Meindl et al., 1985; Shamir, 1992). Thus, leadership provides followers with a plausible explanatory category for a better understanding and a sense of control. This tendency may be reinforced by the fundamental attribution error. Followers' need to understand and make sense of things is particularly high when events of failure are salient or extraordinary. Beyond this, followers' characteristics may explain this need to find simple explanations and to reduce complexity. Hence, followers high in uncertainty tolerance and having a low personal need for structure may be less prone to simplify reality. On the other hand, people high in uncertainty tolerance and low in need for structure feel that they have the abilities to be successful even when they are confronted with uncertainty and ambiguity. Particularly leaders often have to face challenging situations of insecurity and complexity and therefore are supposed to have abilities and strategies to cope with such situations, amongst them uncertainty tolerance and low need for structure. Therefore, people high in uncertainty tolerance and low in need for structure are more prone to romance of leadership, attributing influence to leaders who are frequently dealing with insecurity and complexity. Therefore, it is assumed:

H4:   *Uncertainty tolerance is positively related to romance of leadership.*

H5:   *Personal need for structure is negatively related to romance of leadership.*

Need for Leadership

Persons who believe that they need a leader to accomplish their goals and to get their tasks done may attribute more influence to leaders than persons who feel less dependent. Accordingly de Vries (2000) postulated that romance of leadership and need for leadership are supposed to be conceptually close concepts. In an experimental study de Vries (2000) found that need for leadership influenced the perception of leaders (also see de Vries & Van Gelder, this volume). A higher level of need for leadership had an effect on perceived goal orientation, support orientation, and prototypicality of a focal leader. Although RLS was not directly measured in this study, de Vries extends his approach and postulates "that romance of leadership will occur to a greater extent when performance is high instead of low and when need for leadership of subordinates is strong instead of weak" (p. 417). Consequently, a positive relationship between need for leadership and romance of leadership should be assumed.

On the other hand it was argued that persons with high self-esteem and self-efficacy tend to romanticize leadership. And it can be argued that people with a high need for leadership experience less autonomy and feel more dependent. Consequently, their self-efficacy and self-esteem are supposed to be lower, leading to a lower romance of leadership. In line with this argumentation, a negative relationship between need for leadership and romance of leadership could be expected. As pointed out above, however, there are good reasons to assume that need for leadership is positively related with romance of leadership.

As there are plausible reasons for both directions of correlation, the question must be raised if there is a moderator that determines if the correlation is positive or negative. As outlined before, self-esteem and self-efficacy may be of importance for the understanding of this relation. Accordingly, the relationship between need for leadership and romance of leadership may depend on people's self-esteem as a core evaluation of the self, this being control, positive mood, and autonomy. The direct effect of need for leadership on romance of leadership may be positive, particularly when self-esteem is low. In this case, need of leadership and romance of leadership may be associates as de Vries (2000) assumes. Vice versa, the relationship between need for leadership and romance of leadership should be near zero or even negatively reversed for persons with high self-esteem. Therefore it is assumed that need for leadership interacts with self-esteem when explaining romance of leadership:

H6:   *The relationship between need for leadership and romance of leadership is moderated by self-esteem. Lower self-esteem is associated with a positive correlation whereas higher self-esteem leads to a negative correlation.*

METHOD

Participants

Participants were 184 undergraduate students from different subjects (49.5% Psychology, 39% Economics, 11.4% others) of the Universities of Halle/Saale, Cologne, and Berlin, who had not attended leadership courses yet. Most of them were women (77.7% women and 22.3% men). The mean age was 23.4 ($SD = 3.9$). 68.7% of the students had work experience. All participants in this study were volunteers.

Personality

Extraversion, contientiousness, and *neuroticism* were assessed using a German short version of the NEO-PI developed by Borkenau and Ostendorf (1993), based on the instrument by Costa and McCrae (1985). The scales range from 1 = *not at all true* to 5 = *completely true*. Each scale consists of 12 items. One item was eliminated from the extraversion scale as its item-total correlation was below .20. The internal consistencies (Cronbach's alpha) for extraversion, conscientiousness, and neuroticism were $\alpha = .79$, $\alpha = .83$, and $\alpha = .88$, respectively. Extraversion is negatively correlated with neuroticism ($r = -.39$, $p < .001$).

To measure *self-efficacy* a short version of the occupational self-efficacy scale (OSE) by Schyns and von Collani (2002) was administered. The short version contains 8 items. The scale ranges from 1 = *not at all true* to 5 = *completely true*. The internal consistency (Cronbach's alpha) was $\alpha = .80$.

Self-esteem was measured with the 9-item scale by Rosenberg (1965). The scale ranges from 1 = *not at all true* to 5 = *completely true*. The internal consistency (Cronbach's alpha) was $\alpha = .86$. Self-esteem and OSE are strongly correlated ($r = .51$, $p < .001$).

Uncertainty tolerance (UT) was assessed using an eight-item scale developed by Dalbert (1999). The scale ranges from 1 = *not at all true* to 5 = *completely true*. The internal consistency (Cronbach's alpha) was $\alpha = .74$. UT is positively correlated with OSE ($r = .27$, $p < .001$) and self-esteem ($r = .15$, $p < .01$).

Personal need for structure (PNS) was assessed using an eight-item scale based on the original version from Neuberg and Newsom (1993), translated by Wolfradt, Sommer, and Rademacher (1999). Items were transferred to a work context by the author of this article. The scale ranges from 1 = *not at all true* to 5 = *completely true*. The internal consistency (Cronbach's alpha) was $\alpha = .73$. As expected uncertainty tolerance and PNS are correlated negatively ($r = -.56$). Moreover, PNS is also negatively correlated with OSE ($r = -.25$, $p < .01$), self-esteem ($r = -.19$, $p < .01$), but positively related to neuroticism ($r = .36$, $p < .001$).

Motives were measured with scales from the German Personality Research Form (PRF) (Stumpf et al., 1985). The scale ranges from 1 = *right* to 2 = *wrong*. Five items were removed from the original 16 items power motivation (dominance) scale and 1 item was removed from the achievement motivation scale to improve reliability. The internal consistencies (Cronbach's alpha) were $\alpha = .80$ for dominance and $\alpha = .63$ for achievement. Both scales are positively correlated ($r = .26$).

Need for Leadership was assessed using a German translation of the need for leadership scale from de Vries (2000). The translation was done by the author of this article and checked by de Vries. With this scale, participants were asked to indicate how much they rely on their leaders for different purposes: goal setting, motivation etc. The scale ranges from 1 = *not at all* to 5 = *very much*. The internal consistency (Cronbach's alpha) was $\alpha = .79$. It should be noted that there is a slight difference to the original use of the instrument in this study. Here respondents did not refer or think about a specific leader when filling out the need for leadership questionnaire but were asked to refer to a leader in general. Thus, a more generalized need for leadership was obtained. This may also explain the somewhat lower alpha in contrast to other studies. Need for leadership is negatively related to dominance, and although not significant, need for leadership is negatively correlated with self-efficacy, self-esteem, and work experience.

To measure *Romance of Leadership* the Romance of Leadership Scale (RLS) was administered (Meindl, 1998; German translation by Schyns, Meindl, & Croon, in review). The original scale range from –3 (does not apply at all) to +3 (applies completely) was changed to 1 = *not at all true* to 5 = *completely true*. Schyns et al. (in review) propose three factors whereas the first factor with 17 items appeared to be the most central and stable factor over different samples. This first factor contains items that represent the high perceived causal significance of leadership, and the value of investing in extensive and costly assessment procedures to select applicants for vacant leadership positions. The internal consistency (Cronbach's alpha) of this scale "RLS relevance" was $\alpha = .81$ after removing three items that had only low correlations with this scale. The items of the remaining two scales were combined as they both cover aspects regarding irrelevance of leadership or the importance of other factors besides leadership. The internal consistency (Cronbach's alpha) of this scale "RLS irrelevance" was $\alpha = .75$ after removing two items that had only low correlations with this scale. As expected both scales are correlated negatively $r = -.42$ ($p < .001$).

RESULTS

Preliminary Analyses

As the sample consists of participants from different universities and study subjects, systematic differences were checked. ANOVAS show that there were no significant differences for RLS relevance ($F(2.180) = 2.32$, $p < .101$) and RLS irrelevance ($F(2.180) = .75$, $p < .48$) with regard to the different universities. Moreover, no differences occurred for study subjects: RLS relevance ($F(1.169) = 1.31$, $p < .254$) and RLS irrelevance ($F(1.169) = 2.32$, $p < .130$). Sex, age and work experience were also not related to romance of leadership (see Table 8.1). However, correlations indicate that women had higher values for neuroticism and lower values for dominance than men. Not surprisingly, occupational self-efficacy is positively related to age and to work experience.

Test of Hypotheses

In order to test hypotheses, simple correlations were computed as there were no variables that had to be controlled.

H1.1–H1.2: As expected RLS (relevance) is positively correlated with OSE ($r = .31$, $p < .001$) and self-esteem ($r = .28$, $p < .001$). RLS (irrelevance) is negatively correlated with OSE ($r = -.18$, $p < .05$) and self-esteem ($r = -.22$, $p < .01$). Thus, **H1.1** and **H1.2** are supported.

H2.1–H2.3: As expected RLS (relevance) is positively correlated with extraversion ($r = .15$, $p < .05$) and conscientiousness ($r = .29$, $p < .001$) and negatively correlated with neuroticism ($r = -.21$, $p < .01$). RLS (irrelevance) is negatively correlated with extraversion ($r = -.21$, $p < .01$) and positively correlated with neuroticism ($r = .17$, $p < .05$). The correlation between conscientiousness and RLS (irrelevance) is negative but not significant. Thus, **H2.1–H2.3** are mainly supported.

H3.1–H3.2: Achievement motivation is positively related to RLS (relevance) and negatively correlated with RLS (irrelevance) but correlations do not reach significance. **H3.1** is not confirmed. As expected dominance is positively related to RLS (relevance) ($r = -.21$, $p < .01$) and negatively, though not significantly, related with RLS (irrelevance). Thus, **H.3.2** is partly supported.

H4: The correlation between RLS (relevance) and uncertainty tolerance is nearly zero, whereas there is a significant positive relationship between RLS (irrelevance) and uncertainty tolerance ($r = -.18$, $p < .05$), indicating that people with a high level of uncertainty tolerance consider leadership to be more influential. Therefore, H4 is partly supported.

Table 8.1. Means, Standard Deviations, and Correlations of the Scales

	M	SD	1	2	3	4	5	6	7	8	9	10	11	12	13	14
1. sex																
2. age	23.42	4.12	-.21**													
3. work experience	1.49	1.19	-.20**	.64***												
4. RLS (relevance)	3.51	0.48	.04	-.02	-.04											
5. RLS (irrelevance)	2.33	0.47	.02	-.05	-.04	-.42***										
6. OSE	3.36	0.61	-.10	.15*	.19*	.31***	-.18*									
7. self-esteem	4.12	0.65	-.04	.03	.05	.28***	-.22**	.51***								
8. extraversion	3.58	0.56	-.01	.01	.04	.15*	-.21**	.29***	.39***							
9. conscientiousness	3.77	0.61	.10	-.02	.04	.29***	-.10	.31***	.28***	.09						
10. neuroticism	2.63	0.73	.24**	-.04	-.04	-.21**	.17	-.49***	-.71***	-.39***	-.14					
11. achievement motivation	1.70	0.20	-.04	-.02	.02	.12	-.05	.16*	.15*	.15*	.30***	-.23**				
12. dominance	1.54	0.25	-.15*	-.03	.11	.22**	-.07	.38***	.30***	.38***	.17*	-.31***	.26***			
13. need for leadership	3.35	0.52	.02	.01	-.12	.08	-.04	-.13	-.09	.02	-.08	.06	.03	-.15*		
14. uncertainty tolerance	3.08	0.58	.00	-.02	.05	.02	-.18*	.27***	.15*	.24**	-.16*	-.29***	.19***	.24**	-.08	
15. personal need for structure	3.00	0.58	.07	.03	.06	.01	.00	-.25**	-.19**	-.18*	.18*	.36***	-.16*	-.18*	.06	-.56***

Note: * p < .05, ** p < .01, *** p < .001; sex 1 = male, 2 = female; work experience 1 = no, 2 = yes; OSE occupational self-efficacy

H5:   Correlations between both RLS scales and personal need for structure were near zero. Thus, **H5** is not supported.

H6:   The overall correlations between both RLS scales and need for leadership are near zero. It was postulated that followers' self-esteem moderates the relationship between romance of leadership and need for leadership. To test **H6** the interaction term for NFL and self-esteem (NFL x self-esteem) was computed on the basis of Z-scores and entered in the last step of a hierarchical regression. Z-scores were also used for the other variables in the equation. As can be seen in Table 8.2, after controlling for sex, age and job experience, results showed systematic main effects for the full equation. The interaction term reached significance when entered in the equation for romance of leadership. As predicted the beta weight is negative. Thus self-esteem moderates the relationship between need for leadership and romance of leadership in the predicted direction, i.e., lower self-esteem is associated with a stronger (positive) relation between need for leadership and romance of leadership whereas higher self-esteem weakens or even reverses this relationship. Additional analysis reveal, that the correlation

Table 8.2.   Hierarchical Regression on Romance of Leadership

	Romance of leadership (relevance)		
	beta	R^2	delta R^2
Step 1		.004	.004
sex	.04		
age	.02		
job experience	−.05		
Step 2		$.10^{***}$	$.10^{***}$
sex	.05		
age	−.003		
job experience	−.04		
need for leadership	.12		
self-esteem	$.30^{***}$		
Step 3		$.20^{***}$	$.10^{***}$
sex	.05		
age	−.03		
job experience	−.04		
need for leadership	$.27^{**}$		
self-esteem	$.31^{***}$		
self-esteem × need for leadership	$-.35^{***}$		

Note: $p < .10$, * $p < .05$, ** $p < .01$, *** $p < .001$; sex: male = 1, female = 2

between need for leadership and romance of leadership is $r = -.10$ (n.s.) for people with high self-esteem and $r = .36$ ($p < .001$) for those with low self-esteem. High and low self-esteem groups were defined by median-split. Thus, **H6** is supported.

DISCUSSION

The aim of this study was to examine the impact of followers' characteristics on their romance of leadership. The findings show that followers' tendency to overemphasize the meaning of leaders or leadership for organizational success or failure is related to several characteristics of followers' personality. As expected, findings clearly indicate that followers with higher occupational self-efficacy and higher self-esteem show a higher propensity to romanticize leadership than followers with lower occupational self-efficacy and lower self-esteem. Accordingly, followers' occupational self-efficacy and self-esteem are negatively related to the opinion of irrelevance of leadership. As leaders are supposed to be high in self-esteem and OSE, the results confirm theoretical assumptions and empirical findings that emphasize similarity between followers and their leader prototypes as a basis for their implicit leadership theories. Those who share common traits with leaders in general consider leaders to be powerful and influential. There are several explanations why similarity might play an important role. As pointed out by Meindl (1990), people are able to confirm their own need for control and stabilize their self-concept by attributing and projecting their own qualities on leaders. The development of similarity can also be interpreted in line with Keller's (1999) postulation that leadership is constructed on the basis of the self. Another explanation may be that those who feel like leaders or potential leaders have a more positive and optimistic view on leadership. Alternatively, a general belief system in the sense of the "core self-evaluation" proposed by Judge and Bono (2001) and Bono and Judge (2003) can be of importance. It emphasizes internal control and is based on personality and cognitive attribution styles. This disposition may not only be relevant for the perception of the self but can be also extended to the perception of leaders. Accordingly, the common variance of extraversion, conscientiousness, self-esteem, and romance of leadership can be interpreted in terms of a general belief system in which persons instead of circumstances are responsible for actions and results. Consequently, there is no evidence for the alternative assumption that "weak" followers who are low in self-esteem and self-efficacy tend to romanticize leadership. For example, Yukl (1999, p. 296) stated that "theories suggest that followers are more susceptible [to leadership] if they are insecure, alienated, fearful, ... [if] they lack self-esteem, and [if] they have a weak self identity." Under the assumption that susceptibility is related to RLS, persons who lack control and efficacy project and attribute influence to others. By identifying with such leaders they may substitute their lack of control and self-esteem. However, the results of this study do not support this view.

With regard to the Big-five dimensions of personality, similar results were obtained. People who were higher in extraversion and conscientiousness and low in neuroticism showed a stronger tendency to emphasize the role of leadership than their counterparts. Again, a reversed pattern occurred for irrelevance of leadership. However, the correlation between conscientiousness and irrelevance failed to reach significance. As leaders are also supposed to be high in extraversion, conscientiousness and low in neuroticism, these results again support research that emphasizes similarity between leader and follower as a basis for their perception and attribution.

The results with other followers' characteristics examined in this study were somehow mixed. Though the picture for motives (achievement motivation and power motivation (dominance)) is not as compelling as for Big-five dimensions, results show a congruent pattern. Directions of correlations between romance of leadership and achievement motivation and dominance were as expected. People who rated themselves as more dominant and achievement orientated were found to show more romance of leadership. Again the parallel between subjects' own striving for power and achievement and leaders' attributes may cause the picture of powerful and influential leadership. However, only the correlation between dominance and romance of leadership reached significance.

Uncertainty tolerance is also partly related to romance of leadership. Whereas no significant correlation occurs for the RLS subscale "relevance," there is a significant negative correlation with irrelevance. As predicted, people with a high level of uncertainty tolerance do not believe that leadership is irrelevant for organizational success or failure. These findings also partly confirm the view that similarity between follower and leaders in general may play a crucial role for their implicit leadership theories. Contrary to prediction, no relationship with personal need for structure was found. Obviously, this follower characteristic does not influence romance of leadership in this sample.

To sum up, it can be concluded that personality influences romance of leadership as a specific ILT and there seems to be support for theoretical assumptions that emphasize similarity between leader and follower as a basis for followers' implicit leadership theories (Keller, 1999; Klein & House, 1998). Thus, persons who have similar attributes to leaders (extraverted, self-efficient, dominant etc.) tend to have a more benevolent view of leadership.

With regard to self-esteem, the results of the present study also replicate Meindl's (1990) findings. This evaluation can be extended to self-efficacy which is relatively similar to locus of control which was examined by Meindl (1990). In addition to previous research that has found leaders' extraversion, self-esteem, etc. to be central variables both for leadership emergence and performance (Judge et al., 2002), followers' extraversion, self-esteem etc. seem to influence the construction of leadership. Therefore, there is considerable evidence across different studies that followers' extraversion, self-esteem etc. are positively linked to their romance of leadership.

As pointed out above, there are different reasons that can explain this link between followers' and leaders' personality, which in turn leads to a favorable evaluation of leadership. Firstly, social construction may be a cause for similarity. Positive self assessment with regard to influence and control leads to a positive evaluation of leaders in general. Secondly, the perception of similarity may serve as an explanation for romance of leadership as it is well known that similarity leads to attraction. Alternatively, persons romanticize leaders because in doing so they are able to confirm and stabilize their self-concept by attributing their own qualities to their leaders. Derived from Social Identity Theory, prototypicality for the characteristics of a group could also serve as an explanation (Haslam & Platow, 2001). Keller (1999) proposes that both, the leader and the self, are most salient and therefore similar attributions of responsibility occur. Therefore it is concluded that merely asking the followers about their leaders neglects the role of the self. Yet, with regard to romance of leadership this aspect might have been overlooked. Though the role of leadership is overestimated in comparison to other factors the self seems to be an exception: those who tend to romanticize leaders will probably do the same with regard to themselves.

There were contradicting arguments for the relationship of need for leadership and romance of leadership. Accordingly, there was no hypothesis with regard to the direct relationship. Actually, the correlation was near zero, indicating that no relationship exists or that the influence of another variable suppresses a hidden relation. It was assumed that self-esteem moderates the relationship between NFL and RLS. The results clearly support this assumption. The positive relation between NFL and RLS as proposed by de Vries (2000) can be found only when followers' self-esteem is lower. In contrast for people with high self-esteem this relation does not exist or even tends to be negative. However, the interaction effect can be interpreted in an alternative way. Accordingly, the relationship between self-esteem and romance of leadership is influenced by need for leadership. The positive relationship between self-esteem and romance of leadership is stronger for persons with low need for leadership and lower for persons with high need for leadership.

It has to be noted that the need for leadership scale in this study slightly differs from the original version. Whereas in the original version participants refer to a specific leader, participants in this study thought of a leader in general. This may lead to lower relationships as need for leadership is also influenced by concrete leadership behavior (also see De Vries & Van Gelder, this volume).

There are some ideas as to how the findings of this study can be used for leadership practice. Although the romance of leadership concept primarily refers to leaders in general, it probably will influence the perception and attitudes toward a specific leader. Thus, leaders should be advised to be aware of being romanticized. Being romanticized by certain followers may have consequences for the interaction. First of all leaders may expect more support and commitment from followers, who are high in self-efficacy, self-esteem, extraversion, etc. than from others, as they are more likely to romanticize leadership. Therefore, these followers may be more willing to support their leaders and accept their behavior. This mechanism can be described in terms of a self-fulfilling prophecy. However, they have to be aware that in case of failure they will be made responsible even when other factors should be taken into account. One can assume that the feedback of followers high in extraversion and self-efficacy tend to be positively biased in times of success and negatively biased in times of failure in contrast to feedback from introverts. Leaders should have this in mind when receiving feedback and interacting with their followers because positive feedback should not only be attributed to one's own leadership behavior but must be relativized by followers' upward and downward bias. Thus, they should consider the chances as well as the risks when being romanticized. In particular, they should not neglect their relationships with followers who seem to be less supportive and attractive at first sight because these followers may provide stability and continuity. They may have the ability to serve as a "devil's advocate" when pointing out important circumstances that cannot be controlled by the leader. This is important in times of success as well as in times of failure.

LIMITATIONS AND FUTURE RESEARCH

Some limitations of this study should be mentioned. The major limitation of this study is the fact that similarity between one's own personality and leaders' personality in general served as an explanatory frame to set up the hypotheses but similarity was not directly tested. Although there is some theoretical plausibility for the assumption of similarity this must remain speculative. Similarity can result from social construction in the sense that leaders are construed similar to the self. Similarity can also be the result of a comparison between the self and a leader with regard to personality. Moreover, a general belief system that emphasizes internal control in the sense of the "core self-evaluation" (Bono & Judge, 2003; Judge & Bono, 2001) is responsible for similar evaluations of the self and leaders in general.

Some proposals are provided to overcome parts of these shortcomings. In addition to their own personality ratings participants should also directly estimate their ILT with regard to leaders' personality traits in general. The comparison of both, followers' and leaders' personality traits, enables the direct testing of the influence of similarity on romance of leadership. An alternative way to measure perceived similarity is to include direct items where participants will be asked to indicate how similar they think they are to a leader in general in terms of personality traits. The interpretation in terms of similarity could be supported if similarity between self-rated personality and leaders' personality in general serves as a predictor for romance of leadership. For example, persons with high self-esteem and the belief that leaders in general have a high self-esteem are supposed to show higher romance of leadership than persons with high self-esteem and lower self-esteem ratings for leaders in general. In this vein similarity moderates the relationship between personality and romance of leadership.

Furthermore, the idea of similarity with regard to implicit leadership theories may be useful for future research. In a different approach, Felfe and Schyns (2004b) have shown that perceived similarity between one's own leadership behavior and the direct leader's behavior is positively related to outcome measures. Besides effects of similarity with regard to leadership behavior or personality traits, similarity with regard to implicit leadership theories might also be an important predictor for leadership outcomes. It can be assumed that follower-leader dyads with similar levels of romance of leadership perform better than dyads with divergent beliefs of the role of leadership. Further research should also address the question as to whether people who romanticize leadership in general automatically romanticize their direct leader. If there is evidence that romance of leadership can be transferred to a direct leader, consequences of this direct "romance of the leader" should be examined in more detail. However, as romance of leadership is primarily a concept that reflects a generalized theory of leadership one must be careful if this concept can be applied to a specific, direct superior.

Another limitation refers to the sample of this study. As participants were students this sample was relatively homogenous with regard to age, leadership experience and other characteristics. Probably higher relations between romance of leadership and socio-demographic variables occur with a more heterogeneous sample. However, it is an advantage of this study that different samples were comprised. Participants studied different subjects and attended different universities. As our preliminary analyses show, there were no effects with regard to these variables. Nevertheless, future research should cover a broader range of participants. In particular, job conditions and experiences with leadership should be taken into account. Last but not least the question must be raised if there are other follower characteristics that might influence romance of leadership. On an individual level, variables such as positive mood, positive/negative affectivity, or arousal level should be considered (Meindl, 1998), on a group level norms and network effects (Pastor, Meindl, & Mayo, 2002) should be considered, and on a cross-cultural level individualism/collectivism and power distance may explain the emergence of romance of leadership.

AUTHOR NOTE

Please send requests for reprints to Jörg Felfe, Martin-Luther-Universität Halle-Wittenberg, Institut für Psychologie, 06099 Halle (Saale), Germany. E-mail: j.felfe@psych.uni-halle.de.

REFERENCES

Awamleh, R.A., & Gardner, W.L. (1999). Perceptions of leader charisma and effectiveness: The effects of vision content, delivery, and organizational performance. *The Leadership Quarterly, 10*, 345–373.

Ayman, R. (1993). Leadership perception: The role of gender and culture. In M.M. Chemers, R. Ayman et al. (Eds.), *Leadership theory and research: Perspectives and directions* (pp. 137–166). San Diego, CA: Academic Press.

Bandura, A. (1997). *Self-efficacy: The exercise of control.* New York: Freeman.

Barrick, R.B., & Mount, M.K. (1993). Autonomy as a moderator of the relationship between the Big -five personality dimensions and job performance. *Journal of Applied Psychology, 78*, 111–118.

Bass, B.M. (1985). *Leadership and performance beyond expectations.* New York: The Free Press.

Bono, J.E., & Judge, T.A. (2003). Core self-evaluations: A review of the trait and its role in job satisfaction and job performance. *European Journal of Personality, 17*, 5–18.

Borkenau, P., & Ostendorf, F. (1993). *NEO-Fünf-Faktoren-Inventar (NEO-FFI) nach Costa und McCrae.* (The NEO-Five-Factor-Inventory by Costa and McCrae). Göttingen: Hogrefe.

Costa, P.T., & McCrae, R.R. (1985). *The NEO-Personality Inventory. Manual form S and form R.* Odessa, FL: Psychological Assessment Resources.

Crant, J.M., & Bateman, T.S. (2000). Charismatic leadership viewed from above: The impact of proactive personality. *Journal of Organizational Behavior, 21,* 63–75.

Dalbert, C. (1999). Die Ungewissheitstoleranzskala: Skaleneigenschaften und Validierungsbefunde. *Hallesche Berichte zur Pädagogischen Psychologie, Bericht Nr. 1.* Martin-Luther-Universität Halle-Wittenberg.

De Vries, R.E. (2000). When leaders have character: Need for leadership, performance, and the attribution of leadership. *Journal of Social Behavior and Personality, 15,* 413–430.

De Vries, R.E., Roe, R.A., & Taillieu, T.C.B. (1999). On charisma and need for leadership. *European Journal of Work and Organizational Psychology, 8,* 109–133.

Eden, D., & Leviathan, U. (1975). Implicit leadership theory as a determinant of the factor structure underlying supervisory behavior scales. *Journal of Applied Psychology, 60,* 736–741.

Ehrhart, M.G., & Klein, K.J. (2001). Predicting followers' preferences for charismatic leadership: The influence of follower values and personality. *The Leadership Quarterly, 12,* 153–179.

Ehrlich, S.B., Meindl, J.R., & Viellieu, B. (1990). The charismatic appeal of a transformational leader: An empirical case study of a small, high-technology contractor. *The Leadership Quarterly, 1,* 229–248.

Engle, E.M., & Lord, R.G. (1997). Implicit theories, self schemas, and leader-member-exchange. *Academy of Management Journal, 40,* 988–1010.

Felfe, J. (2003). *Transformationale und charismatische Führung und Commitment im Organisationalen Wandel.* [Transformational and charismatic leadership and commitment in organizational change]. Habilitation thesis: Martin-Luther University of Halle-Wittenberg.

Felfe, J., & Schyns, B. (2004a). Der Einfluss von impliziten Führungstheorien und Persönlichkeitsmerkmalen auf die Wahrnehmung und Akzeptanz transformationaler Führung. [The influence of implicit leadership theories and personality on the perception and acceptance of transformational leadership]. In W. Bungard, B. Koop & C. Liebig (Hg.), *Psychologie und Wirtschaft leben. Aktuelle Themen der Wirtschaftspsychologie in Forschung und Praxis.* München und Mering: Rainer Hampp Verlag.

Felfe, J., & Schyns, B. (2004b). Is similarity in leadership related to organizational outcomes? The case of transformational leadership. *Journal of Leadership and Organizational Studies 10(4), 92–102.*

Felfe, J., & Schyns, B. (in press). Personality and the perception of transformational Leadership: The impact of extraversion, neuroticism, personal need for structure, and occupational self-efficacy. *Journal of Applied Social Psychology.*

Felfe, J., & Petersen, L.E. (in review). *The impact of romance of leadership on decision making in a management context.*

Gardner, W.L., & Avolio, B.J. (1998). The charismatic relationship: A dramaturgical perspective. *Academy of Management Review, 23,* 32–58.

Haslam, S.A., & Platow, M.J. (2001). The link between leadership and followership: How affirming social identity translates vision into action. *Society for Personality and Social Psychology, 27,* 1469–1479.

Hogg, M.A. (2001). A social identity theory of leadership. *Personality and Social Psychology Review, 5,* 184–200.

House, R.J., & Howell, J.M. (1992). Personality and charismatic leadership. *The Leadership Quarterly, 3*, 81–108.

House, R.J., Hanges, P.J., Ruiz-Quintanilla, S.A., Dorfman, P.W., Javidan, M., Dickson, M., Gupta, V., & 170 co-authors (1999). Cultural influences on leadership and organizations: Project GLOBE. In W.F. Mobley, M.J. Gessner, & V. Arnold (Eds.), *Advances in global leadership* (pp. 171–233). Stamford, CT: JAI Press.

House, R.J., Hanges, P., Javidan, M., Dorfman, P.W., & Gupta, V. (2004). *Leadership and organizations: A 62 nation GLOBE study*. Thousand Oaks, CA: Sage.

Judge, T.A., & Bono, J.E. (2001). Relationship of core self-evaluations traits—self-esteem, generalized self-efficacy, locus of control, and emotional stability—with job satisfaction and job performance: A meta-analysis. *Journal of Applied Psychology, 86*, 80–92.

Judge, T.A., & Bono, J.E., Ilies, R., & Gerhardt, M.W. (2002). Personality and leadership: A qualitative and quantitative review. *Journal of Applied Psychology, 87*, 765–780.

Keller, T. (1999). Images of the familiar: Individual differences and implicit leadership theories. *The Leadership Quarterly, 10*, 589–607.

Kenney, R.A., Schwartz-Kenney, B.M., & Blascovich, J. (1996). Implicit leadership theories: Defining leaders described as worthy of influence. *Society for Personality and Social Psychology, 22*, 1128–1143.

Kirkpatrick, S.A., & Locke, E.A. (1996). Direct and indirect effects of three charismatic leadership components on performance and attitudes. *Journal of Applied Psychology, 81*, 36–51.

Klein, K.J., & House, R. (1995). On fire: Charismatic leadership and levels of analysis. *The Leadership Quarterly, 6*, 183–198.

Klein, K.J., & House, R. (1998). Further thoughts on fire: Charismatic leadership and levels of analysis. In F. Dansereau & F.J. Yammarino (Eds.), *Leadership: The multiple-level approaches: Contemporary and alternative* (pp. 45–52). Stamford, CT: JAI Press.

Lord, R.G. (1985). An information processing approach to social perceptions, leadership and behavioral measurement in organizations. In B.M. Staw & L.L. Cummings (Eds.), *Research in organizational behavior* (Vol. 7, pp. 87–128). Greenwich, CT: JAI Press.

Lord, R.G., Brown, D.J., Harvey, J.L., & Hall, R.J. (2001). Contextual constraints on prototype generation and their multilevel consequences for leadership perceptions. *The Leadership Quarterly, 12*, 311–338.

Lord, R.G., De Vader, C.L., & Alliger, G.M. (1986). A meta-analysis of the relation between personality traits and leadership perceptions: An application of validity generalization procedures. *Journal of Applied Psychology, 71*, 402–410.

Lord, R.G., & Emrich, C.G. (2001). Thinking outside the box by looking inside the box: Extending the cognitive revolution in leadership research. *The Leadership Quarterly, 11*, 551–579.

Lord, R.G., Foti, R.J., & De Vader, C.L. (1984). A test of leadership categorization theory: Internal structure, information processing, and leadership perception. *Organizational Behavior and Human Performance, 34*, 343–378.

Lord, R.G., & Maher, K.J. (1993). *Leadership and information processing*. London: Routledge.

Meindl, J.R. (1990). On leadership: An alternative to the conventional wisdom. In B.M. Staw & L.L. Cummings (Eds.), *Research in organizational behavior* (Vol. 12, pp. 159–203). Greenwich, CT: JAI Press.

Meindl, J.R. (1995). The romance of leadership as a follower-centric theory: A social constructionist approach. *The Leadership Quarterly, 6,* 329–341.

Meindl, J.R. (1998). Appendix: Measures and assessments for the romance of leadership approach. In F. Dansereau & F.J. Yammarino (Eds.), *Leadership: The multiple-level approaches, Part B: Contemporary and alternative* (pp. 199–302). Stamford, CT: JAI Press.

Meindl, J.R., & Ehrlich, S.B. (1988). Developing a "romance of leadership" scale. *Proceedings of the Eastern Academy of Management, 30,* 133–135.

Meindl, J.R., Ehrlich, S.B., & Dukerich, J.M. (1985). The Romance of Leadership. *Administrative Science Quarterly, 30,* 78–102.

Neuberg, S., & Newsom, J.T. (1993). Personal need for structure: Individual differences in the desire for simple structure. *Journal of Personality and Social Psychology, 65,* 113–113.

Nye, J.L. (2002). The eye of the follower: Information processing effects on attributions regarding leaders of small groups. *Small Group Research, 33,* 237–360.

Nye, J.L., & Forsyth, D.R. (1991). The effects of prototype-based biases on leadership appraisals. *Small Group Research, 22,* 360–379.

Offermann, L.R., Kennedy, Jr., J.K., & Wirtz, P.W. (1994). Implicit leadership theories: Content, structure, and generalizability. *The Leadership Quarterly, 5,* 43–58.

Pastor, J.C., Meindl, J.R., & Mayo, M.C. (2002). A network effects model of charisma attributions. *Academy of Management Journal, 45,* 410–420.

Rosenberg, M. (1965). *Society and the adolescent self-image.* Princeton, NJ: Princeton University Press.

Rush, M.C., Phillips, J.S., & Lord, R.G. (1981). Effects of a temporal delay in rating on leader behavior descriptions: A laboratory investigation. *Journal of Applied Psychology, 66,* 442–450.

Schneider, D.J. (1973). Implicit personality theory: A review. *Psychological Bulletin, 79,* 294–309.

Schyns, B., & v. Collani, G. (2002). A new occupational self-efficacy scale and its relation to personality constructs and organizational variables. *European Journal of Work and Organizational Psychology, 11,* 219–241.

Schyns, B., Felfe, J., & Blank, H. (in review). *The relationship between romance of leadership and the perception of transformational/charismatic leadership revisited.*

Schyns, B., Meindl, J.R., & Croon, M.A. (in review). *Romantische Führung: Überprüfung eines US-amerikanischen Konzepts im deutschen Sprachraum [The Romance of Leadership: Examination of a US-American concept in Germany].*

Schyns, B., & Sanders, K. (2004). Impliciete leiderschap theorieën en de perceptie van transformationeel leiderschap: een replicatie van Duits onderzoek [Implicit leadership theories and the perception of transformational leadership: A replication of a German study]. *Gedrag en Organisatie, 17,* 143–154.

Shamir, B. (1992). Attribution of influence and charisma to the leader: The Romance of Leadership revisited. *Journal of Applied Social Psychology, 22,* 386–407.

Silverthorne, C. (2001). Leadership effectiveness and personality: A cross cultural evaluation. *Personality and Individual Differences, 30,* 303–309.

Stumpf, H., Angleitner, A., Wieck, T., Jackson, D.N., & Beloch-Till, H. (1985). *Deutsche Personality Research Form (PRF) Handanweisung*. Göttingen: Hogrefe.

Tajfel, H., & Turner, J.C. (1986). The social identity theory of intergroup behavior. In S. Worchel & W. G. Austin (Eds.), *Psychology of intergroup relations* (pp. 7–24). Chicago: Nelson-Hall.

Watson, D. (2000). *Mood and temperament*. New York: Guilford Press.

Wofford, J.C., Whittington, J.L., & Goodwin, V.L. (2001). Follower motive patterns as situational moderators for transformational leadership effectiveness. *Journal of Managerial Issues, 13*, 196–212.

Wolfradt, U., Sommer, S., & Rademacher, J. (1999). Das "Persönliche Bedürfnis nach Struktur" als klinisches differential-diagnostisches Persönlichkeitsmerkmal ["Personal Need for Structure" as personality trait for clinical diagnostic]. *Zeitschrift für Klinische Psychologie, Psychiatrie und Psychotherapie, 47*, 307–316.

Yukl, G. (1999). An evaluation of conceptual weakness in transformational and charismatic leadership theories. *The Leadership Quarterly, 10*, 285–305.

CHAPTER 9

CHILDREN'S IMPLICIT THEORY OF LEADERSHIP

Saba Ayman-Nolley and Roya Ayman

On the shoulder of the youth today rests the future . . .
—(The Baha'i writings: Shoghi Effendi, 1954)

INTRODUCTION

In all societies historically and across the globe leadership has always been the key to the success of all collective endeavors, yet we know very little about how the concepts of leaders and of leadership evolves and forms in the mind of a human (Ayman, 2004, 1993). The profusion of books about leaders and leadership in bookstores or libraries, demonstrates the popularity of these topics for the public and scholars alike (Ayman, 2000). Almost all that is written is based on our knowledge of past or present leaders, but we know very little about our future leaders. Who will be our president in 30 years? Who will be the coach of the best football team in 20 years? Who will lead a great scientific team that will take us to space, or find the cure for cancer? And who will lead our international peace efforts in 40 years? An answer to these questions lies in our understanding of children and youth's concept of leadership.

Implicit Leadership Theories: Essays and Explorations, pages 227–274
Copyright © 2005 by Information Age Publishing
227

This chapter will explore children's current understanding of leadership and their schema of leaders. We open this discussion with a short summary of implicit leadership theory (ILT) in adults. Subsequently a summary of leadership studies in children including those on ILT will be presented. This summary will demonstrate the less explored areas of research in understanding the ILT of children. Following this section we will offer a series of four studies that we have conducted to systematically examine children's ILT in the last 15 years. In conclusion, we will look at patterns of what we have learned and their implications.

IMPLICIT LEADERSHIP THEORY IN ADULTS

Implicit theories in social psychology have evolved from what is referred to as "the lay expectations." In relation to the study of leadership, implicit leadership theory (ILT), leader exemplars, and leader prototypes have been noted (Fischbein & Lord, 2003). The early research by Eden and Leviatan (1975) demonstrated that people have a mental image of a leader and can describe the leader's behavior even if they have never met the leader. This study can be considered a seminal work upon which subsequent studies built. In these studies, researchers explored the understanding of people's expectations of a leader or their ILT, and its effect on the future perception, judgment, and actions by leaders or observers. This section includes a brief review of ILT research in adults, starting with a short summary presenting the importance of an individual's schema on their judgment of others' leadership behavior. We will then review studies on the content and structure of ILT.

Scholars such as Lord and Maher (1991) and Meindl (1990, 1998) have demonstrated the importance of the ILT paradigm. They have shown that people's schema, prototype, and expectation of a leader affect their memory of the leader's behaviors. For example, in series of studies, Lord and his associates demonstrated that when a certain category of a leader is activated (such as effective or ineffective), the observers/participants in the study remembered the behaviors that matched that category (e.g., Larson, 1982; Lord, Benining, Rush, & Thomas, 1978). This phenomenon astonished the researchers, particularly because in these studies, the leaders were actors following a prewritten script. Yet, observers confidently remembered behaviors, which did not occur, and omitted those that did. Thus, they recalled what met their mental model of an effective or ineffective leader regardless of what actually occurred.

Some studies have found that when the observers' expectations (i.e., their ILT) do not match what they see, they tend to rate the observed more negatively (Burgoon, Dillard, & Doran, 1983). Hains, Hogg, and Duck

(1997), as well as Fielding and Hogg (1997) also demonstrated that those leaders who matched the leader-schema of their team members were evaluated more positively. This may mean that if an observer expects a white man in a leadership position, and is instead confronted with a black woman in that position who does not behave as they expected, they may rate that person negatively. For example, the meta-analysis of Eagly, Karau, and Makhijani (1995) demonstrated that when women are engaged in masculine tasks or are a minority in a group, their performance is rated lower than that of men.

To further understand this dynamic the issue of stereotyping and ILT needs to be acknowledged. Both of these phenomena are representation of mental structures of social phenomenon. In the case of ILT, the mental structure is about the attributes and beliefs about leaders. In the case of stereotype, Ashmore and Del Boca (1979) defined it as "a structured set of beliefs about the personal attributes of a group of people" (p. 222). Furthermore, Wegner and Vallacher (1977) in fact identified stereotypes as a form of implicit theories. Therefore, when an individual's implicit leadership theory and stereotype of a group overlap, there is a potential that this person may hold a stereotypic ILT.

In addition to researchers' acknowledgment of the role of stereotyping on gender and leadership (Eagly & Carli, 2003; Heilman, 2001), others have also voiced this concern. In a 1998 publication, Catalyst (a national watch group on status of women) and the United Nations in a white paper from the Beijing Women's Conference (2000) both alluded to the fact that traditional stereotyping is one of the hindering factors to the advancement of women in decision-making roles.

As the number of diverse people in positions of leadership across professions increases, the role of stereotyping becomes of greater importance. Evidence for this can be seen even in the work of scholars and practitioners in performance appraisal and assessment centers, who strongly recommend frame-of-reference training before an evaluation process begins (e.g., Woehr & Huffcutt, 1994). This training provides a common expectation for the raters.

Although many scholars are interested in the impact of ILT, some are in the pursuit of understanding what constitutes people's ILT and the effect of individual differences in ILT. The content of implicit leadership theory and the contextual factors that can influence these expectations will be the focus of the next paragraphs of this section. To explore the image of a leader in the minds of people, two lines of research could be considered. One line of research has examined the similarity and difference of the attributes associated with a manager versus a woman or a man (Schein, 2001). Another is the work that demonstrated that the prototype or image of a leader will vary due to the category of the leader such as men or women leaders, military and political leaders, and leaders and supervisors (Lord, Brown, Harvey, & Hall, 2001).

Schein (1973) conducted research examining the similarity between people's description of men, women, and managers. Across the years, including experienced or less experienced adults, men and women, and across countries, she reported that when people think of a manager, they think of a man (Schein, 1973, 1975; Schein, Mueller, & Jacobson, 1989; Schein, Mueller, Litchey, & Liu, 1996). In her later work she presented evidence from her U.S. sample of women showing that women by the end of the 20th century in the United States had less of a male prototype for a leader than samples in other countries (Schein, 2001). The combined results of these studies attested to a strong image of a leader that does not match the image people have of a woman. It also provided evidence that the image of a leader is more similar to the image of a man than of a woman.

Several scholars have demonstrated that people seem to have differing prototypes of leaders in different contexts. For example, Foti, Fraser, and Lord (1982), and Lord, Foti, and deVader (1984) demonstrated that people differentiated between a generic leader, a political leader, and an effective political leader. In these studies the respondents associated a political leader with being religious and concerned for the poor more than they associated a generic leader with these attributes. Additionally, Offermann, Kennedy, and Wirtz (1994) demonstrated that both experienced and inexperienced respondents' structure of the definition of a leader was similar across context (generic leader, effective leader, supervisor). These definitions included sensitivity, dedication, tyranny, charisma, attractiveness, masculinity, intelligence, and strength. The results showed, however, that sensitivity, dedication, charisma, and intelligence are the characteristics that were shared across the three types of leaders. In this study, on the other hand, generic leaders and supervisors were considered more tyrannical than effective leaders. Offermann et al.'s findings support the previous work of Lord, deVader, and Alliger (1986) where summarizing past research on characteristics of leadership perception found that intelligence, dominance, and masculinity are among the key factors that differentiate leaders from non-leaders in the United States.

The universality of the implicit leadership theory is still under investigation. The GLOBE project, an international study including more than 64 countries' initial results tend to support the finding that certain traits such as charisma, team orientation, and participativeness are favored as qualities associated with effective leaders around the world. However, both the manner in which these traits are expressed and unique traits appreciated in each country vary across-cultures (Den Hartog et al., 1999). To further illustrate cultural variation, examples from China and Iran are presented.

Additionally, in China, Ling, Chia, and Fang (2000) reported that across age, gender, and occupation, Chinese consider four factors when describing a leader, which are personal morality, goal efficiency, interpersonal competence, and versatility. They further stated that among all groups interpersonal competence was the most important factor.

Ayman and Chemers (1983) also demonstrated that Iranians' concept of leader behavior did not fit the same pattern as that of the U.S. population. That is, pre-revolution Iranians' concept of leadership combined considerate and initiating structuring as one factor. This further demonstrated that Iranians expect their leaders to incorporate both interpersonal and task behaviors together. More recently, in Iran as part of the GLOBE project, Dastmalchian, Javidan, and Alam (2001) reported that in terms of leadership, a seven-factor solution was obtained (supportive, dictatorial, planner, familial, humble, faithful, and receptive). Both of the studies in Iran on leadership, though conducted more than 30 years apart, demonstrated that interpersonal relationship is the cornerstone of the concept of leadership in Iran.

Thus, culture as well as leader's occupation may impact expectations of a leader. It is possible to consider children as yet another culture within our society. Though children may be different from adults culturally, as already mentioned they are future adults. Therefore, understanding their image of a leader may give a glimpse of the development of implicit leadership theory, as well as better understanding of the cohort differences.

LEADERSHIP IN CHILDREN

Overall, existing study of leadership in children is quite limited and constitutes a disparate approach to understanding this important social phenomenon in the young and its development across life's stages. This section will be a general historical overview of past research. This presentation includes the studies that validate an adult leadership model for children, as well as those studies that identified children's leadership traits.

Hardy (1976, 1977) and his colleagues (Hardy, Sack, & Harpine, 1973) conducted the only studies that validated an adult theory of leadership (Fiedler's contingency model of leadership effectiveness) among children. He found that similar to adults, children have either orientation toward task or relationship. This trait affected their leadership success (as assessed by independent trained judges) based on their level of control over the situation as defined by Fiedler's model (Ayman, Chemers, & Fiedler, 1995). In addition, he found that firstborn boys were more task-oriented compared to later born boys (Hardy, 1972; Hardy, Hunt, & Lehr, 1978).

Most of the early attempts to understand leadership in children, in the decades between the 1920s and 1960s, focused on studies of child leaders and their characteristics in various settings, such as summer camps and sports teams. Some of these characteristics include high intelligence and a desire for achievement (Caldwell & Wellman, 1926; Fleming, 1935; Gowen, 1955; Harrison, Rawls, & Rawls, 1971; Reynolds, 1944; Wetzel, 1932).

In some cases, personality characteristics associated with child leaders were identified as confidence (Gowen, 1955), popularity, and sociability (Caldwell & Wellman, 1926; Garrison, 1933; Nutting, 1923). Many child leaders were found to demonstrate greater versatility, sense of humor, and social skills in general (Fleming, 1935; Garrison, 1933; Harrison et al., 1971; Reynolds, 1944; Stray, 1934; Terrell & Shreffler, 1958). Many studies identified student leaders to be healthier boys with high levels of vitality, who were active in sports (Fleming, 1935; Gowen, 1955; Harrison, et al., 1971; Reynolds, 1944; Stray, 1934).

It is important to note that in many studies of leadership in children, examination of the concept of leadership was co-mingled with the study of dominance structure in child and youth groups. However, studies that focused on the concept of dominance had primarily concentrated on descriptors such as "tough" and "getting one's way." In 2001, Yamaguchi found that task conditions that promote more dominance in children are different from those that promote leadership. He showed that mastery tasks increase leadership and positive behavior, whereas performance-based tasks bring about dominance.

Another confounding element of children's social structure that can overlap with leadership is popularity. As early as 1969 however, Durojaije in relating popularity to leadership showed that not all popular children are identified as leaders, although child leaders are among the most popular. In addition, Hensel (1983) reported that elected and appointed leaders are also found to be popular. Regardless of their sociometric status however, emerging child leaders were more likely to be effective leaders (managing the group's task well and attending to the group's emotions and needs) than the popular children. Based on these results, it is important to note that although in research on children and leadership a connection is found between popularity and being a leader, these two concepts need to be studied separately.

In the 1980s and 1990s some studies of leadership in children focused on finding the antecedents to leadership in children, especially familial variables predictive of leadership roles. However, the body of work devoted to this topic is very small. Klonsky (1983) conducted the most comprehensive work in this area. He studied sport leaders in a New York high school. Among the complex web of his findings was the fact that male leaders were socialized differently than were female leaders. More specifically, male leaders seem to have emerged from experiences of intense socialization such as high parental achievement demands, maternal principled discipline, and parental authority discipline. In contrast, female leaders emerged partially as the result of having a major voice in familial decision-making processes, low intensity socialization, and low to moderate parental warmth.

About ten years later, Whorton and Karnes (1992) examined the relationship between parent and child leadership styles and their perceptions. They found that those parents who desire their children to assume positions of leadership should utilize a parenting style that could be described as "delegating." Hartman and Harris (1992) found that parents had a stronger influence on boy leaders. Specifically, the boys' perception of parents' leadership seemed to have had more of an influence than parents' actual behavior (as reported by themselves). Karnes, Bean, and McGinnis (1995) found that female students in a leadership program ranked family influence first, followed by teachers, and then their opportunities for involvement in student government.

Although the last three decades have seen an increase in the number of leadership training programs, especially for youth (Karnes & Chauvin, 1985; Richardson & Feldhusen, 1986), most of these efforts are community outreach programs with very little systematic examination of their effectiveness. While full discussion of these programs is not in the scope of this chapter, it is important to note the increasing interest in children's skills as leaders.

The area of leadership least examined in children is their schema of leaders and leadership. It would be the examination of this area that will enlighten the understanding of how the future leaders perceive this social role and its characteristics. It is to this aim that we devote this chapter to discovery of children's implicit theory of leadership.

CHILDREN'S IMPLICIT THEORY OF LEADERSHIP

In the late 1970s and early 1980s, the first studies that shed light on the ILT of children were conducted. These studies were influenced by Piaget's stage theory and an increased interest in cognitive and social cognitive psychology in general. Selman's (1979, 1980) studies of interpersonal awareness in children (Selman & Jaquette, 1978), Daniels-Beirness (1986), and Matthews, Lord, and Walker's (1990) studies of children's definitions of leadership, developed a structural view of the development of leadership concepts in children.

This body of research suggests that children define their understanding and expectations of leaders differently at different ages, which parallel

Piaget's stages of development. Across these studies, when comparing children from kindergarten to sixth grade, it was shown that younger children used more physical characteristics and older children used more affective and motivational characteristics when defining leaders. It should be noted that these studies all employed a verbal interview methodology. Therefore, the presence of concrete versus abstract definitions may be confounded by the children's verbal ability and their conceptual theories.

It is important to mention that Piaget's own theory for the most part assumes social equality among peers, and in fact uses this assumption as a premise to explain why children learn best in the presence of a peer rather than an "unequal" authority figure such as an adult or peer leader. The results of these studies (Selman, 1979, 1980; Selman & Jaquette, 1978; Daniels-Beirness, 1986; Matthews et al., 1990) although initially based on the Piagetian perspective, in fact questioned the Piagetian notion of equality of power among peers. They revealed that children recognize inequality of authority, power, and leadership in their own peer groups and are able to identify their own peer leaders.

By end of the 1980s the field of developmental psychology remained quite barren in relation to understanding children's concept/schema of leaders and leadership. In response to these lacunas, since 1989, we have embarked on a series of studies to understand children's perception and conception of leadership. Building on past research, we used three different approaches to understand children and leadership: children's leadership perception after a naturalistic experience of leadership, children's verbal responses to an interview about their concepts of leaders and leadership, and children's implicit theory of leadership examined through their drawings.

CHILDREN'S PERCEPTION OF LEADERSHIP IN A NATURALISTIC EXPERIENCE

In 1989, we conducted a case study of a third grade classroom in an urban public school, which had just participated in a group drama production project as part of their curriculum. This study examined the children's perception of leadership in general, their perception of actual leadership roles in their group drama projects, and the relationship between these two perceptions.

Method

Subjects

Thirty-six third grade children in a language arts class located in a Midwestern urban school were the subject pool for this study. Students of this class had been involved in a drama production project. Five of the seven groups who had completed their projects constituted the sub-population of the study for interviews on leadership (28 children, 14 boys and 14 girls). They worked in self-selected groups of 4 to 7 members. Each group was responsible for writing and producing a play.

Variables and Measures

Once all the plays were performed, the children participated in two separate interviews. The first interview asked each child about group formation and leadership functions performed by different group members during various aspects of the project. The second interview focused on the children's implicit leadership theory, asking them about their concept of leadership and its functions.

Emergent child leaders. In the post-drama project interview, each child was asked to identify the group member who was responsible for each of the group's functions (i.e., forming the group, writing the script, assigning roles, and leading the practice). At the end of the interview, each child was asked to identify the group member who was overall in charge of the group's project. Each child received a score, which was a ratio of the number of times she or he was identified as the leader, excluding self-rating, over the number of group members.

Implicit leadership theory. Each child was individually interviewed regarding two concepts of leadership: (a) The saliency of the leader in relation to the group and (b) The children's schema of a leader.

To examine the saliency of the leader in relation to the group, the following questions were asked: "Can a person be a leader without a group?", "Can a group function without a leader?", and "Can a group have more than one leader?"

To examine the children's schema of a leader the following questions were asked: "What is a leader?" "How does one become a leader?" "What are leaders supposed to do?" "What makes a good leader?" and "What should a leader be more concerned about, the group being happy or the job being well done or both?" The above sets of questions were asked in the same order for all children.

Results

Leader Saliency and Role

The saliency of leadership in a group was examined by the frequency of the children's responses to the questions examining the role and importance of leaders in groups. Fifty-four percent of the children said that a person cannot be a leader without a group, 39% said that a person can be a leader without a group, and 7% were undecided. On the other hand, when responding to "Can a group function without a leader?" about half of the children said "yes" (52%), about a quarter of the children said "no" (22%), and another quarter said "maybe" (26%). Eighty-two percent of the children believed that a group could have more than one leader.

Implicit Theory of Leadership

To examine the children's implicit concept of leadership, children's responses to each of the four questions describing leaders were Q-sorted. Two experimenters categorized the children's responses based on semantic similarity. The descriptors used in the Q-sort were the children's comments verbatim.

For the question of "What is a leader?" four categories emerged: positive characteristics which are related to task accomplishment (e.g., guiding, organizing, and being in charge); negative characteristics which are related to task accomplishment (e.g., ordering around, being bossy); characteristics that demonstrate being active in the project (e.g., takes care of things, does a lot, makes decisions); and characteristics that showed concern for others(e.g., asking others, giving attention to others, helping others). Eighty-five percent of the children mentioned task-related characteristics—positive and negative—compared to about 10% who mentioned concern for people.

For the question of "How does one become a leader?", eight categories emerged: characteristics related to task accomplishment, having training, concern for people, competence, desire to be a leader, being responsible, being born a leader, being older. The category most often chosen by the children was "concern for people" (46%).

Four major categories emerged from the responses to the question, "What are leaders supposed to do?" These were: concern for people, positive and negative characteristics for accomplishing the task, and competence. More than 71% of the children mentioned task characteristics.

Seven categories emerged from responses to "What makes a good leader?" Two major categories of responses were developed one task orientation (task accomplishment, competence, and sense of responsibility) and the other people orientation (concern for people, communication, humor, and non-authoritarianism). Over half of the children (53.6%) mentioned concern for people at least once as a characteristic of a good leader.

In addition, the response to the question of the concern for the leader yielded the following results. Thirty-nine percent of the children said that the leader should be more concerned with getting the job done than the group being happy. Forty-three percent of children stated that leader should be more concerned with the group being happy than with getting the job done. Only 18% of the children said that the leader should be concerned with both.

Emergent Leadership in Children

Children identified specific members in their group that they saw as the major contributors to the following functions of the group: forming the group, writing the script, assigning roles, and leading the practices. To test the contribution of these functions in a child being identified as the one in charge of the group, a stepwise regression was conducted. The function of "leading practices" was the only significant contributor to the child being identified as "in charge" ($R = .42$, $F(1, 26) = 19.25$, $p < .05$).

To examine gender differences among children chosen by their peers as leaders of the various group functions, a one way multiple analysis of variance was conducted, with the children's scores on the four functions (i.e., leading practices, assigning roles, writing the script, forming the group) acting as dependent variables and gender being the independent variable. The MANOVA was significant ($p < .004$) and two of the four-univariate analyses reached significance using the Bonferroni method. Girls ($M = 2.9$, $n = 14$) received more votes than boys ($M = 2.14$, $n = 14$) for leading the practice, $F(1,26) = 6.03$, $p < .02$. Girls also received more votes ($M = 3.6$) for writing the script than boys ($M = 2.6$), $F(1,26) = 14.16$, $p < .001$. No significant differences were found between girls' and boys' scores on being nominated as in charge of the group, forming the group, or choosing the roles.

The Relationship between Children's ILT and Emergent Leader

To examine the relationship between children's ILT and being identified as a leader, children's responses to each of the four questions about their implicit leadership theory (what is a leader? How does one become a leader? What are leaders supposed to do? and, What makes a good leader?) were categorized into two groups, task and relationship orientations. Task activities, competence, and negative task activities were combined to create a task-oriented score. Caring for people, communication, and humor were combined to create a relationship-oriented score. The more the child mentioned task-oriented descriptors for each question (75% and above), they were identified as having a task-oriented implicit leadership theory. The same process was applied to categorizing children with a relationship-oriented implicit theory. When children's responses equally represented a task-orientation or relationship-orientation, their implicit leadership theory was considered balanced.

Five separate analyses of variances were conducted, where each function was the dependent variable. The independent variables were the responses to the four implicit leadership theory questions. Separate analyses were necessary because of the variability in missing data per variable.

The children with a balance response to the two ILT questions of "What is a leader?" and "How does one become a leader?" were significantly more likely to be rated as practice sessions leader than those with only task or relationship orientation, $F(1,21) = 5.2$, $p < .03$, $F(1,21)$ 4.75, $p < .02$, respectively. Children with a balanced response to the ILT question of "How does one become a leader?" received the highest rating for being chosen as the leader for script writing, $F(2,19) = 5.15$, $p < .02$. Children with a balanced response to the ILT question "What are leaders supposed to do?" were identified significantly more often than those with only task or relationship orientation responses as being in charge, $F(2,22) = 5.25$, $p < .04$.

Summary and Discussion for the Naturalistic Study

The findings of this study demonstrated that most children expected leaders to have followers. More than half of the children state that the group can function without a leader or have more than one leader. As to what is the goal of a leader, half of the children said to get the job done well and half said to keep the harmony of the team. The majority of the children's ILT varied depending on the question asked. When the children were asked "What is a leader?" or "What are leaders supposed to do?", the majority gave task related responses. However, when they were asked "What makes a good leader?" or "How does one become a leader?", the most frequent responses were related to concern for people. The leadership function most contributing to a child being identified as in charge was leading practice sessions. Interestingly, more girls were identified as leaders of practice sessions and script writing. However, no gender differences were found for the children identified as in charge.

The children's implicit leadership theory's relationship to being identified as a leader varied across different functions and various aspects of their ILT. For example, children identified as practice leaders were those whose answers to "What is a leader?" and "How does one become a leader?" were balanced between concern for the task and people. On the other hand, children with a balanced response to "What are leaders supposed to do?" were those chosen as in charge.

This study used a structure interview. Therefore, all questions were asked in the same order. Also, due to the limited number of children we could not use the counterbalance design for the two interviews. This may have an effect on the responses and consequently the results should be taken with caution.

In conclusion, children in third grade had a clear implicit theory of leadership and their theory was contextual. Their identification of leaders in their groups was also contextual. Overall, children with a balanced ILT were more likely to be identified as a leader. An interesting finding regarding gender differences was that of the four functions, girls were perceived as contributing most to two of them (practice session leader and script writing) and practice was the function that was contributing to a child being identified as a leader. Based on these facts it would be logical that girls would be identified more often as the ones in charge. However, the results showed no gender difference in the child being identified as in charge. This might suggest that by this age children already have a gender schema of the leader as a male figure.

CHILDREN'S VERBAL RESPONSES TO WHAT IS LEADERSHIP

To focus more on the children's implicit theory of leadership, in 1993 a second interview study was conducted in the same school.

Methods

Sample

In this study 130 third (34 boys, 29 girls) and sixth (31 boys and 36 girls) graders from a midwestern urban public school in the United States participated. At each grade level three separate classrooms were included. Thirty-three percent of the children were White, 58% Black, 7% Asian, and 2% Hispanic.

Material

Interview protocol for children. The protocol was part of a larger study. Among the questions asked was the question "What is the name of your ideal leader?" This question was coded based on the identifiability of the leader's gender and the categories of the leader's role (e.g., military, person, parent, teacher, Michael Jordan, and Martin Luther King).

Procedure

Student researchers interviewed each child individually for approximately 25 minutes in a private room. The interviewer recorded the responses by taking notes and they were tape-recorded. After the interview the researchers verified the notes with the taped responses.

Results

When the responses of the children of the two grade levels (third and sixth) were considered the gender of the ideal leader varied by the gender of the child χ^2 (2, $N = 130$) = 27.08, $p < .001$. Overall 69% of the mentioned leaders were male. Among the boys, 81.5% mentioned a recognized male name for their ideal leader, whereas among the girls, 37% mentioned a male name for their ideal leader. Also interestingly girls (20%) compared to the boys (8%) mentioned more than twice as many ideal leaders whose gender could not be identified. However, when examining the characteristics of the children with their type of ideal leader across both grades, only the effect of grade was significant. So the results are reported for each grade separately.

Sixth grade.   A significant difference was found for ideal leader's gender, across children's gender χ^2 (2, $N = 67$) = 7.47, $p = .02$. The majority of the children chose a male leader (64%). However, this was more prevalent among the boys (80%) than among girls (50%).

Although the difference between children's gender and their category of ideal leader was not statistically significant, χ^2 (8, $N = 67$) = 11.13, $p = .2$, the following patterns emerged. More boys than girls named sports figures (67%) and religious leaders (67%). Also, boys identified 100% of entertainers or fantasy leaders (e.g., superman). In contrast, girls named 100% of ideal leaders who were teachers and 89% of those who were children. Furthermore, equal number of girls and boys identified ideal leaders who were heads of state, parents, or a generic person.

Third grade.   We found gender difference between the children and the gender of the ideal leader χ^2 (2, $N = 63$) = 24, $p < .0001$. The majority of the children drew a male leader (54%). However, this was more prevalent among the boys (82%) than among girls (21%).

The category of the ideal leader varied across child's gender χ^2 (8, $N = 63$) = 14.45, $p = .07$. Ideal leader categories that were mentioned by at least 10 children included child, parent and political. In these categories gender differences were found for parents (18% of the boys and 31% of the girls) and for political leaders (29% of the Boys and 10% of the girls). All the other categories (military, teacher, entertainment, fantasy and sport) were mentioned by five or less children.

In summary, this interview study demonstrated a strong male image of an ideal leader in the minds of the children in both grades three and six. However, girls less than boys held a strong image of a male ideal leader. It is important to note that this male image of a leader was stronger in sixth grade than in third grade. Also, the leader's categories varied across child's gender and grade.

A CRITICAL ANALYSIS OF THE TWO INTERVIEW STUDIES

In the two interview studies, adults had developed and asked the questions in the interviews based on the literature on leadership in adults. Such interview protocols may have influenced the types of responses children gave. Studying children can be considered as a form of cross- cultural research. In cross-cultural research, two main approaches are identified: the *emic* and the *etic*. The emic approach examines a phenomenon from within a culture, and the etic approach is when a theory or a measure is brought in from another culture (Berry, 1997; Ayman, 2004). Therefore, the interview studies can be considered as an etic approach where adults' views of leadership were imported into the children's social world. Although this line of research contributed greatly to connecting the world of adults to children, it may have masked the reality of the children's think-ing process. Choosing a method that may access the children's emic con-cept of leadership more effectively was warranted.

In addition to the cross-cultural concerns mentioned above, some researchers have shown concern that the use of interviews may be contami-nated with the child's verbal ability (e.g., Matthews et al., 1990). To further expand the understanding of ILT in children and overcome this limitation, we chose a less intrusive method—children's drawings. The following sec-tion will provide the rationale and overview of this methodology.

CHILDREN'S DRAWINGS: AN APPROACH TO THE STUDY
OF CHILDREN'S THOUGHTS

In the last part of the twentieth century, a body of research on social cogni-tion in children that employed drawing as a method of inquiry emerged. Prior to this time, children's drawings had been primarily used to under-stand the development of their artistic ability (Arnheim, 1966, 1974; D'Amico, 1966; Gardner, 1973, 1979, 1980; Golomb, 1973, 1974, 1992; Goodman, 1968, 1976, 1978). Initially when drawings were used to tap into children's minds, researchers typically used "draw a person" as the instruc-tion. These studies focused on understanding children's emotionality

(Koppitz, 1966; Mortensen, 1966) intellectual performance (Goodenough, 1926; Goodnow, 1977; Freeman, 1980) and spatial development (Freeman, 1980; Piaget & Inhelder, 1956). However, the more recent trends have been in using children's drawings as a way of tapping into their social understanding and social values. Dennis (1966) proposes the idea that children's human figure drawing can be used to assess their social images. Many social images and values of children have been studied such as racial identity, concepts of family, old age, schools, friendships, social distance (i.e., Andersson, 1995; Bombi & Pinto, 1994; Dickson, Saylor, & Finch, 1990; Falchikov, 1990; Gramradt & Staples, 1994; Holmes, 1992, 1995; Pinto, Bombi, & Cordioli, 1997). These studies have revealed interesting findings about children's mental model of their social world.

Children's drawings are rich with the reflection of their mental models. They provide information about children's mental models with minimum prompting from outside. Therefore, drawing is a window into the child's mind. This perspective is consistent with Piaget's view that drawing, as a semiotic activity, visualizes children's thoughts and meanings, much as verbal and written language gives them "voice." In fact, Stern (1966) explained that words are an imperfect language for children, whereas drawings are a more effective method for children to express themselves. Children's drawings have a linguistic structure of their own and clearly communicate thoughts and emotions of the producer to the outside world (Stern, 1966; Eubanks, 1997). Furthermore, Gardner (1982) stated that by age five or six children have achieved skills in drawing that enable them to portray their thoughts and ideas in such a way that it can be, for the most part, "read" or decoded.

What a child draws originally comes from the external world, which is then internalized and reproduced within the drawing (Dennis, 1966). Therefore, children's drawings are often representations of their general schema of the world around them, not of a specific object or individual. Hence, drawings are not just a mirror of the environment, but also a reflection of the child's values or preferences (Dennis, 1966). Gramradt and Staples (1994) indicated that in addition to individual thinking, drawings also reveal group-data rich with information about children's collective cultural patterns and their social understanding.

Children's drawings give researchers of social cognition several clear advantages. First, it allows researchers to ask children about social phenomena with very little influence from the adult researcher's own perspective. This allows for maintaining a more pure emic study of the children's world through their own eyes. Second, drawing is an activity that most children enjoy, much more than being part of a complex and abstract interview where they have to answer questions and interact with an unfamiliar adult researcher (Klepsch & Logle, 1982). This positive motivation is almost universal and allows researchers to get rich data from children globally while minimizing verbal and cultural confounds. Third, drawings help in overcoming the difficulties that children may have in fully disclosing their opinions, thoughts, and feelings to an adult researcher. Forth, the act of drawing is private. The child draws on his or her own. Thus, it avoids the potential inhibitions that are omnipresent in interviewing children.

Based on these positive elements of drawing methodology and the desire to gain a better image of children's "pure" implicit leadership theory, we embarked on a collection of children's drawings of leaders. At two separate times, approximately 10 years apart (1992, 2003), we collected drawings of leader/leadership from two cohorts of children in the same midwestern urban school.

Before examining the details of these two studies, it is important to mention a couple of methodological decisions made across both studies. In both of these studies children where asked to produce drawings of "a leader leading." This instruction was in contrast to the traditional drawing studies where children were asked to either draw a person in a general or in a specific role (e.g., scientists). The purpose of this contrast was to capture not just a portray of a leader, which at best may have revealed elements such as gender and ethnicity, but to give children a chance to elaborate on their leaders social roles and styles of leadership by putting them in a context. This approach provided the opportunity to study children's implicit theories of leaders, along with an indication of their concepts about leadership. We asked the children to describe their drawings and identify their leaders on the back of their drawings. These descriptions enriched the drawing data on children's ILT and enhanced the accuracy of coding the drawings. The following sections cover the details of methodology and results of these two cohort studies.

DRAWING STUDY ONE

Method

Sample

In February of 1992, data for this study was collected from 695 children kindergarten through eighth grade at an urban public school. As our study was focused on a leader leading, we only analyzed the data from the 471 children who drew one leader, which was in the form of a human figure. Of the children who participated in the selected drawings 47.8% were boys. The ethnic distribution of these children showed that 51% were African American, 26.4% were Caucasian, 6.2% Asian, 4.7% Hispanic, 3.4% biracial, 6.6% other, 1.1% unknown. The distribution of children across grades was 6.4% in kindergarten, 12.3% in first, 11% in second, 11.3% in third, 11.7% in fourth, 15.1% in fifth, 13.8% in sixth, 11.3% in seventh, and 6.8% in eighth grade.

Materials

Each child was given a sheet of 9 × 12 white paper, one #2 pencil and a box of 12 Crayola color pencils.

Data Collection Procedure

The data was collected in each class's homeroom and the children had approximately 40 minutes to complete their drawings. The research assistants were trained and conducted the data collection under supervision.

The instruction "DRAW A LEADER LEADING" was written on a large poster board located at the front of the classroom. In addition, the children were given verbal instructions to use colored pencils, a #2 pencil, and a white drawing paper to draw "a leader leading." The researchers walked through the room observing and answering students' questions. Research assistants were trained not to explain the phrase "leader leading." They were asked to only repeat the phrase, "draw a leader leading" and tell the children to draw what comes to their mind, and not to worry. If a student expressed concern about their drawing abilities, the researcher assured the student that this was not a drawing contest and to do their best.

Upon completion of the drawing, each student was asked to turn over his or her paper and write two short sentences: (1) describe his or her drawing, and (2) identify which figure in the drawing was the leader. Those in the kindergarten class received a researcher's assistance in writing these sentences. Each student's ethnicity and gender was collected from the child's teacher, and later along with their grade level was recorded on the back of their drawing.

Coding Procedures

Detailed coding procedures were developed and graduate students coded all drawings using the coding instructions. All the identified leaders were coded for gender and color of their face using information in the drawings and in the text written by the children at the back of the drawings. To determine the style of leadership, the leaders were coded for smiling, presence of violence in the drawing, presence of followers, gender of followers, and relative size of the leader compared to that of the followers.

Four coders assisted in coding this study's drawings. They coded the same 15 drawings on all the various variables stated above. The overall inter-rater reliability average across the 4 raters was 92.72% (ranging from 75% to 100%). All disagreements were discussed for further clarifications. As the inter-rater reliability was fairly high, the drawings were divided among the raters for coding and data entry. The coding instructions for all drawings and the inter-rater reliability for each are presented in the Appendix.

Results

The results are presented in the following manner: (1) Distribution for variables describing the drawings characteristics included eight variables such as drawn leader's gender, leader's color, leader's smiling, the drawing's depiction of violence, presence of followers, gender of the followers, comparative size of the leader with followers, and leader's category; (2) Relationship of these variables to each of the child's characteristics (i.e., gender, ethnicity, and grade) and the child characteristics most predictive of each of the drawing's characteristics; (3) Lastly, the results that reveal the style of the drawn leaders based on their categorization will be offered. Their categorizations were the comparison of male and female drawn leaders, drawn leaders depicting the two ethnic backgrounds, and the leader's role categories.

Prior to analysis of the drawings, three chi-square tests were conducted to examine potential confounding relationships between children's gender, ethnicity, and grade. The chi-squares for gender and ethnicity, for gender and grade, and for ethnicity and grade of children were not significant. Therefore, these results demonstrate that there were no confounding relationships between these independent variables.

Frequency of Drawing Characteristics

To summarize the data on the children's ILT, we present the frequency of the drawing characteristics in the order listed above. Overall, majority of children drew a male figure for the leader (63%), 33% drew a female figure, and in 4% of the drawings the leader's gender was unidentifiable. As the percentage of drawn leaders with unidentifiable gender was very small, in subsequent analyses we only focused on comparing those drawings that identified male of female figures of leaders.

About half of the children drew the leader white (58.5%), whereas 25.5% drew or described a black leader, 3% of the drawn leaders' colors were not identifiable, and 12% of children drew the leader in various colors such as yellow, blue, orange, red, and green. Therefore, since the most frequent colors used for drawn leaders were black and white, in subsequent analyses only drawing with these colors were used.

The results show that 47% of the children drew the leader smiling and 83% depicted a nonviolent setting. Most children drew the leader with followers either drawn or implied (85.5%). Almost a third of them drew male followers (35%), 16% drew female followers, 24% drew a mix of males and female followers, and 25% did not identify the gender of the followers. The leader was depicted larger than others in 56% of the drawings, whereas in 32% of the drawings the leader was equal to others, and in only 12% was the leader drawn smaller.

Children overall identified 14 major role categories of leaders including child, generic person, military, parent, teacher, head of state, religious person, Michael Jordan, sports figure, Martin Luther King, fantasy, self, entertainment/parade leader, and famous people. The three role categories with the highest frequency were person (35.5), entertainment and parade leaders (17%), and military (12%).

Comparing Child's Characteristics and Drawings of the Leader Leading

The next set of analysis dealt with examining the relationship between the children's characteristics and the drawing characteristics. To summarize this data we conducted a series of chi-square tests. We also conducted a logistic regression on the drawing characteristics and children's characteristics to assist in further clarifying the most salient relationships.

Comparing child's gender and drawings of leader leading. The child's gender was crossed with the drawing's characteristics (leader's gender, leader's color, leader's smile, presence of violence, presence of followers, gender of the follower, and the comparative size, leader's role categories). The results showed that the child's gender differed significantly on 7 of the 8 possible characteristics. The only characteristic of the drawings that did not yield a significant difference between girls and boys was the relative size of the leader drawn. Boys drew more male than female figures for the leader (89%), whereas 43% of the girls' drawings included male leader figures χ^2 (1, $N = 447$) = 105.14, $p = .0001$. Also, girls drew considerably more smiling leaders (68%) than non-smiling and boys drew slightly fewer smiling (43%) than non-smiling leaders $\chi^2(1, N = 389)$ = 24.8, $p = .04$. The presence of violence in the drawings were very small only 17%, however, the drawing that showed violence varied significantly based on the child's gender χ^2 (1, $N = 467$) = 26.75, $p = .0001$, where boys drew 74.7% of the violent pictures. Boys (42.8%) and girls (57.2%) drew almost equal percentage of the non-violent drawings.

When followers were drawn, the gender of the child affected the depiction of the followers' gender in the drawing χ^2 (3, $N = 375$) = 99.17, $p = .0001$. When children differentiated the gender of the followers, boys drew more male followers (57%) than female (3%), mixed-gender (12%), and neutral (28%); on the other hand, girls' drawings were more evenly distributed in their depiction of the gender of the followers. That is, they drew more mixed-gender followers (33%) than female followers (28.5%), male followers (16%), and neutral (22%).

Comparing girls and boys drawings on the role categories of the leader drawn, we found that categories of leaders for the two groups of children differed significantly χ^2 (13, $N = 466$) = 38.13, $p = .0001$ (see Figure 9.1). Three categories had similar frequencies in girls and boys drawings. These were generic person: boys drew 51.2% of this category; head of state: boys drew half of these drawings; and famous people: boys drew 54.5% of the drawings. These similarities withstanding, for drawings that portrayed other categories, girls and boys varied in the frequency of their depictions. For religious figure, girls drew 80% of the drawings. For those drawings depicting a child as the leader, girls drew 75.7% of the drawings. For drawings that included Martin Luther King as the leader, girls drew 72.7% of them. Girls also drew most of the drawings with a teacher as the leader (61.9%), a parent as the leader (66.7%), and entertainment and parade leader (58.2). Boys, on the other hand, drew more leaders depicted as sports leaders (87.5%), military (70.4%), Michael Jordan (75%), and fantasy (64.7%).

Comparing child's ethnicity and drawings of leader leading. The effect of the child's ethnicity was examined against the drawings' characteristics. Of the eight chi-squares conducted, three were significant. The characteristics that did not yield significant differences due to children's ethnicity

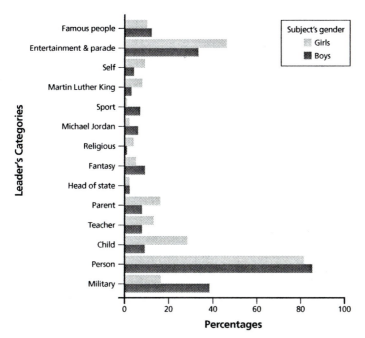

Figure 9.1.   Percentages of Children's Gender and Leader's Role Categories (Study 1).

were leader's gender, smile, presence of violence, followers' gender, and relative size.

The child's ethnicity was significantly related to the drawn leader's color χ^2 (1, $N = 313$) = 15.44, $p = .0001$. African American children drew 62% white leaders and 38% black, the White children drew 84% white leaders and 16% black leaders.

Children's ethnicity significantly effected the drawing of followers' present in the drawings χ^2 (1, $N = 363$) = 6.9, $p < .01$. Although of possible options (i.e., drew the follower, implied, and did not draw followers) both White (92%) and Black children (81.6%) drew more drawing with followers present. Among those who did not draw followers more were African American children (81.5%) than Whites.

The leader's role categories also varied significantly due to the child's ethnicity χ^2 (13, $N = 363$) = 29.34, $p < .01$ (see Figure 9.2). The similar categories drawn by both White and African American children were parent, fantasy, sport, Martin Luther King, self, and famous people. These similarities with-standing, children drew different frequencies of leader categories, though the categories except one stayed the same. The White children's top four categories were person (31%), entertainment (27%), military (14%), and teacher (7%). The top categories of leaders drawn by African American children were person (41%), entertainment and parade leader (11%), military (11%) and child (9%).

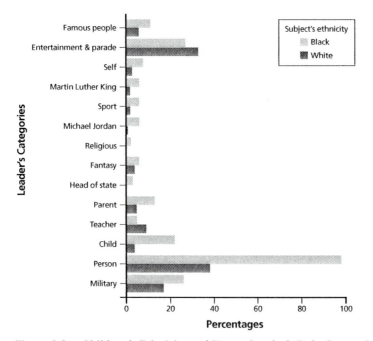

Figure 9.2.   Children's Ethnicity and Drawn Leader's Role Categories (Study 1).

Relationship of children's grade and drawing characteristics.   To examine closely the effects of grade on children's drawings of a leader leading, we analyzed the variables against both the full range of the grades (all kept separate) as well as a combined range of grades (K, 1–2, 3–5, 6–8). Combining grades gave us larger cell sizes as well as a comparison across the Piagetian developmental levels of late pre-operational (Kindergarten), early concrete operational (grade one and two), well-established concrete operational (grades three through five, middle childhood) and early formal operational (grades six through eight). The combined grade analysis yielded the same overall results of significance as separated grades; therefore, in the interest of expedience we will only present the combined grade results. The only independent variables that showed significant differences across grades were leader category, leader smile, and presence of followers.

The analysis examining the relationship between leader's role categories and grade yielded significant results χ^2 (39, $N = 470$) = 77.8, $p < .0001$. It is important to mention that in the cross tabulation table for this analysis there were cell sizes of zero in 10 cells. However, it is valuable for theoretical reasons to examine closely the patterns of choice of leader roles across grades. The presence zero cells became progressively less frequent as grade level increased. Kindergarten children did not draw five of the leader's role categories (self, famous people, Michael Jordan, religion, and head of state). First and second graders did not draw three of the leader categories (Michael Jordan, religion, and fantasy). Finally, third to fifth graders did not draw religious figures, and drawings of the sixth to eighth graders showed all leader categories.

The choice of a more stereotypic known leader increased by grade. The best example of this is the famous people category that went from zero in Kindergarten to 1.8% in first and second grade, 3.9% in third through fifth grade, and 8.7% in sixth through eighth grade, with this last group giving 60% of the responses in this category, seconded by third through fourth graders (32% of the responses). The other example may be seen in the portrayal of Michael Jordan as a leader. He was identified as a leader only in third grade and up (note this data was collected at the time when he was at the height of his fame). Religious leaders only appeared up in 3.4% of the sixth to eighth grade group's drawings. For all developmental levels generic person, military, entertainment, and child were categories with the highest frequency but they did not gain the same order across grades (see Figure 9.3).

Presence of smile on the leaders varied significantly by grade χ^2 (3, $N = 392$) = 17.92, $p<.0001$. In Kindergarten through second grade, children drew more smiling leaders than not smiling (see Figure 9.4). This difference is less noticeable in the higher grades.

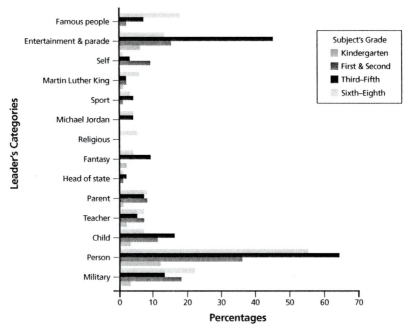

Figure 9.3. Children's Grade and Drawn Leader's Role Categories (Study 1).

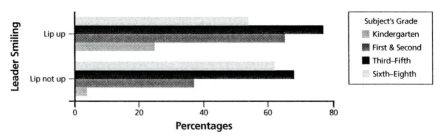

Figure 9.4. Children's Grade and Drawn Leader with Smile (Study 1).

The analysis of presence of followers against grade was significant χ^2 (3, $N = 471$) = 42.52, $p < .0001$. Presence of followers showed the highest representation in the middle grades (93.6% of first and second graders and 92.8% of third to fifth graders). Only 56.7% of leaders drawn by kindergarteners included followers. Sixth through eighth graders although had less incidences of drawn followers than middle graders, showed higher frequency of presence of followers than kindergarteners (77.3%).

Child's characteristics that best describe drawing characteristics. To further understand when the child's characteristics (i.e., gender, ethnicity, and grade) are present which had the most effect on the drawings, we conducted five binary logistic regressions and three multinomial logistical regressions using the SPSS statistical package. The only drawing characteristic that was not related to children's characteristics was drawn leader's comparative size. The pattern of the detailed results was the same as that reported in the bivariate analyses.

First, we regressed the leader's gender on the child's characteristics. The results showed that child's gender and grade yielded significant results χ^2 (3, $N = 349$) = 94.11, $p = .0001$. That is, if the child was a boy it was more likely that he would draw a male (Wald = 67.07, $B = 2.5$, $p = 0001$) and if the child was from the higher grades, it was less likely that male leader would be drawn (Wald = 2.8, $B = -.112$, $p = .05$).

When we regressed the leader's color on the child's characteristics, the results showed that the model with all variables was significant χ^2 (3, $N = 349$) = 30.411, $p < .001$. That is if the child was a boy it was more likely that the leader was drawn white (Wald = 10.267, $B = -.830$, $p = .001$). Also, if the child was White, it was more likely that the leader was also drawn white (Wald = 12.78, $B = 1.14$, $p < .0001$), and when all variables were included grade's significance became marginal (Wald = 3.37, $B = .11$, $p = .07$).

When we regressed the leader drawn smiling on all of the child's characteristics, the results were significant χ^2 (3, $N = 349$) = 44.16, $p < .0001$. That is, if the child was a girl, it was more likely that the leader was drawn smiling (Wald = 23.08, $B = 1.21$, $p < .0001$). The lower the grade of the child, the more likely it was that the leader was drawn with a smile (Wald = 19.06, $B = -.24$, $p < .0001$).

When we regressed violence on the child's characteristics, the model with gender as the predictor was significant χ^2 (1, $N = 349$) = 22.52, $p < .0001$. This result showed if the child was a boy it was more likely that violence was present in the drawing (Wald = 17.9, $B = 1.33$, $p < .0001$), but grade and ethnicity were not significant predictors of drawings with violence.

When presence of followers was regressed on children's characteristics, the model was significant χ^2 (3, $N = 363$) = 14.45, $p = .002$. If the child was a girl it was more likely that followers were drawn (Wald = 6.5, $B = .79$, $p = .01$). If the child was African American it was more likely that the followers were not drawn (Wald = 6.4, $B = -.96$, $p = .01$). Grade of the child did not have a significant effect on the child drawing followers.

Using multinomial logistic regression, when followers' gender was regressed on the children's characteristics, the model was significant χ^2 (30, $N = 288$) = 101.75, $p < .0001$. The gender of the child was the main contributor to this result χ^2 (3, $N = 288$) = 77.97, $p < .0001$, so that if the child was a boy it was less likely that female followers were drawn (Wald = 19.42, $B = -2.92$, $p < .0001$) or mixed gender followers were drawn (Wald = 10.58, $B = -1.26$ the highest, $p < .001$). However, if the child was a boy it was more likely that they drew male followers (Wald = 6.97, B = .91, p < .01).

When leader's category was regressed on children's characteristics, the model was significant for all three child characteristics χ^2 (130, N = 363) = 220.37, p < .0001. See Table 9.1 for detailed results on each child characteristic.

Table 9.1. The Multinomial Logistic Regression for the Leader's Role Categories and Children's Characteristics (Study 1)

Effect	−2 Log Likelihood of Reduced Model	Chi-Square	df
Intercept	485.57[a]	.000	0
Child's Gender	525.48	39.91[****]	13
Child's Ethnicity	515.56	29.99[**]	13
Child's grade	637.88	152.31[***]	104

Note: The chi-square statistic is the difference in −2 log-likelihoods between the final model and a reduced model. The reduced model is formed by omitting an effect from the final model. The null hypothesis is that all parameters of that effect are 0.
[a] This reduced model is equivalent to the final model because omitting the effect does not increase the degrees of freedom.
[****] p < .0001, [***] p < .001, [**] p < .01

The Drawn-Leader's Characteristics and Leadership Style

To examine if the drawn leaders' behavior varied due to context we first identified the leader's style. For leader's style we examined the presence of smile, violence, relative size, and followers. In this analysis, leader's gender, color, or category represented the leadership context.

Using binary logistic regression, when the drawn leader's gender was regressed on drawing with smile, violence, and presence of followers, the model was significant χ^2 (4, N = 383) = 36.76, p < .0001. If the child drew a male leader, it was less likely that it was smiling, more likely that it involved with violence, and less likely that followers were present (see Table 9.2).

Table 9.2. Binary Logistic Regression Results for Drawn Leader's Gender by Smiling, Violence and Presence of Followers (Study 1)

	B	S.E.	Wald	df	Exp(B)
Smiling	.806	.227	12.640[****]	1	2.238
Violence	−1.422	.404	12.370[****]	1	.241
Follower present	.743	.353	4.430[*]	1	2.102
Constant	−2.230	.508	19.263	1	.108

[****] p = .0001, [*] p < .05

When the leader's color was regressed on drawing with smile, violence, and presence of followers, the model was significant χ^2 (3, $N = 337$) = 18.2, $p < .0001$. Overall, the results show that if the leader was drawn as black, it was more likely that the drawing had less violence, less followers present, and that the leader was less likely to smile (see Table 9.2).

Using multinomial logistic regression, when the drawn leader's category was regressed over the drawing characteristics the model was significant χ^2 (39, $N = 391$) = 135.78, $p < .0001$. Since some cells were empty, the result should be considered cautiously. All three predictors yielded significance results: smiling χ^2 (13) = 38.88, $p < .0001$; presence of violence χ^2 (13) = 48.91, $p < .0001$; and presence of followers χ^2 (13) = 48.68, $p < .0001$. Results showed that if the leader was drawn as a military figure it was more likely that the drawing showed violence. If the leader was drawn as a generic person or parade leader/entertainer, it was more likely that the leader was drawn smiling and that there were followers present. If the leader was drawn as a child, teacher, or parent, it was more likely that the leader was drawn smiling. Other categories did not show significant differences based on these drawing characteristics.

DRAWING STUDY TWO

Method

Sample

In February 2003, data was collected from all the children kindergarten through eighth grade, at the same midwestern urban public school as the first study. At this time, due to board of education reorganization, this school did not have a seventh grade classes. Of 500 drawings collected, only 352 had one human leader. This study included all drawings with one human leader leading. The demographic of the sample in this study included 46% boys and 51% girls. The ethnicity of the subjects were 21% White, 58% African American, 14% Asian American, and 5% Hispanic. Among the students in the African American and Asian American categories some were foreign-born. The distribution of the children across grades was 11.9% in kindergarten, 12.8% in first, 13.9% in second, 9.4% in third, 17.6% in fourth, 15.9% in fifth, 11.9% in sixth, 6.5% in eighth grade.

Materials

Identical to the first study, each child was given a 9 × 12 white paper, one #2 pencil, and a box of 12 Crayola color pencils.

Data Collection Procedure

Data was collected in the school library, during each class's weekly library hour, which was approximately 40 minutes. The research assistants were trained and conducted the data collection under supervision. The procedures of the second study were identical to those of the first study, except in two cases where we fine-tuned the data collection process to increase accuracy of information and ease of coding.

First, children sat four or five at the same large library table. In order to avoid the sharing of ideas, the children were asked to remain quiet, avoid talking to the other students in the room, and to raise their hand if they had any questions. Second, we put in place a careful checkpoint when children handed in their drawings. Each drawing was checked carefully for interpretable identification of the drawn leader(s). If the child had missed this information on the back of the drawing, we asked that they add that information before we took the drawing.

Coding Procedure

The coding procedure was identical to the first study. The reliability per variable is available in the Appendix, along with the coding scheme. However, for this study there were two raters and the average reliabilities agreement across variables was 92.61% (ranging from 75% to 100%). All disagreements were discussed for further clarification. As the inter-reliability was fairly high, the drawings were divided among the two coders for coding and data entry. This coding procedure therefore yielded exactly the same variables as in study one.

Results

The results are presented in the same manner as in Drawing Study One. Similar to Drawing Study One, three chi-square tests were conducted to examine potential confounding relationships between children's gender, ethnicity, and grade. All chi squares were not significant. Therefore, these results demonstrate that there is no relationship between children's gender, ethnicity and grades.

Frequency of Drawing Characteristics

To summarize the data on the children's ILT, we present the frequency of the drawing characteristics as listed above.

Overall, majority (54%) of children drew a male figure for the leader, 37% drew a female figure, and in 9% of the drawings the leader's gender was unidentifiable. As the percentage of leader's drawn without identifying gender was very small, in subsequent analyses on drawn leader's gender, we only focused on comparing those drawings that identified male or female figures of leaders.

Half of the drawings drew the leader white (50%), whereas 40% drew or described a black leader, 5% drew the leader in other colors, and 5% of the drawn leaders' colors were not identifiable. Therefore, since the most frequent colors used for a drawn leader were black and white, in subsequent analyses only drawings with these colors were included.

The distribution of the characteristics of the drawings was examined. The results showed that 54% of the children drew the leader smiling and 87% depicted a non-violent setting. Most children drew the leader with followers either drawn or implied (77%). Although 43.4% of the children drew the followers with no gender designation, 16.4% drew male followers, 21.9% drew female followers, and 18.4% drew a mix of males and female followers. The leader was depicted larger than others in 50.8% of the drawings, whereas in 42.5% of the drawings the leader was equal to others and only 6.7% drew the leader smaller than followers.

Children overall identified about 10 major categories of leaders including child, person, military, parent, teacher, head of state, sports figure, Martin Luther King, fantasy, self, entertainment/parade leader, and famous people. The three with the highest frequency were person (31.6%), Martin Luther King (13.7%), and child (10.8%).

Comparing Child's Characteristics and Drawings of Leader Leading

The next set of questions dealt with the relationship between the children's characteristics and the drawing characteristics. To summarize this data we conducted a series of chi-square tests. We also conducted a binary regression on the drawing characteristics that had two levels to assist in further clarifying the most salient relationships.

Comparing child's gender and drawings of leader leading. The child's gender was cross-tabulated with the drawing characteristics. The results showed that the child's gender differed significantly on 5 of the 8 possible characteristics. The results of the chi-squares showed no gender difference on drawing the leader's color, presence of followers, and the comparative size of the leader.

Boys drew more male figures for the leader (93%), while 32% of the girls' drawings depicted the leader as a male figure χ^2 (1) = 119.890, $p = .0001$. Also, girls drew considerably more smiling leaders (71%) than non-smiling, and boys drew only slightly more smiling (59%) than non-smiling (41%) leaders χ^2 (1) = 4.30, $p = .04$. The level of violence in the drawings varied significantly based on the child's gender χ^2 (1) = 21.23, $p = .0001$, where boys drew 85% of the violent pictures compared to 15% drawn by girls. The non-violent drawings were drawn almost equally by boys (44%) and girls (56%).

When followers were drawn, the gender of the child affected the depiction of the followers' gender in the drawing χ^2 (3) = 74.81, p = .0001. When children differentiated the gender of the followers, boys drew more male followers (31%) than female (2.5%); similarly, girls drew more female followers (40%) than males (3%). Also, boys (52%) drew more undifferentiated follower's gender than girls (35%). Girls (21%) and boys (15%) drew almost equal numbers of mixed gender followers.

Comparing girls' and boys' drawings on the category of the leader drawn, we found that role categories of leaders for the two groups of children differed significantly χ^2 (11) = 58.094, p = .0001 (see Figure 9.5). They had three categories with similar representations. These categories were generic person: boys (31%) and girls (32%); Martin Luther King: boys (15%) and girls (13%); parents: boys (7%) and girls (4%). These similarities withstanding, girls drew more frequently themselves (11%) and teacher (9%); whereas boys' more frequently drew military (11%) and famous people (9%) as leader categories.

Comparing child's ethnicity and drawings of leader leading.   The effect of the child's ethnicity was examined against the drawings characteristics. Of the eight chi-squares conducted four were significant. Those drawing characteristics that did not show significant difference due to the child's ethnicity

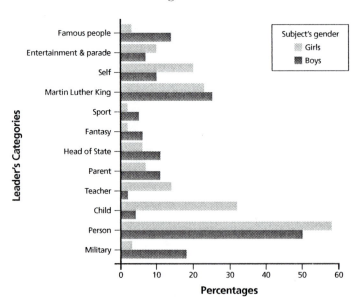

Figure 9.5.   Comparing Children's Gender and Drawn Leader Role Categories (Study 2).

were drawn leader's gender, smile, presence of follower, and gender of the follower present.

The child's ethnicity was significantly related to the drawn leader's color χ^2 (11) = 23.514, p = .0001. African American children drew 44% white leaders and 56% black; the White children drew 79% white leaders and 21% black leaders.

Although the number of drawing depicting violence was very small (13%), presence of violence in drawings varied significantly by the child's ethnicity χ^2 (1, N = 265) = 9.34, p < .002. Of the drawings that the White children drew, 80% depicted non-violence and 20% violence; in contrast, 93% of the African American children's drawings depicted non-violence and 7% violence.

The size of the leader drawn was also related to the child's ethnicity χ^2 (2, N = 202) = 5.82, p < .05. The White children's drawing showed that 2% of their drawings had portrayed the leader smaller, 49% equal, 49% larger than other figures in the drawing. On the other hand, among the African American children drawings 11% drew the leader smaller, 38% drew the leader equal, and 50% larger than the follower in the drawing.

The leader's role category also varied significantly due to the child's ethnicity χ^2 (11, N = 276) = 20.74, p < .036 (see Figure 9.6). For the White children, the top four categories of leaders drawn were person (23%), military (13.5%), child (12.2%), and Martin Luther King (9.5%). For the African American children the top categories of leaders drawn were person (32.2%), Martin Luther King (15.8%), and child (9.9%).

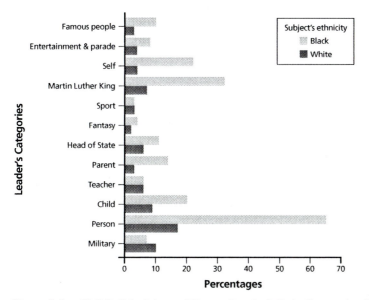

Figure 9.6.   Child's Ethnicity and Drawn Leader's Role Categories (Study 2).

Relationship of child's grade and drawing characteristics.   Only the following four (drawn leader's color, presence of violence, leader smiling and presence of followers) of the eight tests were significant; the drawn leader's gender, smile, followers' gender, comparative size of the leader, and leader role categories did not differ significantly across grades. Even in most cases where significant levels of difference were found, the relationship was not linear. To examine closely the effects of grade, we analyzed the drawing characteristics against both the full range of the grades (all kept separate) as well as a combined range of grades (K, 1–2, 3–5, 6–8). This combined grade variable gave us larger cell sizes as well as a comparison across the Piagetian developmental levels of late pre-operational (Kindergarten), early concrete operational (grades one and two), well established concrete operational (grades three through five, middle childhood), and early formal operational (grades six through eighth).

Grade and the drawn leader's color (focusing on only black and white leaders) yielded only significant results when all grades are kept separate χ^2 (7, N = 317) = 15.67, p < .03. When examining the cells, all grades showed a general pattern of 60% (range from 57%–73%) white leaders and 40% black leaders (ranging from 26%–42%) with the exceptions of third grade (drawing 50% of each category), and fifth and eighth grade drawing the reverse pattern, 40% white and 60% black. It is important to note that there were no differences in these grades as far as distribution of child ethnicity or presence of drawings of Martin Luther King as the leader.

The presence of violence in children's drawings increased by grade during the middle grades and then decreases in upper grades. Of the drawings that had violence 4% where drawn by children in kindergarten through second grade, 83% were drawn by third through fifth grades. However, the percentage of drawings containing violence done by sixth through eighth graders decreased to 11%. This pattern was significant with χ^2 (3, N = 340) = 27.3, p < .0001.

Presence of smile on the leaders varied significantly by grade χ^2 (3, N = 293) = 25.07, p < .0001. In kindergarten through second grade, children drew more smiling leaders than not smiling. This difference is less noticeable in the higher grades.

Although the comparison of grade by presence of followers was significant χ^2 (7, N = 350) = 21.51, p < .005, the pattern could not explain any developmental change. The percentage of those who did not draw followers began at 9.8% and 7.3% in kindergarten and first grade, increasing to 15.9% in second grade, and subsequently dropping to 3.7% in third grade. The percent of children who did not draw followers increased again for fourth (19.5%), fifth (11%), and sixth grade (19.5%). This fluctuation continued for the eighth grade with a drop in percentages (13.4%) of drawing with no followers. When grades were combined the same level of significance was obtained for the grade effect, and a large jump in the percentage of drawings with no followers was obtained in the upper grade category (sixth through eighth grade) at 33%.

Child's characteristics that best describe drawing characteristics. To further understand which of the child's characteristics (i.e. gender, ethnicity, grade) had an effect on the drawings, we conducted five logistic regressions. First, we regressed the leader's gender on the child's characteristics. The results showed that child's gender was the only child characteristic that yielded significant results χ^2 (3, $N = 250$) = 97.05, Wald = 62.52, $B = 3.1$, $p = .0001$. Similar to the bivariate findings, the detail analysis showed that if the child was a boy it was more likely that he would draw a male.

Table 9.3.   Binary Logistic Regression Results for Drawn Leader's Color (White and Black) by Smiling, Violence and Presence of Followers (Study 1)

	B	S.E.	Wald	df	Exp(B)
Smiling	−.626	.251	6.206[**]	1	.535
Violence presence	−.426	.383	1.239	1	.653
Followers present	−1.168	.347	11.299[***]	1	.311
Constant	1.116	.512	4.745	1	3.053

[***]$p < .001$ and [**]$p < .01$

When we regressed the leader's color on the child's characteristics, the results were significant χ^2 (3, $N = 249$) = 29.67, $p = .0001$. However, the only characteristic that contributed significantly was the child's ethnicity. This mirrored the bivariate finding that if the child was White, it was more likely that the leader was also drawn white (Wald = 20.23, $B = 1.57$, $p = .0001$).

When we regressed the leader's smile on all of the child's characteristics, the result was significant χ^2 (3, $N = 226$) = 24.64, $p = .0001$ and demonstrated that grade was the characteristic that contributed most significantly to drawing the leader with a smile (Wald = 18.59, $B = −.76$, $p = .0001$). The detail analysis reflected that if the child was of higher grade it was less likely that the drawing depicted a smiling leader.

When we regressed violence on the child's characteristics the result was significant χ^2 (3, $N = 265$) = 35.48, $p = .0001$. All three characteristics of the children contributed significantly to the drawing of violence. The detail analysis is reflective of the bivariate analyses presented earlier. That is, if the child was a boy or was White, it was more likely that the drawing would show violence. If the child was from higher grades, it was more likely for the drawing to portray violence (see Table 9.4).

Table 9.4.   Binary Logistic Regression Results for Drawn Presence of Violence and Children's Characteristics (Study 2)

	B	S.E.	Wald	df	Exp(B)
Child's gender	−2.420	.634	14.577[****]	1	.089
Child's ethnicity	−1.058	.437	5.873[*]	1	.347
Child's grade	.588	.268	4.798[*]	1	1.800
Constant	−.776	.879	.779	1	.460

[****]p < .0001, [*]p < .05

Using multinomial logistic regression, we regressed the leader's relative size on the children's characteristics. The result was significant χ^2 (18, $N = 202$) = 32.06, $p = .02$. Ethnicity was the only characteristic contributing significantly χ^2 (2) = 7.3, $p = .03$. If the leader drawn was smaller than the followers it was more likely that it was drawn by an African American child (Wald = 2.97, $B = −1.83$, $p = .08$).

Using multinomial logistic regression, we regressed presence of followers on the children's characteristics. The result was significant χ^2 (9, $N = 275$) = 18.46, $p = .03$. Grade was the only characteristic contributing significantly χ^2 (7) = 16.42, $p = .02$. The detailed findings were reflective of the bivariate results mentioned earlier.

The Drawn-Leader's Characteristics and Leadership Style

As in Study 1, leader's style was defined by the presence of smile, violence, and presence of followers. Three logistic regression analyses were conducted where the drawn leader's characteristics (leader's gender, color, or category) were regressed over the leader's style indicators.

Using binary logistic regression, when the leader's gender was regressed on drawing with smile, violence, and presence of followers, the model was significant (χ^2 (3, $N = 267$) = 15.82, $p = .001$). If the child drew a female leader, it was more likely that it was smiling, and less likely that there was violence in the drawing (see Table 9.5).

Table 9.5.   Binary Logistic Regression of Drawn Leader's Gender and Leader's Style (Study 2)

	B	S.E.	Wald	df	Exp(B)
Smiling	.561	.270	4.321[*]	1	1.753
Violence present	−1.744	.641	7.392[**]	1	.175
Follower present	−.208	.313	.441	1	.812
Constant	−.969	.540	3.222	1	.379

[**]p < .01, [*]p < .05

When the leader's color was regressed on drawing with smile, violence, and presence of followers, the model was significant χ^2 (3, $N=264$) = 18.72, p =.0001. Overall the results show that if the leader was drawn as black, it was more likely that the drawing had less violence, and the drawn leader was less likely to smile (see Table 9.6).

Table 9.6.   Binary Logistical Regression for Drawn Leader's Color and Leader's Style (Study 2)

	B	S.E.	Wald	df	Exp(B)
Smiling	−.667	.269	6.126[*]	1	.513
Violence presence	−1.973	.643	9.401[**]	1	.139
Follower presence	−.077	.325	.056	1	.926
Constant	.958	.542	3.117	1	2.606

[*]$p < .05,$ [**]$p < .01$

Using multinomial logistic regression, when the drawn leader's category was regressed over presence of smile, violence, and followers, the model was significant χ^2 (33, $N = 284$) = 156.47, $p = .0001$. Since some cells were empty the result should be considered cautiously. Only presence of violence yielded significance results χ^2 (11) = 209.13, $p = .0001$. The details of the results showed that when military and fantasy leaders were drawn there was more violence in the drawings.

Discussion

The highlight of the results of the studies of the last fifteen years with children can be categorized into two main issues. One issue is the contextual nature of the children's ILT's content and structure. The second issue is the significant impact the methodology and study's design had on information collected.

Implicit Theory and Context
The most salient finding of the four studies over fifteen years, with different methodologies was the role of gender in ILT theory. Not only is this effect true in the difference between boys' and girls' ILT, but it also affected the children's ILT about male and female leaders. Furthermore, the ILT of children affected their decisions when rating boys or girls as leaders.

In the naturalistic study of children in teams, no significant gender differences were found for the gender of the team leader. However, the function that was most associated with being identified as the team leader was a function in which girls rather than boys were most often identified as its leader. Consequently, this demonstrated that even though girls more than boys were noticed for their contribution to a specific and important function (i.e. leader of the practice sessions), they only ended up with an equal chance to boys in being identified as a team leader.

This finding supports the well-established phenomenon in adult literature where it has been reported that women state that they have to work twice as hard to get the same promotions as men. This challenge has been associated with presence of a male stereotype of leadership (Catalyst, 1998; Eagly & Karau, 2002; Schein, 2001). Therefore, these findings suggest that children, as young as elementary school, already have an ILT that portrays a male image.

Furthermore, in the initial study, the results showed that children who were chosen as team leaders most often had an ILT that represents both attention to task and to people. This also indicates that ILT is playing a role in the child's own leadership. Thus, a focus on understanding children's ILT became an imperative next step.

In fact the findings of the two drawing studies, with sole focus on ILT, supported the above-mentioned hypotheses. The results showed that children have an ILT theory and that their implicit theories are contextually defined. In summary, these two studies ten years apart, demonstrated that a male leader was drawn most often, and that this is only due the fact that boys almost always drew male leaders. It is important to note that even in the case of girls, less than half in the first study and a third in the second study drew a male leader. Additionally, in the 1993 interview study results showed the same pattern for the children's ILT of an ideal leader. Thus, these results further extend Schein's recent findings to children in the U.S.—"Think manager think male" (Schein, 2001). Schein in her international study demonstrated that across countries the "Think manager think male" was validated. However, in the United States the trend is changing where more women hold female ILT of a manger.

It is valuable to compare these gender effects on ILT from children's drawings with general findings on gender effects on children's Human Figure Drawings (HFD) in general. Although there are some controversies among HFD scholars, a majority of the studies have shown that children primarily draw self-sex (i.e., sex-typed) humans—that is boys draw males and girls draw females. However, boys more than girls seem to draw self-sex humans (Brown, 1979; Heinrich & Treible, 1972; Jolles, 1952; Phelan, 1964). This is mostly an accepted finding, even across cultures (i.e. Pfeffer's 1985 study among the Yorubas of Nigeria). There are very few exceptions such as Dickson et al. (1990) who found no sex differences in children drawings of self-sex human figures.

Self-sex HFD is also found among adults (Granick & Smith, 1953; Teglasi, 1980). However, studies on adults have found that drawing of men by women is more prevalent among "traditional" and less educated women (Teglasi, 1980). It is interesting that similarly, Nigerian Yoruba girls who were less educated and from low income families compared to the girls of elite families also drew more men in their HFD.

Comparing the findings of the recent drawing study with children to the research in adults shows a similar but not identical pattern. The predominant preference for self-similarity in ILT, which was found among adults (Keller, 1999) was replicated in children only in case of gender. When examining ethnicity, only Whites demonstrated self-similarity in their ILT.

It is important to recognize that in a more context-specific drawing of a "leader leading", the gender differences were replicated. The most salient result in the drawing studies was the self-sex attachment of the boys, whether they are focusing on a general image of a human or their ILT. As for the girls, in the ILT studies the percentage of girls drawing self-sex figures was lower than most of those reported in HFD studies. Less than half of the girls had the same stereotypic image of "think manager, think male" as boys. On the other hand, more than half of the girls had an ILT that represented a female image.

In addition, the results demonstrated that children hold different ILT regarding the style of a drawn male or a drawn female leader. Across the two studies male leaders were more likely than female leaders to be drawn in a violent context, not smiling, and without followers. This is similar to the findings of the adult literature that the implicit theory for male and female leaders is different (e.g., Heilman, Block, & Martell, 1995). Also, the differences in the drawings of male/female leaders' style are analogous to the findings from meta-analysis study of adult leaders. In these meta-analyses Eagly and her colleagues demonstrate that women leaders compared to men leaders are perceived as slightly more participative leaders (Eagly & Johnson, 1990) and are slightly more transformational than men leaders (Eagly, Johannesen-Schmidt, & van Engen, 2003). Among many characteristics of the transformational leaders is the attention and care for the development of the individual follower. It seems that adults and to some extent children believed that women leaders are more kind and inclusive.

Approximately half of the children drew the leader in a particular role or context such as military, teacher, parent, or sports leader. Though both boys and girls drew generic leaders, they did differ in the categories of leaders they chose to draw. Girls drew more authority figures such as religious leaders, teachers and parents, whereas boys drew more masculine roles such as sports and military. For example, in 1992, girls drew more Martin Luther King and boys drew more Michael Jordan.

We did find some cultural/ethnic differences among the White and African American children. This finding is in line with past research that children draw from their own cultural perspective. Therefore, in this case their ILT is culture specific (Alland, 1983; Deregowski, 1989; Wilson, 1985; Wilson & Wilson, 1977, 1984). White children more than African American children drew leaders who were of same color as themselves (self-ethnic). As about half of the African American children drew white leaders, the self-ethnic drawing was less common among them than among White children. We also found differences in the style of the leader based on its color. Black drawn leaders were less expressively (smile and violence) drawn than white ones. This could demonstrate cultural differences in children's ILT.

The developmental changes across the age groups and across the studies were not linear. From the studies on ILT of children, it can be observed that children even as young as kindergarten have an implicit idea of a leader. The characteristics of this ILT more often than not stay the same across grades. Certainly as children's general knowledge of the world increases so does their inclusion of more categories of leaders and more socially recognizable leaders. Unfortunately, with this increased knowledge comes an increased chance of drawing a more "stereotypic" and more "cynical" view of leaders, with less smiles and more violence.

In several cases we found the relationship between grade and ILT to be what may be called a "U" shaped or "J" (or inverted J) shaped changes across grades. These cases showed more similarity between kindergarten and oldest grades in contrast to either one compared to middle grades. Others studying various aspects of children's drawings have reported this phenomenon (Davis, 1991).

Methodology

One of the major conclusions from the review of these studies is the importance of a multi-method approach to the study of ILT in children. The inclusion of a verbal and non-verbal methodology allowed us to tap into larger expanse of children's thinking in general and their ILT in specific. If the interviews had probed for these details they would have been too intrusive to achieve genuine responses. It is also valuable to note that by going beyond portrait drawing of leaders to drawings of active leaders we have been able to get more contextual information.

Although the use of children's drawings has its own challenges and limitations, it is clear that inclusion of drawing methodology increases the amount and accuracy of information from children (Drucker et al., 1997; Gross & Hayne, 1999). In contrast to what some may believe, scholars have stated that interpretation of social meaning in children's drawing is not related to children's drawing ability (Cox & Key, 1993; Dennis, 1966;

Golomb, 1992; Krampen, 1991). Therefore, we suggest that when studying children's social concepts, we employ nonverbal measures in addition to verbal measure.

GENERAL CONCLUSION

The existing studies on children and ILT have shown that children as young as kindergarten have implicit leadership theory. We have made major progress in the last two decades towards understanding the origins of ILT. Certainly more complex analysis and cross-examination is warranted to understand the full story of this important schema in children—our work has just begun.

As gender and ethnic stereotypes seem to be prevalent in our society, change is vital in the interest of a future egalitarian society. The elimination of gender and ethnic stereotypes of people in positions of decision-making is critical. Education can be seen as a significant tool to bring about this change.

We found that girls and boys, Whites and Blacks seem to hold different role models of leaders. Therefore, in order to be effective in eliminating prejudice and stereotypes, the changes must emphasize equal representation of both genders and all ethnic categories in all societal roles. This further supports the existing efforts by employment regulation and campaigns in media and the film industry to enhance their inclusion of men and women of all ethnicities in all roles. Only then can we hope to see women and men of diverse backgrounds in roles such as president of a country, noble prizewinning scientists, and leaders of industry.

ACKNOWLEDGMENT

We would like to thank the following students for their assistance in data collection and coding Mary Dyer, Dan Dowhawer, Jeff Becker, Jennifer Runkle, Joseph Bast, Nancy Friedman, Heather Leffler, Adam Ackerman, Pamela Barnes, Karen Kozminski, Jessica Kitchner, Melinda Scheuer. We also would like to thank Gene McFadden for his contribution in the editing process.

APPENDIX

Definitions of Drawing characteristic variables and coding instructions are presented below. All these instructions required the drawing to be of a human figure and draw or describe the following information.

Variables	Descriptions	Inter-rater agreement study 1 (%)	Inter-rater agreement study 2 (%)
Human	Those drawings of leaders that represented figures that were nonhuman (i.e., animals, spaceships, etc.) were differentiated from those drawings of leaders that were human. Drawings of nonhuman leaders were not of interest to the researchers and coding of these drawings ceased at this variable.	92.21	100.00
One leader	This variable represents how many leaders the child indicated within the drawing: no leader (i.e., "there are no leaders in my drawing"), one leader (i.e., Martin Luther King, Jr.), or multiple leaders (i.e., "Both my parents are the leaders").	96.65	100.00
Gender	Items in the drawing considered analogous to predetermined male or female characteristics determined the leader's gender. Representation of figures as male consisted of leaders wearing pants, having short hair, and void of any characteristics typical of a female such as long eyelashes, skirts, and jewelry. Furthermore, if the child's sentences identified the leader as a male or female the leader was coded accordingly. This may include pronouns, labels such as "mother" or "father," and/or identifying the drawing as oneself.	100.00	93.00
Color	Six categories were utilized to determine the leader's color: (a) *not identifiable,* (b) *White/no color,* (c) *colored black/brown,* (d) *described Black,* (e) *colored black/brown and described Black,* and (f) *other colors* (i.e., purple, green, etc.). The leaders coded as *colored black/brown, described Black,* and *colored black/brown and described Black* were combined to formulate the Black leader's race category (for our study). Criteria to classify leaders within this category required that the child: colored the leader black or brown, described the leader as black, named a famous person such as Martin Luther King as the	94.42	100.00

Variables	Descriptions	Inter-rater agreement study 1 (%)	Inter-rater agreement study 2 (%)
	leader that is known to be black, or identified themselves as the leader and the teacher identified the child as black. Leaders coded as *White/no color* represent the White leader's race category.		
Leader smiling	Three categories reflected the smile of the leader: (a) *not identifiable*, (b) *lips not upward*, and (c) *lips upward*. If there was no identifiable mouth/lips drawn on the leader, *not identifiable* was selected. If there was an identifiable mouth/lips (i.e., straight line, circle) that did not have an elliptical shape, *lips not upward* was selected. If there was an identifiable mouth/ lips that had an elliptical shape (corners of mouth/lips turning upward), *lips upward* was selected.	91.09	75.00
Presence of violence	Four categories indicated whether or not the drawing was violent in nature: (a) *none*, (b) *verbal*, (c) *physical*, and (d) *both*. If there was no violence depicted within the drawing, *none* was selected. If there was verbal violence (i.e., words "I'm going to kill you," "die"), *verbal* was selected. If there was physical violence (i.e., figures fighting), *physical* was selected. If there was both verbal and physical violence present in the drawing, *both* was selected.	93.31	93.75
Follower presence	Three categories indicated whether or not there were followers: (a) *none*, (b) *implied*, and (c) *drawn*. If there were no followers drawn, *none* was selected. If there were followers drawn, *drawn* was selected. If the child indicated that there were followers in the drawing from their written remarks, yet there were no followers drawn, *implied* was selected	96.65	96.65
Follower gender	Coded the same as "leader's gender"	93.34	93.75
Comparative size	Three categories indicated the size of the drawn follower relative to the size of the drawn leader: (a) *larger*, (b) *equal*, and (c) *smaller*. If the follower was over $\frac{1}{2}$ inch longer larger than the leader, larger was selected. If the follower was equal in height to the leader, *equal* was selected. If the follower was over $\frac{1}{2}$ inch shorter than the leader, *smaller* was selected.	75.55	87.50

Variables	Descriptions	Inter-rater agreement study 1 (%)	Inter-rater agreement study 2 (%)
Leader categories	**Description for coders**	82.21	87.50
Military personnel	a soldier, a member of an army, policeman, fireman, wearing military/police/fireman fatigues		
Generic person	If the figure drawn failed to fall into any of the other categories.		
Child	a child ("this is a child"), as a sibling of the drawer, labeled as a "boy" or "girl" versus "man" or "woman."		
Self	If in the description it said: the leader is me, I am the leader, the leader is the one——, that's me, the leader is _____ (the child's name). Or, if the child pointed to him/herself as the leader in the drawing.		
Teacher	*drawn or described* as any of the following: a teacher, leading a class (classroom setting).		
Parent	*described* as any of the following: a parent, mother, father		
Entertainer/parade	*drawn or described* as any of the following (void of any specific mention of "famous" people): comedian, talk show host, singer, actor, clown, musician, etc. Also: a band, individuals marching with instruments (batons not considered an instrument), a parade		
Head of state	leader of a country/state		
Fantasy/story	a leader/prince/princess (of a fantasy world—"Princess of the Purple People Eaters"), member of an imaginary civilization (made up of a group of people), possessing non-human abilities (fly, beyond natural strength, etc.), "famous" fairy-tale image (Cinderella, Snow White, Superman, etc.), all comic characters, any character out of a story (i.e., Star Wars, Lord of the Rings, etc.)		
Religious	described as any of the following (void of any specific mention of "famous" people): preacher, leading a congregation (obvious church setting)		
Sports leader	leader of a sports team, team captain		
Famous people	with a name of a famous star and/or image with some identifying information (must be able to identify the name of the star) (i.e., Hilary Duff, Olsen twins, etc.); a name of a famous politician and/or image with some identifying information (must be able to identify the name of the politician); with a name of a sports star and/or image with some identifying information (jersey number) (void of the mention of Michael Jordan) (i.e., Tiger Woods, Joe Montana, Summer Sanders, etc.)		
Michael Jordan	Michael Jordan (or jersey number)		
Martin Luther King	with a name of a Martin Luther King, MLK, "I have a dream"		

REFERENCES

Alland, A. (1983). *Playing with form: Children draw in six cultures*. New York: Columbia University Press.

Andersson, S.B., (1995). Social scaling in children's family drawings: A comparative study in three cultures. *Child Study Journal, 25*(2), 97–121.

Arnheim, R. (1966). *Toward a psychology of art*. Berkeley: University of California Press.

Arnheim, R. (1974). *Art and visual thinking*. Berkely: University of California Press.

Ashmore, R.D., & Del Boca, F.K. (1979). Sex stereotypes and implicit personality theory: Towards a cognitive-social psychological conceptualization. *Sex Roles, 5*, 219–248.

Ayman, R. (1993). Leadership perception: The role of gender and culture. In M. M. Chemers & R. Ayman (Eds.), *Leadership theory and research: Perspectives and directions* (pp. 137–166). New York: Academic Press.

Ayman, R. (2000). Leadership. In E.F. Borgatta & R.J.V. Montgomery (Eds.), *Encyclopedia of sociology* (2nd ed., Vol. 3, pp. 1563–1575). New York: Macmillan Reference U.S.A.

Ayman, R.(2004). Situational and contingency approaches to leadership. In J. Antonakis, A.T. Cianciolo, & R.J. Sternberg (Eds.), *The nature of leadership* (pp. 148–170) Thousand Oaks, CA: Sage.

Ayman, R.(in press). Culture and leadership. In C. Spielberger (chief ed.), *Encyclopedia of applied psychology* (Vol. 2, pp. 507–519). San Diego, CA: Elsevier Ltd.

Ayman, R., & Chemers, M.M. (1983). The relationship of supervisory behavior ratings to work group effectiveness and subordinate satisfaction among Iranian managers. *Journal of Applied Psychology, 68*, 338–341.

Berry, J.W. (1997). An ecocultural approach to the study of cross-cultural industrial/organizational psychology. In P.C. Earley & M. Erez (Eds.), *New perspectives on international industrial/organizational psychology* (pp. 130–147). San Francisco: The New Lexington Press.

Bombi, A.S., & Pinto, G. (1994). Making a dyad: Cohesion and distancing in children's pictorial representation of friendship. *British Journal of Developmental Psychology, 12*, 563–575.

Brown, E.V. (1979). Sexual self-identification as reflected in children's drawings when asked to "draw-a-person." *Perceptual and Motor Skills, 49*, 35–38.

Burgoon, M., Dillard, J.P., & Doran, N.E. (1983). Friendly or unfriendly persuasion: The effects of violations of expectations by males and females. *Human Communications Research, 10*(2), 283–294.

Caldwell, O.W., & Wellman, B. (1926). Characteristics of school leaders. *Journal of Educational Research, 14*, 1–15.

Catalyst. (1998). *Advancing women in business—the Catalyst guide: Best practices from corporate leaders*. San Francisco: Jossey Bass.

Cox, M.K., & Key, C.H. (1993). Post hoc pair-wise comparisons for the chi-square, test of homogeneity of proportions. *Educational and Psychological Measurement, 53*, 951–962.

D'Amico, V. (1966). The child as painter. In E. Eisner & D. Ecker (Eds.), *Readings in art and education* (pp. 232–237). Waltham, MA: Blaisdell Publishing.

Daniels-Beirness, T. (1986). *Children's understanding of leadership: Conceptual differences with age.* Unpublished doctoral dissertation, University of Waterloo, Canada.

Dastmalchian, A., Javidan, M., & Alam, K. (2001). Effective leadership and culture in Iran: An empirical study. *Applied Psychology: An International Review, 50,* 532–558.

Den Hartog, D., House, R.J., Hanges, P.J., Ruis-Quintanilla, S.A, Dorfman, P.W., Abdulla, I.A., et al. (1999). Culture specific and cross-culturally generalizable implicit leadership theories: Are attributes of charismatic/ transactional leadership universally endorsed? *The Leadership Quarterly, 10,* 219–256.

Davis, J. (1991). *Artistry lost: U-shaped development in graphic symbolization.* Doctoral dissertation, Harvard Graduate School of Education.

Dennis, W. (1966). *Group values through children's drawings.* New York: Wiley.

Deregowski, J.B. (1989). Real space and represented space: Cross-cultural perspectives. *Behavioral and Brain Sciences, 12,* 51–119.

Dickson, J.M., Saylor, C.F., & Finch, A.J., Jr. (1990). Personality factors, family structure, and sex of drawn figure on the draw-a-person test. *Journal of Personality Assessment, 55,* 363–366.

Drucker, P.M., Greco-Vigorito, C., Moore-Russell, M., Avaltroni, J., & Ryna, E. (1997, April). *Drawing facilitates recall of traumatic past events in young children of substance abusers.* Paper presented at the Biennial Meeting of the Society for Research in Child Development, Washington, DC.

Durojaije, M.O.A. (1969). Patterns of friendship and leadership choices in a mixed junior school: A sociometric analysis. *British Journal of Educational Psychology, 39,* 88–89.

Eagly, A., & Carli, L.L. (2003). Female leadership advantage: An evaluation of evidence. *The Leadership Quarterly, 14,* 807–834.

Eagly, A., & Johnson, (1990). Gender and leadership style: A meta-analysis. *Psychological Bulletin, 108,* 233–256.

Eagly, A., Johannesen-Schmidt, M.C., & van Engen, M.L. (2003). Transformational, transactional, and laissez-faire leadership styles: A meta-analysis comparing men and women. *Psychological Bulletin, 129,* 569–591.

Eagly, A., & Karau, S. (2002). Role Congruity Theory of prejudice toward female leaders. *Psychological Review, 109,* 573–598.

Eagly, A., Karau, S., & Makhijani, M. (1995). Gender and the effectiveness of leaders: A meta-analysis. *Psychological Bulletin, 117,* 125–145.

Eden, D., & Leviatan, U. (1975). Implicit leadership theory as a determinant of the factor structure underlying supervisory behavior scales. *Journal of Applied Psychology, 60,* 736–741.

Eubanks, P. K. (1997). Art is a visual language. *Visual Arts Research, 23,* 31–35.

Fielding, K.S., & Hogg, M.A. (1997). Social identity, self-categorization, and leadership: A field study of small interactive groups. *Group Dynamics: Theory, Research, and Practice, 1,* 39–51.

Fischbein, R., & Lord, R.G. (2003). Implicit leadership Theory. In J. MacGregor Burns (Senior ed.). *Encyclopedia of leadership* (Vol. 2, pp.700–706). Thousand Oaks, CA: Sage.

Falchikov, N. (1990). Youthful ideas about old age: An analysis of children's drawings. *International Journal of Aging and Development, 31*(2), 79–99.

Fleming, E. G. (1935). A factor analysis of the personality of high school leaders. *Journal of Applied Psychology, 67*, 326–333.

Foti, R.J., Fraser, S.L., & Lord, R.G. (1982). Effect of leadership labels and prototypes on perceptions of political leaders. *Journal of Applied Psychology, 67*, 326–333.

Freeman, N. (1980). *Strategies of representation in young children*. London: Academic Press.

Gamradt, J., & Staples, C. (1994). My school and me: Children's drawings in postmodern educational research and evaluation. *Visual Arts Research, 20*, 36–49.

Gardner, H. (1973). *The arts and human development*. New York: John Wiley & Sons.

Gardner, H. (1979). Entering the world of the arts: The child as artist. *Journal of Communication, 29*(4).

Gardner, H. (1980). *Artful scribbles: The significance of children's drawings*. New York: Basic Books.

Gardner, H. (1982). *Art, mind, and brain*. New York: Basic Books.

Garrison. K. C. (1933). A study of some factors related to leadership in high school. *Peabody Journal of Education, 11*, 11–17.

Golomb, C. (1973). Children's representation of the human figure: The effects of models, media, and instruction. *Genetic Psychology Monographs, 87*, 197–251.

Golomb, C. (1974). *Young children's sculpture and drawing: A study in representational development*. Cambridge, MA: Harvard University Press.

Golomb, C. (1992). *The child's creation of a pictorial world: Studies in the psychology of art*. Berkely: University of California Press.

Goodman, N. (1968). *Languages of art*. Indianapolis, IN: Bobbs-Merrill.

Goodman, N. (1976). *Languages of art*. Indianapolis, IN: Hackett Publishing Co.

Goodman, N. (1978). *Ways of worldmaking*. Indianapolis, IN: Hackett Publishing Co.

Goodenough, F. L. (1926). *Measurement of intelligence by drawing*. New York: World Book Co.

Goodnow, J. (1977). *Children drawing*. Cambridge, MA: Harvard University Press.

Gowen, J.C. (1955). Relationship between leadership and personality measures. *Journal of Educational Research, 48*, 624–627.

Granick, S., & Smith, L. J. (1953). Sex sequence in the draw-a-person test and its relation to the MMPI masculinity-femininity scale. *Journal of Consulting Psychology, 17*, 71–73.

Gross, J., & Hayne, H.(1999). Drawing facilitates children's verbal reports after long delays. *Journal of Experimental Psychology: Applied, 5*(3), 265–283.

Hains, S.C., Hogg, M.A., & Duck, J.M. (1997). Self-categorization and leadership: Effects of group prototypicality and leader stereotypicality. *Personality and Social Psychology Bulletin, 23*, 1087–1100.

Hardy, R.C. (1972). A developmental study of relationships between birth order and leadership style for two distinctly different American groups. *Journal of Social Psychology, 87*, 147–148.

Hardy, R.C. (1976). A test of the poor leader-member relation cells of the contingency model on elementary school children. *Child Development, 46*, 958–964.

Hardy, R.C. (1977). Stability and consistency of factor structure of least preferred co-worker scale for different age groups. *Perceptual & Motor Skills, 4,* 139–146.

Hardy, R.C., Hunt, J., & Lehr, E. (1978). Relationship between birth order and leadership style for nursery school children. *Perceptual & Motor Skills, 46,* 184–186.

Hardy, R.C., Sack, S., & Harpine, F. (1973). An experimental test of the contingency model on small classroom groups. *Journal of Psychology: Interdisciplinary & Applied, 85,* 3–16.

Harrison, C.W., Rawls, J.R., & Rawls, D.J. (1971). Differences between leaders and non-leaders in six-to-eleven year old children. *Journal of Social Psychology, 84,* 269–272.

Hartman, S.J., & Harris, O.J. (1992). The role of parental influence in leadership. *Journal of Social Psychology, 132*(2), 153–167.

Heilman, M.E., Block, C.J., & Martell, R.F. (1995). Sex stereotypes: Do they influence perceptions of managers? *Journal of Social Behavior & Personality, 10,* 237–252.

Heilman, M.E. (2001). Description and prescription: how gender stereotype prevent women access up the organizational ladder. *Journal of Social Issues, 57,* 657–674.

Heinrich, P., & Triebel, J.K. (1972). Sex preferences in children's human figure drawings. *Journal of Personality Assessment, 36,* 263–267.

Hensel, N. (1983). Developing emergent leadership skills in elementary and junior high school students. *Roeper Review, 5*(4), 33–35.

Holmes, R.M. (1992). Children's artwork and nonverbal communication. *Child Study Journal, 27*(3), 157–165.

Holmes, R.M. (1995). *How young children perceive race.* Thousand Oaks, CA: Sage.

Karnes, F., Bean, S., & McGinnis, J.C. (1995). Perceptions of leadership held by young females. *Journal of Secondary Gifted Education, 6*(2),113–119.

Karnes, F., & Chauvin, J. (1985). The leadership skills. *G/C/T, 9*(3), 22–23.

Keller, T. (1999). Images of the familiar: Individual differences and implicit leadership theories. *The Leadership Quarterly, 10,* 589–607.

Klepsch, M., & Logle, L. (1982). *Children draw and tell.* New York: Brunner/Mazel.

Klonsky, B. (1983). The socialization and development of leadership ability. *Genetics Psychology Monographs, 108,* 97–135.

Koppitz, E. M. (1966) Emotional indicators on human figure drawings of shy and aggressive children. *Journal of Clinical Psychology, 22,* 466–469.

Krampen, M. (1991). *Children's drawings: Iconic coding of the environment.* New York: Plenum Press.

Larson, J.R., Jr. (1982). Cognitive mechanisms mediating the impact of implicit theories of leader behavior on leader behavior ratings. *Organizational Behavior and Human Decision Processes, 29,* 129–140.

Ling, W., Chia, R., & Fang, L. (2000). Chinese implicit leadership theory. *Journal of Social Psychology, 140,* 729–739.

Lord, R. G., Benining, J.F., Rush, M.C., & Thomas, J.C. (1978). The effect of performance cues and leader behavior on questionnaire ratings of leadership behavior. *Organizational Behavior and Human Performance, 21,* 27–39.

Lord, R.G., Brown, D.J., Harvey, J.L., & Hall, R.J. (2001). Contextual constraints on prototype generation and their multilevel consequences for leadership perception. *The Leadership Quarterly, 12,* 311–338.

Lord, R.G., Foti, R.J, & deVader, C.L. (1984). A test of leadership categorization theory: Internal stucture, information processing, and leadership perceptions. *Organizational behavior and Human Performance, 34,* 343–378.

Lord, R.G., deVader, D.L., & Alliger, G.M. (1986). A meta-analysis of the relation between personality traits and leadership perceptions: An application of Validity generalization procedures. *Journal of Applied Psychology, 71,* 402–401.

Lord, R.G., & Maher, K.J. (1991) *Leadership and information processing: Linking perceptions and performance.* Boston, MA: Unwin Hyman.

Matthews, A.M., Lord, R.G., & Walker, J.B. (1990). *The development of leadership perception in children.* Unpublished manuscript, University of Akron.

Meindl, J.R. (1998). The romance of leadership as a follower-centric theory: A social constructionist approach. In F.D. Dansereau & F.J. Yammarino (Eds), *Leadership: The multiple-level approach—Contemporary and alternatives* (pp. 285–298). Stamford, CT: JAI Press.

Meindl, J.R. (1990). On leadership: An alternative to the conventional wisdom. In L.L. Cummings & B.M. Staw (Eds.), *Research in organizational behavior* (Vol. 12, pp. 159–203). Greenwich, CT: JAI Press.

Mortensen, K.V. (1966). Formal aspects of children's drawings as a projective technique test method. *Nordisk Psykologi, 18,* 275–299.

Nutting, L.R. (1923). Some characteristics of leadership. *School and Society, 18,* 387–390.

Offermann, L.R., Kennedy, J.K., & Wirtz, P.W. (1994). Implicit leadership theories: Content, structure and generalizability. *The Leadership Quarterly, 5,* 43–58.

Pfeffer, K. (1985). Sex-identification and sex-typing in some Nigerian children's drawings. *Social Behavior and Personality, 13,* 69–72.

Phelan, H.M. (1964). The incidence and possible significance of the drawing of female figures by sixth-grade boys in response to the Draw-A-Person test. *Psychiatric Quarterly, 38,* 488–503.

Phillips, J.S., & Lord, R.G. (1982). Schematic information processing and perceptions of leadership in problem-solving groups. *Journal of Applied Psychology, 67,* 486–492.

Piaget, J., & Inhelder, B. (1956). *The child's concept of space.* London: Routledge and Kegan Paul.

Reynolds, F.J. (1944). Factors of leadership among seniors of Central High School, Tulsa, Oklahoma. *Journal of Educational Research, 37,* 356–361.

Richardson, W., & Feldhusen, J. (1986). *Leadership education: Developing skills for youth.* New York: Trillium Press.

Schein, V.E. (1973). The relationship between sex role stereotypes and requisite management characteristics. *Journal of Applied Psychology, 57,* 95–100.

Schein, V.E. (1975). The relationship between sex role stereotypes and requisite management characteristics among female college students. *Journal of Applied Psychology, 60,* 340–344.

Schein, V.E. (2001). A global look at psychological barriers to women's progress in management. *Journal of Social Issues, 57,* 675–688.

Schein, V.E., Mueller, R., & Jacobsen, C. (1989). The relationship between sex-role stereotypes and requisite management characteristics among college students. *Sex Roles, 20,* 103–110.

Schein, V., Mueller, R., Lituch, T., & Liu, J. (1996). Think manager—think male: A global phenomenon. *Journal of Organizational Behavior, 17,* 33–41.

Selman, R.L. (1979). *Assessing interpersonal understanding: An interview and scoring manual.* Cambridge, MA: Harvard-Judge Baker Social Reasoning Project.

Selman, R.L. (1980). *The growth of interpersonal understanding.* New York: Academic Press.

Selman, R.L., & Jaquette, D. (1978). *Stability and oscillation in interpersonal awareness: A clinical developmental approach.* In C. B. Kearsy (Ed.), Twenty-fifth Nebraska symposium on motivation (pp. 261–304). Lincoln, Nebraska: University of Nebraska Press.

Stray, H.F. (1934). Leadership traits of girls' camps. *Sociology and Social Research, 18,* 240–250. (Abstract obtained from *Psychological Abstract,* 1934, *8,* Abstract No. 3349).

Teglasi, H. (1980). Acceptance of the traditional female role and sex of the first person drawn on the draw-a-person test. *Perceptual and Motor Skills, 51,* 267–271.

Terrell, G., & Shreffler, J. (1958). A developmental study of leadership. *Journal of Educational Research, 52,* 69–72.

United Nations. (2000). *FWCW platform for action: Women in power and decision-making.* Retrieved October 30, 2000, from http://www.un.org/womenwatch/daw/beijing/platform/decision.htm

Wegner, D.M., & Vallacher, R.R. (1977). *Implicit psychology.* New York: Oxford University Press.

Wetzel, W.A. (1932). Characteristics of pupil leaders. *School Review, 40,* 532–534.

Whorton, J.E., & Karnes, F. (1992). Comparison of parents' leadership styles: Perceptions of parents and student leaders. *Perceptual and Motor Skills, 74,* 1227–1230.

Wilson, B. (1985). The artistic Tower of Babel: Inextricable links between culture and graphic development. *Visual Arts Research, 11,* 90–104.

Wilson, B., & Wilson, M. (1977). An iconoclastic view of the imagery sources of young people. *Art Education, 30,* 5–11.

Wilson, B., & Wilson, M. (1984). Children's drawings in Egypt: Cultural style acquisition as graphic development. *Visual Arts Research, 10,* 13–26.

Woehr, D.J., & Huffcutt, A.I. (1994). Rater training for performance appraisal: A quantitative review. *Journal of Organizational and Occupational Psychology, 67,* 189–205.

Yamaguchi, R. (2001). Children's learning groups: A study of emergent leadership, dominance, and group effectiveness. *Small Group Research, 32,* 671–697.

PART IV

**BROADENING UP OUR VIEWS
ON IMPLICIT LEADERSHIP THEORIES:
IMPLICIT FOLLOWERSHIP THEORIES
AND IMPLICIT ORGANIZATIONAL THEORIES**

CHAPTER 10

LEADERSHIP AND NEED FOR LEADERSHIP

Testing an Implicit Followership Theory

Reinout E. de Vries and Jean-Louis van Gelder

ABSTRACT

In this chapter, we describe and test an implicit followership theory. In contrast with the implicit leadership theory, which is guided by leader-centered or outcome-centered considerations, the implicit followership theory relies on a follower-centered approach and focuses on the causes and effects of subordinates' need for leadership. Two scenario studies are presented to test the theory. The first scenario study shows that observed need for leadership has a strong influence on leadership ratings. The second scenario study shows that, in turn, perceived charismatic leadership has strong effects on observers' perceptions of subordinates' need for leadership. Together, the studies suggest that need for leadership plays an important role in the reciprocal relation between perceptions of followership and leadership. In the discussion, we argue that need for leadership may also play an important role in social contagion processes.

Implicit Leadership Theories: Essays and Explorations, pages 277–303
Copyright © 2005 by Information Age Publishing

INTRODUCTION

What makes a leader a leader? All along, the answer may have been looked at in the wrong quarter. In the end, leaders do not determine the outcomes of a group or organization, but the people that do the actual work. Subordinates or followers of a leader allow the influence process to take place and allow their behaviors to be changed. Additionally, subordinates determine whether the supervisor is called a "real" leader. Basically, of course, it takes two to tango, but probably for too long leadership scholars have neglected the subordinate side of the equation. Recently, a number of articles have appeared to right this "wrong" by putting the subordinate squarely in the center of our attention (Hollander & Offermann, 1990; Meindl, 1995). These follower-centered theories of leadership posit that instead of focusing on the characteristics of the leaders, scholars should focus on the characteristics of subordinates that may or may not determine leadership attributions. One of these follower-centered theories is the need for leadership theory. This theory argues that "need for leadership" is a central variable that may enable both leadership attributions and leadership effectiveness (De Vries, 2000; De Vries, Roe, & Taillieu, 2002). In this chapter we will argue that apart from an implicit theory about the relationship between performance and leadership, people also have an implicit theory about the relationship between subordinates' needs and leadership itself. We will present two studies that offer preliminary support for what we will call an "implicit followership theory." In the discussion, we take an additional step and propose that performance criteria, together with need for leadership and social identity may facilitate the social contagion of leadership perceptions. First, however, we will take a look what attribution theories have offered us so far and why it makes sense to include need for leadership as an additional variable in attribution theories.

ATTRIBUTION OF LEADERSHIP

In 1953, Carter argued that leadership consists of behaviors that experts define as leadership behaviors. This hasn't prevented scholars from trying to conceptualize and operationalize the construct. However, the lack of agreement between scholars in the leadership field on how to conceptualize leadership may well be staggering to outsiders. There are probably more scales by different authors to measure leadership and less agreement about how to measure the construct than in any other area of social science. It is no wonder that leadership scholars have had such a problem in defining what exactly leadership is, since there may be no really fixed behaviors associated with leadership.

Perception theorists have taken issue with the lack of consensus in the leadership field by taking an entirely different approach. One of the main tenets of leadership perception theories is the argument that leadership may be more in the eye of the beholder than being really "out there." An extreme perception theorist rejects the notion that there are fixed leadership behaviors and embraces a social constructionist approach. Lord and Maher (1993), for instance, define leadership as "the process of being perceived by others as a leader" (p. 11), which leaves room for anybody to label any other person a leader or not, and to label any behaviors as leadership behaviors or not. Most perception theorists, including Lord and Maher (1993), recognize that some behaviors, such as "dedicated," "goal-oriented," "decisive," and "intelligent," are more prototypical or leader-like, leading observers to categorize a person who is perceived to exhibit these behaviors as a leader. The word "social" in "social constructionism" implies that these prototypes are shared among people within one culture and even among cultures. As Den Hartog et al.'s (1999) research shows, there are indeed several leadership attributes, such as "trustworthy," "dynamic," and "decisive," that are endorsed by people around the globe, although there are a number of attributes for which there is no universal endorsement, such as "subdued," "intragroup conflict avoider," and "sensitive."

Whether people agree about the labels that are associated with leadership is something else than whether people agree about a person having leadership characteristics or not. People may watch the same person and perceive either the proverbial full or empty glass when assessing leadership, noticing for instance either the rhetorical qualities associated with the presence of leadership qualities or the lack of sincerity associated with a lack of leadership qualities. According to Lord and Maher (1993), leadership perceptions are based on two types of processes that are used to select and interpret social information: recognition-based processes and inferential processes. Recognition-based processes are grounded in automatic categorization processes, while inferential processes are grounded in controlled attribution processes. In recognition-based processes of leadership, social impressions are compared with pre-existing categories and prototypes that are part of a person's implicit leadership theory (Offermann, Kennedy, & Wirtz, 1994). Through categorization, observed persons are assigned positional leadership labels such as "president," "chairman," "head of school," or behavioral labels that are associated with leadership actions, such as the above-mentioned adjectives "dynamic" and "decisive." Behavioral labels, such as "dynamic," that are strongly associated with leadership are also called prototypical of leadership. Prototypical information with respect to leadership is processed much faster than non-prototypical information (Lord, Foti, & De Vader, 1984). The stronger a person is matched in one's memory with some prototypical leadership labels, the more likely that person is to be perceived as a leader or having leader-like attributes. Additionally, if a person is assigned a positional leadership label, that person is also more likely to be rated using behavioral leadership labels, even when almost no other information is present (Eden & Leviatan, 1975; Rush, Thomas, & Lord, 1977).

In inferential processes of leadership, outcomes and circumstances associated with a group or organization and the presence of positional and/or behavioral leadership labels are ascertained at the same time (Meindl, 1990; Meindl, Ehrlich, & Dukerich, 1985; Mitchell, Larson, & Green, 1977; Pavitt & Sackaroff, 1990; Phillips & Lord, 1981; Shamir, 1992). Research shows that there is a straightforward and reciprocal relation between the perception of success and the presence of behavioral leadership labels. On the one hand, the presence of prototypical behavioral leadership labels can lead to an enhancement of performance perceptions (Lord et al., 1984). On the other hand, positive performance cues can cause a stronger prototypical behavioral leadership labeling process to take place (Phillips & Lord, 1982; Puffer, 1990; Rush et al., 1977). Meindl and colleagues (Meindl, 1990; Meindl et al., 1985) show that the perceived success of a person in a leadership position depends on the extremity of the perceived outcomes. Both highly positive and highly negative outcomes are more likely to be attributed to a person in a leadership position. Intermediate— neither positive nor negative—outcomes are more likely to be attributed to environmental circumstances. Consequently, with negative outcomes, a schism may evolve between the position of the leader (or, positional leadership perceptions) and behavioral leadership perceptions. If this schism is too broad, for instance when a person is in a leadership position but is labeled as adynamic and untrustworthy, that person is more likely to be either forced to resign from the position, to resign him/herself, or to be considered a "lame duck."

External success factors such as positive or negative performance outcomes are of course but one of many possible situational cues that may impact leadership perceptions and perceptions of leadership success. However, surprisingly, not much research has devoted itself to the exploration of other situational characteristics (Pillai & Meindl, 1998). The main characteristics that may impact leadership perceptions are the characteristics of the subordinates themselves and their position vis-à-vis the leader (Hollander & Offermann, 1990; Meindl, 1995). Puffer (1990) for instance found that people in a management position were more likely to make charismatic attributions than people in non-management positions. In an experimental study, Phillips and Lord (1981) found that perceptions of the ability and motivation of employees, together with performance cues, significantly influenced leadership perceptions. When ability and motivation were low, observers were much more likely to judge the leader to be an important determinant of a group's performance than when ability and motivation were high. Thus, the evidence so far indicates that subordinate characteristics may play an important role in leadership attributions.

NEED FOR LEADERSHIP

One of the most important subordinate characteristics that affect leadership attributions may be subordinates' need for leadership. Need for leadership is the extent to which an employee wishes the leader to facilitate the paths toward individual, group, and/or organizational goals (De Vries et al., 2002). De Vries et al. (2002) argue that need for leadership is a social-contextual need, which is triggered by contextual cues and expressed in social settings. The context determines whether a person would like guidance and supervision to fulfil his or her needs, since some situations contain elements that a person finds harder to cope with or feels more insecure about. The amount of expertise a person has relative to the situation, for instance, depends on the context. Relative to a younger and less experienced person, somebody may have a weak need for leadership in a situation that is relatively simple and familiar to him/her. However, relative to an older and more experienced person, in a relatively unfamiliar and complex situation, a person may find him or herself to be highly dependent on a leader. For employees, job-related expertise may thus be one of the most important predictors of need for leadership.

According to De Vries et al. (2002), need for leadership is a "catchall" variable, which combines the effects of a great number of contextual and personal characteristics. In a review of findings, De Vries et al. (2004) showed that the most important personality and background predictors are a subordinate's emotional stability, his/her age, and education. Subordinates who scored higher on emotionality (as opposed to emotional stability), who were younger, and who had a higher education, were found to have a stronger need for leadership than subordinates who were less emotional, older, and who had received a lower level of education.

Apart from these, De Vries et al. (2004) looked at the relation of need for leadership with the substitutes for leadership (Kerr & Jermier, 1978), since these were theorized to make the effects of leadership unnecessary or impossible (Howell, Dorfman, & Kerr, 1986). The substitutes come in three categories: (1) individual characteristics, such as ability/experience, professional orientation, need for independence, and indifference toward organizational rewards; (2) task characteristics, such as unambiguous tasks, task-feedback, and intrinsically satisfying tasks; and (3) organizational characteristics, such as organizational formalization, organizational inflexibility, staff support, workgroup cohesiveness, leaders lack of control of

rewards, and leaders spatial distance. Howell et al. (1990) argued that organizations can overcome ineffective leadership by replacing the ineffective
leaders by effective substitutes for leadership. Consequently, substitutes
should reduce the need for leadership of subordinates by improving the
context in which they function or by changing—through training—the
skills and attitudes of subordinates themselves.

Surprising enough, the substitutes were only weakly related to need for
leadership (De Vries et al., 2004). The strongest relation was between
employees' expertise and need for leadership, with—as expected—expert
subordinates having a weaker need for leadership than subordinates with
less expertise, followed by a negative relation between need for independence and need for leadership. However, the total explained variance of
the substitutes for leadership was only 9% and two of them, professional
orientation and staff support, were positively instead of negatively related
to need for leadership. Further lack of support for the substitutes is provided by tests of the moderator hypotheses inherent in the substitutes for
leadership theory (De Vries, 1997; Howell et al., 1986; Podsakoff, MacKenzie, Ahearna, & Bommer, 1995). Podsakoff and colleagues (Podsakoff,
MacKenzie, & Fetter, 1993; Podsakoff, Niehoff, MacKenzie, & Williams,
1993) show that, contrary to expectations, the substitutes do not substitute
leadership much more than chance would predict. Consequently, apart
from expertise and need for independence, the substitutes do not seem to
have a major impact on subordinates' need for leadership.

Although at first glance, these results seem to invalidate the social-contextual definition of need for leadership, according to De Vries et al.
(2004), some of the assumptions underlying the substitutes for leadership
may be incorrect. Basically, to act as a substitute, the functions of leadership and the substitute should be similar enough to be able to replace each
other. Although a leader himself/herself is easy to replace, some of the
functions or roles of leaders are extremely difficult to replace, because
these functions or roles are by themselves labeled as *leadership* functions or
roles. Even without a formal leader, the person who fulfils coordinating,
networking, social-emotional, and inspirational functions may sooner or
later be labeled as an (albeit) informal leader. However, in a situation
where no fixed leader is present, this labeling process is bound to be less
pronounced, weakening also subordinates' reliance on and need for supervision. Indeed, De Vries (1997) found that in the absence of a leader, need
for leadership was considerably lower than in the presence of a leader,
even when corrected for unit size. Thus, the presence of hierarchical labels
and positions may act as a prerequisite for leadership needs to develop.
According to Vanderslice (1988), such leadership labels may actually be
counteractive to organizational effectiveness, since power-differentiating
labels (such as supervisor and subordinate) may decrease the self-concept

of subordinates (while increasing those of the supervisors), may decrease subordinates' responsibility for the task, and may lead to acts of resistance toward authority. Most likely, however, the presence of leadership labels acts in tandem with the presence of leadership roles or functions. Leadership labels without corresponding roles and functions will probably lead to resistance, notably when the leadership labels are felt to be undeserved. But if roles and functions are specialized, and some of these roles are more central to the group than others, leadership labels may lead to exaggeration and over-generalization of the impact of these roles, resulting in an increase in subordinates' felt need for leadership.

An example of such a functional specialization in which needs develop and are expressed in similar ways as need for leadership is the family situation. As the social-contextual specification of need for leadership implies, need for leadership can only be expressed in social situations, in which a target is available to facilitate need fulfilment. The earliest situation in which such a need expression occurs is the parent-child interaction. Parental figures evoke dependency or, one could say, a need for leadership, by fulfilling a child's basic needs, such as the need for food and safety, by offering rewards for desired and appropriate behaviors, by exposing them to and protecting them from new stimuli, and by increasing the child's competence through role modeling and provision of feedback. In turn, a child expresses his or her need for leadership by asking for food (e.g., crying), safety (e.g., clinging behavior), rewards (e.g., nagging), by taking the parents by the hand to explore something, by asking questions, and by showing frustration when not being able to perform a task.

These parental functions and children's responses are in many ways similar to the functions leaders fulfil toward their subordinates and the way subordinates react to these functions. In fact, Popper and Mayseless (2003) argue that there is a strong correspondence between parenthood and leadership. Just like parents, leaders may give individual attention, show trust, set challenging goals, and provide opportunities for new experiences. Just like children, subordinates may ask for attention, guidance, and inspiration and may react to the leader's behaviors by feeling more (or less) secure, by increased autonomy, self-efficacy, and self-esteem, and by displaying "appropriate" behaviors.

More important, the parent may function as a template to which future leadership figures are compared. Implicit theories of leadership may thus be very much based on the role models that parents provide (Keller, 1999) and these may in turn affect the attachment styles of both leaders (Popper, Mayseless, & Castelnovo, 2000) and subordinates (Keller, 2003) and the satisfaction of both leaders and subordinate in their dyadic relationships (Keller, 2003). For instance, in the Netherlands, former Prime Minister Wim Kok was very much regarded as a father figure and (maybe consequently) seen as a very well liked charismatic and supportive leader. The parental leadership template may provoke specific attributions of leadership, in which attributions are based on a person's earlier experiences with parental figures. Based on these earlier experiences, expectations may form with respect to the dyadic interactions between leaders and subordinates and what types of interactions are satisfactory or adequate or not. Leaders' styles may thus become intrinsically linked to subordinates' needs and responses in leadership scripts and prototypes (Lord & Maher, 1993). For instance, a script based on "adequate" parent–child interaction may contain supportive acts, such as: child gets hurt—child starts crying—parent talks soothingly to child—child stops crying. In a similar way, the expectations of subordinates with respect to supportive leader behaviors could be part of a following script: subordinate has problems at home—subordinate talks to leader about it—leader listens supportively and suggests subordinate take time out to sort things out—subordinate is relieved and motivated to sort things out. To provide another example, a script for external relations could be as follows: work by subordinate is not processed by member of other department—subordinate asks department head to help him out—head of department talks to a member of other department—subordinate's work is quickly processed. As may be evident, an innumerate number of scripts can be thought of that represent adequate and inadequate leader–member exchanges. Most of these scripts probably involve some appeal to the needs, wishes, goals, values, or expectations of subordinates. Or, if we consider distant leaders, these scripts involve a leader's appeal to the needs, wishes, goals, values, or expectations of whole groups or nations.

What do subordinates need from a leader and what kinds of needs are expressed? De Vries (De Vries, 1997; De Vries et al., 2004) makes a distinction between 17 subordinate needs that are based on leadership functions, roles, and behaviors distinguished by Yukl (1994), Quinn (1988), and Luthans and Lockwood (1984). These 17 leadership needs, that all have bearings on close (instead of distant) leader–subordinate dyads, are the following: need for a leader who sets goals, who decides what work should be done, who transfers knowledge, who motivates, who coordinates, plans and organizes work, who maintains external contacts, who provides information, who gears all activities of the team for one another, who creates a good team spirit, who provides support, who arranges things with upper management, who handles conflicts, who gives work-related feedback, who corrects mistakes, who helps solve problems, who recognizes and rewards contributions, and who inspires. Of these leadership functions, the most needed by subordinates appear to be the ones related to upward influence and provision of information; the least needed are the ones relating to the coordinating and decision making functions (De Vries et al., 2004). This may be the case because an individual subordinate has more to gain from a leader who can help him/her individually through linking pin functions or through the provision of important information than she or he has to gain from a leader who mainly helps the group through coordination and (group) decision-making.

Underlying these different functions are a general need for leadership. The strongest correlates of this need for leadership are the perceived leadership characteristics themselves, with need for leadership positively related to leader's expertise, charismatic leadership, human-oriented leadership, and task-oriented leadership (De Vries, 1997; De Vries et al., 1999, 2002; De Vries, et al., 2004). In experimental research, need for leadership was found to predict leadership ratings, with higher prototypical leadership ratings given to a leader who had subordinates with a strong need for leadership than to a leader who had subordinates with a weak need for leadership (De Vries, 2000). Thus, it appears that need for leadership may influence leadership perceptions. Vice versa, it may also be the case that prototypical leadership behaviors influence need for leadership. Consequently, as with an implicit theory about the relationship between success and leadership prototypicality, there may very well be an implicit theory about the relationship between subordinate characteristics, such as need for leadership, and leadership prototypicality.

AN IMPLICIT FOLLOWERSHIP THEORY

At the basis of the implicit followership theory are the expectations concerning the exchanges that take place between a subordinate and a leader. The implicit followership theory model is exhibited in Figure 10.1 and involves three different stems that combine to form perceptions of success, leadership, and followership. In the model, (prototypical) leadership perceptions are determined by: (a) the perception of the situation and the implicit theory about positive outcomes (i.e., success), and (b) the perception of the behavior of a focal group member and the implicit theory about what constitutes leader behaviors and what doesn't. For example, in sports, perceptions of leadership can result from watching a sports team win a game and seeing a person (labeled: coach) talking to players on the side.

The implicit leader theory determines which person is viewed as a leader in the group. A person can exhibit a great number of behaviors, but some of these, such as dynamic behavior, are regarded as more leader-like than others. Additionally, the implicit leadership theory may also contain a link between the behavioral and positional attributes of a person. These positional attributes do not necessarily have to refer to a formal leader role with the accompanying label, but may also refer to more informal leadership

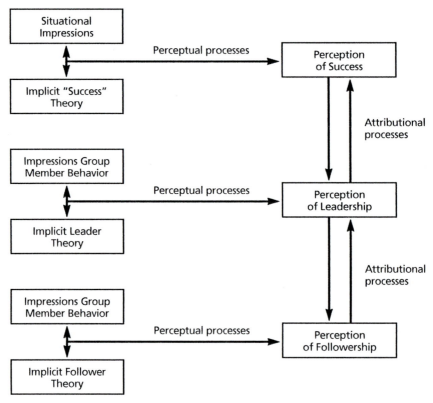

Figure 10.1.   The Implicit Followership Theory.

roles. Thus, behavior that is prototypical for a leader may lead to perceptions of leadership roles and, vice versa, leadership roles may lead to perceptions of leadership behaviors.

The implicit "success" theory determines what situational stimuli are perceived as successful outcomes (e.g., a winning score) and which factors are likely to cause these successful outcomes. As is argued in the romance of leadership theory (Meindl, 1990, 1995; Meindl & Ehrlich, 1987; Meindl et al., 1985), simplification is one of the main mechanisms to deal with the complexity of the world around us. A leader serves as a focal attribute in the perceptual field and is thus more likely to serve as an attributional anchor. Especially in the case of clear or overwhelming success or failure and a highly visible focal person, attribution to a person's leadership qualities is more likely to take place than in the case of mediocre performance and no visible person (Meindl, 1990).

Perceptions of followership are determined by perceptions of group member behaviors in combination with an implicit follower theory. Behaviors such as "being silent," "asking questions," "showing rapt attention," "making a suggestion," or "showing deference" may be associated more with a followership than with a leadership role. The implicit follower theory thus contains the link between behavioral and positional attributes of followers or subordinates in a similar way but opposite to those of the implicit leader theory. Together, these perceptions determine whether observers and group members alike perceive the group members or themselves to be categorized as followers or not.

In the model a reciprocal relation between perception of leadership and perception of followership is drawn, signifying that these perceptions may strengthen the categorization and attribution of leadership and followership qualities. Perceptions of followership imply stronger perceptions that the subordinates need their leader. These needs and displays of need for leadership, in turn, imply that somebody is present to fulfil them. Thus, the implicit followership theory assumes that need for leadership only exists in a situation in which a strong leader is present or is wanted to be present to fulfil these needs.

If the previous are true, not only followers themselves, but also observers will be more likely to perceive need for leadership in the face of a strong leader and perceive strong leadership when faced with subordinates' high need for leadership. Thus, not only own need for leadership, but also observed need for leadership may lead to more prototypical perceptions of leadership. In turn, when a leader is perceived to have strong prototypical leadership qualities, not only subordinates themselves but also observers may infer that the subordinates have a strong need for leadership. In the following section, these two assumptions (i.e., the effects of observed need for leadership on perceptions of leadership and the effects of observed leadership on perceptions of need for leadership) will be tested in two separate scenario studies.

STUDY 1

In study 1, we examined the effects of observed need for leadership and performance on leadership perceptions. This study can be considered a replica and extension of an earlier study into the effects of perceived need for leadership on leadership perceptions (De Vries, 2000), but in contrast to that study, in which prototypical leadership adjectives were used (Lord & Maher, 1993), in this study we used existing leadership scales as dependent variables. Furthermore, we tested the effects of need for leadership and performance information on leadership perceptions using a different scenario. Thus, in terms of Figure 10.1, this study investigates the two arrows from respectively followership and "success" perceptions to leadership perceptions. We expected that both observed need for leadership and observed performance will have positive main effects on perceived charismatic, expert, human-oriented, and task-oriented leadership.

Method Study 1

Sample and Procedure

The sample consisted of 113 students, 48 men (42.5%) and 65 women (57.5%), with an average age of 22.6 years (sd = 4.8). The students were asked to participate in the study for credit points. Students who participated entered a room in which they were presented with one of four randomly distributed written vignettes about a banking company with a fictitious team leader and his subordinates. An approximately equal number of subjects (between 27 and 30) participated in each of the four conditions. The respondents were asked to form a mental image of the leader and his subordinates. After carefully reading, the vignette was removed and a questionnaire on leadership was presented followed by a number of background variables and manipulation check items. After filling out the questionnaire, the respondents were thanked and debriefed.

Variables

The one-page vignette described a Bank and one of its teams. Apart from the manipulation, the text of the vignette was identical for all respondents. The manipulation in the vignette consisted of a number of sentences on the subordinates of a "Young Capital Team" led by Willem Verburg and their performance in a 2 (strong versus weak need for leadership) by 2 (high versus low performance) design. Strong need for leadership was manipulated using the following sentence: "It appeared that the subordinates had a strong need for Verburg's leadership," while weak need for leadership was manipulated with: "It appeared that the subordinates hardly had any need for Verburg's leadership." High performance was manipulated using the following sentence: "Compared to other teams, the Young Capital Team contributed very much to the success of the bank and were very effective in executing and winding up assignments." Low performance was manipulated in the following way: "Compared to other teams, the Young Capital Team contributed little to the success of the bank and were not very effective in executing and winding up assignments."

The following dependent variables were measured: charismatic leadership, human-oriented leadership, task-oriented leadership, and leader's expertise. The scale measuring charismatic leadership is derived from the Multifactor Leadership Questionnaire (MLQ: Bass, 1985; Den Hartog, Van Muijen, & Koopman, 1997) and consists of 10 inspirational leadership items. This scale has been proven to be very reliable (De Vries, 1997), with Cronbach alpha's exceeding .90. In this study, the Cronbach alpha of the charismatic leadership scale is .95. The human- and task-oriented leadership scales are derived from the Supervisor Behavior Description Questionnaire (Fleishman, 1953; Syroit, 1979). Cronbach alpha's for these scales have been reported to be greater than .90 for human-oriented leadership and greater than .70 for task-oriented leadership (De Vries, 1997). In this study the reliabilities are .90 for the 13-items human-oriented leadership scale and .88 for the 10-items task-oriented leadership scale. The scale measuring leader's expertise is an extended Dutch version of the scale by Podsakoff, Todor, and Schuler (1983; De Vries, 1997). In the original version it had 3 items; in the Dutch version 2 items were added. In earlier studies this 5-items version had a reliability of .87 (De Vries, 1997). In this study, the reliability of leader's expertise is .90.

Manipulation Checks

At the end of the questionnaire, six items were added to check whether the manipulations were effective. The need for leadership manipulation check consisted of three items, such as "The team has a strong need for Verburg's leadership," with a Cronbach alpha of .91. The performance manipulation check also consisted of three items, such as "The team contributes to the success of the bank," with a Cronbach alpha of .93. The effect of the manipulation on the manipulation check scales was checked using a MANOVA. Both of the manipulations were highly effective. The need for leadership manipulation had a highly significant effect on the need for leadership manipulation check ($F(1, 109) = 374.26$, $p < .001$) with the following means and standard deviations for need for leadership on respectively the weak need for leadership manipulation ($m_{weak} = 2.00$, sd = 1.02) and the strong need for leadership manipulation ($m_{strong} = 4.65$, sd = 0.43). The performance manipulation had a similar strong effect on the performance manipulation check, $F(1, 109) = 364.70$, $p < .001$, with the following means and standard deviations for performance on respectively the low performance manipulation ($m_{low} = 1.72$, sd = 0.86) and the high performance manipulation ($m_{high} = 4.48$, sd = 0.65). Although the need for leadership manipulation did not have an effect on the performance manipulation check ($F(1,109) = 1.93$, $p = .167$), the performance manipulation did have an effect on the need for leadership manipulation check ($F(1,109) = 10.72$, $p = .001$; $m_{low} = 3.53$ (sd = 1.43) and $m_{high} = 3.09$ (sd = 1.65)). Additionally, although the interaction of the two manipulations was not significant with the performance manipulation check as dependent variable ($F(1,109) = 0.63$, $p = .431$), there was a significant interaction effect on the need for leadership manipulation check ($F(1,109) = 8.54$, $p = .004$), with notably lower need for leadership in the weak need for leadership—high performance condition. All in all, the manipulations appear to be successful, although in interpreting the results, one should bear in mind that, apparently, ideas about a team's need for leadership are accentuated by ideas about the team's performance.

Results Study 1

Similar analyses as above were used to inspect the effects of the manipulations on perceived leadership. The MANOVA's were followed by Univariate ANOVA's and Scheffé's post-hoc test in order to interpret the findings. The findings, which are shown in Table 10.1 and Figure 10.2, indicate a strong effect of both the need for leadership and the performance manipulation on leadership perceptions. The MANOVA's indicate that need for leadership has an especially strong effect on perceptions of charismatic leadership perceptions ($F(1, 109) = 255.89$, $p < .001$, $\eta = .70$) and perceptions of the leader's expertise ($F(1, 109) = 189.67$, $p < .001$, $\eta = .64$). The effects of performance on charismatic leadership perceptions ($F(1, 109) = 6.65$, $p = .011$, $\eta = .06$) and perceptions of leader's expertise ($F(1, 109) = 4.07$, $p = .046$, $\eta = .04$), although just significant, are relatively meager. Actually, according to Scheffé's post-hoc test, within the same need for leadership condition, the differences between the high and low performance conditions are not significant (see Table 10.1). Additionally, a test of the difference in the effects of need for leadership and performance on perceived charismatic leadership and leader's expertise using Fisher's r-to-z transformations of the partial eta's (_) shows that the effect of need for leadership is significantly stronger than the effect of performance ($F = 8.52$, $p < .01$) for the difference in effects on charismatic leadership and $F = 7.49$, $p < .01$ for the difference in effects on leader's expertise. The results clearly show that, in this study, observed need for leadership has a stronger effect on leadership perceptions than observed performance has.

Both need for leadership and performance have significant effects on human- and task-oriented leadership. The following effects are observed: there is a significant effect of need for leadership on perceived human-oriented leadership ($F(1, 109) = 27.32$, $p < .001$, $\eta = .20$) and on perceived task-oriented leadership ($F(1, 109) = 19.21$, $p < .001$, $\eta = .15$), and there is a significant effect of performance on perceived human-oriented leadership ($F(1, 109) = 12.63$, $p = .001$, $\eta = .10$) and task-oriented leadership ($F(1, 109) = 21.14$, $p < .001$, $\eta = .16$). In contrast with perceived charismatic leadership and leader's expertise, need for leadership does not appear to have a significant stronger effect than performance on perceived human-oriented and task-oriented leadership. Additionally, Table 10.1 shows that

Table 10.1.   The Effects of Need for Leadership and Performance on Leadership Perceptions (N = 113)

		Weak Need for Leadership		Strong Need for Leadership	
		Low Performance	High Performance	Low Performance	High Performance
Charismatic Leadership	Mean	1.99[a]	2.23[a]	3.73[b]	4.08[b]
	Sd	0.66	0.69	0.56	0.45
Human-oriented Leadership	Mean	2.61[a]	2.89[a,b]	3.06[b]	3.53[c]
	Sd	0.52	0.55	0.58	0.57
Task-oriented Leadership	Mean	2.41[a]	2.85[a]	2.82[a]	3.57[b]
	Sd	0.81	0.51	0.84	0.46
Leader's Expertise	Mean	2.11[a]	2.20[a]	3.62[b]	4.01[b]
	Sd	0.65	0.55	0.74	0.59

Note: Means in the same row that do not share the same subscript are significantly different at $p < .05$.

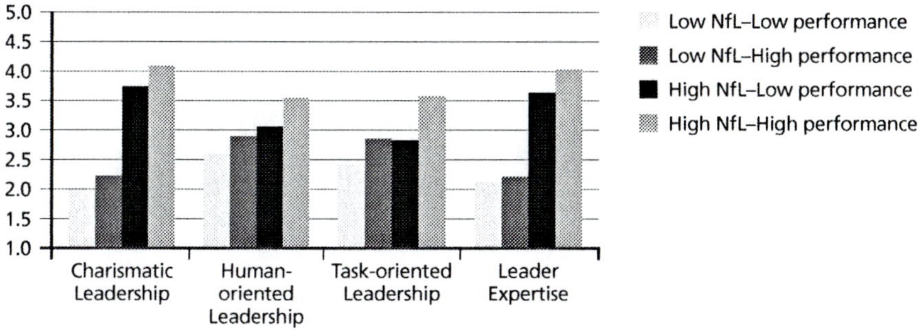

Figure 10.2.   The effects of need for leadership and performance on leadership perceptions.

especially the strong need for leadership—high performance condition obtains high leadership ratings.

Conclusion Study 1

This first study shows that people have a strong implicit followership theory, which links impressions about subordinates to prototypical leadership assessments. Especially observed need for leadership is shown to have a powerful effect on leadership perceptions. These effects are most pronounced on charismatic leadership and ratings of the leader's expertise, which can be considered most prototypical aspects of leadership. Thus, not only does the study confirm both attributional processes in Figure 10.1, but it also shows that the effects of need for leadership are stronger than those of performance for these two variables. Consequently, information on subordinates is an important determinant of whether people view "high-quality leadership" or not, and this information may be more important than situational cues related to success or performance.

STUDY 2

In study 2, we examined the effects of observed leadership and subordinates' expertise on perceived need for leadership. This study is almost a mirror study of study 1 and complements it by exploring the reciprocal relationship between leadership and need for leadership perceptions (see Figure 10.1). Apart from the effect of leadership on need for leadership, we investigated subordinates' expertise as a predictor of need for leadership to see which of the two, proximal subordinate characteristics or more distal leadership characteristics, have the strongest effect on perceived need for leadership. In terms of Figure 10.1, in this study the arrow from leadership perceptions to followership perceptions and the lowermost arrow from the interaction between impressions of group member expertise and implicit follower theory to followership perceptions are investigated. Apart from the manipulation of subordinates' expertise, we decided to use charisma as the other to be manipulated variable, since charismatic leadership can be considered the most prototypical form of leadership. We expected that both observed charismatic leadership and observed subordinates' expertise would have positive main effects on perceived subordinates' need for leadership.

Method Study 2

Sample and Procedure

The sample of study 2 consisted of 120 students, 46 men (38.3%) and 74 women (61.7%), with an average age of 21.7 years (sd = 4.7). Again, the design consisted of four conditions, in which between 29 and 32 students participated. Apart from different vignettes, the procedure was similar to the one employed in study 1.

Variables

The one-page vignette described a security company and one of its departments. Again, apart from the manipulation, the text of the vignette was identical for all respondents. The manipulation in the vignette consisted of a number of sentences on leadership of Peter Van Velzen and the expertise of his subordinates in the human resource department in a 2 (high versus low charismatic leadership) by 2 (high versus low expertise of subordinates) design. High charisma is manipulated using the following sentences: "Van Velzen is known for his inspirational speeches. When people have work-related problems, Van Velzen always finds insightful and new ways to deal with them. Additionally, Van Velzen is very committed to his people and will do all he can to accommodate to his employees' wishes." Low charisma is manipulated using the following sentences: "Van Velzen is known for his dry speeches. When people have work-related problems, Van Velzen most of the time comes up with standard, well known, solutions. Additionally, Van Velzen doesn't care for individual wishes of his employees; according to him people should conform to the existing rules." High expertise is manipulated using the following sentences: "Van Velzen's employees have built up a tremendous amount of expertise over the years. Their file knowledge is extremely high. When tested by a co-worker, employees were, without any effort, able to cite name, facts, and procedures when given a file number." Low expertise was manipulated using the following sentences: "Van Velzen's employees did not yet have any opportunity to build up expertise on Human Resource issues. File knowledge in the department is relatively low. When tested by a co-worker, employees were not able to cite name, facts, and procedures when given a file number."

The following dependent variables were used: need for leadership, leader dependency, and idealized styles of supervision. Need for leadership (De Vries, 1997; De Vries et al., 2002) consists of 17 items with a similar stem and different endings. An example of a need for a leadership item in this study is: "The employees in the HR department need Van Velzen to set goals." Reliability of the need for leadership is consistently high in other studies; often reaching levels of .90 and higher (De Vries et al., 2004). In this study, the reliability of the need for leadership scale is .87. Leader dependency (Kark, Shamir, & Chen, 2003) is a scale consisting of 10 items. An example of a leader dependency item in this study is: "If Van Velzen goes on vacation, the employees' functioning would deteriorate." In Kark et al. (2003) research, this scale had a reliability of .84. In this study, the Cronbach alpha is .90. Idealized styles of supervision (Vecchio & Boatwright, 2002) consists of 10 items, five of which belong to an idealized structuring scale and five of which belong to an idealized consideration scale. In Vecchio and Boatwright's (2002), these two scales have reliabilities of .70 and .74 respectively. The items in our study were somewhat reworded to fit our purpose. An example item of idealized structuring in our study is: "According to you, the ideal supervisor in this narrative should assign group members to particular tasks." Although the reliability of idealized consideration (.76) is better than the one reported by Vecchio and Boatwright (2002), the Cronbach alpha of idealized structuring is a paltry .53.

Manipulation Checks

Eight items were used to check whether the manipulations were successful. The charismatic leadership manipulation check consisted of four items, such as: "Van Velzen is an inspiring leader." This scale had a Cronbach alpha of .95. The subordinate expertise manipulation check consisted of four items, such as the recoded item: "The employees of the HR department have little expertise." This scale has a reliability of .93. Both manipulations were highly successful. The charismatic leadership manipulation had a highly significant effect on the charismatic leadership check $(F(1, 116) = 379.89, p < .001)$, with the following means (and standard deviations) for the respectively low and high charisma conditions: $m_{low} = 1.40$ (sd = 0.55) and $m_{high} = 4.03$ (sd = 0.89). The charismatic leadership manipulation had a marginal, but just not significant, effect on the subordinate expertise manipulation check $(F(1, 116) = 3.44, p = .066)$, with high charisma associated with a somewhat lower perceived expertise of subordinates: $m_{low} = 3.15$ (sd = 1.48) and $m_{high} = 3.05$ (sd = 1.49). The subordinate expertise manipulation had a strong effect on the subordinate expertise manipulation check $(F(1, 116) = 676.49; p < .001)$, with the following means (and sd's): $m_{low} = 1.77$ (sd = 0.62) and $m_{high} = 4.48$ (sd = 0.53). There was no significant effect of the subordinate expertise manipulation on the charismatic leadership manipulation check $(F(1, 116) = 0.55, p = .459)$. No significant interactions were found between the charismatic leadership and the subordinate expertise manipulations. Consequently, the manipulations in this study were highly effective.

Results Study 2

The findings of study 2 are shown in Table 10.2 and Figure 10.3. The charismatic leadership manipulation had significant effects on need for leadership $(F(1, 116) = 37.32, p < .001, \eta = .24)$ and leader dependency $(F(1, 116) = 71.19, p < .001, \eta = .38)$, but did not have a significant effect on idealized structuring $(F(1, 116) = 0.24, p = .622, \eta = .00)$ and only a marginally significant (at $p < .10$) effect on idealized consideration $(F(1, 116) = 3.04, p = .084, \eta = .03)$. The subordinate expertise manipulation had significant effects on need for leadership $(F(1, 116) = 13.64, p < .001,$

$\eta = .11$), leader dependency ($F(1, 116) = 5.39$, $p = .022$, $\eta = .04$), and idealized structuring ($F(1, 116) = 8.61$, $p = .004$, $\eta = .07$), but did not have a significant effect on idealized consideration ($F(1, 116) = 1.89$, $p = .172$, $\eta = .02$). None of the interactions between the charismatic leadership and subordinate expertise manipulations were significant.

When comparing the effects of charismatic leadership and subordinate expertise, we found a significant difference between the effects of charismatic leadership versus subordinates' expertise on leader dependency ($F = 3.85$, $p < .01$), with charismatic leadership ($\eta = .38$) having a stronger effect on leader dependency than subordinates' expertise ($\eta = .04$). Although for need for leadership, the effects were in the same direction, there was no significant difference between the two effects ($F = 1.54$, $p > .05$), neither were there any differences between the effects on the idealized styles of supervision scales. The one-way ANOVA's in Table 10.2 also show that, especially with respect to leader dependency and need for leadership, charismatic leadership had the most pronounced effect on the dependent variables, with higher need for leadership and leader dependency especially associated with high charismatic leadership, and also, but to a lesser extent with low subordinates' expertise. Post-hoc, the ANOVA's did not reveal any significant differences between the idealized styles of supervision in the four conditions.

Table 10.2. The Effects of Charismatic Leadership and Subordinates' Expertise on Perceived Need for Leadership, Leader Dependency, and Idealized Structuring and Considerate Styles of Supervision ($N = 120$)

		Low Charismatic Leadership		High Charismatic Leadership	
		High Expertise	Low Expertise	High Expertise	Low Expertise
Need for Leadership	Mean	2.69[a]	3.13[b]	3.37[b,c]	3.65[c]
	Sd	0.59	0.61	0.48	0.43
Leader Dependency	Mean	2.09[a]	2.37[a]	3.03[b]	3.25[b]
	Sd	0.47	0.59	0.64	0.65
Idealized Structuring	Mean	3.68[a]	3.98[a]	3.78[a]	3.97[a]
	Sd	0.49	0.33	0.54	0.43
Idealized Consideration	Mean	4.36[a]	4.25[a]	4.54[a]	4.39[a]
	Sd	0.49	0.49	0.54	0.51

Note: Means in the same row that do not share the same subscript are significantly different at $p < .05$.

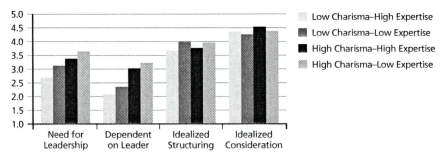

Figure 10.3.   The effects of charismatic leadership and subordinates' expertise on perceived need for leadership, dependency, and idealized supervision.

Conclusion Study 2

The second study shows that charismatic leadership and subordinates' expertise have significant effects on perceived need for leadership and leader dependency. Although one could argue that especially subordinates' expertise is most proximate to subordinates' need for leadership, it appears that charismatic leadership has a more pronounced effect on these two variables than subordinates' expertise does. Combined with study one, this study clearly shows a reciprocal relation between leadership and subordinates' needs and wishes and again it strongly endorses the view that there is an implicit theory of observers linking the two, with respondents believing charismatic leadership to be strongly associated with subordinates' need for leadership.

DISCUSSION AND CONCLUSIONS

Both studies offer strong support for the presence of an implicit followership theory as described in Figure 10.1. The first study shows that leadership perceptions are strongly influenced by knowledge about subordinates' need for leadership. In this study, the attribution of leadership from knowledge about a group's need for leadership is actually much stronger than the attribution of leadership based on the knowledge of a group's success. Consequently, followership perceptions seem to play an important, and up until now almost ignored, part in leadership perception theories. The second study shows the reverse effects of knowledge about a leader's behavior and group members' expertise on need for leadership perceptions. Again, the relation between leadership and need for leadership is strong, with observers inferring high need for leadership and high leader dependency whenever a charismatic leader is around.

Recently, Felfe and Schyns (2003) argued that leader-subordinate simi-larity might be more important than complementarity in predicting leader-ship ratings. Since followership is diametrically opposed to leadership, and stronger followership perceptions seem inextricably linked to stronger leadership perceptions, the results of our studies do not offer much sup-port for their stance. On the contrary, our results offer strong support for a complementarity effect. The difference can be resolved if we look at the type of situation in which ratings are made. Ratings of speeches of leaders, such as in Felfe and Schyns' (2003) study, may invite similarity ratings, because watching someone perform, without being involved oneself (like watching television), may involve identification processes. Ratings of leader-subordinate interactions, whether observed, such as in these two studies, or experienced, such as in De Vries et al. (1999) study, may evoke complementarity ratings, because of social comparison mechanisms.

Actually, with respect to the leader-subordinate dyadic interactions there may be three effects that can be distinguished. First of all, some-one's personality, needs, and/or attitudes may have a direct effect on the way a person perceives and rates a leader with whom one interacts. Conse-quently, when interacting with others, insecurity, fearfulness, and lack of self-esteem, which may be associated with the personality traits emotional-ity and introversion, may positively affect leadership susceptibility and per-ceptions (Yukl, 1999). Secondly, the real-life interaction between a subordinate and a leader may actually be affected by a subordinate's per-sonality, needs, and attitudes. In line with the LMX theory (Graen, Novak, & Sommerkamp, 1982; Maslyn & Uhl-Bien, 2001), based on a subordi-nate's needs, a leader may actually act differently toward a subordinate and, as a consequence, be perceived differently by the subordinate in turn. Thus, actual leadership behaviors may mediate the relationship between personality traits, needs, and attitudes on the one hand and leader perceptions on the other. Thirdly, and also in line with LMX think-ing, leadership itself may have an impact on subordinates' needs and atti-tudes, by making them for instance aware of important deficiencies between the present state and a desirable future state and convincing them that these deficiencies can be solved through leadership. This heightened awareness of deficiencies, which may be equated to need for leadership, in turn may lead to more favorable perceptions of leadership, since by virtue of him/her pointing out the deficiencies she or he is also believed to know the way to handle them.

It should be noted that this study does not support the actual existence of the mechanisms described above. One of the main limitations is that our studies only focused on the observers' viewpoint of a supervisor–subordi-nate dyad; they did not actually investigate the mechanisms that underlie such a relationship. Additionally, scenario studies may engender simplistic cognitive heuristics that are less likely to occur in real life settings. However, both studies reported in this chapter do strongly suggest that observers have an implicit theory about (1) what kind of leadership is exhibited when faced with subordinates with either high or low need for leadership—as has been shown in study 1—and (2) to what extent subordinates need leadership when they are faced with a charismatic leader—as has been shown in study 2. Consequently, the two studies combined do suggest that the implicit followership theory suggested in this chapter may be a valuable extension of the implicit leadership theory.

To take the implicit followership theory a step further, and to overcome some of the limitations of scenario studies, a suggestion for future research would be to use real life actors who play act subordinates who need leadership and let observers rate perceived (charismatic or other) leadership (cf. study 1). Conversely, a similar design can be used in order to observe the real-life effect of observed (charismatic) leadership on perceived need for leadership (cf. study 2). Additionally, to more fully investigate the relationship between the follower characteristics and perception of followership, in line with work on the attachment theory (Bowlby, 1988; Hazan & Shaver, 1990; Keller, 2003), it would be worthwhile to invest the relation between subordinates' attachment styles and need for leadership. It is plausible that subordinates with an anxious-ambivalent attachment style have a higher need for leadership than securely attached subordinates, in line with the finding that emotionality is positively related to need for leadership (De Vries et al., 2004), but it may be worthwhile to ask whether observers attribute higher need for leadership to anxious-ambivalent individuals than to secure leadership or even to look at the effect of observers' attachment style on others' perceived need for leadership.

SOCIAL CONTAGION OF FOLLOWERS' NEED FOR LEADERSHIP

Another potentially fruitful area of research involves the effect of (perceived) need for leadership on social contagion. Social contagion is defined as "the spread of affect, attitude, or behavior from Person A (the "initiator") to Person B (the "recipient"), where the recipient does not perceive an intentional influence attempt on the part of the initiator" (Levy & Nail, 1993). According to Meindl (1990, 1995) and Weierter (1997), social contagion may play an important part in the spread of followers' expressive behaviors. Extreme examples of these expressive behaviors are the screaming and fainting in the presence of pop and/or television idols, but social contagion may invite all sorts of behaviors, such as either respectful distance or wanting to touch a leader figure, rapt attention or drawing attention to oneself, etc...., depending on the reactions of other people around. The most important characteristic of social contagion is, that it is not the leader, who is primarily responsible for the behaviors in question, but the other followers or onlookers that are present. Social modeling, not of the leader, but of the followers, thus plays an important part in the spread of the "charismatic affect" (Meindl, 1990).

In the process of social contagion, both need for leadership and identification may play an important role. For instance, somebody who identifies with a group of people and observes some members of this group to act demurely toward another person, submissively asking questions, listening, and noting down everything the person says, may be more likely to echo these actions than someone who doesn't identify with these group members. A similar point is made in the charismatic contagion model of Meindl (1990), which is based on the social contagion phases observed by Kerckhoff and Back (1968) in a clothing mill in which a belief about being infected by a mysterious disease spread quickly through the social (rather than the physical) network of the plant. Meindl (1990) makes a distinction between a latency phase, a social isolate phase, a social network phase, and a normative phase of charismatic contagion. The first two phases refer to the arousal of fringe group members in the presence of a salient leader-like figure. While the arousal is attributed to the leader figure, it may also stem from other sources. The third phase refers to the spread of the contagion through the social network, while the fourth phase refers to the norming of behaviors associated with the charismatic "movement" within the population. Arousal is more likely to occur when one needs someone (like one needs an object of love), and a stronger social identity (i.e., a stronger social network) occurs when people strongly identify with a particular in-group (De Vries, 2003). A simple model of Meindl's (1990) phase model would thus predict that attribution of leadership is stronger when need for leadership in others and the identification with those others is stronger.

Some research already points in this direction. In a study of the distribution and dispersion of charismatic attributions, Pastor, Meindl, and Mayo (2002) show that over time in friendship networks (i.e., networks in which strong identification occurs) charismatic attributions converge to a greater extent than in task networks, in which less identification occurs. In a field study of an outward-bound group, Fielding and Hogg (1997) found that identification with a group enhanced the relation between social attraction and prototypicality of a leader and his/her perceived effectiveness. These studies and recent theorizing (Hogg, 2001; Van Knippenberg & Hogg, 2003), seems to suggest that social identity is an important addition to models of leadership perception.

CONCLUDING REMARKS

As other studies before (Hollander & Offermann, 1990; Meindl, 1995; Shamir, 1992; Weierter, 1997), this study points to the importance of the development of a follower-centered model of leadership. We propose such a model in this chapter and show its strength in two studies. Both studies show the existence of a strong implicit theory of the reciprocal relation between subordinates' need for leadership and leadership perceptions. These relations appear to be stronger than the relation between performance and leadership perceptions, which thus far has been the main focus of implicit theories of leadership. Future research needs to establish whether social identity may enhance the effects of observed need for leadership, causing social contagion of leadership to occur.

REFERENCES

Bass, B.M. (1985). *Leadership and performance beyond expectations.* New York: Free Press.

Bowlby, J. (1988). *A secure base: Parent-child attachment and healthy human development.* New York.

Carter, L.F. (1953). Leadership and small group behavior. In M. Sherif & M.O. Wilson (Eds.), *Group relations at the crossroads.* New-York: Harper.

De Vries, R.E. (1997). *Need for leadership: A solution to empirical problems in situational theories of leadership.* Tilburg: Tilburg University.

De Vries, R.E. (2000). When leaders have character: Need for leadership, performance, and the attribution of leadership. *Journal of Social Behavior & Personality, 15*(4), 413–430.

De Vries, R.E. (2003). Self, in-group, and out-group evaluation: Bond or breach? *European Journal of Social Psychology, 33*(5), 609–621.

De Vries, R.E., Roe, R.A., & Taillieu, T.C.B. (1999). On charisma and need for leadership. *European Journal of Work & Organizational Psychology, 8*(1), 109–133.

De Vries, R.E., Roe, R.A., & Taillieu, T.C.B. (2002). Need for leadership as a moderator of the relationships between leadership and individual outcomes. *Leadership Quarterly, 13*(2), 121–137.

De Vries, R.E., Roe, R.A., Taillieu, T.C.B., & Nelissen, N.J.M. (2004). Behoefte aan leiderschap in organisaties: wie heeft het en waarom? [Who needs leadership in organizations and why?]. *Gedrag en Organisatie, 17*(4), 204–226.

Den Hartog, D.N., House, R.J., Hanges, P.J., Ruiz-Quintanilla, S.A., Dorfman, P.W., et al. (1999). Culture specific and cross-culturally generalizable implicit leadership theories: Are attributes of charismatic/transformational leadership universally endorsed? *Leadership Quarterly, 10*(2), 219–256.

Den Hartog, D.N., Van Muijen, J.J., & Koopman, P.L. (1997). Transactional versus transformational leadership: An analysis of the MLQ. *Journal of Occupational and Organizational Psychology, 70*(1), 19–34.

Eden, D., & Leviatan, U. (1975). Implicit leadership theory as a determinant of the factor structure underlying supervisory behavior scales. *Journal of Applied Psychology, 60*, 736–741.

Felfe, J., & Schyns, B. (2003). *Personality and the perception of transformational leadership: The impact of extraversion, neuroticism, personal need for structure, and occupational self-efficacy.* Unpublished manuscript.

Fielding, K.S., & Hogg, M.A. (1997). Social identity, self-categorization, and leadership: A field study of small interactive groups. *Group Dynamics, 1*(1), 39–51.

Fleishman, E.A. (1953). The description of supervisory behavior. *Journal of Applied Psychology, 37*, 1–6.

Graen, G.B., Novak, M.A., & Sommerkamp, P. (1982). The effects of leader-member exchange and job design on productivity and satisfaction: Testing a dual attachment model. *Organizational Behavior and Human Performance, 30*, 109–131.

Hazan, C., & Shaver, P.R. (1990). Love and work: An attachment-theoretical perspective. *Journal of Personality and Social Psychology, 59*(2), 270–280.

Hogg, M.A. (2001). A social identity theory of leadership. *Personality and Social Psychology Review, 5*(3), 184–200.

Hollander, E.P., & Offermann, L.R. (1990). Power and leadership in organizations: Relationships in transition. Special Issue: Organizational psychology. *American Psychologist, 45*, 179–189.

Howell, J.P., Bowen, D.E., Dorfman, P.W., Kerr, S., & Podsakoff, P.M. (1990). Substitutes for leadership: Effective alternatives to ineffective leadership. *Organizational Dynamics, 19*, 21–38.

Howell, J.P., Dorfman, P.W., & Kerr, S. (1986). Moderator variables in leadership research. *Academy of Management Review, 11*, 88–102.

Kark, R., Shamir, B., & Chen, G. (2003). The two faces of transformational leadership: Empowerment and dependency. *Journal of Applied Psychology, 88*(2), 246–255.

Keller, T. (1999). Images of the familiar: Individual differences and implicit leadership theories. *Leadership Quarterly, 10*(4), 589–607.

Keller, T. (2003). Parental images as a guide to leadership sensemaking: An attachment perspective on implicit leadership theories. *Leadership Quarterly, 14*(2), 141–160.

Kerckhoff, A., & Back, K. (1968). *The June bug: A study of hysterical contagion.* New York: Appleton-Century-Crofts.

Kerr, S., & Jermier, J.M. (1978). Substitutes for leadership: Their meaning and measurement. *Organizational Behavior and Human Performance, 22*, 375–403.

Levy, D.A., & Nail, P.R. (1993). Contagion: A theoretical and empirical review and reconceptualization. *Genetic, Social, and General Psychology Monographs, 119*(2), 233–284.

Lord, R.G., Foti, R.J., & de Vader, C.L. (1984). A test of leadership categorization theory: Internal structure, information processing, and leadership perceptions. *Organizational Behavior and Human Performance, 34*, 343–378.

Lord, R.G., & Maher, K.J. (1993). *Leadership and information processing: Linking perceptions and performance.* New York: Routledge.

Luthans, F., & Lockwood, D.L. (1984). Towards an observation system for measuring leader behavior in natural settings. In J.G. Hunt, D. Hosking, C.A.

Schriesheim, & R. Stewart (Eds.), *Leaders and managers: International perspectives on managerial behavior and leadership.* New York: Pergamon Press.

Maslyn, J.M., & Uhl Bien, M. (2001). Leader-member exchange and its dimensions: Effects of self-effort and other's effort on relationship quality. *Journal of Applied Psychology, 86*(4), 697–708.

Meindl, J.R. (1990). On leadership: An alternative to the conventional wisdom. In L.L. Cummings & B.M. Staw (Eds.), *Research in organizational behavior* (Vol. 12, pp. 159–203). Greenwich, CT: JAI Press.

Meindl, J.R. (1995). The romance of leadership as a follower-centric theory: A social constructionist approach. *Leadership Quarterly, 6*(3), 329–341.

Meindl, J.R., & Ehrlich, S.B. (1987). The romance of leadership and the evaluation of organizational performance. *Academy of Management Journal, 30*(1), 91–109.

Meindl, J.R., Ehrlich, S.B., & Dukerich, J.M. (1985). The romance of leadership. *Administrative Science Quarterly, 30*, 78–102.

Mitchell, T.R., Larson, J.R., & Green, S.G. (1977). Leader behavior, situational moderators, and group performance: An attributional analysis. *Organizational Behavior and Human Performance, 18*, 254–268.

Offermann, L.R., Kennedy, J.K., & Wirtz, P.W. (1994). Implicit leadership theories: Content, structure, and generalizability. *Leadership Quarterly, 5*, 43–58.

Pastor, J.C., Meindl, J.R., & Mayo, M.C. (2002). A network effects model of charisma attributions. *Academy of Management Journal, 45*(2), 410–420.

Pavitt, C., & Sackaroff, P. (1990). Implicit theories of leadership and judgments of leadership among group members. *Small Group Research, 21*, 374–392.

Phillips, J.S., & Lord, R.G. (1981). Causal attributions and perceptions of leadership. *Organizational Behavior and Human Performance, 28*, 143–163.

Phillips, J.S., & Lord, R.G. (1982). Schematic information processing and perceptions of leadership in problem-solving groups. *Journal of Applied Psychology, 67*, 486–492.

Pillai, R., & Meindl, J.R. (1998). Context and charisma: A "meso" level examination of the relationship of organic structure, collectivism, and crisis to charismatic leadership. *Journal of Management, 24*(5), 643–671.

Podsakoff, P.M., MacKenzie, S.B., Ahearne, M., & Bommer, W.H. (1995). Searching for a needle in a haystack: Trying to identify the illusive moderators of leadership behaviors. *Journal of Management, 21*(3), 422–470.

Podsakoff, P.M., MacKenzie, S.B., & Fetter, R. (1993). Substitutes for leadership and the management of professionals. *Leadership Quarterly, 4*, 1–44.

Podsakoff, P.M., Niehoff, B.P., MacKenzie, S.B., & Williams, M.L. (1993). Do substitutes for leadership really substitute for leadership? An empirical examination of Kerr and Jermier's situational leadership model. *Organizational Behavior and Human Decision Processes, 54*, 1–44.

Podsakoff, P.M., Todor, W.D., & Schuler, R.S. (1983). Leader expertise as a moderator of the effects of instrumental and supportive leader behaviors. *Journal of Management, 9*, 173–185.

Popper, M., & Mayseless, O. (2003). Back to basics: Applying a parenting perspective to transformational leadership. *Leadership Quarterly, 14*(1), 41–65.

Popper, M., Mayseless, O., & Castelnovo, O. (2000). Transformational leadership and attachment. *Leadership Quarterly, 11*(2), 267–289.

Puffer, S.M. (1990). Attributions of charismatic leadership: The impact of decision style, outcome, and observer characteristics. *Leadership Quarterly, 1*(3), 177–192.

Quinn, R.E. (1988). *Beyond rational management: Mastering the paradoxes and competing demands of high performance.* San Fransisco: Jossey-Bass.

Rush, M.C., Thomas, J.C., & Lord, R.G. (1977). Implicit leadership theory: A potential threat to the internal validity of leader behavior questionnaires. *Organizational Behavior and Human Performance, 20,* 93–110.

Shamir, B. (1992). Attribution of influence and charisma to the leader: The Romance of Leadership revisited. *Journal of Applied Social Psychology, 22,* 386–407.

Syroit, J. (1979). Mens- en taakgerichtheid: constructie en validering van een verkorte leiderschapsschaal. *Gedrag, Tijdschrift voor Psychologie, 3,* 176–192.

Van Knippenberg, D., & Hogg, M.A. (2003). *Leadership and power: Identity processes in groups and organizations.* London: Sage Publications.

Vanderslice, V.J. (1988). Separating leadership from leaders: An assessment of the effect of leader and follower roles in organizations. *Human Relations, 41,* 677–696.

Vecchio, R.P., & Boatwright, K.J. (2002). Preferences for idealized styles of supervision. *Leadership Quarterly, 13*(4), 327–342.

Weierter, S.J.M. (1997). Who wants to play "follow the leader?" A theory of charismatic relationships based on routinized charisma and follower characteristics. *Leadership Quarterly, 8*(2), 171–193.

Yukl, G. (1999). An evaluation of conceptual weaknesses in transformational and charismatic leadership theories. *Leadership Quarterly, 10*(2), 285–305.

Yukl, G.A. (1994). *Leadership in organizations* (3nd ed.). Englewood Cliffs, NJ: Prentice-Hall International, Inc.

CHAPTER 11

EFFECTS OF HIERARCHICAL POSITIONS OF TARGET PERSONS ON SOCIAL INFERENCE

Schema Use and Schema Content in Perceiving Leaders and Subordinates

Dorien Konst and Wim van Breukelen

ABSTRACT

People are limited in their capacity and motivation to process information about others. To simplify perception, they use various strategies, like schema use and stereotyping. This chapter focuses on the differences between judgments made of leaders and of subordinates. We first describe the relevant literature on social perception and social-cognitive leadership approaches. We pay attention to the function of the role schemas and the personality schemas that people use in judging other people's traits and behaviors. We then relate these general insights from the literature to more specific lines of thought, develop two hypotheses and describe a series of three studies in which these

Implicit Leadership Theories: Essays and Explorations, pages 305–331
Copyright © 2005 by Information Age Publishing

hypotheses were tested. Our first hypothesis was that leaders are judged as more competent than subordinates. The second hypothesis was that leaders are also judged as more sociable than subordinates. The findings of our studies offer support for the first hypothesis, but not for the second. With regard to the first hypothesis a further qualification is in order. In particular, subordinates were downgraded on the competence dimension, while we expected that leaders would be upgraded. In trying to explain our findings, we refer to the literature on implicit leadership theories, implicit performance theories of subordinates, and prototypes. We conjecture that the label "leader" instigates more thoughtful and less schema-based processing than the label "subordinate." We give some suggestions for organizational practice, especially for leaders, to improve the accuracy of their impression formation. In addition, we describe some potential avenues of further research.

SOCIAL PERCEPTION: HOW DO WE PERCEIVE OTHERS?

Generally speaking, there are two ways in which people are perceived and judged. On the one hand, people can be perceived on the basis of pre-existing schemas, i.e., organized collections of knowledge about a certain stimulus (e.g., a specific supervisor) or a category of stimuli (e.g., supervisors in general). On the other hand, people can be perceived as individuals, as unique persons. Fiske and Neuberg (1990) have proposed a continuum of impression formation, ranging from more schema-based to more attribute-based or individuated processes. Depending on the situation, perceivers can move from one end of the continuum to the other.

Fiske and Taylor (1991) distinguish several kinds of social schemas, all of which may influence the encoding of new information, retrieval and memory of old information, and inferences about missing information. In this chapter, we focus on two types, namely role schemas and personality schemas, and their relevance for the perception of leaders and subordinates. We investigate the effects of the hierarchical position of organizational members (leaders and subordinates), both as target persons and as perceivers, on several aspects of social perception and social inference. We test the hypothesis that people make less use of role schemas in perceiving leaders than in perceiving subordinates.

Like a stereotype, a *role schema* is a cognitive structure that contains expectations about members of a certain social category. The difference between stereotypes and role schemas is subtle: stereotypes refer more or less to well-defined categories, such as women, Catholics, or soccer hooligans. Role schemas refer to categories that are associated with the role or function the target person fulfils at that moment (often a professional role), e.g., supervisor, mother, teacher.

So a role schema refers to the cognitive structure that organizes one's knowledge about behaviors and traits that are appropriate for a certain role (Fiske & Taylor, 1991). Role schemas contain the traits and behaviors expected from a person in a particular social position. Two kinds of roles can be distinguished: ascribed roles and achieved roles. At birth, and as we grow up, we acquire ascribed roles, related to our sex, race and age. Expectations for behavior emanate from these roles. Ascribed roles can be a rich source of stereotypes (cf. Allport, 1954). Achieved roles refer to social roles people can acquire by effort and intent (Fiske & Taylor, 1991). A leadership role, for instance, is an achieved role. A leader is supposed to behave in an intelligent, goal-oriented, and in a responsible way (Lord & Maher, 1991).

Just like any other schema, role schemas can be distinguished by different levels of abstraction. With regard to role schemas about leaders, for instance, we have expectations about leaders in general, but we can also specify subschemas about a political leader, military leader, sports coach, or a manager in an advertising agency (see Lord & Maher, 1991).

Person or personality schemas (or implicit personality theories, IPT; Bruner & Tagiuri, 1954) constitute a different type of schema used in judging others. A personality schema contains general knowledge about personality traits which may or may not go together, and about behavior-trait associations. It offers a framework with which—on the basis of one or more perceived personality traits or behaviors—inferences can be made about other traits and behaviors. Trait inferences almost seem inevitable when encountering behavioral information that has clear trait implications. Trait inferences may even be qualified as an automatic process (Carlston, Skowronski & Sparks, 1995; Smith & Miller, 1983; Uleman & Moskowitz, 1994). For example, if a person frequently asks for the advice of others, even with regard to trivial matters, it is generally assumed that this person is insecure. Another example of a trait inference is that one infers that a person who is sociable may also be cooperative and helpful. This example illustrates that positive traits are mutually associated. Likewise, negative traits are mutually associated (Schneider, 1973). Personality schemas can be distinguished from role schemas or stereotypes by their starting points. In the case of personality schemas it is not the social category of the person that is the main starting point, but one or more personality traits or behaviors which form the basis for conclusions about other characteristics (Ashmore & Del Boca, 1979; Vonk, 1996). The starting point for role schemas, however, is the membership of a social category.

Research on perceived associations between personality traits shows that traits can be organized in terms of two universal dimensions or types of evaluation (Rosenberg, 1977; Vonk, 1993). The one dimension can be called social evaluation, likeability or sociability, and included traits like friendliness and spontaneity as opposed to arrogance and hostility. The other dimension is called competence or ability. Competence is strongly related to Osgood, Suci and Tannenbaum's (1957) potency dimension, which can be defined as the ability to initiate behavior and change the environment.

Competence and potency are especially relevant for leadership. Consequently, this dimension encompasses more than just certain capacities: it concerns all traits that refer to strength, be they in the form of specific skills such as problem solving aptitudes, or in the form of the ability to influence the environment, e.g., by being enterprising or dominant (cf. Vonk, 1996).

Both competence and social evaluation are dimensions of evaluation and, as such, may in practice be related: a positive judgment on one dimension is often accompanied by a positive assessment on the other (Kim & Rosenberg, 1980). Thus, people who are seen as competent are generally also assumed to be friendly. These people benefit from the halo effect: the tendency to assume that people who have certain positive characteristic must have others as well (Thorndyke, 1920).

When Do We Use Schemas?

Information about others can be processed in a schema-based fashion, but also in a systematic and elaborated manner (cf. Petty & Cacioppo, 1986), which is called individuation (Fiske & Neuberg, 1990). Individuating processes only occur under two conditions. Perceivers must be motivated to make the cognitive effort to integrate all data into an accurate and detailed impression, and they must have the cognitive capacity to do so.

Perceivers do not rely on schema-based impressions when they are dependent on someone's actions for their own outcomes. Individuation is motivated by dependency on someone else for obtaining outcomes like gaining rewards and benefits and avoiding costs and punishment (Fiske, 1993; Fiske, Morling & Stevens, 1996; Fiske & Neuberg, 1990; Neuberg & Fiske, 1987). Outcome-dependent persons are motivated to obtain an accurate impression of the other person, because the other person's actions can influence (positively or negatively) their own outcomes. To obtain an accurate impression, one cannot exclusively rely on schemas: the cost of being wrong and consequently making false predictions, is too high. So outcome dependency motivates people to pay close attention to the other, seeking to obtain an accurate impression and predict the behavior of the other, in order to improve their chances of reaching the desired outcomes (Erber & Fiske, 1984).

Dependency between people can be either symmetrical or asymmetrical (cf. Kelley & Thibaut, 1978). The social context in which leaders and subordinates operate is usually characterized as a situation of asymmetrical outcome dependency. Subordinates are more outcome-dependent on their leader than vice versa. As a result, it can be expected that subordinates are more motivated to form individuated rather than schema-based impressions of leaders, while leaders tend to use schemas to organize their impressions of subordinates (see Fiske, 1993).

Generally speaking, several cognitive constraints obstruct individuation. When people have to perform under time pressure, their cognitive capacities are limited, leading to schema-based processing (Kruglanski & Freund, 1983; Sanbonmatsu & Fazio, 1990). Another cognitive restraint follows from the information that is available about the target. If perceivers have ambiguous information about someone, schemas direct their interpretations: schemas are then something to go by. Also, if complex information is available about a person, perceivers can become "cognitively overloaded" (see Bodenhausen & Lichtenstein, 1987). Since it takes a lot of cognitive effort to integrate all the pieces of information, observers try to simplify the evaluation process, consequently making use of schemas.

Causal Inferences from Behavior

Inference is the process of collecting and combining often diverse and complex information into a judgment (Fiske & Taylor, 1991, p. 404). Attribution research investigates the cognitive processes through which individuals infer causation from observed behavior and events (Jones & Nisbett, 1972; Kelley & Michela, 1980). People's perception of the behavior of others is largely determined by the causes to which they attribute that person's behavior (Heider, 1958).

Why do we make causal attributions? Why are we interested in the motives and intentions of others? According to attribution theorists, we want to explain and understand events, and to predict the future and thus "control" future events (Heider, 1958; Jones & Davis, 1965; Kelley, 1967, 1972). Understanding what factors give rise to a certain outcome or action enables us to control the likelihood of that outcome or action, or at least to predict when it will happen (Fiske & Taylor, 1991).

Intriguing though the issue of causal inferences is in the research and theory on leadership, we will confine our present analysis to the use and content of schemas (cf. Hastie, 1984; Weiner, 1985). Elsewhere we described the results of a study in which inferences about the causes and consequences of performance-related behavior of leaders and subordinates were investigated (Konst, Vonk & Van der Vlist, 1999).

Since we are interested in the intersection between leadership and social perception, the next section will highlight some research on leadership that has included social-cognitive phenomena such as schemas and prototypes.

SOCIAL COGNITION AND LEADERSHIP

In this section we focus on some leadership approaches that emphasize social perception processes in organizations. As we will see, most research focuses on how leaders behave, how they should behave according to followers, and how they are perceived to behave by followers. Much less attention has been devoted to the question of how subordinates are perceived by leaders, and it is in this area that our research adds to the existing literature.

Cognitive Categorizations about Leaders

Lord and Maher (1991) define leadership as the process of being perceived by others as a leader. This view is based upon Eden and Levitan's (1975, p. 741) conclusion that "leadership factors are in the mind of the respondent." Therefore, it is important to discover what followers are thinking (Lord & Emrich, 2000). Leadership perceptions are formed through automatic or deliberate processes. According to Lord and his colleagues (e.g., Lord, Foti, & De Vader, 1984), leaders are categorized in the same hierarchical fashion as objects are (see also Cantor & Mischel, 1979; Rosch, 1978). At the superordinate level, a distinction is made between leaders and non leaders. Moving down the hierarchy, basic level leadership categories represent leaders in specific social contexts, e.g., political leaders, business leaders, religious leaders, and so forth. At the lowest level, we might categorize basic-level politicians as liberal or conservative, or business leaders as authoritative or democratic. People are categorized according to their similarity to prototypical categories. A prototype is a mental representation or abstract collection of the attributes most commonly shared by category members (Kenny, Blascovich, & Shaver, 1994; Lord, De Vader, & Alliger, 1986). Phillips (1984, p. 126) defines a prototype as an "abstract conception of the most representative member or most widely shared features of a given cognitive category." According to Lord and Maher (1991), the prototype of a successful leader, at least in the United States, is someone who is intelligent, goal-oriented, and responsible. People develop prototypes of both effective and ineffective leaders. These prototypes can be considered a special type of schema containing information about the traits and behaviors of an effective or ineffective leader (Phillips

& Lord, 1981). They are held in the long-term memory and are accessed when triggered by a stimulus in the environment. Prototypes of good and poor leaders are part of a person's implicit leadership theory (ILT). In Hollander and Offermann's words (1990, p. 180): "basically, implicit leadership theories are followers' preconceptions of what a leader ought to be like, such as competent and considerate." A worldwide study undertaken by Kouzes and Posner (1995) showed that people want their leaders to be credible and to have a sense of direction. In their study the most important traits and behaviors of leaders included honesty, competence, vision and inspiration. Studies by Offermann, Kennedy and Wirtz (1994) and Epitropaki and Martin (2004) have focused on the content, structure and generalizability of implicit leadership theories. When people encounter an assigned leader, they compared his or her behaviors and observed or inferred traits with the relevant prototype. On the basis of this comparison, a particular leader is categorized as a successful or an ineffective leader. A study by Smith and Foti (1998) emphasized that prototypes involve patterns of traits and behaviors, which contain important information that goes beyond their specific elements.

The process can also work the other way. When we label someone a (good) leader, we look for traits that are consistent with this label. The label which is initially attached to a stimulus guides subsequent information processing (Sande, Ellard, & Ross, 1986). Once a stimulus is categorized, much of the subsequent information about this object or person is processed in terms of that category. This may also cause difficulty in distinguishing between observed and unobserved, i.e., inferred, behaviors (cf. Lord & Maher, 1991). Finally, we make responses and decisions based upon the category. Thus, someone once categorized as a poor leader has a hard time to persuade the perceiver that he or she also has the qualities of a good leader.

Subordinates as Non-leaders

Given that we have articulate schemas about those who are in control, expectations must also exist about those who are being controlled. Fiske and Taylor (1991, p. 146) note that peoples general treatment of those without power overlaps with their treatment of specific examples of such people, such as children, women and other minority groups. The role schema for subordinates is less well defined than the schema for leaders, but since individuals are categorized into groups perceived in relation to each other (see Mackie, Hamilton, Susskind & Rosselli, 1996), subordinates are mostly described in terms opposite to those applied to leaders, and are attributed traits such as compliance and passivity (cf. Hollander & Offermann, 1990). As a result of the stereotype of leaders as high on personal potency, we may infer that the behavior of subordinates is expected to be more externally controlled and less autonomous (e.g., Deci & Ryan, 1987; Kipnis, 1976; Kipnis, Castell, Gergen & Mauch, 1976; Kruglanski, 1975). Leaders seem especially inclined to hold this assumption; they appear to think that they are the cause of the performance of their subordinates (Green & Mitchell, 1979; Kipnis 1976). The more leaders' attempts to influence subordinates' behavior by using directive and controlling means are followed by compliance, the more likely they are to believe that subordinates' behavior is not self-controlled, but is controlled by them (Kipnis, 1976, p 184; Raven & Kruglanski, 1970).

Along similar lines, leaders often make evaluations about subordinates that are negative in tone (Argyris, 1964; Baron, 1983; Kipnis, 1976; Lawler, 1989; Van der Vlist, 1991; Walton, 1985). According to Baron (1983), many leaders still endorse the assumptions of McGregor's theory X (1960) about subordinates as basically lazy people who must be controlled, and who are unwilling or unable to accept responsibility. Miles (1965) stresses the fact that leaders are often convinced that their own supervisors ignore their competences and capabilities, while they themselves think of their subordinates as relatively incompetent and passive too. Engle and Lord (1997) contend that, from a supervisor's perspective, a subordinate's performance is more important than the subordinate's leadership qualities. That is why supervisors rely on *implicit performance theories* to form impressions of subordinates. Leaders develop prototypes of effective subordinates and then compare subordinates to this prototype. Depending on the result of this comparison, subordinates are labeled as effective or ineffective.

Thus, differential expectations exist about the traits and behaviors of leaders and subordinates. Specifically, subordinates may be seen as less competent and less dominant than leaders. In addition, their behavior may be regarded as resulting from situational causes, while leaders' behavior is considered to be more internally motivated.

In summary, these cognitive leadership approaches show that we hold expectations about the personality traits and behaviors of leaders, and illustrate the importance of a fit between observations and expectations about traits and behaviors. Given that schemas and prototypes about leaders exist, and that individuals are often categorized into contrasting groups, people also hold expectations about subordinates. Assumptions about subordinates can thus be expressed in opposite terms to those used of leaders: subordinates are typically assumed to be passive and incompetent.

In the next section we describe three studies of the effects of the hierarchical position of targets (leaders, subordinates) on evaluation (schema use and schema-content). Before introducing the hypotheses and the research designs, we will outline, in more detail, the specific literature underlying our hypotheses.

EFFECTS OF HIERARCHICAL POSITION ON SOCIAL INFERENCE: THE RESULTS OF THREE STUDIES

As we mentioned previously, an impression of a person can vary in its degree of positivity or negativity on two universal dimensions or types of evaluation. The first dimension concerns competence, and the second refers to social evaluation (Osgood et al., 1957; Rosenberg, 1977; Rosenberg & Sedlak, 1972; Schneider, Hastorf, & Ellsworth, 1979; Vonk, 1993). So in evaluating others, two crucial questions are asked: Is this person likable? and, Is this person good at the things he or she is supposed to be good at? Social evaluation involves traits like friendliness and spontaneity as opposed to arrogance and hostility. Examples of competence would include traits like persistence and confidence as opposed to passivity and insecurity.

Leaders often make negative evaluations about subordinates (Baron, 1983; McGregor, 1960). There are three possible explanations for this outcome. The first is concerned with the different roles that leaders and subordinates fulfil and the personality traits that go with those roles (see Katz & Kahn, 1978). When judging someone in a lower or higher position, a role schema is activated (cf. "prototypes of leadership"; Rush & Russell, 1988). Negatively evaluated traits are associated with the role of subordinates, at least on the competence dimension (e.g., passivity and compliance). The role of leaders on this dimension is associated with positive traits (e.g., purposefulness and confidence) (Pfeffer, 1977; Pfeffer & Salancik, 1978; Yukl, 1994, 2002).

A second explanation has to do with the motives of the one who judges. A leader is judged as relatively competent, because that way the difference in authority can be legitimized. According to this explanation, the perceiver assumes that persons with tools of power have earned and deserved these tools and are therefore probably competent ("belief in a just world"; Lerner, 1980). Leaders legitimize the power relation by judging their subordinates as being relatively incompetent (Kipnis, 1976). Their position is justified when they find their subordinates require supervision because they lack competence and initiative (cf. Miles, 1965).

A third explanation can be based on the "mere exposure effect" (Zajonc, 1968): the more often one is exposed to a stimulus, the more positive the judgments of this stimulus will become (cf. Guns, 1985). This is relevant because leaders, being a minority in an organization, receive more attention on average than subordinates. A person who belongs to a minority is salient and attracts more attention than a majority member (Fiske & Taylor, 1991; Kanter, 1977). Moreover, leaders must divide their attention among several subordinates, while this is not usually the case the other way around. Because subordinates pay more attention to the superior, then vice versa, in a sense leaders are "exposed" more intensively and frequently, which can lead to more positive judgments

Hence, the main hypothesis that is tested in these studies is that leaders are judged as more competent than subordinates (1). A second question that is posed is whether leaders are judged more positively than subordinates on the social evaluation dimension as well (2). This dimension can provide insight into the three explanations mentioned above for the predicted difference in competence judgments. If role schemas are the cause of the mutual differences in judgments between leaders and subordinates, it is to be expected that judgments only differ on the competence dimension. After all, according to role schemas, leaders and subordinates only differ in competence: the schema does not imply that one group is more likeable than the other. According to the legitimizing explanation too, one would only expect differences in judgments to arise on the competence dimension. Socially evaluative traits are irrelevant in this explanation, because they do not sufficiently legitimize the hierarchical difference between leaders and subordinates. On the other hand, following the "mere exposure" explanation, differences in judgments should appear on both the competence dimension and the social evaluation dimension. If the increased exposure of leaders causes more positive judgments, then evaluations of leaders should be higher on both dimensions, because the mere exposure effects involve evaluations in the broad sense of the word.

These hypotheses were tested in three studies, outlined below. An additional question addressed in these studies, regarded the origin of the hypothesized differences between leaders and subordinates as targets. We expected that leaders would be upgraded on the competence and sociability dimensions, in comparison with subordinates. We did not expect that subordinates would be downgraded. To investigate this issue, in studies 2 and 3 we introduced a control group, used as a reference group of status-neutral targets.

Study 1: A Field Study

Method

The first study was a field study. A questionnaire was administered during a meeting for leaders from about 25 different organizations. The respondents (N = 32) were randomly assigned to two groups. Members of the one group were asked to give their impressions of a subordinate by means of 20 personality traits (a stimulus person was a subordinate). They were instructed to arbitrarily choose one of their subordinates as a target, based upon the first letter of the last name of the particular subordinate. Members of the other group were asked to give an impression of their direct superior (a stimulus person/target was a leader/supervisor). Thus, in both groups there were authentic outcome dependencies between subjects and target persons. Table 11.1 shows the characteristics of the three studies on which this chapter is based.

The respondents in the first study were mainly males (90.6%) who judged male subordinates or superiors (87.5% of the stimulus persons/targets were male). Of the respondents 6.3% had a supervisory position at a lower echelon level; 28.1% worked at a middle echelon level while the largest group (65.6%) supervised at a higher echelon level. There were no differences in this regard between the two groups of respondents.

Dependent Variables and Results

For all studies the dependent variables were derived from ratings on a series of 7-point scales (from "not at all" to "highly") on a number of personality traits. Table 11.2 shows the exact wording of the 20 traits used in study 1 and 2, as well as the two-factor solution after varimax rotation based upon the answers of the respondents who took part in study 1 and 2. Each factor contains five positively worded traits and five negatively worded traits.

The socially negative traits and the incompetence traits were recoded and two scale scores were calculated. For the resulting competence scale, Cronbach's alpha was .77 in study 1 and .80 in study 2. The sociability scale had alphas of .83 and .81, respectively.

In the first study, differences between impressions of leaders and of subordinates were examined with a one-way analysis of variance. As hypothesized, the evaluations of leaders on the competence dimension were higher than of those of subordinates: $M = 5.26$ versus $M = 4.69$; $F(1,30) = 5.58$; $p < .05$. The effect size (Cohen's d) was quite substantial: $d = 0.86$. However, the means on the sociability dimension did not differ significantly: $F(1,30) = 0.04$; $p > .05$.

Discussion

A possible explanation for the differences in competence ratings in this field study is that the judged subordinates were in fact less competent than the judged leaders, in which case the differential judgments reflected real differences. This seems a plausible explanation since there were two hierarchical levels between the supervisors and subordinates who served as targets in this study, all participants being managers who were asked to give an impression of their direct supervisor or one of their direct subordinates. As a rule, supervisor targets and chosen subordinate targets held ranks that differed two hierarchical levels.

The possibility that real competence differences were responsible for the findings could only be ruled out by creating an experimental situation.

Table 11.1. Study Type, Design, Respondents, Study Issues, and Dependent Variables for Three Studies

Study	Type of study	Respondents (Number and kind)	Objects/targets	Study issue	Dependent variable
1	field study (N = 32)	16 managers > 16 managers >	16 subordinates 16 supervisors	dependency authentic	competence and sociability of targets
2	experiment (N = 69)	19 students as "supervisors" > 18 students as "subordinates" > 32 students as "colleagues" >	19 "subordinates" 18 "supervisors" 32 "colleagues"	dependency manipulated	competence and sociability of targets
3	field-experiment (N = 50)	11 leaders and # 39 subordinates #	26 in leader position 13 "subordinates" 11 in control group	scenario about fictitious target person	competence evaluation of targets

**Table 11.2.   Two-factor Solution (after varimax rotation) of the 20
Traits Employed in Study 1 and 2 (N = 101)**

	Factor 1	Factor 2
Sociable	.78	.08
Friendly	.72	−.08
Hostile	−.69	−.05
Helpful	.69	.06
Arrogant	−.67	−.11
Cooperative	.66	−.01
Selfish	−.62	.02
Spontaneous	.53	.24
Indifferent	−.39	−.12
Irritable	−.38	−.12
Confident	.05	.75
Submissive	−.03	−.73
Insecure	−.27	−.70
Independent	.13	.66
Purposeful	.08	.67
Easily to influence	.33	−.56
Persistent	−.03	.56
Stupid	−.23	−.36
Passive	−.05	−.36
Competent	.33	.23
Eigenvalue	4.20	3.50
% explained variance	21.10	17.60

In this experiment (study 2) all participants were given exactly the same information about the stimulus person/target, while only the hierarchical position of the target person was varied (the stimulus person/target was either a subordinate or a leader). This experimental design also offered the opportunity to add a control condition, in which the hierarchical differences between judge and target person were eliminated. The judgments made by the participants in the control group provided information about their impressions of status-neutral target persons (colleagues), and served as a reference.

Study 2: An Experimental Study

Method

The second study was a laboratory study with 69 freshmen from the Psychology Department of the University of Leiden, the Netherlands. The experimental manipulation, outcome dependency, was based upon an announced interaction between two persons, the subject and a target person (stimulus). The power relation that would be in effect between these persons simulated, in the one case, the relation between a leader and a subordinate and in the other case (control condition) the relation between two colleagues. The subjects sat behind a computer in individual cubicles and were given instructions via the screen. They were told they would be working at a task with another participant (stimulus person/target). In studies on stereotypes by Fiske (1993), outcome dependency was induced by making the financial outcome for the less powerful person dependent upon the behavior of a more powerful person. This form of outcome dependency was also used in this study. In the conditions where the power was unequally distributed, subjects were told either that they would be in charge of this person ($N = 19$) or that the other person was in charge of them ($N = 18$). It was made clear that participants were randomly assigned to one of these two roles. The one in charge (supervisor) would assign tasks to the other (subordinate) and judge the other's work, which was to have financial consequences for him or her. The financial consequences were either fixed or variable (in a range from 2 to 5 euros) and their possible confounding effects were thoroughly investigated by using two control groups, one in which the outcomes were fixed ($N = 16$) and another one in which the outcomes were variable ($N = 16$). In both control conditions, the power was equally distributed. All control subjects ($N = 32$) were told that they would be working with the target person as colleagues.

After this explanation, subjects were given some information on the target person (T) in the form of 12 descriptions of behavior, supposedly recorded during an earlier study in which this target person had participated. The descriptions consisted of 4 moderately negative, 4 moderately positive, and 4 neutral behaviors. These descriptions were pretested and controlled for meaning (positive or negative). An example of a moderately positive description was, "T. put someone at ease who was waiting in his room for a moment." The reason for using moderately positive, negative and neutral descriptions were to allow the formation of a diverse range of impressions, so that the effects of power would not be overruled by diagnostic target information.

After reading both the instructions on the work relationship the subject was to have with the target person and the behavior descriptions, participants were asked to rate T. on the same 20 traits used in study 1. There was no actual interaction between the participants and the target persons. After judging T. and answering some control questions, subjects were debriefed.

Results

Study 2 also showed that subordinates were thought of as less competent than leaders. Additional analyses showed that the manipulated financial consequences (fixed or variable) did not have any confounding effects (for further details, see Konst, 1998, pp. 24–31). Again, the competency judgments of the leader targets were higher ($M = 5.16$) than those of the subordinate targets ($M = 4.64$): $F(1,35) = 6.97$, p < .05). Cohen's d was 0.88. The colleague targets, too, were rated higher on the competence judgments ($M = 5.03$) than the subordinate targets ($M = 4.64$): $F(1,49) = 4.84$, $p < .05$. Here, Cohen's d was 0.62. The competence judgments of the leader ($M = 5.16$) and colleague targets ($M = 5.03$) did not differ significantly: $F(1,48) = 0.62$, $p > .05$. Apparently, the differences between leaders and subordinates on the competence dimension were caused by a devaluation of the competence rating of the subordinates and not by an enhancement of the leaders' competence rating. With regard to the judgments on the sociability dimension, there were no significant differences among the three conditions (leaders, subordinates, or colleagues as target persons).

Conclusions and Discussion of Studies 1 and 2

The judgments of leaders and subordinates in these studies did not differ on the social evaluation dimension. In particular, study 1 indicates that the different evaluations of leaders and subordinates cannot be explained by the "mere exposure"-explanation, because according to this explanation, the judgments of leaders should have been more positive on both sociability and competence dimensions. Thus, the assumption that leaders are judged more positively because they receive more attention is not supported by our data. The results of the second study cannot clarify this issue, because in this experimental study the amount of information participants received about the target persons was kept constant, and equal attention was given to subordinate and superior stimulus persons.

Despite the absence of any actual interaction between subjects and target persons in study 2, the same differences in judgments on the competence dimension were found as in study 1. Therefore, it may be concluded that the differences in competence evaluations in study 2 were based upon interpretations by the perceiver and not on actual differences.

Taking this into account, it seems plausible that the effect emanates from the use of role schemas and the legitimation of differences in power.

According to the role schema explanation, differences in judgment are based on implicit ideas about the traits associated with the roles of leader or subordinate. For example, leaders are assumed to be more confident, while subordinates are thought of as more passive. The legitimation explanation tells us about the motives of the judge. For subordinates it is more comfortable to believe that a leader, on whom they are dependent, is competent. Correspondingly, leaders will feel themselves confirmed in their leading role if they think that their subordinates need guidance, being relatively incompetent.

Finally, study 2 showed that participants' judgments of leaders did not deviate from their judgments of persons in an equal power situation (such as colleagues). Only the judgments of subordinates deviated from the other groups. In sum these studies demonstrate a hierarchical effect on competence evaluations. More specifically, these findings suggest that it was not the competence of leaders as target persons which were upgraded, but the competence of subordinates which was downgraded, in comparison with the control group.

Research by Kipnis (1976) shows that the *use* of power by leaders leads to devaluation of the less powerful person. Our experiment (study 2) shows that the *illusion* alone *of having* power (in subjects who did not actually exercise their power) is enough for a relatively negative judgment on the competence of the subordinate (cf. Sande et al., 1986). There seems to be a "mere power effect": the fact that one had power, regardless of whether one used this power or not, led to a distortion in the judgment on the competence of the less powerful person.

Study 3

Method

In a third study a field experiment was conducted in which the hypothesis was tested that mere position labels of target objects can result in differential competence evaluations of these targets. This study investigated whether differences in competence evaluations could originate from implicit ideas about traits associated with position labels. Respondents were merely observers of targets whose hierarchical position varied: they included leader targets, subordinate targets, and status-neutral targets. So in study 3 there were neither real nor simulated outcome dependencies between the observers and the target persons. In study 3 position effects were investigated by mere variations in the position labels of the target persons.

Respondents were 50 civil servants of a municipality in The Netherlands. They were asked to answer a questionnaire. The first part of the questionnaire consisted of questions on hierarchical position and sex. Twenty-five participants were women, and twenty-five were men. Thirty-nine employees had a subordinate position and eleven had a supervisory position. Respondents read a scenario about a fictitious target person. The following instruction was given in every case: "You are now asked to participate in a study about how people form impressions of others. You will be given a description of a leader we call T./a subordinate we call T./a person we call T." Respondents were also asked to imagine that T. had to work on a task with someone else. The task was described as developing ideas on how to make the department work more efficiently by making an inventory of the number of activities that needed to be done. In the first case T. was a leader target and in the second case T. was a subordinate target. In the control case no information was given about the power relation between T. and the other person: targets were status-neutral persons.

These instructions were followed by an evaluatively mixed description of the target person. At present T. has been working for the company for a few years. T. is largely satisfied with the job, however T. is sometimes in a bad mood. In general, T. finishes the job in time. T. finds it difficult to cope with severe pressure. Now and then, at the end of the week, T. goes to the pub with colleagues. This behavioral description had some relevance to the task, and hence provided respondents with the opportunity to form an impression. At the same time, it was sufficiently uninformative to avoid allowing the effects of the role schema to be overruled by diagnostic target information (for instance sex). Respondents were asked to rate the target on five competence-related traits also used in studies 1 and 2: confident, independent, persistent, purposeful, and competent. These traits refer to positive competence (cf. Rosenberg & Sedlak, 1972). The traits were scaled and used as the dependent variable. Cronbach's alpha was .90. See Table 11.1 for the study characteristics.

Results and Discussion of Study 3

The pattern of results was exactly the same as in study 2: subordinate targets received lower competence evaluations than leaders ($M = 3.50$ versus $M = 4.53$; $F(1,37) = 7.09$, $p < .05$) and than control targets ($M = 3.50$ vs. $M = 4.28$; $F(1,22) = 3.53$, $p < .05$). Again, the effect sizes were substantial: Cohen's d's were 0.87 and 0.79, respectively. Competence evaluations of leaders and controls (status-neutral persons) as target persons did not differ significantly: $F(1,35) = 0.94$, $p > .05$.

The present study indicates that mere position labels can result in differential competence evaluations, and, more specifically, in the downgrading of target persons with a low status position. This does not imply that dependency between subject and object is not an important variable. Dependency, as we mentioned previously, has several effects. The point here is that some of these effects could be established by mere variations in the position labels of the target persons.

As we have seen, the trait inferences of subordinates deviated negatively not only from those of leaders, but also from those of control targets. Unfortunately, respondents were not asked about the assumptions they made about the hierarchical position of control targets. If they assumed that control targets were leaders, this would explain the asymmetry in judgment. Therefore, in a small follow-up study, we asked fifteen civil servants of another municipality in The Netherlands about their expectations of the hierarchical position of the control target. The same information was given to them as to the subjects in the control case in study 3. The respondents unanimously expected the target to be a subordinate. Thus, assumptions about the hierarchical position of the control target probably do not explain the asymmetry between competence judgments of subordinates and of status-neutral target persons.

CONCLUSIONS AND GENERAL DISCUSSION

The three studies outlined in the preceding paragraphs show that both outcome dependency (studies 1 and 2) and the use of mere position labels (study 3) influence social perception. In the first study, a field study, outcome dependency and social perception were explored in a natural setting: organizational members, i.e., managers, were asked to rate one of their subordinates or their leader on competence-related and sociability-related traits. The results showed that leaders and subordinates were differently rated on competence but not on sociability. The size of the effect on the competence ratings was rather strong.

In the second study, an experimental study in which the leader—subordinate relationship was simulated, it was also found that the competences of leader and subordinate targets were evaluated differently. In addition, this study showed that subordinates were downgraded: their competence was judged as significantly lower than that of both the leader targets and the colleague targets, while the competence of these two groups was evaluated at a similar level. In this study the effect sizes were substantial, too. In study 1 there was a real outcome dependency between the participants and the target persons (their leaders or subordinates; all participants being managers), while in study 2 the outcome dependency between observer and target was manipulated. Here, the participants were 69 college freshmen from the psychology department from the University of Leiden, the Netherlands.

The third study, a field experiment, examined whether the results from study 2 could also be obtained by using mere position labels without inducing outcome dependency. If so, we would know that cognitive variables, e.g., schema-effects, accounted for the differential scores on competence evaluation of target persons. The results showed again that subordinates were downgraded on their competence. Here, too, the effect sizes were strong. These results suggest that even before power is actually exercised (cf. Fiske, 1993; Kipnis, 1976) and even before perceivers have participated in an asymmetrical power interaction, impressions are biased due to categorization processes based upon the position label of the target person. Variations in the position label of a target person proved sufficient to evoke expectations about the attributes or traits of those assigned to that position.

The pattern of results was exactly the same in these three studies, despite the fact that the studies were totally different in many ways. In the first two studies, in which subjects were involved with targets, motivational variables could explain the findings, e.g., the legitimizing of power differences (cf. Kipnis, 1976; Lerner, 1980), and the motivation to develop more favorable impressions of a person one depends upon (e.g., Berscheid, Graziano, Monson & Dermer, 1976). In the first study, the results could also be caused by the tendency of leaders to use more schema-based impressions of subordinates than vice versa, because of their relatively low need to make accurate predictions about the traits and behavior of less powerful others (see Fiske, 1993).

For the findings of the third study these explanations are less appropriate. Given the absence of personal involvement (dependency) between subjects and targets in this study, cognitive explanations seem more plausible. Obviously, perceivers have different stereotypes about leaders than about subordinates. The situation is complicated, however, by the asymmetry of schema-use: differences between leader and subordinate targets can be explained by cognitive references, but the reason why perceivers are more likely to use schemas for targets with a subordinate position label, and not for targets with a leader position label, is less clear.

One possible explanation is that the stereotypes of leaders and subordinates differ in extremity levels, i.e., the stereotype of subordinates may be seen as more extreme because it is negative in tone. It has been established that negative information carries more weight in judgments than positive information, because of its diagnostic value (e.g., Reeder & Brewer, 1979). Further, negative labels often result in confirmation effects (e.g., Darley & Gross, 1983). The asymmetry, then, might be caused by this negativity effect, resulting in more extreme inferences.

Another, more speculative, explanation might be that the schemas about leaders and subordinates are similar in extremity and strength, but that they are used differentially by perceivers. Concepts referring to power can generate "automatic vigilance" (cf. Pratto & John, 1991), even when the stimulus does not personally affect the perceiver (Vonk, 1996). Because of perceivers' frequent prior experiences with leaders as powerful persons who can affect others' outcomes, the label "leader" may not only activate a role schema, but also power-related or dependency-related concepts. This is in accordance with results from a study by Palich and Hom (1992) who found that leader schemas also connote power basis (cf. Hollander & Offermann, 1990). By the same token, the subordinate position might have generated the opposite image: the picture of harmless persons who do not exert control, and who are dependent on others', i.e., leaders', actions. Automatic vigilance when perceiving leaders could have resulted in the motivation to form accurate impressions, because of a generalized need to predict and control behavior that can affect others. This could have resulted in less schema use. Subordinate targets, on the other hand, "allow" perceivers to take cognitive shortcuts: relatively moderate risk is involved when perceivers make false predictions about powerless persons. This explanation can clarify the results of the asymmetry in schema use, by assuming that the label "leader" activates control motivation even when there is no personal involvement, whereas the label "subordinate" does not. As a result, judgments of leaders are less schema-driven and more data-driven.

In addition, in a study on causal attributions on the basis of leaders' and subordinates' behavior descriptions, it was found that people perceiving subordinates are less concerned with attributional elaboration than people perceiving leaders (Konst et al., 1999). This confirms the control motivation hypothesis (cf. Fiske, 1993). Another intriguing conclusion in this study was that the processing strategies of leaders were more simplistic than those of subordinates. These effects appear to be additive, implying that subordinates perceiving leaders are more likely to engage in elaborative processing, whereas leaders perceiving subordinates are less likely to do so.

The everyday hazards and turbulence of organizational life interfere with people's motivation and ability to form accurate impressions of others. Leaders in particular often lack the motivation, the cognitive resources, and the time required to stop and think when a person's behavior runs counter to stereotypical expectations (Fiske, 1993). In these cases, it is more likely that stereotypes will be confirmed than disconfirmed. The overall picture that emerges from our data is that in perceiving subordinates, people (leaders as well as colleague-subordinates) hold negative competence-related expectations, and are not particularly motivated to abandon these schemas and to engage in a more extensive processing.

In practice, leaders might be especially vulnerable to cognitive shortcuts in observing the behavior of subordinates. The asymmetrical outcome-dependency in real life relations between leaders and subordinates might enhance these position effects, for instance in situations of time pressure (see Kruglanski, 1975; Fiske, 1993; Kruglanski & Freund, 1983). Several other mechanisms can obstruct the individuation of impressions, including ambiguous information about someone, or complex information causing perceivers to become cognitively overloaded (see Bodenhausen & Lichtenstein, 1987).

Nevertheless, we do not know how problematic these inferential errors and biases are for organizational behavior. Three relevant perspectives on this issue are described by Fiske and Taylor (1991). First, it is possible that the shortcuts are more apparent than real (cf. Funder, 1987). Our studies barely involve ecological conditions and do not involve interpersonal conditions at all. As a consequence, people might have looked worse than they really are (see also Murphy, Herr, Lockhart & Maguire, 1986).

Secondly, inferential errors and simple strategies may be corrected by feedback from the situation. In organizational life, for instance, the biases of leaders about their subordinates might disappear when leaders are made accountable for their evaluations, through performance appraisal systems, for example. Accountability can result in more complex information processing (see Tetlock & Boettger, 1989). Inferential errors can, on the other hand, also be reinforced by the features of the organizational culture. For instance, the way leaders talk among themselves about their subordinates or about other social categories such as female or black organizational members, might encourage stereotyping (Fiske, 1993).

Thirdly, given the risk of judgmental errors having serious consequences, people might try to correct them. Suppose subordinates were aware of their leaders' negative evaluations of them: would they then be motivated to perform extra role behavior? It therefore does not seem strategically wise for leaders to express their negative assumptions about subordinates, as this is likely to demotivate them. Unfortunately, many people are probably not particularly aware of their inferential shortcomings and stereotypes (see Fiske & Taylor, 1991; Nisbett & Wilson, 1977).

Traditionally, implicit ideas about leadership have viewed the leader role and the subordinate role as representing two extremes on the potency-continuum. Although an imbalance of power exists, influence can be exerted in both roles: effective organizational behavior depends on reciprocity and two-way influence and power sharing between leaders and subordinates (cf. Keller & Dansereau, 1995). Perhaps organizations can create conditions in which the differences in power are de-emphasized and the relevance of the contributions from both parties is emphasized. In this context it might also be worth considering replacing labels like subordinate and follower with more neutral labels like coworker, fellow worker or assistant.

This way, traits like passivity, inactivity and dependency are rendered schema-inconsistent.

In the comparison between subordinates, leaders, and status-neutral persons as targets, we did not find evidence indicating that leaders' competence was upgraded (on the ILT-traits: competent, active, purposeful, persistent and independent). We did find, however, that subordinate targets were downgraded on the competence dimension. This was an unexpected finding, since, based upon the generally held prototype of leaders as dedicated, strong (dynamic), and intelligent (cf. Epitropaki & Martin, 2004; Offermann et al., 1994), we assumed that leaders would be characterized as more competent, in comparison with status-neutral targets and subordinates. Given these findings, a fruitful approach might be to further investigate the content and dimensions of the "implicit subordinate theories" held by leaders as well as by colleague subordinates, i.e., fellow coworkers. Elaborations on this theme could build on the work by Engle and Lord (1997), who studied the content of what they call an *implicit performance theory* in relation to successful subordinates. However, we would prefer to use the term *implicit subordinate theory*, because performance also is part of the implicit *leadership* theories developed by managers, supervisors and subordinates. Epitropaki and Martin (2004), for example, showed that traits like dedicated, hard-working and energetic belonged to the leader prototype held by British employees. The study by Engle and Lord (1997) employed 17 traits which were found prototypical of successful subordinates. It is noticeable that six of these seventeen traits refer to the relationship dimension between supervisors and subordinates: the "good" subordinate is reliable, punctual and cooperative, gives/takes suggestions, and communicates effectively.

In further clarifying this issue, it seems important to distinguish between the prototype of "the successful subordinate" and the prototype of "the common or average subordinate." This difference runs parallel with the difference between the prototype of a "good leader" and that of an "average leader" (cf. Lord & Emrich, 2000). Many studies, in our opinion, do not pay enough attention to the exact wording and definition of the target object in research on prototypes. Our research suggests that a profound schema exists about the average subordinate as an actor who is relatively incompetent and whose behavior is caused by external sources.

An interesting avenue of research might be to compare the differences between the prototypes of leaders and the prototypes of subordinates, not only with respect to the evaluation as such (i.e., positive or negative), but also with regard to the core dimensions of the prototype (cf. Engle & Lord, 1997; Offermann et al., 1994). It is, for instance, highly likely that the prototype of the effective subordinate contains such traits as loyalty, cooperation and dedication, in addition to potency traits like competence and persistence. Traits such as loyalty and cooperation refer to the relationship dimension, which is especially relevant for leader-subordinate interactions (cf. Dienesch & Liden, 1986) and thus for organizational effectiveness in general.

REFERENCES

Allport, G.W. (1954). *The nature of prejudice*. Reading, MA: Addison-Wesley.

Argyris, R.D. (1964). *Integrating the individual and the organization*. New York: Wiley.

Ashmore, R.D., & Del Boca, F.K. (1979). Sex stereotypes and implicit personality theory: Toward a cognitive-social psychological conceptualization. *Sex Roles, 5*, 219–248.

Baron, R.A. (1983). *Behavior in organizations*. Boston: Allyn & Bacon.

Berscheid, E., Graziano, W., Monson, T., & Dermer, M. (1976). Outcome dependency: Attention attribution and attraction. *Journal of Personality and Social Psychology, 34*, 978–989.

Bodenhausen, G.V., & Lichtenstein, M. (1987). Social stereotypes and information processing strategies: the impact of task complexity. *Journal of Personality and Social Psychology, 52*, 871–880.

Bruner, J.S., & Tagiuri, R. (1954). The perception of people. In G. Lindzey (Eds.), *Handbook of social psychology* (Vol. 2, pp. 634–654). Reading, MA: Addison-Wesley.

Cantor, N., & Mischel, W. 1979. Prototypes in person perception. In L. Berkowitz (Ed.), *Advances in experimental social psychology* (Vol. 12, pp. 3–52). New York: Academic Press.

Carlston, D.E., Skowronski, J.J., & Sparks, C. (1995). Savings in relearning: On the formation of behavior-based trait association and inferences. *Journal of Personality and Social Psychology, 69*, 420–436

Darley, J.M., & Gross, P.H. (1983). A hypothesis-confirming bias in labeling effects. *Journal of Personality and Social Psychology, 44*, 20–33.

Deci, E., & Ryan, R.M. (1987). The support for autonomy and the control of behavior. *Journal of Personality and Social Psychology, 53*, 1024–1037

Dienesh, R.M., & Liden, R.C. (1986). Leader-member exchange model of leadership: A critique and further development. *Academy of Management Review, 11*, 618–634.

Eden, D., & Levitan, U. (1975). Implicit leadership theory as determinant of the factor structure underlying supervisory behavior scales. *Journal of Applied Psychology, 60*, 736–741.

Engle, E.M., & Lord, R.G. (1997). Implicit theories, self-schemas, and leader-member exchange. *Academy of Management Journal, 40*, 988–1010.

Epitropaki, O., & Martin, R. (2004). Implicit leadership theories in applied settings: factor structure, generalizability, and stability over time. *Journal of Applied Psychology, 89*, 293–310.

Erber, R., & Fiske, S.T. (1984). Outcome dependency and attention to inconsistent information. *Journal of Personality and Social Psychology, 47*, 709–726.

Fiske, S.T. (1993). Controlling other people: The impact of power on stereotyping. *American Psychologist, 48,* 621–628.

Fiske, S.T., Morling, B., & Stevens, L.E. (1996). Controlling self and others: A theory of anxiety, mental control and social control. *Personality and Social Psychology Bulletin, 22,*115–123.

Fiske, S.T., & Neuberg, S.L. (1990). A continuum of impression-formation, from category based to individuating processes. In M.P. Zanna (Ed.), *Advances in experimental social psychology* (Vol. 23, pp. 1–74). New York: Academic Press.

Fiske S.T., & Taylor, S.E. (1991). *Social cognition.* New York: McGraw-Hill.

Funder, D.C. (1987). Errors and mistakes: Evaluating the accuracy of social judgment. *Psychological Bulletin, 101,* 75–90.

Green, S.G., & Mitchell, T.R. (1979). Attributional processes of leaders in leader-member interactions. *Organization Behavior and Human Performance, 23,* 429–458.

Guns, N. (1985). *Women on board.* Dissertation. Amsterdam: Free University.

Hastie, R.(1984) Causes and effects of causal attribution. *Journal of Personality and Social Psychology, 46,* 44–56.

Heider, F. (1958). *The psychology of interpersonal relations.* New York: Wiley.

Hollander, E.P., & Offermann, L.R (1990) Power and leadership in organizations: Relationships in transition. *American Psychologist, 45,* 179–189.

Jones, E.E., & Davis, K.E. (1965). From acts to dispositions: The attribution process in person perception. In L. Berkowitz (Ed.) *Advances in experimental social psychology* (Vol. 2). New York: Academic Press.

Jones, E.E., & Nisbett, R.E. (1972). The actor and the observer: Divergent perceptions of the causes of behavior. In E.E. Jones, D.E. Kanouse, H.H. Kelley, R.E. Nisbett, S. Valins, & B. Weiner (Eds.), *Attribution: Perceiving the cause of behavior* (pp. 79–94). Morristown, NJ: General Learning Press.

Kanter, R.M. (1977). *Men and Women of the corporation.* New York: Basic Books.

Katz, D., & Kahn, R.L. (1978). *The social psychology of organizations.* New York: Wiley and Sons.

Kelley, H.H. (1967). Attribution theory in social psychology. In D. Levine (Ed.), *Nebraska symposium on motivation* (Vol. 15, pp 192–240). Lincoln: University of Nebraska Press.

Kelley, H.H. (1972). Attribution of social interaction. In E.E. Jones, D.D. Kanouse, H.H. Kelley, R.E. Nisbett, S. Valins, & B. Weiner (Eds.), *Attribution: Perceiving causes of behavior* (pp 1–27). Morristown, NJ: General Learning Press.

Keller, T., & Dansereau, F. (1995). Leadership and empowerment: A social exchange perspective. *Human Relations, 48,* 127–146.

Kelley, H.H., & Michela, L.L. (1980). Attribution theory and research. *Annual Review of Psychology, 31,* 457–501.

Kelley, H.H., & Thibaut, J.W. (1978). *Interpersonal relations: A theory of interdependence.* New York: Wiley-Interscience.

Kenney, R.A., Blascovich, J., & Shaver, P.R. (1994). Implicit leadership theories: Prototypes for new leaders. *Basic and Applied Social Psychology, 15,* 409–437.

Kim, M.P., & Rosenberg, S. (1980). Comparison of two structural models of implicit personal theory. *Journal of Personality and Social Psychology, 38,* 375–389.

Kipnis, D. (1976). *The powerholders.* Chicago: The University of Chicago Press.

Kipnis, D., Castell, P.J., Gergen, M., & Mauch, D. (1976). Metamorphic effects of power. *Journal of Applied Psychology, 61,* 127–135.

Konst, D. (1998). *Effects of hierarchical positions on social inference.* Dissertation, Leiden University, The Netherlands.

Konst, D., Vonk, R., & Van der Vlist, R. (1999). Inferences about causes and consequences of behavior of leaders and subordinates. *Journal of Organizational Behavior, 20,* 261–271.

Kouzes, J.M., & Posner, B.Z. (1995). *The leadership challenge.* San Francisco: Jossey-Bass.

Kruglanski, A.W. (1975). The endogeneous-exogeneous partition in attribution theory. *Psychological Review, 82,* 387–406.

Kruglanski, A.W., & Freund, T. (1983). The freezing and unfreezing of lay-inferences: Effects of impression primacy, ethnic stereotyping, and numerical anchoring. *Journal of Experimental Social Psychology, 19,* 448–468.

Lawler, E.E. (1989). Participative management in the US: Three classics revisited. In C.J. Lammers & G. Széll (Eds.), *International Handbook of Participation in Organizations* (Vol. 1). (pp. 91–97). Oxford: Oxford University Press.

Lerner, M.J. (1980). *The belief in a just world: A fundamental delusion.* New York: Plenum Press.

Lord, R.G., DeVader, C.L., & Alliger, G.M. (1986). A meta-analysis of the relationship between personality traits and leadership perceptions: An application of validity generalization procedures. *Journal of Applied Psychology, 71,* 402–410.

Lord, R.G., & Emrich, C.G. (2000). Thinking outside the box by looking inside the box: Extending the cognitive revolution in leadership research. *Leadership Quarterly, 11,* 551–579.

Lord, R.G., Foti, R., & de Vader, C.(1984). A test of leadership categorization theory : Internal structure, information processing and leadership perceptions. *Organizational Behavior and Human Performance, 34,* 343–378.

Lord, R.G., & Maher, K.J. (1991). *Leadership and information processing: Linking perceptions and performance.* Boston: Routledge.

Mackie, D.M., Hamilton, D.L., Susskind, J., & Rosselli, F. (1996). Social psychological foundations of stereotype formation. In C.N. Macrae, C. Stangor, & M. Hewstone (Eds), *Stereotypes and stereotyping.* New York: The Guilford Press.

McGregor, D. (1960). *The human side of enterprise.* New York: McGraw Hill.

Miles, R.E. (1965). Human relations or human resources? *Harvard Business Review, 43,* 148–163.

Murphy, K.R., Herr, B.M., Lockhart, M.C., & Maguire, E. (1986). Evaluating the performance of paper people. *Journal of Applied Psychology, 71,* 654–661.

Neuberg, S.L., & Fiske, S.T. (1987). Motivational influences on impression formation: Outcome dependency, accuracy-driven attention, and individuating processes. *Journal of Personality and Social Psychology, 53,* 431–444.

Nisbett, R.E., & Wilson, T.D. (1977). The halo effect: Evidence for unconscious alteration of judgments. *Journal of Personality and Social Psychology, 35,* 250–256.

Offerman, L.R., Kennedy, J.K., & Wirtz, P.W. (1994). Implicit leadership theories: Content, structure, and generalizability. *Leadership Quarterly, 5,* 43–58.

Osgood, C.E., Suci, G.J., & Tannenbaum, P.H. (1957). *The measurement of meaning.* Urbana: University of Illinois Press.

Palich, L.E., & Hom, P.W. (1992). The impact of leader power and behavior on leadership perceptions: A LISREL test of an expanded categorization theory of leadership model. *Group and Organization Management, 76*, 279–296.

Petty, R.E., & Cacioppo, J.T. (1986). *Communication and persuasion: Central and peripheral routes to attitude change.* New York: Springer-Verlag.

Pfeffer, J. (1977). The ambiguity of leadership. *Academy of Management Review, 2*, 104–112.

Pfeffer, J., & Salancik, G.R. (1978). *The external control of organizations: A resource dependence perspective.* New York: Harper & Row.

Phillips, J.S. (1984). The accuracy of leadership ratings: A cognitive categorization perspective. *Organizational Behavior and Human Performance, 33*, 143–163.

Phillips, J.S., & Lord, R.G. (1981). Causal attributions and perceptions of leadership. *Organizational Behavior and Human Performance, 28*, 143–163.

Pratto, F., & John, O.P. (1991). Automatic vigilance: The attention-grabbing power of negative social information. *Journal of Personality and Social Psychology, 61*, 380–391.

Raven, B.H., & Kruglanski, A.W. (1970). Conflict and power. In P. Swingle (Ed.), *The structure of conflict.* New York: Academic Press.

Reeder, G.D., & Brewer, M.B. (1979). A schematic model of dispositional attribution in interpersonal perception. *Psychological Review, 86*, 61–79.

Rosch, E.H. (1978). Principles of categorization. In E.H. Rosch & B.B. Lloyd (Eds.), *Cognition and categorization.* Hillsdale, NJ: Erlbaum.

Rosenberg, S. (1977). New approaches to the analysis of personal constructs in person perception. In J.K. Cole & A.W. Landfield (Eds), *Nebraska symposium on motivation* (pp. 179–242). Lincoln: University of Nebraska Press.

Rosenberg, S., & Sedlak, A (1972). Structural representations of implicit personality theory. In L. Berkowitz (Ed.), *Advances in experimental social psychology* (Vol. 6). New York: Academic Press.

Rush, M.C., & Russell, J.E. (1988). Leader prototypes and prototype-contingent consensus in leader behavior descriptions. *Journal of Experimental Social Psychology, 24*, 88–104.

Sanbonmatsu, D.M., & Fazio, R.H. (1990). The role of attitudes in memory-based decision making. *Journal of Personality and Social Psychology, 59*, 614–622.

Sande, G.N., Ellard, J.H., & Ross, M. (1986). Effect of arbitrarily assigned status labels on self-perceptions: The mere position effect. *Journal of Personality and Social Psychology, 50*, 684–689.

Schneider, D.J. (1973).Implicit personality theory: A review. *Psychological Bulletin, 79*, 294–309.

Schneider, D.J., Hastorf, A.H., & Ellsworth, P.C. (1979). *Person perception* (2nd ed.). Reading, MA: Addison-Wesley.

Smith, J.A., & Foti, R.J. (1998). A pattern approach to the study of leader emergence. *Leadership Quarterly, 9*, 147–160.

Smith, E.R., & Miller, F. (1983). Mediation among attributional inferences and comprehension processes: Initial findings and a general method. *Journal of Personality and Social Psychology, 52*, 689–699.

Tetlock, P.E., & Boettger, R. (1989). Accountability: A social magnifier of the dilution effect. *Journal of Personality and Social Psychology, 57*, 388–398.

Thorndyke, E.L. (1920). A constant error in psychological ratings. *Journal of Applied Psychology, 4,* 25–29.

Uleman, J.S., & Moskowitz, G.B. (1994). Unintended effects of goals on unintended inferences. *Journal of Personality and Social Psychology, 66,* 490–501.

Van der Vlist, R. (1991). *Leiderschap in organisaties: kernvraagstuk voor de jaren '90.* Utrecht: Lemma B.V.

Vonk. R. (1993). Individual differences and common dimensions in Implicit personality theory. *British Journal of Social Psychology, 32,* 209–226.

Vonk, R. (1996). Negativity and potency effects in impression formation. *European Journal of Social Psychology, 26,* 851–865.

Walton, R.E. (1985). From control to commitment in the workplace. *Harvard Business Review, 63,* 76–84.

Weiner, B. (1985). Spontaneous causal thinking. *Psychological Bulletin, 92,* 74–84.

Yukl, G. (1994). *Leadership in organizations* (3d ed.). Englewood Cliffs, NJ: Prentice-Hall.

Yukl, G. (2002). *Leadership in organizations* (5th ed.). Englewood Cliffs, NJ: Prentice-Hall.

Zajonc, R.B. (1968). Attitudinal effects of mere exposure. *Journal of Personality and Social Psychology,* Monograph Supplement, 9 (2), 1–27.

CHAPTER 12

THE ROLE OF IMPLICIT ORGANIZATION THEORY IN THE START-UP PHASE OF NEW FIRMS

Brigitte Kroon

ABSTRACT

Entrepreneurs start organizations that reflect their knowledge and experience, and that fit with the expectations of other people and institutions that are involved with the start-up organization. To understand the relationship between the cognition of entrepreneurs and the firms they develop, the concept of implicit organization theory is introduced in this chapter. Implicit organization theories are structured cognitive schemas that help make sense of organizations. Everybody holds implicit organization theories; the entrepreneur therefore has to deal with the implicit organization theories of others when realizing his or her idea. These others can potentially reject the new venture idea of the entrepreneur, depending on the implicit evaluations they hold upon the idea of the entrepreneur. In the interaction and communication about a new venture, implicit organization theories melt together into an accepted organizational blueprint: the socially legitimate core of a new organization. It is reasoned that these early cognitions and decisions have a

Implicit Leadership Theories: Essays and Explorations, pages 333–348

lasting impact on de core of the organization as it develops further on. Implicit organization theory thus sheds light on understanding the development of entrepreneurial firms.

INTRODUCTION

Entrepreneurs build new organizations, and that is viewed as important, because this generates new jobs and economic growth. There is a vein of innovativeness over the words *new organization*; it implies a fresh idea, a challenge to exploit a truly original opportunity in a very unique way. And, certainly in theory, entrepreneurs have no limits in to build any organization they would like.

In practice, however, the innovativeness of entrepreneurs seems rather limited. Entrepreneurs prefer to start a new business within their own knowledge and experience (Aldrich, 1999). Their knowledge is limited to the information they can obtain, and based on this limited information and knowledge, they need to make their best guesses about for example the market and the competition they will meet (Atherton, 2003). No wonder that the primary source of knowledge and information that entrepreneurs use to find business opportunities is their previous work experience (Romanelli & Schoonhoven, 2001). Another indication that the richness of possible new organizations isn't fully utilized can be derived from institutionalism theory. This theory states that organizations accommodate themselves to their environments, in order to be accepted as a recognizable and legitimate player in the market in which the organization operates (DiMaggio & Powell, 1983). So on the one hand entrepreneurs have a limited view of all possibilities, and on the other hand there are forces in the environment of the entrepreneur that are normative for the legitimation of the new organization that frame the choices of entrepreneurs.

The question raises in what way the ideas for new organizations of entrepreneurs are framed. And, if the roots for a business idea are grounded in the knowledge and experience of entrepreneurs, how will this knowledge and experience infer with the actual creation of new organizations? Although the question of entrepreneurship has produced a long tradition of research, little work is known that answers these questions. A good deal of entrepreneurship research has focused on characteristics of entrepreneurs like personality (e.g., Ciavarella, Buchholtz, Riordan, Gatewood, & Stokes, 2004), human capital (e.g., Colombo, Delmastro, & Grilli, 2004), or ambitiousness (e.g., Gundry & Welsch, 2001). These characteristics are often used to explain for example the venture creation decision (e.g., Chen, Greene, & Crick, 1998), or the growth of the new venture (e.g., Gundry & Welsch, 2001). Only some research has related the content of the cognitive frames of entrepreneurs to the actual form of new organizations (e.g., Baron, Burton, & Hannan, 1999).

This chapter will take a cognitive approach to entrepreneurship. I introduce the concept of implicit organization theory in this chapter to indicate that entrepreneurs don't start with a *tabula rasa* while developing their organizations, but that they take their decisions based on framed knowledge about organizations. In short, an implicit organization theory is an organized configuration of knowledge about organizations, derived from past experience that is used to interpret experiences. Implicit organization theories unconsciously infer with start-up decisions of entrepreneurs.

Attention to the impact of implicit organization theories on decision processes of entrepreneurs in starting organizations is important, because it is thought that these early decisions lay the foundation of the later firm (Aldrich, 1999; Baker, 2000). Decisions taken in the start-up phase of new ventures build the organization, not only in terms of product, market and financial position, but also lay the foundations for the social infrastructure of the organization, such as human resource practices (Baker, 2000; Baron et al., 1999), power balance (Greenwood & Hinings, 1996) and the kind of external relations build up by the organization (Nicholls-Nixon, Cooper, & Woo, 2000).

The influence of implicit organization theories on entrepreneurship is twofold. First, entrepreneurs have to deal with the expectations and perceptions of customers, venture capitalists, employees and competitors. Implicit theories of others therefore define the context in which the new venture will exist.

Besides, implicit organization theories of the founder him- or herself interfere with start-up decisions. The room for innovativeness seems thus to be limited by the cognitive frames of entrepreneurs and by the wish to meet expectations of others in order to gain legitimation.

A following question concerns how implicit theories of both the founder and others involved, together develop into a socially legitimate idea of an organization. In this chapter, the concept of a blueprint will be used to refer to a shared meaning of a new organization. A blueprint is a story of the why, what and how of the organization, that legitimates the new organization (Lounsbury & Glynn, 2001). Blueprints are shared cognitions between the entrepreneur and the new organization's stakeholders. Without an actual organization present, all people involved with the entrepreneur share a quite explicit idea about what the organization-to-be will be like.

The blueprint forms the basis on which the actual organization will develop. The core of the blueprint seems reluctant to change. As organizations face challenges, they try alternative strategies on non-core aspects of the organization, but these alternative strategies seldom touch the core of the organization (Nicholls-Nixon et al., 2000). The blueprint of the founder thus seems to have a lasting impact on organizations. The blueprint becomes a quite stable dominant logic (Prahald & Bettis, 1986), or deep-level structure of the organization, that doesn't really change anymore even after the founder has left the organization (Baron et al., 1999).

The chapter will first explore the concept of implicit organization theory and how it applies to everybody who deals with organizations. Next is examined what frames the implicit organization theories of entrepreneurs. Then the linkage of implicit organization theory to organizational blueprint is described. Finally it is described how the blueprint transfers into a dominant logic of the new organization.

IMPLICIT ORGANIZATION THEORY

An implicit theory is a cognitive schema: an organized configuration of knowledge, derived from past experience, which is used to interpret experiences (Hastie, 1980). These individual schemas are unconscious memory processing structures, applied to encode and retrieve information (Fiske & Taylor, 1991). Cognitive schemas are more or less structured, depending on the familiarity of the event (Goia & Poole, 1984). In novel situations, bottom up information processing will occur: all parts of the information are observed equally to understand the event. In most events however, some kind of top-down information processing is taking place: by observing only certain aspects of an event, our minds make up for the missing information by applying schematic restored experiential information (Walsh, 1995). When an event has a high degree of familiarity, almost automatically the prototypical schema is activated (Goia & Poole, 1984). Fiske and Taylor (1991) define a prototype as a strong schematic representation about (a group of) people. Prototypes are activated when people are confronted with only a few characteristics of other people, thus providing the missing information (Fiske & Taylor, 1991). Implicit theories are strong prototypes: with only a few characteristics, a whole picture of the subject is filled, and associated with typical behaviors and consequences. Implicit theories help to interpret stimuli and consequently provide meaning and, finally, help to make sense of the world. The sense making process involves observing events, detecting or abstracting patterns of relationships between events and interpreting these events and their relationships in psychologically meaningful terms (Goia & Poole, 1984). Although cognitive schemas obviously offer advantages in terms of the speed of information processing and the provision of meaning, the downside can be that some information is overlooked or misinterpreted, as a simplified version of the reality is taken for real (Walsh, 1995).

Implicit theories have been successfully applied to explain a diverse range of events, such as the perception of other people's personality (Bruner & Taguiri, 1954; Schneider, 1973), leadership (Eden & Leviatan, 1975), employees (e.g., De Vries & Gelder, this volume), work relationships (Uhl-Bien, this volume), and the attribution of the success or failure of organizations to top managers (e.g., Meindl, 1985). An extension of implicit theory, is the application of implicit theory to non-people events, such as organizations. Goia and Poole's (1984) description of automatic schematic responses of employees to highly typical organizational events can be perceived in this light. Also, from research to the perception of applicants, venture capitalists and consumers, the concept of implicit organization theory makes sense. For example, Lievens and Highhouse (2003) showed the importance of organizational attributions of applicants in the perception of the attractiveness of the organization as an employer. For consumers, Balmer (2004) for example showed that the attribution of the organizational identity plays a role in consumer buying behavior.

Implicit organization theory means that people hold stereotyped ideas about organizations. That is, when confronted with some organization characteristics, people fill in the gaps about the organization with their implicit organization image, and consequently have opinions about, for example, the type of employees working there, the relationships the organization holds with internal and external parties, the behavioral patterns within the organization, the organizational structure, and the organizational culture. Implicit organization theories differ from organizational images. Organizational image is always related to an existing firm (e.g., Lievens & Highhouse, 2003). An implicit organization theory is a schema that applies to "prototypical" firms. Little research is known that explores the perceptions of organizations in terms of prototypes. One exception is the work done by Philips (1994). Her study evaluated perceptions of employees in two different industries (wineries and museums), and compared their conceptualizations of their own industry and the other industry. Substantial differences were found in conceptualizations of membership, competition, the origins of "truth," the purpose of work, and the nature of work relationships (Philips, 1994).

These conceptualizations are the shared stereotypes of "typical" firms in an industry.

People evaluate these stereotypical aspects positively or negatively. For example, a venture capitalist will look for stereotypes of proven successful organizations while judging a business plan of a potential new venture, and when the business plan doesn't fit to a success-theory, it will have a greater chance to be rejected (Lounsbury & Glynn, 2001).

Consequently, implicit theories interfere with the creation of new ventures. Implicit theories of customers, bankers, suppliers and other stakeholders define the social context of the new organization, and the implicit organization theory of the founder, in the form of previous experience, knowledge, and personal characteristics, interferes with decisions to be taken while building up the firm. In the next section, the role of implicit theories of the founder of an organization is described.

IMPLICIT ORGANIZATION THEORY OF ENTREPRENEURS

Entrepreneurs create organizations. This means that they have quite some freedom to build any organization they can imagine. Lacking a real organization, there is not an emergent implicit schema that applies automatically. However, implicit theories will intervene with the rationality of the entrepreneur because a complete experience-free context simply doesn't exist. Some events will always be there to evoke some kind of implicit theory, like the type of product or service, the location, or the necessity of fund raising with venture capitalists. Besides known events, entrepreneurs have to make guesses about the future, and for this unfamiliar situation no stereotypical frame exists. So on the one hand, there may be some implicit schemas available concerning the known aspects of the start-up but, on the other hand, there is quite some uncertainty because it is hard to predict organization success without organization history. Atherthon (2003) states that under highly uncertain conditions, entrepreneurs trust upon previous experience, and on information gathered with key relationships in their networks. They *elaborate* on this fragmented knowledge, to *create* a schema that makes sense of their business plan for success (Atherton, 2003). Compared to implicit theory, in starting a business, founders are building a frame instead of simply applying an implicit theory. In this light it is sensible to discern typical from untypical situations (Goia & Poole, 1984). Typicality refers to the frequency with which people are confronted with an event. Starting a business is a partially atypical situation because most entrepreneurs start a business only once in their lives, although they may have (management) experience in other businesses. In more atypical situations, the cognitive structure of information becomes more conscious, people think about their options and compare or adjust possible scripts (Goia & Poole, 1984). So, the awareness of the situation and the accompanying scripts leads to the possibility to evaluate stereotypical aspects of implicit theories. Scott (1991, p. 181) theorizes that all founders of organizations exercise some choice to puzzle out their optimal structure by combining information from multiple institutional sources. He states that the combination of imposed (obligatory), authorized (strong pressures to build organization in a certain way), induced ("best practice" in a given organizational community), acquired (by education or experience) and imprinted (time-bound fashions of organizing) sources leads to a prevailing organization structure in an industry. However, Scott (1991) acknowledges that there are different paths to combine these institutional sources. This means, the entrepreneur can make choices from the aspects of the implicit theories accompanying the potential firm, and decide to continue with these aspects (which now become explicit instead of implicit or automated) or to take an alternative route.

To understand entrepreneurial cognition and the subsequent construction of implicit theory by entrepreneurs, it is helpful to gain some understanding about the content and structure of cognitive frames of entrepreneurs (Walsh, 1995). Aldrich (1999) summarizes the information resources that define the cognition of entrepreneurs, namely: former work experience, the consultation of experts, and the imitation and copying of successful others. First, former work experience defines for a large part the human capital of an entrepreneur. Human capital is hard to imitate, and is therefore seen as a valuable resource for gaining competitive advantage. Work experience within an industry also means that entrepreneurs are familiar with the norms within their industry, which makes it more likely that their cognition will reflect these norms. Second, entrepreneurs frequently consult (Aldrich, 1999). Most entrepreneurs seek for advice from experts in their network, which, depending on the strength of the network, can also lead to reinforcing cognitive structures in an industry (Aldrich, 1999). Third, the imitation and copying of successful other organizations also play a role in the cognition of entrepreneurs. Some entrepreneurs have a vision of building an organization like "[...] Hewlett-Packard, coupled with writings on Japanese management styles in the 1980's" (Baron et al., 1999, p. 542).

CONTENTS OF THE COGNITION OF ENTREPRENEURS

Some research has been carried out to predict the venture creation decision or on venture success in terms of financial growth or wealth by investigating the content of the cognition of entrepreneurs. For example, Mitchell, Smith, Seawright, and Morse (2000) cross-culturally researched cognitive scripts of managers, entrepreneurs, and students in seven countries, that relate to the venture creation decision. It was found that the decision to start a venture relates to willingness, ability, and arrangement scripts. Willingness means that entrepreneurs, more than other managers, look for opportunities, are prepared to work hard to achieve results, and keep an open eye at business opportunities (Mitchel et al., 2000). Chen et al. (1998) found that founders significantly varied from non-founding owners of businesses in their perceived capabilities in innovation and risk taking. Gundry and Welsch (2001) found a positive relation between the founder's commitment to the firm's success and the speed of growth of the venture. Hence, willingness has to do with the ambition that people have to make their business a success. The more ambitious the schema of the entrepreneur is, the more likely their firm will succeed (Gundry & Welsch, 2001).

Ability means that entrepreneurs quickly diagnose situations, business decisions and opportunities (Mitchel et al., 2000). The venture arrangement script helps the entrepreneur to protect an idea, to build and maintain a venture network, to have access to general business resources and to have venture specific skills. These scripts were the same all over the seven countries, and only a small effect was found for cultural factors, which indicate that entrepreneurs internationally share similar implicit theories (Mitchell et al., 2000). Kets de Vries, Shekshnia, Korotov, and Florent-Treacy (2004) illustrate, with a series of case studies of new Russian ventures, the influence of country (culture) on business creation. Their descriptions also indicate a mixture of Mitchell et al.'s (2000) generic entrepreneurial arrangement scripts, with an amount of Russian institutional inheritance. This cultural inheritance seems mainly to be reflected in the management structure (Kets de Vries et al., 2004). Suthcliffe and Huber (1989) found that a large part of the variance in individual top-level executives' perceptions of aspects of their respective organizations environment is explained by their organizational and industry membership, which again indicates that implicit theories are formed by experience.

Thus, besides implicit theories of entrepreneurs that relate to the venture creation decision or the determination to venture success, theories about the form of the future organization define the ground for the actual building of the firm. Implicit theories about organization form are also related to organization success (Gundry & Welsch, 2001; Jenkins & Johnson, 1997). Entrepreneurs that hold the idea of the necessity of structuring the management of the organization that have a vision on the business (Jenkins & Johnson, 1997; Gundry & Welsch, 2001), on team-based work, on leadership and on the use of financial sources are more successful than entrepreneurs that hold a more ad-hoc vision (Gundry & Welsch, 2001).

In summary, entrepreneurs build their theories of organizations by relying on experience, by consulting others and by looking at other organizations. The success of the start-up is thus related to the cognitive frames of the entrepreneur. Cognitive frames of successful entrepreneurs reflect attributions like ambition, opportunity seeking, networking and persistence. Besides these entrepreneurial attributions, cognitive schemas about the form of the organization have a relation with organization success. The combination of the founder's implicit organization theories and entrepreneurial attributions are the ground for the formation of a more explicit story of a new organization: the organizational blueprint. In the next paragraph the concept of a blueprint will be explained.

BLUEPRINT

A large part of the creation of a new organization by an entrepreneur is convincing others about the viability of the business idea. In the communication process a story of the new organization is shaped. This story is reinforced by all people involved, and, as a result, even without the actual existence of the organization, a clear picture about the "why," "what," and "how" of the new firm comes to life: the so-called blueprint. This blueprint is the basis to provide legitimation of the new firm in the society (Lounsbury & Glynn, 2001).

An important difference between implicit organization theory and organizational blueprint is that the latter builds on the cognitive contents of the first, but is tested and adjusted in the interaction with others. This process of testing and reinforcing provides meaning to the blueprint. Meaning is a necessary construct to understand behaviors and decisions and to get meaning. People negotiate it with members in their social system (Rentsch, 1990).

Another effect of this interaction process, which provides meaning to the blueprint, is that this meaning becomes the shared perception of the new firm (Lounsbury & Glynn, 2001). So, where the implicit organization theory is mainly a personal construct, the blueprint is a shared cognitive framework of an organization. This shared cognitive aspect is important for the viability of organizations, because it functions as the legitimation card to the society in which the organization will operate.

In the process from implicit organization theories of a founder to an explicit and viable blueprint of a new firm, the implicit ideas of the entrepreneur are tested to the context of the new firm. Communication is the platform at which the ideas are tested, and the story is the form. An entrepreneurial story consists of: "[a] *narrative subject* as the individual entrepreneur or the new venture, *the ultimate object or goal of the narrative* as a successful new enterprise, profitability, funding by venture capitalists, or a positive reputation with potential stakeholders; and the *destinator* as the corporate and societal environment in which the narrative subjects operates" (Lounsbury & Glynn, 2001, p. 549). The story develops over time, its fundaments raise from the implicit organization theory of the founder, but at the time of going public, these theories are strongly intermingled with societal expectations into a blueprint (Lounsbury & Glynn, 2001). Entrepreneurs that insufficiently succeed to create a linkage in their blueprint to external expectations will have smaller opportunities to gain resources, and will be less viable. Reynolds and White (1997) expect that only half of the people with an idea to start a business, actually take the next step from idea to the start-up of a company. One reason for this could lay in the lack of attractiveness of the founder's implicit organization theory.

The blueprint becomes the core of the new venture. For the entrepreneur, it is the sense-making framework of the enterprise, and the more it is used, the more automatic and internalized this cognition becomes, forming a new implicit organization theory about their own venture. Also, in a larger social context, the blueprint has provided meaning to the new venture. Thus stated, it seems logically unwise to drastically change a socially accepted blueprint of an organization, and endanger the acquired legitimation. Some empirical research to young enterprises supports the idea of the persistence of the blueprint as the deep level structure of the organization (Baron et al., 1999; Nicholls-Nixon et al., 2000).

Baron et al. (1999) interviewed founders of new enterprises in Sillicon Valley about the blueprints of their organizations, and found a significant relation between the founder's blueprint of the employment system in their organizations, and the way that the administration and management were structured in the organization. Founders holding a blueprint that emphasizes formal control mechanisms like procedures and systems earlier led to a bureaucratic and layered organization than organizations whose founders hold a vision of committing people to their organization by providing a family like culture. Besides, they showed that this effect only counted for the founder of the organization and not for a CEO that succeeded the founder. Founder effects were still measured even if the founder had left the organization (Baron et al., 1999). These results indicate a continued reinforcement of the original blueprint by all members of an organization.

Other empirical evidence supporting the persistence of founder blueprints on organizations comes from Nicholls-Nixon et al. (2000). In a longitudinal study of 400 young businesses, it was found that under the perception of great environmental hostility, such as aggressive competition and scarcity of resources, entrepreneurs start to experiment with alternative strategies to survive. However, it was found that this strategic experimentation mainly applied to the peripheral dimensions of the organization. These are operational decisions, the allocation of time and effort and the competitive emphasis chosen.

The core dimensions of the organization's strategy, which define the purpose of the organization and the legitimation to organizational members and others, were more stable, even under a perceived hostile environment. Nicholls-Nixon et al. (2000) assume that this is because peripheral dimensions are easier to change than the core dimensions of the organization.

Baron et al. (1999) found similar results in an investigation to the adoption of standard HR policies and management titles by new ventures. It was found that these superficial policies were adopted by the organization to satisfy external relations, but that this did not affect the deep level blueprint of the organization. It was found that the imprint of the founder's blueprint had the strongest effect on the core culture of the organization, namely the propensity to rely on self-management by employees, versus a specialized regime to control the organization.

In this paragraph, the development of a shared blueprint as the founding condition of a new venture was discussed. A blueprint is a narrative story of a new venture that provides meaning of the venture to both the entrepreneurs and the social environment they are dealing with. The blueprint consists of parts of the implicit organization theories of founders, mingled with aspects of implicit theories from the social context of the founder. The blueprint thus reflects unique characteristics of the founder, and provides legitimation of the new venture in the society. The blueprint has enduring effects on the new venture. It creates the deep level structure of the firm, which is unlikely to change in the first years of the firm, because the new firm is dependent on the legitimation gained by a socially accepted blueprint.

In the next paragraph the emergence of a shared cognition in a new organization is discussed.

BLUEPRINT TO DOMINANT LOGIC

When the new organization grows further, the blueprint becomes a dominant way of thinking within the organization. Some longitudinal studies have shown that this dominant logic is decisive for the way organizations manage their business (Côté, Langley, & Pasquero, 1999). The concept of the "dominant logic" of the organization was originally developed by Prahaled and Bettis (1986). Their definition of the concept was "the way in which *managers* conceptualize the business and make critical resource allocation decisions—be it in technologies, product development, distribution, advertising, or human resource management (...). The dominant logic is stored via schemas and hence can be thought of as a structure. However, some of what is stored is process knowledge" (Prahaled & Bettis, 1986, p. 490, italics added). The dominant logic can be viewed as a shared cognitive structure. Shared cognitive structures of employees of an organization shape a context for appropriate thinking and acting (Goia & Poole, 1984). Some research is known to the effect of the dominant logic of a management team on the performance of an organization. Löwstedt (1993) found a relationship between key decision makers' organizing framework and the way three comparable organizations differed in implementing new technologies. Côté et al. (1999) showed that the acquisition strategies of a Canadian engineering firm were affected by the dominant logic of the organizational decision makers, and that the origins of this logic were to be found in the early years of the organization. This indicates a linkage between the blueprint of the start-up firm and the dominant logic of the key decision makers.

However, it may be obvious that there is a linkage between the blueprint that helped founding the organization, and the shared cognitive structure of the top management team of a (new) firm that extends to the lower regions of the organization. In other words, how dominant is the dominant logic within the organization?

Walsh (1995) provides some cognitive logic when he writes: "when a group of individuals is brought together, each with their own knowledge structure about a particular information environment, some kind of emergent collective knowledge structure is likely to exist" (Walsh, 1995, p. 291). Thus it is assumed that within organizations, people tend to have similar cognitive structures. There is empirical evidence that employees within an organization share ideas about the organization identity, which influences how they perceive and deal with issues (Dutton & Dukerich, 1991). Rentsch (1990), however, has found evidence that the level at which these cognitions are shared is the strongest at groups that work together intensely.

Obviously, the downside of a shared dominant logic is a misperception because of memory discrimination. Memory discrimination occurs when strong prototypical stimuli are present in an event, that lead to an imperfect or misconceived picture of the situation (Walsh & Ungson, 1991), which ultimately can lead to wrong decisions.

A shared dominant logic within organizations certainly hold advantages as well: the more strongly the images are shared, the better the behaviors of employees can be aligned and predicted (Bowen & Ostroff, 2004). Bowen and Ostroff (2004) suggest that a strong climate helps to align people's behavior to the desired outcomes of the organization. Climate is defined here as: "a shared perception of what the organization is like in terms of practices, policies, procedures, routines, and rewards—what is important and what behaviors are expected and rewarded (...)—and is based on shared perceptions among employees within formal organizational units" (Bowen & Ostroff, 2004, p. 205). From the evolutionary perspective of this chapter, it can be questioned whether a strong climate really is as designable as Bowen and Ostroff (2004) suggest, or if, at the contrary, climate is a consequence of organization history. Process theorists take the latter perspective: an organizational climate is formed in the history of an organization (Baron et al., 1999; Côté et al., 1999; Suthcliffe &

Huber, 1998). This is in line with the reasoning about the persistence of the founders' blueprint on the organization.

In return, the organizational climate is an important source for the development of individual cognitive frames (Walsh, 1995), which makes it difficult for any change agent to treat an organization as if it were a clean sheet on which a new climate could be designated. Change management literature supports the view that organizational climate tends to be reinforced by organizational members (Molinsky, 1999; Greenwood & Hinings, 1996).

So, the circle is complete. From the implicit organization theory of one founder through the socially accepted new venture blueprint, a new organization is formed that in turn creates an environment that shapes the implicit organization theories of its members.

CONCLUSION/DISCUSSION

In this chapter the idea of implicit theories was extended to the field of the perception of organizations, and especially on the effect that implicit theories play in the foundation of new organizations. The chapter started by defining implicit organization theories of individuals, and built on the concept to demonstrate a lasting impact of implicit theories of founders, stakeholders and organization members on the deep level climate of the organization.

There is little doubt that new ventures play a vital role in the global economy. However, the explanation for entrepreneurial activity and new venture development is still unclear. The cognitive perspective taken in this chapter seems promising, because it builds a bridge between cognition and the social environment in a field that is dominated by economic perspectives.

Entrepreneurs will have to be made aware of their lasting impact on the organization, and can be stimulated to think about their blueprint by consciously looking into the future and picturing a clear vision for their organization. As with attributions, implicit organization theories may change when people are given more information about organizations. To understand the importance of entrepreneurial implicit organization theory, it will be helpful to research the effects of different types of implicit organization theories on the performance of developing organizations.

To do so, however, we must first gain further understanding about the concept of implicit organization theory. It will be interesting to find out if, similar to implicit leadership theories, patterns of cognitions are traceable over groups of people. Moving away from organization image research, which focuses on the image of specific firms, the accent must be laid on the attributions people apply to prototypes of organizations. Some similar work has been done on the existence of industry culture (Philips, 1994), which may count as a guideline for researching implicit organization theories. One explicit perspective will need to focus on implicit organization theories of founders, and find out if there are differences in the implicit organization theories of entrepreneurs and non-entrepreneurs.

Additional questions that come to mind concern the structure of implicit organization theories, their stability over time, and events that lead to adaptation of the implicit organization theory.

Next, the development of an organizational blueprint will need to be on the research agenda. Launsbury and Glynn (2001) have importantly pointed out the role of social interaction at the start-up phase of a firm. It will be interesting to find out the importance of implicit organization theory, and find out when, why, and how implicit theories are changed to meet expectations and other challenges from reality. To date, there is no research known that investigates the ideas provided by Lounsbury and Glynn (2001) on the development of a shared meaning of an organization (i.e., a blueprint).

Finally, to investigate the evolutionary development from a founder's implicit organization theory, via a shared blueprint into a dominant logic or deep-level organization climate, longitudinal studies that follow founders and their organizations are desirable. The SPEC study of Baron et al. (1999) gives some direction for the impact that blueprints have on HR practices and organizational climate. Their results are consistent and promising, but need to be tested in other industries and countries.

This chapter has taken a bird's-eye view on a complicated topic. I have thought it to be important to theoretically relate topics that not have received attention in a path-dependent relation. This means however that is has become a theoretical sketch of the impact of cognition on both the perception, creation, and becoming of organizations, both on individual and organizational level. No justice is done to extensively discuss these separate parts. As suggested in the topic list for further research, it will be impossible to test the bird's-eye view without fully understanding the parts that create the whole. The challenge now is to tackle the parts and to discover the whole picture.

ACKNOWLEDGMENTS

I would like to thank Birgit Schyns for the opportunity to contribute a chapter to this book, and both her and Mary Uhl-Bien for their helpful suggestions on the manuscript.

REFERENCES

Aldrich, H.E. (1999). *Organizations evolving.* London: Sage.

Atherton, A. (2003). The uncertainty of knowing: An analysis of the nature of knowledge in a small business context. *Human Relations, 56,* 1379–1398.

Baker, E.A. (2000). *Responses to dependence: A social exchange model of employment practices in entrepreneurial firms.* Dissertation, University of North Carolina, Chapel Hill.

Balmer, J.M.T., & Gray, E.R. (2003). Corporate brands: What are they? *European Journal of Marketing, 37,* 972–997.

Baron, J.N., Burton, M.D., & Hannan, M.T. (1999). Engineering bureaucracy: The genesis of formal policies, positions, and structures in high-technology firms. *The Journal of Law, Economics & Organization, 15,* 1–41.

Baron, J.N., Hannan, M.T., & Burton, M.D. (1999). Building the iron cage: Determinants of managerial intensity in the early years of organizations. *American Sociological Review, 64,* 527–547.

Bowen, D.E., & Ostroff, C. (2004). Understanding HRM-firm performance linkages: The role of the "strength" of the HRM system. *Academy of Management Review, 29,* 203–221.

Bruner, J.S., & Tagiuiri, R. (1954). Person perception. In G. Lindzey (Ed.), *Handbook of Social Psychology* (Vol. 2). Reading, MA: Addison-Wesley.

Ciavarella, M.A., Buchholtz, A.K., Riordan, C.M., Gatewood, R.D., & Stokes, G.S (2004). The Big Five and venture survival: Is there a linkage? *Journal of Business Venturing, 19,* 465–483.

Chen, C.C., Greene, P.G., & Crick, A. (1998). Does entrepreneurial self-efficacy distinguish entrepreneurs from managers? *Journal of Business Venturing, 13,* 295–316.

Colombo, M.G., Delmastro, M., & Grilli, L. (2004). Entrepreneurs' human capital and the start-up size of new technology based firms. *International Journal of Industrial Organization, 22,* 1183–1211.

Côté, L., Langley, A., & Pasquero, J. (1999). Acquisition strategy and dominant logic in an engineering firm. *Journal of Management Studies, 36,* 919–952.

DiMaggio, P.J., & Powell, W.W. (1983). The iron cage revisited: Institutional isomorphism and collective rationality in organizational fields. *American Sociological Review, 48,* 147–160.

Dutton, J.E., & Dukerich, J.M. (1991). Keeping an eye on the mirror: Image and identity in organizational adaptation. *Academy of Management Journal, 34,* 517–554.

Engsley, M.D., & Pearce, C.L. (2001). Shared cognition in top management teams: Implications for new venture performance. *Journal of Organizational Behaviour, 22,* 145–160.

Fiske, S.T., & Taylor, S.E. (1991). *Social cognition.* New York: McGraw-Hill.

Goia, D.A., & Poole, P.P. (1984). Scripts in organizational behaviour. *The Academy of Management Review, 9,* 449–459.

Greenwood, R., & Hinings, C.R. (1996). Understanding radical organizational change: Bringing together the old and the new institutionalism. *Academy of Management Review, 21,* 1022–1054.

Gundry, L.K., & Welsch, H.P. (2001). The ambitious entrepreneur: High growth strategies of women owned enterprises. *Journal of Business Venturing, 16,* 453–470.

Hastie, R. (1980). *Person memory : The cognitive basis of social perception.* Hillsdale, NJ: L. Erlbaum Associates.

Jenkins, M., & Johnson, G. (1997). Entrepreneurial intentions and outcomes: A comparative causal mapping study. *Journal of Management Studies, 34,* 871–894.

Kets de Vries, M., Shekshnia, S., Korotov, K., & Florent-Treacy, E. (2004). The new global Russian business leaders: Lessons from a decade of transition. *European Management Journal, 22,* 637–648.

Lounsbury, M., & Glynn, M.A. (2001). Cultural entrepreneurship: Stories, legitimacy, and the acquisition of resources. *Strategic management Journal, 22,* 545–564.

Lievens, F., & Highhouse, S. (2003). The relation of instrumental and symbolic attributes to a company's attractiveness as an employer. *Personnel Psychology, 56,* 75–103.

Löwstedt, J. (1993). Organizing frameworks in emerging organizations: A cognitive approach to the analysis of change. *Human Relations, 46,* 501–526.

Meindl, J.R. (1985). Romance of leadership. *Administrative Science Quarterly, 30,* 78–102.

Mitchell, R.K., Smith, B., Seawright, K.W., & Morse, E.A. (2000). Cross-cultural cognitions and the venture creation decision. *Academy of Management Journal, 43,* 974–993.

Nicholls-Nixon, C.L., Cooper, A.C., & Woo, C.Y. (2000). Strategic experimentation: Understanding change and performance in new ventures. *Journal of Business Venturing, 15,* 493–521.

Phillips, M.E. (1994). Industry mindsets: Exploring the cultures of two macro-organizational settings. *Organization Science, 5,* 384–402.

Reynolds, P.D., & White, S.B. (1997). *The entrepreneurial process: Economic growth, men, women and minorities.* Westport, CT: Quorum Books.

Rentsch, J.R. (1990). Climate and culture: Interaction and qualitative differences in organizational meanings. *Journal of Applied Psychology, 75,* 668–681.

Romanelli, E., & Schoonhoven, C.B. (2001) *The local origins of new firms.* In C.B. Schoonhoven & E. Romanelli (Eds.), *The entrepreneurship dynamic.* Stanford, CA: Stanford University Press.

Schneider, D.J. (1973). Implicit personality theory: A review. *Psychological Bulletin, 79,* 294–309.

Sutcliffe, K.M., & Huber, G.P. (1998). Firm and industry as determinants of executive perceptions of the environment. *Strategic Management Journal, 19,* 793–807.

Scott, W.R. (1991). Unpacking institutional arguments. In W.W. Powell & P.J. DiMaggio (Eds.), *The new instititutionalism in organizational analysis.* Chicago: The University of Chicago Press.

Walsh, J.P. (1995). Managerial and organizational cognition: Notes from a trip down memory lane. *Organization Science, 6,* 280–321.

Walsh, J.P., & Ungson, G.R. (1991). Organizational memory. *The Academy of Management Review, 16,* 57–91.

Weick, K.E. (1995). *Sensemaking in organizations.* Thousand Oaks, CA: Sage.

Printed in the United States
44042LVS00001B/19

9 781593 113605